D0999526

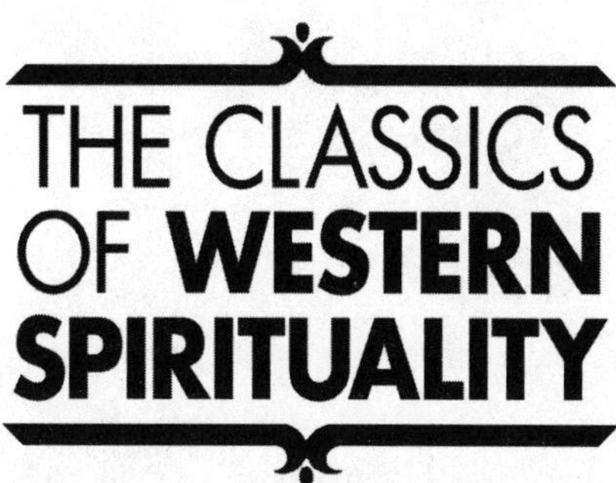
THE CLASSICS
OF WESTERN
SPIRITUALITY

THE CLASSICS OF WESTERN SPIRITUALITY
A Library of the Great Spiritual Masters

Azim Nanji—Director, The Institute of Ismaili Studies, London, England.

Seyyed Hossein Nasr—Professor of Islamic Studies, George Washington University, Washington, DC

Raimon Panikkar—Professor Emeritus, Department of Religious Studies, University of California at Santa Barbara, CA

Jaroslav Pelikan—Sterling Professor of History and Religious Studies, Yale University, New Haven, CT

Sandra M. Schneiders—Professor of New Testament Studies and Spirituality, Jesuit School of Theology, Berkeley, CA

Michael A. Sells—Emily Judson Baugh and John Marshall Gest Professor of Comparative Religions, Haverford College, Haverford, PA

Huston Smith—Thomas J. Watson Professor of Religion Emeritus, Syracuse University, Syracuse, NY

John R. Sommerfeldt—Professor of History, University of Dallas, Irving, TX

David Steindl-Rast—Spiritual Author, Benedictine Grange, West Redding, CT

David Tracy—Greeley Professor of Roman Catholic Studies, Divinity School, University of Chicago, Chicago, IL

The Most Rev. and Rt. Hon. Rowan D. Williams—Archbishop of Canterbury.

Fénelon

SELECTED WRITINGS

EDITED, TRANSLATED, AND INTRODUCED BY

CHAD HELMS

PAULIST PRESS

NEW YORK • MAHWAH

Cover art: The portrait of François de Salignac de la Mothe-Fenélon, Archbishop of Cambrai (1651–1715), was painted by Joseph Vivien (1657–1734) in 1689 and is now located in Versailles, France. Photo: D. Arnaudet/G. Blot. Réunion des Musées Nationaux/Art Resource, NY.

Cover and caseside design by A. Michael Velthaus

Library of Congress Cataloging-in-Publication Data

Fénelon, François de Salignac de La Mothe-, 1651-1715.
[Selections. English. 2006]
Fénelon : selected writings / edited and translated by Chad Helms.
p. cm. — (The classics of Western spirituality)
Includes bibliographical references and index.
ISBN 0-8091-4151-5 (pbk. : alk. paper); ISBN 0-8091-0555-1 (cloth : alk. paper)
I. Helms, Chad. II. Title. III. Series.
BX2182.3.F4613 2006
282—dc22

2006010353

Published by Paulist Press
997 Macarthur Boulevard
Mahwah, New Jersey 07430

www.paulistpress.com

Printed and bound in the
United States of America

Contents

CONTENTS

Editor and Translator of This Volume

CHAD HELMS earned his PhD in French from the University of Virginia in 1987. A recipient of a DuPont fellowship for doctoral research at the University of Virginia and the BCLE scholarship from the French Ministry of Education, he has taught French at Presbyterian College in Clinton, South Carolina, since 1992.

ACKNOWLEDGMENTS

The list of people deserving thanks for their assistance in this project of bringing Fénelon's major writings within reach of an English-speaking public is a very long one. I must especially thank Dr. Bernard McGinn of the University of Chicago, my editor for this volume. His judicious comments, his patience, and his support throughout the writing and revising of this book have been of inestimable value. I would be remiss in not thanking Dr. Gladys Saunders of the University of Virginia and Dr. Stacey Hahn of Oakland University for their encouragement and their friendship; Father Chris Kirchgessner of Belmont Abbey, who was kind enough to take time out of his schedule to read and comment upon portions of the manuscript dealing with specific theological issues; Ms. Sharon Byrd of Davidson College for her kind assistance in locating articles from various reference sources; Dr. Rob Howiler for the preparation of the manuscript; Ms. Teresa Inman and her colleagues at Presbyterian College for their help in procuring materials and answering reference questions throughout this process; Mr. Jim Holland of the Cleveland County Memorial Library for his generous help in locating and obtaining books through interlibrary loan from universities far and wide; Mr. Alan Greenberg, formerly of Winthrop University, for his very valuable suggestions in finding research materials as well as for his constant friendship. And, finally, warm thanks to Ms. Genell Gamblin for all her help with pesky computer questions as well as her friendship and support throughout this process.

This book is dedicated to my mother, Virginia Marie Ellis,
for her constant love and support.

Introduction

François de Salignac de la Mothe-Fénelon was born on August 6, 1651, in the familial château near Sarlat in the Périgord region of southwest France, the son of Pons de Salignac and his second wife, Louise de la Cropte de Saint-Abre. Pons had established the reputation of being the profligate sort who, with his pleasures, his financial speculation, and his large brood of children, had reduced the family's finances from what had been a most enviable position on the death of Bertrand de Salignac, Fénelon's grandfather, in 1599, to a state of what might be best described as genteel poverty. The family's domestic staff had been cut to a bare minimum—three to four servants in the entire château—and they were reduced at one point to selling their silver and eating off pewter plates.[1] Yet, in spite of this unfortunate turn of affairs, we must not see the Salignac-Fénelon as minor provincial nobility with no history or prospects. On the contrary, from the outset young François de Fénelon was very conscious of his family's exalted history and his subsequent social position. This is a fact that cannot be overemphasized in considering the nature of Fénelon's mature world view.

Fénelon's family tree extended back to beyond the tenth century. If obliged to eat off pewter and to make do with only one valet, young François nevertheless grew up looking at the portraits of thirty-three of his most illustrious ancestors hanging on the walls of château Fénelon. When at the peak of his power and influence as preceptor of the *enfants de France*, Fénelon will always be able to sit down at the same table as his royal charges and to ride as an equal in the same royal carriages (unlike the bourgeois Bossuet, who had occupied the same post a generation earlier). Fénelon himself, although the quintessence of humility before his God, never forgot his illustrious origins—nor would he let others forget this fact. When, for example, in 1694 his brother sought an office reserved traditionally for the highest nobility, this pride of family showed itself as Fénelon writes: "We have had in our family many governors, kings' chamberlains [...] ambassadors to all the principal courts and almost all the offices of war that people of quality had in past times."[2] This citation is representative of an important aspect of Fénelon's personality—that of *grand seigneur*. This Fénelon could easily have looked around at his imposing familial château—even to this day called "the jewel of the Périgord" in guidebooks—and decided, as his father had, that social success and its incumbent pleasures outweighed other values. Such was not to be the case, however. The Almighty took a hand in Fénelon's educational and psychological formation by removing his father's influence from him at the age of twelve. Upon Pons de Salignac's death, Fénelon was given over to the care of two uncles, the marquis Antoine de Fénelon and the bishop of Cahors, François de Fénelon.

According to Fénelon's earliest biographers François's upbringing and education were simple, reasonable, and Christian. They agree that there was nothing remarkable or unusual in Fénelon's earliest experiences in church or school for a member of his class. Tradition attributes him a tutor among the local parish clergy, and most modern historians, among them Carcassonne and Richardt, find nothing to discount in this tradition, although documentary evidence is lacking.[3] Another story tells of the infant François being dedicated to the care of Our Lady of Rocamadour, a local pilgrimage site in the Périgord. The plain, albeit disconcerting, truth of the matter is that we know practically nothing for certain about the intellectual and spiritual education of young François de Fénelon. There are—to be sure—many pious legends that have been passed down from generation to generation, and indeed many of these have been included in standard biographies of Fénelon. Only the most recent scholars, such as Jean Orcibal, have pointed out the necessity of prudence in accepting the various family legends and traditions that have attached themselves to the Fénelonian saga. Often what has been printed in even standard biographies of Fénelon is in fact little more than anecdote or conjecture.

It is commonly believed that Fénelon studied for a time with the Jesuits of Cahors—men eminent for their learning and wisdom.[4] One of Fénelon's recent biographers, Jeanne-Lydie Goré, claims that the Jesuit institution at Cahors was at the "height of its prosperity" at the time Fénelon would have been in attendance and that the Jesuit fathers who taught there were reputed far and wide for their eloquence and learning. She concludes, "Fénelon was happy there."[5] After spending two years with the Jesuits (1663–65)

Fénelon studied at the Collège du Plessis in Paris where he deepened his knowledge of the classics and began his serious study of theology. Carcassonne, in his authoritative *Fénelon: l'homme et l'oeuvre*, maintains that young François—with the help of his uncle the marquis—was introduced as a student into the seminary of Saint Sulpice in 1672, during which time he was initiated into the writings of the mystics by M. Louis Tronson, the seminary's director.[6]

How factual the biography of Fénelon's youth is, however, remains an open question. Orcibal has proven that the François entrusted to the care of Our Lady of Rocamadour, for example, was actually a cousin.[7] And scholars will probably never discover the real identity of Fénelon's first tutor.[8] As for Fénelon's studies at the Collège du Plessis in Paris, there are finally documents attesting that Fénelon was indeed a student at the college and that he, furthermore, enjoyed the guidance of Charles Gobinet, the director of the school and well-known scholar. However, for the far more important link between Fénelon and Saint Sulpice there is oddly once again no documentary evidence to support this part of the Fénelonian biography, much less the assertion that he remained—as most biographers have maintained—at the seminary for five years or more.

What we do know, based on Fénelon's correspondence, is that he must have met Louis Tronson, superior of Saint Sulpice, early during his stay in Paris and that their relationship must have been a particularly affectionate one because Fénelon would later say in a letter to Tronson that he had looked upon him for many years as a father. Such a relationship is important to note because Fénelon's sense of family and his psychological need, evidenced from his earliest youth, for the paternal affection he associated with his uncles and father figures such as Tronson would affect both his life and his work. Until their deaths he would maintain an exceptionally warm relationship with his two foster fathers, the marquis de Fénelon and the bishop of Sarlat. After 1689, when called to positions of increasing influence and patronage, he would be quick to bring his nieces and nephews to share in his prosperity.

This need for closeness from family and friends was perhaps due to the fact that Fénelon had lost both parents so early in life. These relationships are, however, significant in that all the surrogate paternal and maternal figures with which he would surround himself throughout his life would not only provide him with emotional support but would also influence to a great degree Fénelon's spiritual development and theological understanding. Since these three father figures—the marquis, the bishop, and the seminary director—were undoubtedly crucial to his formative years, a short consideration of each is in order.

Antoine de Fénelon, known in history as the marquis, was at this time a middle-aged courtier who had lived life to the fullest. Having been one of the most dashing young soldiers and most fearless duelists of Louis XIII's court, the marquis by 1663 was a changed man. Through the influence of Olier,[9] his spiritual director, the marquis had given up dueling and even sworn on his honor to eradicate this practice from the realm. He had furthermore become a member of the Compagnie du Saint Sacrement and was one of the most fervent partisans of this secretive organization, endeavoring always to live up to the company's motto: "to do away with all evil—to do the most good." His ardor was so intense that some scholars believe he served as the model for Molière's *Tartuffe*. Unlike the protagonist of Molière's comedy, however, the marquis's conversion seems to have been quite sincere and his desire to direct his nephew's feet onto the path of righteousness unswerving.

Apart from being under the spiritual direction of M. Olier, the marquis de Fénelon was also a friend of Vincent de Paul and frequented the most devout circles in Paris. Fénelon, in fact, would later write in favor of de Paul's canonization, saying that although he had not personally known the saint in his youth, from his uncle he had often heard of Vincent's holiness within his family circle.[10] Indeed, Antoine de Fénelon was almost passionate in his admiration of the saintly men whose company he sought. And his circle does not stop in Paris; he also frequented such saintly bishops as Alain de Solminihac, bishop of Cahors, and the Jesuit mystic Père Surin.

Fénelon's other uncle, François de Fénelon, was equally well suited to encourage the young Fénelon's incipient piety. François de Fénelon was in 1663 bishop of the small diocese of Sarlat, near the Fénelon's château in the Périgord. There had been fifteen Salignacs and Fénelons before him in the episcopal see. In fact, so many members of the family had occupied the position that it had begun to be considered as practically a familial apanage to which the Salignac-Fénelon had a right as seigneurs of the locality. There is no doubt that François de Fénelon, upon consecration as bishop, brought to Sarlat a certain ease of manners. He was comfortable in his position and felt no qualms about refurbishing the episcopal mansion, having the gardens landscaped, and entertaining local dignitaries and travelers.[11]

In spite of what might seem to be an opulent lifestyle, however, François de Fénelon was an able and pious bishop. Like his brother, Antoine, the bishop of Sarlat numbered among his friends Vincent de Paul and Jean-Jacques Olier. Bishop Fénelon was also on intimate terms with the provincial clergy and had been especially close to the sainted bishop of Cahors, Alain de Solminihac, who although recently deceased still exerted a powerful spiritual influence on the province.

At the time young Fénelon lost his father and left the family's château to further his education in Cahors, Solminihac had been dead only four years. His memory remained very much alive in the region during these formative years of the young student. Solminihac was revered especially in his episcopal see of Cahors where his spirituality, which emphasized the pure love of God, was still influential. Jean Calvet notes that a biography of Solminihac had just been published in 1663 and was, moreover, read during mealtimes at the Jesuit college in Cahors. Calvet adds that "Fénelon, who had just arrived, did not miss a word of it."[12]

Although we can not state with certainty how deeply young François was affected by Solminihac's example, it is known that both of his uncles were associated with the Cadurcian bishop. In a letter dated October 23, 1655, Solminihac writes of the marquis de Fénelon and the abbé de Fénelon (this is the future bishop, not yet named bishop of Sarlat) visiting him in order to "follow lectures on the means of staying united in order to procure the glory of God."[13] And there are frequent mentions in Solminihac's correspondence of both Antoine and François de Fénelon. Indeed, Solminihac had been one of the provincial clergy to write the Queen Mother strongly urging the nomination of François de Fénelon to the vacant see of Sarlat. Orcibal assures us, moreover, and the correspondence bears this out, that once a bishop François de Fénelon worked in harmony with Solminihac in Cahors and venerated his memory after his death.[14]

Alain de Solminihac provides a fascinating case study of a dedicated bishop in the post-tridentine tradition of the Catholic Counter-Reformation. He is a complex figure. Judged by some to be too harsh in his zeal to extirpate clerical abuses in his diocese, he came, nevertheless, to be venerated as a saint by the vast majority of his flock due to his charity and personal virtue. A number of salient traits can be gleaned from his biographies. First, in spite of calumny and accusations Solminihac seems to have remained a kindly man who always preferred the path of persuasion to that of force. Speaking of his role as superior of the Austin canons in his diocese, one of his biographers writes that he constantly told his novices that they should only obey him through "love, not constraint; by the joy of pleasing God and not from the fear of displeasing him."[15]

Solminihac worked zealously and indefatigably for the salvation of his flock. He regularly visited parishes to give confirmation, admonish lax clergy, and encourage devout priests in their functions. He also regularly held diocesan councils, which were attended by Fénelon's uncle, François, before he became bishop, in his quality as Prior of the abbey of Carennec. These synodal councils offered opportunities for Solminihac to enlist the support of his clergy for his favorite causes, among which were winning Calvinists back to the fold and extirpating Jansenism. Indeed, he seems to have been particularly zealous in his crusade against the Jansenists, regularly preaching against them and writing the Holy See to encourage the pope to move more forcefully against them. During one of the meetings attended by François de Fénelon he would say that he was the first among French bishops to have publicly condemned Jansenism as a heresy.[16]

If Solminihac reminds us of the mature Fénelon in his anti-Calvinist and anti-Jansenist zeal, he also reminds us of Fénelon in his pro-Jesuit and ultramontane sympathies. One contemporary ecclesiastic is quoted as saying, "I have never seen anyone more attached to the Holy See than he is."[17] This view of the church was shared by few of his colleagues, since the seventeenth century in France was the heyday of Gallicanism. Solminihac's view of the church, however, was universal and humanistic, as Fénelon's would be, and he venerated the memory of Francis de Sales, in favor of whose canonization he wrote Pope Alexander VII. He stated that de Sales's writings had the same effect as those of Thomas Aquinas: "Of the bishop of Geneva's books, I can say that in each sentence there are as many miracles."[18]

Although the exact nature of Fénelon's educational formation at Cahors is unclear due to the dearth of documentary evidence, it seems very likely that he was indeed influenced in his spirituality by both his uncle, François, bishop of Sarlat, and by the friends and disciples of Solminihac among the Jesuits of Cahors. In later life Fénelon would run counter to Gallican sympathies in being a faithful ally of the Jesuits, and like Solminihac, he would always be a zealous foe of Jansenism. It is clear that by the time Fénelon set off for Paris to further his studies he would have instilled in him the sentiment that humanism and moderation were choices more agreeable to God than rigorism and austerity. The more esoteric mystical doctrine of pure love would await him in Paris, where he would meet the two people, Louis Tronson and Jeanne Guyon, who would arguably influence his spiritual direction more than any others.

In 1665 Fénelon left Cahors for Paris at the urging of his uncle, Antoine, the marquis, who thought that the sophisticated Parisian atmosphere would broaden his nephew's intellectual horizons. At this time Paris was a spiritually effervescent city that was home to many of those who would become leaders of the church in France. Still in the flush of Counter-Reformation piety, the city had only recently witnessed the ministries of Vincent de Paul, Francis de Sales, Pierre de Bérulle, Madame Acarie, Benoit de Canfield, Charles de Condren, and Jean-Jacques Olier, all luminaries of the French School of Spirituality, many of whom would be declared saints by the Catholic Church.[19] Paris could indeed in this period be called the school for saints. Bossuet, France's leading theologian; Mabillon, the internationally known Benedictine scholar; and Tronson, who had taken over Olier's role as superior of the seminary of Saint Sulpice—all were alive and either full-time or part-time residents of Paris. So it is to Paris that Fénelon will direct his steps during the fifteenth year of his life, and it is in Paris that he will begin to learn of the writings of the mystics as interpreted by the French School.[20]

After staying some time with his uncle Antoine (and undoubtedly being introduced to Bossuet who, like the marquis, was an active member of the Company of the Holy Sacrament) Fénelon was placed in the Collège du Plessis under the direction of Charles Gobinet. Gobinet's possible influence over Fénelon is open to conjecture. Most biographers, in fact, pass over him in silence, concluding his influence negligible. It is true that in later years Fénelon never speaks of him in his voluminous correspondence. Yet Goré, for one, has pointed out that Gobinet was known as a Christian humanist and admirer of Francis de Sales. She points out as well that the choice of books he made for Fénelon's spiritual reading is suggestive of the humanistic, Salesian spirituality that will form such a large part of Fénelon's beliefs as an adult. The *Confessions* of Saint Augustine, the *Imitation of Jesus Christ* by Thomas à Kempis, and the *Introduction à la vie dévote* by de Sales were prominent on the list. Although it is unlikely that Fénelon was initiated into Salesian spirituality by Gobinet—as we have seen, his uncles both venerated de Sales and had probably spoken often of him—it seems safe to say that Fénelon's stay at the Collège du Plessis probably deepened his appreciation of de Sales's work and strengthened the proclivities he had already toward Christian humanism and Christian mysticism. Monsieur Tronson would continue to encourage these proclivities in Fénelon for the next several years in which he would be under his direction.

At this time Saint Sulpice, under the leadership of Tronson, was reputed to be one of the finest seminaries in France. Founded by Jean-Jacques Olier in the 1640s, Saint Sulpice was a center of French School devotion and was infused with Bérullian spirituality as interpreted by Olier. Monsieur Tronson, the superior, Olier's successor, had formerly been his student and disciple. Indeed, during Fénelon's stay at Plessis, M. Tronson had been in the process of giving lectures on Olier's spirituality and publishing his literary works.

Saint Sulpice was a logical choice for young Fénelon to begin his serious theological training. Not only is there a consensus among historians extolling the Sulpicians' "nobility," "selflessness," and "piety," but we remember the intimate connection that existed between the marquis Antoine de Fénelon and the Sulpician seminary. M. Olier had been the marquis's confessor and friend, and after his death M. Tronson came to fill this same role. It was inevitable that his uncle should encourage Fénelon to study with Tronson and the Sulpicians. Indeed, he may have introduced his nephew to M. Tronson upon his arrival in Paris before enrolling at the College du Plessis.

This widely respected and saintly man was quickly to exert an influence on Fénelon as great as that of his own cherished uncles. Indeed, Fénelon would later write his uncle Antoine that he had grown to feel more open and at ease with Tronson than with anyone else in his life. The letter is undated, but Orcibal surmises that it was written as early as 1669, only four years after Fénelon's arrival in Paris. In the letter Fénelon writes that although his openness and relationship with his uncle "seems perfect," he nevertheless is able to be "even more open with M. Tronson."[21] He goes on to say that he cannot find words to express how close their union is, and he thanks his uncle profusely for having introduced him to Tronson and placed him under his spiritual tutelage.

Indeed, Fénelon would always consider Tronson a father, in similar but even deeper manner than he considered his two uncles as his foster fathers. Why Fénelon would feel this strong attachment to Tronson is perhaps a question for historians trained in psychology to answer. Whatever the psychological dynamic in play here between Fénelon and Tronson, the same sort of ineffable spiritual attraction would lead him later to Jeanne Guyon. Whereas Tronson would exert a positive influence on Fénelon, Guyon would exert a questionable one.

Therefore, the man whom Fénelon would later write, saying, "you have always been like a father to me,"[22] would play a decisive role in forming the sensitive, almost tormented conscience of his young seminarian. This man who had lived in conversation with the saints, as it were, having personally known so many of the French School of Spirituality, from Olier to de Paul, would teach Fénelon their doctrine and inculcate in him their spirituality. As Carcassonne maintains: "By their conversations, by the collection of Olier's spiritual letters that he had published in 1672, the novice was initiated in a high and very pure form of piety."[23] This melding of the Salesian spirituality with which Fénelon was already familiar with the Berullian/Olierian spirituality taught to him by Tronson would form an amalgam of mystical beliefs that would reach fruition in the mature Fénelon.

In many ways these two spiritual traditions were perfectly suited for Fénelon. His aristocratic heritage and humanist education echo the life of Francis de Sales. Fénelon, indeed, throughout his life would show himself to be a courageous defender of his family's honor, and many historians have suggested that his chivalric defense of Madame Guyon when she came under attack in the 1690s can best be understood in light of his aristocratic forbears and their *point d'honneur*. Like de Sales, Fénelon's concept of God would be that of loving father and munificent prince. Like de Sales he would love learning, especially the classics, and would temper his faith with charity and moderation.

Fénelon was a complex individual, however, and one always senses in his writings an uncertainty, a searching for a mystical relationship with God, which he felt eluded him. Even as a young seminarian Fénelon suffered an almost debilitating *noche oscura*, dark night of the soul, and ongoing periods of "dryness" stretching over years. In this he reminds us more of Saint John of the Cross or Olier, who was often anguished at his lack of closeness with God in spite of his personal sanctity. As a disciple of Olier, Tronson understood Fénelon's need for reassurance during his periods of uncertainty and anguish, and as a disciple of Bérulle, he understood Fénelon's yearning for ecstatic union with a loving Father. He urged his pupil to engage in a study of the mystical tradition of the church and to develop a life centered around Christ. Since mystical theology will play such a prominent role in Fénelon's later life and work, this is perhaps a good point to give the reader a brief overview of the mystical tradition in France before his birth.

Mysticism before Fénelon

The mystical tradition in Christianity may be said to have begun with the origins of Christianity itself. The Hellenistic world into which Christianity was born was already permeated with the teachings of the Greek philosophers. As a consequence, it was doubtless inevitable that the Christian *kerygma*, the proclamation of the good news of Jesus' victory over death and sin should be interpreted by his early disciples in light of Greek thought patterns and ideas.

Scripture, of course, would be the touchstone of church doctrine on mysticism, and scripture abounds in experiences and terminology that would be taken up throughout the centuries by mystics as prooftexts in defense of their understanding of Christian perfection and union with God. The Johannine vocabulary of the Logos, Saint Paul's vision of being lifted to the third heaven, Christ's injunction that his disciples should strive for union with the Father—all these texts were capital in encouraging the growth of mysticism in the early church.[24] As is well known, many theologians and mystics have emphasized the literal sense of the biblical texts speaking of Christian perfection and divine union and have not shirked from speaking of Christian deification, *theosis* in Greek, as the goal of the church.[25]

Fénelon, who had a firm grounding in the Bible and the church fathers, was imbued with an appreciation for the church's mystical tradition even as a child studying with the Jesuits. Later, as a seminarian at Saint Sulpice in Paris under Tronson's direction, he would delve more deeply into the works of mystical theology. Authors such as Clement of Alexandria and Dionysius the Areopagite would fuel his imagination. Although this period of Fénelon's life is somewhat murky, it is likely that it was at Saint Sulpice as well that Fénelon would come into contact with the works of the medieval mystics such as the Dominicans Henry Suso and John Tauler and the Italian saint Catherine of Genoa, all of whom he would later cite in his work.[26]

The exact nature of the influence of these ancient and medieval mystics on Fénelon's developing spirituality is impossible to know, of course. And, indeed, his study of mystical authors and their theology was a lifelong process. Saint Teresa of Avila, for example, and Saint John of the Cross—two authors whom he will quote extensively in his *Maxims of the Saints*—he apparently discovered as an adult, long after his seminary studies. The same appears to be the case with the Rheno-Flemish mystics—especially Tauler—who also find echoes in Fénelon's mystical theology of pure love and willingness to suffer all for God's sake. Although we may never know exactly when Fénelon began his serious reading of the mystics, the list of authors that can be culled from his references in his correspondence and his writings, such as the *Maxims*, is a very impressive one. Augustine of Hippo joins Clement of Alexandria. The great Scholastic Thomas Aquinas is cited alongside Bernard of Clairvaux, one of Fénelon's saints of predilection. We find Gregory Nazianzen, John Chrysostom, Cassian, Leo the Great, Gregory the Great, Anselm, Hugh of St. Victor, Richard of St. Victor, Denis the Carthusian. Among the more modern authors the list includes Cardinal Bellarmine, the great Jesuit theologian, Balthazar Alvarez, and Cardinal Bona.[27]

The authors who influenced Fénelon more immediately, however, were those mystics and saints of the Catholic Counter-Reformation who had lived in the century before his birth and who had expressed themselves in French. First and perhaps foremost among these authors was Saint Francis de Sales (1567–1622), bishop *in partibus* of Geneva, who, along with Jeanne de Chantal, founded the Order of the Visitation and was instrumental in propagating a fervent devotion and intense love of God that he expressed most famously in his *Introduction to the Devout Life*.[28] Published in 1609, this guide, along with the 1616 *Treatise on the Love of God*, summarizes de Sales's theology of Christian perfectibility and ultimate goal of union with God. These intensely personal works describe his own experiences of mystical union.

De Sales neither lived nor wrote in a vacuum, however, and he seems to have been indebted, as Fénelon would later be, for much of his understanding of his mystical experiences and the terminology he used to express them to the writings of the Spanish mystics, Saint Teresa of Avila and Saint John of the Cross. De Sales apparently came to knowledge of these Spanish Carmelites through Barbe Acarie (1566–1618), a Parisian wife and mother of six children, who was also a fervent mystic. She was instrumental in introducing the Discalced Carmelites into France along with her cousin Pierre (later Cardinal) de Bérulle, who had lodged at her house and witnessed her raptures firsthand. As the Spanish mystics were celebrated for their intense spirituality and vivid poetic style, de Sales's work would likewise be noted for his brilliant use of metaphor.

One example of de Sales's use of metaphors is that of sculptor and statue. God has created us and placed us in a certain location for reasons known only to God, just as a sculptor would fashion a statue and set it up in a certain place. Like clay or rock, we must allow ourselves to be molded by God and passively await God's will in a state of holy indifference. Another frequent Salesian metaphor compares the flowing of the soul into God to a drop of water flowing into the sea to describe the soul's necessity for annihilation and "liquefaction" in order to unite with God.

De Sales, moreover, will elaborate a system of two levels of the soul, speaking of the "fine point of the soul" (a term frequently cited by Fénelon in the *Maximes des saints*) to describe metaphorically that part of the soul, its essence, that communicates with God. All of these Salesian themes exerted a profound influence on de Sales's contemporaries in the French School—from Bérulle to the next generation of Olier and Condren. Fénelon considered these authors to be his immediate mentors in the mystical tradition. He greatly admired their life and work and was deeply imbued with their spirituality. Therefore, both directly, since Fénelon himself became a student of de Sales's work, and indirectly, through the influence of his predecessors in the French School, Salesian spirituality indelibly marked Fénelon's theology and spirituality.

One aspect of Salesian mystical teaching that Fénelon adopted was to be problematic later on, however. This was the concept of the so-called *demande impossible* or impossible case.[29] According to de Sales, and echoing ideas already found in Saint Catherine of Genoa and mystics such as Tauler, the truly passive soul would be willing to suffer torment, even eternal damnation, if it knew that damnation were more pleasing to God than its salvation. This supposition came to be known as the impossible case, since Christian doctrine teaches that God desires the salvation of sinners, not their damnation. Although de Sales is careful in his work to formulate this concept and express it in a Catholic sense and was never condemned by Rome for it, other authors such as Miguel de Molinos in Spain and Jeanne Guyon in France were neither so careful in their expressions nor so lucky with the Roman Curia.

By the seventeenth century the fervor of the first wave of Counter-Reformation spirituality had waned and with it a waning appreciation for the fervid terminology often used by even "approved" mystics such as Saint Teresa and Francis de Sales. Guyon and Fénelon would later discover to their misfortune that the France of Louis XIV—a more rational and less enthusiastic environment than sixteenth-century Spain—was unwilling to accept such excesses of emotion and "impossible" musings, even when intended in a sincerely Catholic sense. In fact, these emotional excesses and extravagant imagery would be grouped together and condemned under the term *Quietist*.

Fénelon, who adopted de Sales's views and those of the French School on annihilation of self and holy indifference, found himself at pains through the years in which he was involved in the Quietist controversy to distinguish what he considered sound, authorized doctrine on these subjects from the excesses he admitted had crept into the teachings of certain Quietist authors. Indeed, the *Maximes des saints* may primarily be seen as a defense of the doctrines of the French School of spirituality as opposed to Quietist perversions of these themes.

The next great theologian and mystic to influence Fénelon was Pierre de Bérulle, archbishop of Paris and founder of the French Oratorians. The future cardinal and leader of the French School was born in 1575 on the Burgundian frontier to minor nobility. As a child Bérulle showed signs of a priestly vocation that ran counter to the wishes of his family, who had chosen a career in the magistrature for him. His father finally relented, and Bérulle was allowed to study theology at the Collège de Clermont, a Jesuit school in Paris. Like Fénelon, Bérulle always was indebted to the Jesuits for their instruction and humanistic imprint. After studying at the Sorbonne, he was ordained in 1599.

The Jesuits' influence on Bérulle's theology was profound. Historians have noted his acceptance of the Society's theological positions in many areas. For example, he often seems to have borrowed verbatim from Suarez and other Jesuit theologians, particularly in expressing beliefs on creation and the nature of grace.[30]

Bérulle showed evidence from an early age of seeking mystical union with God. He poured over the writings of the mystics and borrowed his vocabulary from many sources. It is said that he greatly admired, for example, the "pure love" with which Saint

Catherine of Genoa burned. He venerated Saint Francis of Assisi as well and stood in awe of God's signal favor to him in the bestowal of the stigmata. From his earliest days as priest Bérulle chose his spiritual directors, such as Benoit de Canfield, and friends, such as Madame Acarie, from among the mystics. As early as 1597, under Canfield's influence, he wrote a treatise on *Abnégation intérieure*, or inner abnegation, in which he delineated themes that he would perfect over the years into what we know as characteristic Bérullian spirituality. In this work Bérulle maintains that it is every Christian's duty to deny himself or herself in order to unite with God. Even though he acknowledges the importance of human free will in cooperating with God in salvation, he insists that in order to renounce evil completely and to opt for salvation we must first recognize our *néant* or "nothingness," for only God truly possesses "being."

In this same treatise the future cardinal also raised the themes of holy indifference and *passivité absolue* (complete passivity to God's will). He insists, moreover, on God's greatness and transcendence and God's love for humanity in the willingness to take on human form in the incarnation. Thus, on the threshold of the seventeenth century, Bérulle as a young man is already elaborating themes of "grandeur de Dieu" (God's greatness) and "néant de l'homme" (man's nothingness) that will inform all of his mature theological works, especially the *Grandeurs de Jésus.*

This is the best known of Bérullian works, published in 1622 when he was cardinal-archbishop and uncontested leader of the church in France. The *Grandeurs of Jesus* is a meditation on the love of God as expressed in humbling himself and taking flesh as the baby Jesus. This elaboration of Bérulle's Christocentric spirituality takes up themes already seen in the *Abnegation intérieure* and shapes them into lyrical prose that would impact French mystics throughout the seventeenth century. "Pulled out of nothingness by the Creation, cast back into nothingness by the Fall," humankind is a *néant*, according to Bérulle, "a nothingness surrounded by God, indigent of God, capable of God and filled with God if it wants to be."[31] Bérulle is deeply moved by the magnitude of God's sacrifice in making himself human and returns again and again to the image of Almighty God suffering the indignities of infancy. Translating

Philippians 2:6 "exinanivit semetipsum" as "Il s'est anéanti" (he made himself a nothingness) *Grandeurs* describes the incarnation as "a mystery of love."[32] In another passage in the book he exclaims: "God loved mankind to the point of lowering himself and making himself man. O love of God for the world! O Love!"[33]

The third member of the French School to influence Fénelon's developing spirituality was Jean Jacques Olier. Olier, as mentioned already, was the founder of Saint Sulpice and Louis Tronson's teacher and mentor. Born in Paris in 1608, Olier was destined to the clerical state as a child. A devout youth, he apparently never gave his parents reason to question their decision for him. Olier's early biographers relate that as a child his mother took him to see Francis de Sales, who was passing through Lyon, where the family was living at that time. Having qualms as to whether she and his father had made the right decision in choosing the church as her son's career, she supposedly asked de Sales's advice. He reassured her, saying that far from being unsuited for the priestly life Olier would become a great light to the church "because God had chosen this child for his glory and for the good of his church."[34]

Olier studied theology at the Sorbonne in Paris, after which he was ordained in 1633. Shortly thereafter he fell under the influence of Bérulle and Vincent de Paul and, at their urging, led several missions in Auvergne to evangelize the poor. These missions were a great success and led Bérulle and later Condren (Bérulle's disciple who had succeeded him as superior of the Oratory) to entreat Olier to found a seminary. This seminary was Saint Sulpice, where Fénelon would study for the priesthood thirty years later.

The founder of Saint Sulpice was not content to be a teacher and preacher. His piety found expression in several devotional works, one of which is entitled *Introduction to the Christian Virtues.* This work summarizes themes typical of Olier's spirituality—themes common to the French School, such as humankind's "nothingness" and God's "greatness." Like de Sales and Bérulle, Olier also underlines the capital importance of the incarnation as proof of God's ineffable love for humanity. Unlike his two illustrious predecessors, Olier's spirituality is often tortured. He suffered many periods of spiritual aridity in which he would spend days fasting, wearing a hairshirt, and flagellating himself in attempts to quell the spiritual combat raging in himself between God and the devil.

"To sacrifice everything to God" is the theme that Olier announces at the beginning of the *Introduction to the Christian Virtues*, and this theme is echoed and elaborated throughout the book.[35] "Let the creature perish," says Olier, in order to make room for grace. Indeed, the treatise is pervaded with expressions such as "lose oneself," "bury oneself," "empty oneself," "purge oneself," "allow oneself to become an abyss," "crucify oneself," and "destroy oneself." We must, according to Olier, destroy our ego and empty ourself completely in order to become a receptacle for God.

This theme of total sacrifice of personal ego to God is perhaps most lyrically expressed in Olier's image of the holocaust. In vocabulary that calls to mind visions of Old Testament priestly sacrifice in the Temple, Olier emphasizes the necessity of our making ourselves a "bouc émissaire" (scape goat) in order to sacrifice ourselves completely to God: "He wants our soul and mind to be united to him so that he possesses them...so that they neither love, nor breath, nor desire anything other than total possession and entire consummation in him."[36]

It is just this sort of fervent spirituality evinced by Olier, inherited and developed from Bérulle and de Sales, that forms the ethos of the French School. The sacrifice of one's self, as a burnt offering to God, in order to be consumed entirely by God's pure love in union with God is at the very core of Fénelon's spirituality as well. And even though Fénelon was claimed by philosophers and theologians as one of their own for bringing a brilliant intellect to bear on questions of grace and salvation, free will, and determinism, his most personal and impassioned writings will always deal with the spiritual concerns evident in all French School authors. As a student and disciple of the French School, it can be said of Fénelon—as Bremond said of the French School in general—that these churchmen were members of "a school, yes, but of the inner life, one of elevated spirituality, and not of theology." He concluded that even though many were considered to be intellectuals and even subtle theologians, "their apparent intellectualism, their apparent subtleness both bow down before the inspiration of the simplest mystics."[37]

Fénelon's Studies at Saint Sulpice and Ordination

It is with this background in mysticism that the instruction and spiritual direction Fénelon received at the hands of M. Tronson can best be understood. Tronson, as a member of the French School with mystical leanings himself, influenced Fénelon in a direction that heavily relied on the Bérullian insistence on total abandonment of self to the loving God as personified in Christ and the Olierian insistence on "holocaust" and "annihilation" of one's personal ego in order to achieve divine union.

One letter of direction from Tronson to Fénelon may serve to elucidate the direction typically found in the correspondence between them. In this letter Tronson attempts to ally Fénelon's recurring doubts about his relationship to God, his "sécheresse" (dry period), as he termed it. In a flow of argument echoing both the themes and the style of French School authors, Tronson writes:

> If in some occasions you are not as faithful to him as you ought to be...if you fear having even committed some sin, humble yourself before him, but do not be troubled. For anxiety always increases the pain that humiliation could cure. And since you do not wish to separate yourself from God, and only want what he wants, never forget that he is called the God of peace, Deus pacis...And if with all these precautions and all your care you cannot prevent your interior sometimes to be troubled, abandon yourself to God in order to carry that pain in satisfaction of your past infidelities, but take care that you do not change your outward appearance.[38]

In this short passage of spiritual direction we have in microcosm some of the major tenets of French School spirituality. We see the typical Salesian imagery of "devoir" or "duty," reminding us that Christians, like soldiers or courtiers, have a duty to their Prince. Salesian, as well, is the injunction to interior austerity versus outward shows of piety. We see the characteristically Bérullian vocabulary of humbling oneself in order to be raised up to God. We also see the use of "abandon yourself," a phrase found in Bérulle, Olier, and Condren. Another echo of Olier is the advice to suffer pain and spiritual aridity as satisfaction for past infidelities. However, we also see the comforting advice of "do not be troubled," calling to mind de Sales's message to Philothée in his *Introduction to the Devout Life*, reminding her that God's name is not "he who damns" but "he who saves": "nomen meus non damnator est sed Jesus!"

In 1685 Louis XIV revoked the Edict of Nantes, which had granted religious liberty to French Protestants for a hundred years. Although Fénelon personally had reservations about the efficacy of forced conversions, he accepted the mission of evangelizing the Calvinist areas of Saintonge and Poitou in southwest France. He spent the next three years at this arduous, and ultimately frustrating, task. Although he was known as one of the most able and compassionate of the "missionaries" to the Protestants, Fénelon finally realized that conversion must come from the heart and cannot be coerced. The numbers of sincere, lasting conversions from this mission remained dismally small.

It was therefore time for the young abbé to return to Paris, where he was increasingly in demand as a lecturer, preacher, and spiritual director. Although the dates are uncertain, it is doubtless during the years between his seminary studies and the mission to Poitou that he met and became friends with the Duc de Beauvillier and the Duc de Chevreuse. He had even composed *Treatise on the Education of Daughters* for Beauvillier's young girls. Scions of ancient and influential families, both dukes had married daughters of Colbert, Louis XIV's famous finance minister. Colbert had been one of the king's most trusted advisers, and on his death his two sons-in-law came to fill this position as well. There were no aristocrats in greater favor with the king than these two.[39] As a sign of his confidence in them, in 1689 Louis XIV named Beauvillier governor of his three beloved grandsons' education. It was certainly through his friendship with the duke that Fénelon was appointed in the same year *précepteur*, preceptor or chief tutor, to the three young boys: the dukes of Bourgogne, Anjou, and Berry.

But before discussing the works that define Fénelon's period with the young dukes, it is perhaps appropriate to pause to consider his reputation as a preacher.

Early Preaching

Nearly all of Fénelon's extant sermons are undated. The consensus among historians is that he began to preach at an early age.[40] Some say that he was preaching trial sermons as early as age nineteen, but what may be termed his mature preaching is commonly held to have occurred after his ordination. The sermon included in this volume is entitled *Sermon for the Feast of the Epiphany on the Vocation of the Gentiles.* The sermon was preached on January 6, 1687, at the church of the Missions étrangères (foreign missions) in Paris. It was commonly believed to be his greatest success in the pulpit to that date. The occasion was the commissioning of four new missionaries to Siam (now Thailand). The king of Siam had recently sought diplomatic relations with France, and contemporary witnesses say that this sermon was attended by the Siamese ambassadors to Versailles. The feast day could not have been more appropriate for the task at hand since the feast of the Epiphany commemorates the visit of the Magi to Bethlehem and, metaphorically, the unveiling of the gospel to the Gentiles.

The sermon genre was not one to which Fénelon applied himself as assiduously as others. In his own time he would never eclipse the masters of pulpit eloquence: Bourdaloue, the great Jesuit preacher; or Bossuet, bishop of Meaux. Indeed, Fénelon would achieve fame in later life primarily from his literary works composed for the Duc de Bourgogne and his polemical works in defense of mysticism written during the time of the Quietist controversy. This sermon, nevertheless, was well received when it was preached and is considered one of Fénelon's best.

Throughout the sixteenth and seventeenth centuries the preaching of sermons had been seen as an art form, an opportunity for the most gifted writers to showcase their talent for composition and reasoned argument from a scriptural text. Sermons were also considered ideal vehicles to demonstrate lyrical and poetic gifts. Most preachers embellished their sermons with brilliant conceits and literary devices such as metaphor, enallage, hypallage, and allusions to ancient mythology and history. By the beginning of the seventeenth century the most popular preachers were drawing large crowds to hear their sermons, and these were judged successful relative to how clever they were and how many rhetorical devices they included. They had become works of literature and oratory but had lost the simplicity of the gospel message.

The sermon had taken on a rigid form of its own. A well-constructed sermon had to include the following elements. It began with a recitation of the scriptural text on which the sermon would be based, called the *texte*, usually quoted in the Latin of the Vulgate. Afterward, opening remarks introducing the main thesis of the sermon would be made. These were called the *exordes*, and they were meant to situate the subject and the spirit of the sermon. These opening remarks would inevitably end with a transition to the recitation of the *Ave Maria*. This transition was called the *chute*, and the more ingenious the chute was, the more applauded the sermon was. Following the *exordes* came the main body of the sermon, divided into two or more sections, called *points*. These sections would develop the main ideas of the sermon in a thesis-antithesis pattern and were usually pervaded with literary and rhetorical devices. Finally, the preacher would conclude the sermon with an ingenious synthesis of his main points in what was termed the *péroraison*.

Although sermons were well attended and often subsequently published by their authors, gaining literary fame for many of them, by the early decades of the seventeenth century a reaction arose to what was considered the artificial, overly literary quality of the sermon structure. This reaction was championed by such lights of the Catholic Counter-Reformation as Cardinal Bérulle and more especially Vincent de Paul and Saint Jean Eudes. These preachers proposed the use of simpler models for sermons, a type of preaching that relied solely on the scriptural text and eschewed mythological allusions and poetic conceits. Their goal was the conversion of sinners, and the means they employed were above all simplicity and sincerity.

Fénelon's *Sermon on the Vocation of the Gentiles* is indicative of the simpler, more apostolic approach to preaching favored by the French School. Although Fénelon does not abandon what had become the traditional structural elements of text, exordium, chute, divisions, and peroration, he insists exclusively on the text of his sermon, taken from Isaiah, and avoids any contrived use of rhetorical or poetic devices, avoiding all allusions of a mythological nature. Gods and goddesses will not people the Fénelonian sermon; rather, he presents the clear, simple message of the gospel.[41]

The *Sermon for the Feast of the Epiphany on the Vocation of the Gentiles* is representative of Fénelon's approach to forensic discourse in general. As in his letters of spiritual direction and in his other works for the pulpit (funeral orations, panegyrics, exhortations, and so forth), he will progress stylistically in this sermon from the rational exposition to the emotional appeal. In this sermon Fénelon, the preacher, bemoans the loss of northern Europe to the Catholic faith and decries the sinful ways of his French contemporaries. Indeed, he paints a portrait of sin with an apocalyptic tint, to borrow the phrase from Carcassonne, alternating between the reasoned exposition of "an expiatory calamity" to the emotional "vision of regenerated humanity."[42] And, although one of the earliest works included in this volume, it remains one of the most popular of all Fénelon's sermons and is still considered an excellent example of what the 17th century called "l'éloquence de la chair."

Pedagogical Works

THE *FABLES*

The period from 1689 to 1695 was perhaps the happiest of Fénelon's life. This was the period of the preceptorate, the directing of the education of the three young dukes, the eldest of whom, Louis, Duc de Bourgogne, was, after his father, the heir to the throne. It was a period in Fénelon's life in which he felt fulfilled professionally, being the chief educator in France; intellectually, composing the literary works for which he would become famous; and emotionally, being the spiritual director of the group of devout courtiers calling themselves the *petit troupeau.* This group, which included Mme. de Maintenon, had formed around the Beauvilliers and Chevreuses. Its members were known as the *parti dévot* (the devout group) at court and were decidedly under Fénelon's spell. Although Mme. de Maintenon would break with Fénelon at the time of the Quietist controversy in 1697, the Beauvilliers and Chevreuses would remain loyal and lifelong friends to the man both families considered chosen by God to lead them along the mystical paths.

As soon as he was appointed tutor, Fénelon decided to direct the education of his three young charges in the most active way possible, by composing textbooks for their instruction. In his *Treatise on the Education of Daughters* he had already proposed methods of instruction for children involving visual, emotional, and intellectual components. According to the treatise, children are naturally sincere and confident, wanting to please and malleable to formation if that formation comes in a shape that is attractive and interesting to the pupil. "Pleasure must do everything," he wrote.[43] He immediately set out, therefore, to compose didactic works for his charges that would be interesting to them and serve the dual purposes of his educational program: (1) to instruct the princes academically in such subjects as history, geography, literature, mythology, and art; and more important (2) to inculcate in them the moral values that he felt were essential to ruling a kingdom.

Of the three major pedagogical works Fénelon composed for the education of the *enfants de France—The Fables*, *The Dialogues of the Dead*, and the *Adventures of Telemachus*—the first to be written was the *Fables*. Composed for the most part between 1689 and 1691 when Louis, Duc de Bourgogne, would have been between seven and nine years old, the fables are a prime example of what Fénelon termed "attractive education." These fables would all be short, as befitted the attention span of a child, and would be peopled with creatures from ancient legend and mythology to appeal to the young duke's imagination. To personalize the fables even further and make them more attractive to their reader, Fénelon often inserted Louis as a protagonist in the fables themselves under the guise of one or another mythological character. For, although theoretically Fénelon was responsible for the education of all three grandsons of Louis XIV, there was never any question that his attention would be focused on the eldest, Louis, destined to become ruler of France. So, in composing what seem to be innocuous fables—simplistic and charming—he had actually begun a program of instruction and indoctrination that would last ten years. His goal was nothing less than forming the heart and mind of a king of France according to Christian principles.

Never being intended for publication, the *fables* form a loosely organized group, including works of differing length and literary sophistication, and yet the book provides us with Fénelon's first schema for the development of the ideal prince, a schema to be more fully elaborated in the *Dialogues of the Dead* and the *Adventures of Telemachus*. If contemporary sources are to be believed, Louis himself collaborated in the composition of some of the fables, contributing an idea here and a story line there. One of the first tasks Fénelon had put to Louis was translating Jean de La Fontaine's fables into Latin. This fabulist, "the best known and best loved" of all French writers,[44] had achieved celebrity with the publication of his *Fables* beginning in the 1660s. Louis had been so impressed by them that he had insisted on meeting the celebrated fabulist. Later La Fontaine would dedicate the 1692 edition of his *Fables* to Louis.

The *Fables* is characterized by a style that is remarkably unaffected and spontaneous. The lack of artifice, one of Fénelon's hallmarks, is never so apparent as in these pedagogical fables; there was no need for redaction because they were never intended to be seen outside the circle of friends that constituted the tutorial staff. Thus, in these fables we are treated to perhaps the most disarmingly endearing writings of all the Fénelonian corpus, consisting of ingenuous stories of pagan myth and antique legend.

Knowledge of the ancient world was a mark of a culture in the seventeenth century. A smattering of Latin along with a cursory knowledge of ancient history and mythology were considered the essential cultural baggage of an *homme de race*. The fables ostensibly serve this end. They have as their protagonists heroes and gods of the ancient Greco-Roman pantheon and are permeated with allusions to ancient history and polity. Thus, at first glance, these fables may seem childishly simple. However, more careful analysis reveals that each of these seemingly simplistic fables harbors a moral quite literally fit for a prince (*ad usum delphini*, in the expression of the time), each simple character illustrating a value worthy of royal emulation. A superficial knowledge of the Olympian deities or Attic history may be gleaned from reading the fables, but in order to understand their essence one must carefully consider them individually and as groups. Such an analysis will permit us to locate recurring themes and to appreciate the didactic and moral import of these fictional works, which have as their goal the teaching of ethics by means of attractive literature.

The thirty-six short fictional works that form the corpus of the extant *Fables* are a very incoherent lot.[45] They were written, scholars agree, at various times for the purposes of ad hoc instruction. They contain, therefore, many different images and themes, and they treat diverse situations as they arose. It is clear that the fables could be approached in a number of different ways, using various methods of analysis and interpretation. A folklorist, for example, might choose to study differing motifs, such as that of the invisible ring, which appears in several fables (V, VI, and VII).[46] A literary historian, conversely, might be more interested in tracing the fables' sources back to Aesop or Phaedrus. For practical purposes, however, it seems logical to group the fables into various configurations according to Fénelon's pedagogical and didactic purposes in composing them. Of various possible groupings, I propose the following three. While subjective and somewhat arbitrary, they are nevertheless useful in isolating certain recurring themes throughout the collection. The fables, according to this proposed schema, would be divided into (1) general animal fables, (2) fables concerning the successful governing of a state and the character traits of an ideal prince, and (3) fables extolling the virtues of the simple life.

The general animal fables, as the grouping indicates, deal with animals as the main protagonists. These fables seem to have been the earliest of the three groups in date of composition; thus they tend to be short and simple. They are not much different stylistically or didactically from the fables of Aesop or La Fontaine, and they serve to point out obvious and conventional distinctions between vice and virtue. In the tradition of the fable, animals represent human beings, having the same strengths and suffering from the same weaknesses. In these general animal fables Fénelon often intrudes as authorial judge, commenting upon the vices and virtues common not only to princes but to all human beings. Among the fables in this first grouping we find numbers IX, X, XI, XII, XVI, XVII, XVIII, XIX, XX, XXIV, and XXVIII. A close analysis of each fable would be repetitious and unwieldy. Let us therefore examine two representative fables from this grouping to get a sense of the type of moral instruction Fénelon intended to inculcate by means of these animal characters.

Fable IX, "Patience and Education," is indicative of the many fables having animals as their protagonists in two respects: it is short and simple, and its moral is obvious and conventional. This fable tells the tale of a mother bear who, having given birth to a deformed cub *(une masse informe et hideuse)*, decides to kill it. She is dissuaded by a wise crow, who advises the mother to lick her cub tenderly. In time this approach brings about good results as the cub becomes more presentable. The mother hastens to thank the wise crow saying, "If you had not moderated my impatience, I would have cruelly torn my son apart, he who now is all the pleasure of my life." Fénelon, the narrator, adds the moral: "Oh! How easily impatience blocks good things and causes great evils."[47]

Although the story line of this fable is simple, as befits the attention span of the child for whom it was written, and its moral conventional, this fable reveals one of the most characteristic and recurring of Fénelonian themes: simplicity. Choosing nature as the backdrop to his fables, although conventional in the classic fable as opposed to the city or the court (two popular settings for seventeenth century fiction), the fabulist uses natural simplicity as a metaphor for virtue. To Fénelon's mind, a bucolic setting suggested the ideals of simplicity, honesty, industry, and humility. Moreover, the moral of this particular fable—the importance of patience and compassion—is typically Fénelonian. He had already praised these methods of bringing up children in his *Treatise on the Education of Daughters.* Throughout his dealings with young Louis, who was notoriously temperamental and strong willed, Fénelon put the moral of the fable into practice, and, like the mother bear, consistently used patience and kindness to overcome the repugnance felt by his young pupil for discipline and self-examination.

Another of the animal fables, XXIV of the Gosselin edition, "Nightingale and Warbler,"[48] is atypical of the general animal grouping in that its structure is more complex (indicating a later composition than the other fables in this group). Moreover, animals are not the principal protagonists. Yet it seems to fit in the grouping because the title indicates the continuing importance of nature and animals.

INTRODUCTION

In this fable we have the story of a young shepherd who lives in a sacred grotto near the ever-fragrant pastures next to the Alpheus River. It is an idyllic home for the shepherd, surrounded by nymphs and fauns. In this paradise Philomela, the nightingale, and a warbler sing of the joys and pains of love when they discover the presence of our shepherd. Astounded by his beauty and grace, and thinking he might be Apollo in disguise, they exclaim: "Who is this shepherd, or this unknown god who comes to grace our copse? He is attentive to our songs. He loves poetry." Philomela, more perspicacious than her feathered friend, divines a royal career for this young shepherd and predicts a golden age under his rule. At her prompting the warbler joins in singing the shepherd's praises, wishing him the strength of Hercules and the wisdom of Orpheus: "May the wisdom of Minerva reign in his heart! [...] May he be good and wise; beneficent, tender toward men and beloved of them."[49] While the two birds are singing the praises of the shepherd, flowers begin to bloom all around him, and the woodland deities come close to admire this boy so praised by nature's representatives.

This fable can be chronologically situated by virtue of the internal stylistic evidence among the last fables that Fénelon would write for Louis, around 1693–94, when the Duc de Bourgogne was twelve years old. We see the typical Fénelon emphasis on nature and simplicity in this text, but it is obviously a more complex and mature fable than the previous one. Here we see the use of two of Fénelon's favorite devices: (1) the use of indirect, agreeable instruction in proposing his moral through fictional characters, and (2) Fénelon's penchant for inserting either himself or Louis into the works of pedagogical fiction. Here, for example, Louis is represented under the guise of the young shepherd. This is a very telling allegorical representation for the reader familiar with Christian symbolism and, more specifically, Guyonian/Fénelonian political aspirations.

The shepherd is a traditional biblical symbol for Christ, and Minerva here (as she will later in the *Adventures of Telemachus*) symbolizes divine grace. Historically, we know that both Fénelon and Mme. Guyon had hopes of a new Christian golden age under the reign of Louis. In his edition of the fables Jacques Le Brun notes that the expectation of a golden age was an important theme in what he terms the "messianic atmosphere" surrounding the Duc de

Bourgogne.[50] The adjective *messianic* is apposite since Fénelon saw nothing less than a regenerated, sanctified kingdom in France once his pupil took the throne. "May the golden age return through him," the nightingale prays. Louis himself would be a saintly king, another Saint Louis, who would reign with Fénelon by his side, as *alter Mentor* or *alter Christus,* to dispense holy counsel whenever needed. Nor was this dream confined only to the inner circle surrounding the duke. Etchings dating from this period actually picture the Duc de Bourgogne as a shepherd, archetype of Christ leading his flock. Continuing his method of attractive, indirect instruction, Fénelon succeeds in this fable in teaching mythology (presenting classical deities), geography (the Alpheus River), and literature (allusions to Virgil's *Georgics*). More important, however, Fénelon intensifies his moral instruction. In putting Louis on stage as the embodiment of virtue, Fénelon anticipates the more elaborate allegorical representations found in the *Adventures of Telemachus,* wherein we see Louis as the archetype of hero and savior, fighting for right, seconded by Fénelon as Mentor/Minerva, the incarnation of divine wisdom and grace, aiding the young hero in his pilgrim's progress toward salvation.

Written later than the animal fables and stylistically more complex, the second grouping, fables of the ideal prince, address in a more specific manner than the previous works the duties of royalty. While the general animal fables deal with such human problems as the need for patience, the importance of honesty, and acceptance of God's providence, these lessons are important to a royal student only inasmuch as they would be useful to any student. Fénelon was not just dealing with a little boy, however. His mission was to educate a future king of France, and he felt keenly his responsibility to instill a sense of Christian ethics in his pupil. For this reason, in the second grouping of fables the moral lessons become much more limited to the problems unique to a prince. These fables delineate, for the first time in the pedagogical works, themes that will come to predominate in the *Dialogues of the Dead* and the *Adventures of Telemachus:* the duty of a king to sacrifice for his people and, conversely, the horrors brought upon a kingdom by rulers who, neglecting their duties, abandon themselves to their passions.

The characters that make up this group of fables are an eclectic lot, composed of animals, mythological personages, and forces of nature. They all serve, however, to present important lessons in the art of ruling. The fables that most easily classify themselves as dealing with the duties of the Christian prince in the Gosselin edition are XI, XIV, XV, XXI, XXVI, XXVII, XXIX, XXX, XXXI, and XXXII. Let us analyze several fables from this grouping in order to understand the moral direction intended by Fénelon in these political fables.

Fable XXIX, "The Two Lion Cubs," tells the story of two lion cubs born in the same forest at the same time. One of the cubs is captured and taken to court, where the attentions he receives serve to make him vain and indolent. "He looked down on all the other lions...who were not in favor as he was."[51] The other cub grows up brave and strong in the pristine goodness of nature. One day the King of the lions dies, and all the lions assemble to elect a new ruler. The two protagonists present themselves for consideration, and the animals choose the city lion because "he had studied the politics of the court." He proves to be vain and cruel, however, and soon the lions come to regret their decision; they rebel and put the country lion on the throne because of his virtue and strength. At this point an old, wise lioness moralizes: "I knew that he was unworthy of being king, but I wanted you to have a king spoiled by luxury and indolence so that you might better appreciate the worth of another who deserves royalty due to his patience and his worth."[52]

The moral of the fable is clear, and the allegory is suited to the moral. Louis, as metaphorically represented in the classic symbol of royalty, the lion, will have a choice in life: to be a corrupt king, indulging his own vices and shirking his duty to his people, or to be a brave, selfless king who protects his people and sacrifices his own interests for their prosperity. The question was not a merely theoretical one for either Fénelon or anyone else in France in the 1690s. Louis XIV, the great Sun King, was old, and hardly anyone expected him to live past the end of the century. His son and heir, Louis (called the Grand Dauphin), was despised by most of those who knew him. Although tutored by Bossuet, he had never grown to appreciate learning or to take his duties as heir and future king seriously. He was said to have never read a book after his instruction from Bossuet was concluded, and he was so adverse to writing that

Chamfort relates the story of the Dauphin saying with relief on learning of the death of his mistress, who had been fond of love letters, "At least I'll never have to write another letter."[53]

In fable XXXII, "Indiscreet Prayer of Neleus," we find the goddess Minerva offering to Neleus any wish he desires. Neleus rashly asks for satisfaction of all his sensual appetites, which Minerva sadly grants him. Having lived for a time in debauchery and having brought ruin to his people, Neleus repents, seeing that sensual satisfaction without virtue is empty and meaningless. "In grasping at the vain, chimerical illusion of happiness," he admits, he ended up losing both "tranquility and peace of mind."[54]

Both of these fables represent virtues to be emulated by young Louis and vices to be shunned. As in all of the *fables* we are presented with protagonists who allegorically represent either Louis or Fénelon under fictional disguise. Thus, Fénelon applies his method of indirect instruction by presenting morality in a striking and memorable way by having his pupil participate vicariously in the trials the wicked invariably undergo in Fénelon's moralistic universe before they can be redeemed. Indeed, the quintessential Christian doctrine of redemption through suffering is ubiquitous in the *Fables,* either in the foreground or the background. This doctrine will become even more explicit in the later pedagogical works.

Patience and self-restraint are virtues often proposed, as in the character of the country lion that patiently awaits his call to rule. These virtues are again proposed in fable XXI, the story of the young god Bacchus, whose arrogance and petulance are put in place by a faun. This fable is particularly interesting because it seems to have been based on an actual incident. Louis was a temperamental, strong-willed child, prone to outbursts of anger and fond of reminding people of his social rank.[55] One day after an argument with his tutor, it appears that Louis abruptly exclaimed, "Monsieur, you forget who you are and who I am!" Fénelon replied calmly that he was very aware of his position vis-à-vis His Highness and withdrew from the room, saying that if Louis was displeased with him he could no longer continue in his service. After a cooling-down period Louis, who was genuinely attached to Fénelon, came looking for him to ask him to stay. Fénelon, however, in order to derive a moral lesson from the episode, reminded him that the Duc de

Bourgogne was displeased with him and that he would only talk to little Louis, his pupil and friend. Louis, the story goes, with tears in his eyes meekly opened the door to Fénelon's apartments, saying, "I'm leaving behind the door the Duc de Bourgogne, and I am no longer for you anyone other than little Louis."[56]

In fable XXXII Louis appears in the form of Neleus, from Greek mythology, and Fénelon in the form of Minerva. This representation is interesting since this is the same symbolism used later in the *Adventures of Telemachus*, where once again Louis will appear under the guise of a young Greek hero and Fénelon again will appear as Mentor/Minerva. This fable is interesting, furthermore, in that the *mollesse* imagery, a recurring theme throughout the later pedagogical works, occurs in this fable for the first time. *Mollesse* indeed will become a key word, almost a leitmotiv, in the Fénelonian moral vocabulary of the pedagogical works. It translates many nuances of vice that Fénelon will attack in all three works. Depending on context, *mollesse* can be translated, for example, as "indolence," "sloth," "pusillanimity," "shirking of duty," or "weakness of character." In some occasions it can mean even "corruption" and "dissipation." In this fable it is Neleus's "indiscreet prayer" to have rashly wished for satisfaction of sensual desires, thus spending his life in *mollesse.* The author uses the verb form as well, writing that Neleus's spirit becomes weak and indolent; "Son esprit s'amollit..." Moreover, Neleus's subjects begin to imitate the lifestyle of their king, as children emulate their father. "But what was worse, the inhabitants, following Neleus's example, only [...] sought after dissipation and voluptuousness."[57]

This image of the king as father to his people is an important one in Fénelon's work. Under various guises in the *Fables*, the *Dialogues of the Dead*, and, particularly in the person of Minerva in the *Adventures of Telemachus*, he will hold up a heroic, Christian ideal for Louis and will consistently warn his pupil of the dangers of *mollesse.* A weak, dissolute king, in Fénelon's vision of the ideal Christian polity, is seen as corrupting not only himself but his people as well and, in a very real sense, perverting the natural order that God has established for humankind. In like manner, therefore, we see the city lion in fable XXIX as corrupted after having been raised *mollement* (the adverbial form of *mollesse*). He grows up to be hated and despised by his subjects because he wallows in corrupt pleasures (Il s'amollit dans les plaisirs).[58] He ends up as a willing sycophant in the court of his country lion and ignominiously accepts the fawning, servile role that his weakness and corrupt character have destined for him. Virtue has nothing of the weak, indolent, or corrupt about it. Minerva, Fénelon's mouthpiece and alter-ego in the pedagogical works, is described as "a beauty who had nothing of the weak or effeminate about her." The word used here is *mou*, the adjectival form of *mollesse*. As in the fables and later in the *Dialogues* and the *Telemachus*, idle luxury and sensual pleasure are seen as antitheses to virtue. In the later two pedagogical works, as in the fables, nature is always preferred by Fénelon over the city or the court. Simplicity is always preferred over opulence.

The general animal fables and the fables concerning the ideal prince both present important moral lessons for young Louis. Both praise virtue and condemn vice; the second group highlights certain virtues as being proper for a prince. The third group of fables continues this same line of moral instruction and complements the first two groupings by giving them a philosophical cadre, a backdrop against which the workings of virtue and vice may be seen. It is the third group of fables that particularly extol the simple life over that of the court. By insisting that happiness and peace of mind can only be found in simplicity, they furnish a philosophically Christian universe in which not only the animals of the *fables* interact, but also in which the dead souls of the *Dialogues* and the mythological personages of the *Telemachus* will live and proffer their moral instruction.

In the third group, fables extolling the simple life, peasants and monarchs share the stage with gods and goddesses, nymphs and shepherds. There is an absence of animals. It is perhaps more than coincidental that the human dominates the bestial characters in this grouping, for the human nature of the characters lends poignancy to the stories, some of which are very melancholy. They prepare the reader for the two later fictional works that will deal entirely with human characters. This third group of fables, emphasizing the ideal of simplicity, is informed by the ethos of *contemptio mundi*, a scorn for the world's luxuries and corruption. They equate the simplicity of nature with goodness; conversely, the luxury of the city and court is equated with vice. The fables falling in this category are I, II, IV,

V, VI, VII, VIII, XXV, XXXIII, XXXIV, XXXV, and XXXVI of the Gosselin edition of Fénelon's works.

A fable typical of this grouping is fable I, "An Old Queen and a Young Peasant." In this tale we find a queen "so old that she no longer had either teeth or hair"[59] who agrees to exchange her kingdom for the youth of a country girl, Peronelle. Both soon weary of their new lives and so agree to revert to their former status. The old queen immediately regrets her decision, but Peronelle had learned her lesson. "It is better to dance on the grass or the heather than in a palace, and to be Peronelle in the village than an unhappy lady in wealthy society."[60]

The moral of the fable is clear and serves to reiterate the didactic message found in the other groups of fables, particularly the second: simplicity and humility in good health are more to be valued than riches and opulence when old and decrepit. The same moral is repeated in fable II, in which we find a young maid who again realizes that it is better to be poor and happy than old and miserable. "I'd rather be young and eat black bread," she states, "than be a queen in misery."[61] Again, in fable XII, a young, virtuous shepherd discovers a miraculous ring that gives him the power to be invisible. He uses this power to win himself a place at court but realizes ultimately that riches and power cannot alone bring happiness or peace of mind. "His talisman procured him everything except peace and happiness, because they can only be found within oneself."[62]

In all these fables the moral is similar: natural simplicity is good; luxury is evil. However, Fénelon's moral teaching of simplicity is more complex than a superficial reading would suggest. For the author of the *Fables* natural simplicity translates not only the simplicity of nature but also the simplicity of the heart. Christ speaks in the gospel of the necessity of childlike simplicity for salvation: "Let the little children come to me; do not stop them; for it is to such as these that the kingdom of God belongs. Truly I tell you, whoever does not receive the kingdom of God as a little child will never enter it" (Mark 10:14–15). It is this simplicity above all that Fénelon wishes to inculcate in Louis by means of the fables. Simplicity of dress, manners, and morals—all these are desirable in and of themselves, but they are truly significant only in that they are exterior signs of interior grace. Thus, when a character in the

Fénelonian fables renounces the simple life in order to live in luxury, this renunciation is a metaphor for those who turn their back on virtue in order to wallow in vice. As the author of the *Fables* says: "When, in opulence and grandeur, we lose simplicity, innocence, and moderation, then our heart and our conscience—true seats of happiness—become prey to anxiety, worry, shame, and remorse."[63]

The *fables* were all written rapidly with little attention to style. As they were never intended for publication, coherence and symmetry were often neglected by their author. The three groupings proposed here are therefore an attempt to bring some measure of coherence to a rather inchoate group of stories. These disparate fables were written at various times and in various styles over a five-year period and are ultimately impossible to classify in a completely logical fashion. Some fables, such as XI and XXVII, for example, overlap the groupings proposed above. Others steadfastly refuse to be placed in any category. Nevertheless, most of the fables do fit conveniently into classes and allow the reader to locate recurring themes and images.

"Children love amusing stories," Fénelon had opined in his treatise *On the Education of Daughters.*[64] It was for this end that he composed the fables to amuse the Duc de Bourgogne while at the same time instructing him in ethical values. Critics have disagreed over the ultimate success of the *Fables* as either literature or as morality. Some critics see the fables as overly didactic and moralizing. Louis Cognet, for example, in his *Littérature française*, while recognizing that certain passages in the fables are not without charm, nevertheless states that "the artifice of the literary device is too obvious for our tastes today."[65] James Davis, however, cites the "variety of form and subject matter" of the *fables* and maintains that they, indeed, succeed as works of literature. He calls for the reconsideration of the literary merit of the fables by the critical public and for their inclusion in their "rightful place" in the body of French literature.[66] Fénelon's earliest pedagogical work may, therefore, be considered successful on three levels: literature, pedagogy, and moral instruction. The *Fables* serves, furthermore, as a starting point for the next two better-known pedagogical works that we can now consider.

THE DIALOGUES OF THE DEAD

Sometime after the completion of the *Fables*, probably between 1692 and 1695, the Duc de Bourgogne's tutor began writing the *Dialogues of the Dead* for his continuing instruction. This genre, very popular in the seventeenth century, is characterized by the following literary conventions: the participants must be dead, and the setting for the action must be the Underworld. The genre was not new to Fénelon; it had been invented by Lucian, a Greek author of the late Classical period, and had more recently been popularized in France by Fontenelle with the publication of his *Nouveaux Dialogues des morts* in 1683. There is no reason to doubt that Fénelon was inspired by his two predecessors or that he borrowed liberally from them. One student of Fénelon's dialogues, having studied the history of the genre in France, maintains that Fénelon was not only inspired by Lucian and Fontenelle as to choice of genre, but that Fontenelle especially influenced him in his structure of the dialogues and the limitation to two characters instead of the several often found in Lucian as well as in the inclusion of recently deceased historical figures.[67] Even if we admit Lucian's inspiration and Fontenelle's considerable influence, the reader is still faced in the Fénelonian *Dialogues* with a work that is different in both tone and purpose from the works of his predecessors.

In his dialogues Fontenelle provides all the information about the two participants of each dialogue that the reader needs to know to be able to appreciate the dialogue by itself.[68] Fontenelle's dialogues are further characterized by the refined manner in which he writes and the inevitably enigmatic epigram that closes each selection. In contrast with these well crafted, witty dialogues, the *dialogues* of Fénelon present practically no prefatory information to introduce the protagonists to the reader; the tutor assumed that his pupil would have the knowledge requisite to grasp the mythological and historical allusions. Moreover, they are stylistically less refined and more didactic than Fontenelle's dialogues. The most striking difference, however, between Fénelon and his predecessors is the emphasis he places on the infernal tone of the genre he uses. In contrast to the satiric atmosphere of Lucian and the refined, almost precious, atmosphere of Fontenelle, Fénelon's dialogues are permeated with the somber presence of death.

Like the *Fables*, the *Dialogues of the Dead* was not intended for publication. The dialogues, therefore, show a natural lack of organization; even so, there is remarkable cohesiveness among them that delivers the clear thrust of Fénelon's didactic goal. Fénelon's intent was to continue inculcating in the Duc de Bourgogne the virtues of simplicity and charity already seen in the fables and to inspire in him a greater moral repulsion toward the evils of corruption, weakness (the *mollesse* of the fables), sensuality, violence, and tyranny.

The dialogue form is eminently suited to Fénelon's didactic purpose. By presenting the reader with two or more interlocutors who, stripped of their rank and power by death, the great equalizer, meet in the Underworld to converse about their former conditions, the author is able to give the impression of spontaneity and veracity that one expects from impromptu conversations. The interlocutors may be ancient or modern figures and may represent completely different cultures. This fictional framework, while remaining faithful to Fénelon's theories of "attractive education," is well suited for an adolescent pupil easily bored with a formal study of ethics but able to read with interest these lively conversations between exotic historical personages. Fénelon further heightens the inherent drama of the genre by juxtaposing several of history's most victimized figures with their persecutors. Thus the *Dialogues* presents a stage on which we see murderers meet with their prey (LVI), debauched students with their former teachers (XVI), and abused ministers with their royal persecutors (XXIII). Throughout these conversations there is the ubiquitous, inescapable presence of death and the almost palpable sensation of hopelessness. This is the pagan Underworld at its most vivid, brought to life by an ardent lover of the classics, yet molded to present a moral lesson by a Christian priest and spiritual heir of Bérulle and Olier.

In all seventy-nine dialogues that have come down to us, all but four were published after Fénelon's death in 1715.[69] Nearly all of them deal with actual historical figures. The preponderance of historical characters, as opposed to mythological or legendary characters, for example, is easily understandable if we keep in mind the didactic purpose of the works. Historical figures lend themselves easily and with greater realism than other possible subjects to the purpose of teaching ethics. Fénelon's technique of proposing models for Louis's moral instruction overrode all considerations he might have had in the aesthetic domain, had he been writing these dialogues for the general public. Thus, what sometimes appears as heavy-handed moralizing was unavoidable given the single-minded nature of Fénelon's endeavor. What is remarkable, however, is that the *Dialogues of the Dead*, written as a collection of minor treatises of political ethics and with no pretense of being polished works of literature, can still hold the interest of a modern reader.

One of the most charming of the dialogues is atypical in that characters taken from contemporary fiction are the protagonists, and for that reason it can be considered apart from the rest. Dialogue LXXIX, "Harpagon and Dorante," presents us with two famous characters from Molière's theater, the protagonist of *The Miser* and a character from *The Would-be Gentleman*. We find them *in medias res* at the beginning of the dialogue, already discussing the desirability of amassing wealth. Harpagon insists that he loves his children more than himself. It is for this reason, he claims, that he has been a miser all his life. Dorante, however, counters by arguing that Harpagon really loves only himself, since he has spent all his time on business and left his children unsupervised and uneducated. When Harpagon replies that tutors would have cost dearly and it is more important that he leave his children a rich inheritance, Dorante—here the *porte-parole* of Fénelon—replies that he should have given them the most important inheritance, virtue.

This dialogue is significant for several reasons. As mentioned above, it is atypical of the dialogues in presenting characters taken from fiction as its protagonists rather than historical figures. Was this perhaps an attempt by his chief tutor to inspire an appreciation of contemporary literature in his pupil? We know that Louis had read and appreciated La Fontaine, Fontenelle, and other contemporary French authors up to this time. Molière is a curious choice in that Fénelon, along with most clerics at this time, criticized the theater as inciting immorality. Bossuet actually wrote a polemic against theater going, and Fénelon's position, although more ambivalent than that of Bossuet (mellowing considerably over the years), was nevertheless condemnatory of the theater in general.[70]

This dialogue, if atypical in its protagonists, is nevertheless typically Fénelonian in the moral lesson it teaches. Harpagon, the archetype of the selfish miser, is condemned not only for his own character flaw but equally, and perhaps more important, for the fact that his sinful love of money has affected the welfare of his children. They have grown up without formal education because their father was too miserly to provide them with proper tutors. Here we see Fénelon once again as a Christian humanist, implying that study of the classics is not antithetical to—indeed can be an aid to—virtue. In taking this position Fénelon shows himself once again a faithful disciple of the French School theologians, such as Bérulle (a noted humanist himself), who opposed the rigorist position of many seventeenth-century Catholics, who favored education only within a tightly controlled Christian curriculum.[71]

The Fénelonian dialogues cover practically all stages of history, from earliest times up to contemporary France. It is apparent even from a cursory reading that their author has a definite agenda for moral instruction. More than any other pedagogical work by Fénelon, the dialogues seem to shine a harsh light on what lies underneath the rocks of history. This method is, of course, consistent with Fénelon's intent throughout the pedagogical works of proposing positive models for Louis's emulation and negative models for his avoidance. This indirect method of instruction might be called negative instruction, especially in the dialogues in which Fénelon exposes not only the faults of rulers such as Nero and Caligula, execrated by common consent of humanity, but also those of traditionally respected rulers such as Marcus Aurelius and Henri IV. In the case of these men Fénelon seems to want to point out to his pupil the inherent flaws of humankind. Even as diamonds can have flaws, good people can also have serious character failings when they seek to live by rules of secular morality without the grace of the Christian gospel.

Not everyone will appreciate the efficacy of such a cynical depiction of life, especially when presented as a norm of human behavior to an impressionable pubescent boy. In fact, the lack of understanding for human frailty has led some critics to marvel at the harshness of the *Dialogues*. Madeleine Daniélou, for example, in her study of the Duc de Bourgogne's educational program, comments on the paradoxical nature of a work by a Christian mystic in which "no Christian softness modifies his judgments."[72] Such a critical appraisal shows little understanding of Fénelon the man. Fénelon was both Christian and a Humanist, and, in his role as preceptor, both mentor[73] and guide to his charges in the context of Versailles' corrupting environment. If some of the dialogues seem anti-humanistic, it must be remembered that he was reacting to the temptations of court life in which he and his young pupils found themselves. This was an environment of flattery, sensuality, and ambition. In the *Fables* Fénelon had already attempted to demonstrate that happiness and peace of mind can only be found in the love of simplicity and reason. Now, in the *Dialogues*, the preceptor seeks to show the fate of those throughout history who did not follow the path of virtue. This doubtless explains why there are no saints among in the characters in the dialogues, for in this work Fénelon constantly proposes to Louis a negative ideal and thus holds up to the young prince a mirror of what he could become if, failing to follow the lessons of the *Dialogues*, he should allow himself to become a slave to his passions.

As far as subject matter is concerned, the dialogues are decidedly eclectic. Their source material is derived from many different times and cultures. However, Fénelon's mind seems to have repeatedly returned to three major periods of history for inspiration for the majority of the dialogues: classical Greece, the early Roman Empire, and the European Renaissance. Of these periods the dialogues are heavily weighted in favor of the Ancients (fifty-one of the dialogues treat personages from Antiquity as opposed to twenty-seven dealing with more contemporary figures). This preponderance of Ancients clearly indicates Fénelon's interest in classical history and his desire to teach it to his pupil. As far as the moderns are concerned, the group is largely French—fifteen French characters as opposed to only four English, and even fewer Germans, Italians, or Spanish. This is not surprising, since Fénelon's primary purpose was to teach ethics to a young French prince in the context of his role in history. The history that was to be taught would logically be that which would be most useful to Louis, once a king. Classical history was central, because this formed the culture common to all educated Europeans. The history of France was important because France was the country over which he would rule and with whose history he needed to be familiar.

Since the dialogues were not intended for publication, Fénelon left no plan for their presentation in print, nor did he edit them to present a central theme or idea. They have been found as he wrote them, hastily—in his words "à la hâte." Critics for the most part have not been able to reach any consensus as to a definitive manner of their organization. For the purposes of convenience, however, it seems useful to attempt a classification similar to the one proposed for the *Fables* in order to better comprehend certain key Fénelonian preoccupations in the *Dialogues.* With few exceptions they fall into three categories: (1) pedagogical dialogues written primarily to teach some factual information, (2) moral dialogues written to condemn a particular moral flaw, and (3) political dialogues having as their primary purpose the teaching of a virtue proper to a ruler or, conversely, the condemnation of royal abuse of power. Like the *Fables,* of course, they are not so simple as to be pigeonholed into rigid, preconceived categories. As with any other work of good literature, the dialogues are complex and oftimes so fluid that they defy easy labels.

By far the smallest of the three groups is the pedagogical dialogues. As in the *Fables* and later in the *Adventures of Telemachus,* Fénelon's purpose in the *Dialogues* is not primarily to instruct but to educate in a moral sense. Nevertheless, they are not wholly without interest. Fénelon weighs in on art appreciation in dialogue LII, a conversation between the artists Parrhasius and Poussin in which the protagonists debate the relative merits of modern (that is, the seventeenth century) art as opposed to the art of the Ancients. He opines on the relative merits of different schools of philosophy in dialogue XXIX, wherein Pyrrho and his "neighbor" discuss skepticism as a philosophy. These dialogues are interesting in that they reveal Fénelon's approach to teaching Louis to distinguish between the worthwhile and the useless in art, music, literature, and philosophy.

The moral dialogues, in contrast to the pedagogical dialogues, form a large part of the *Dialogues of the Dead.* Although a diverse group, they are cohesive in that they concern themselves with personal moral issues as opposed to political morality. They set forth moral lessons in personal virtue, apart from qualities that would affect a prince's behavior toward his subjects. These moral dialogues are among the most straightforward in terms of theme and purpose.

Fénelon has been taken to task by some critics who accuse him of having distorted history in order to serve his didactic aims. This criticism, however, is overly facile in that it ignores both Fénelon's avowed didactic purpose and the status of historical knowledge in the seventeenth century, which lacked the critical and scientific apparatus of modern historians. Indeed, the genre itself, in presenting imaginary conversations by people who obviously could not have engaged in these conversations, is open to criticism if a rigid standard of historical veracity were to be imposed. The *Dialogues of the Dead*, however, if not factually accurate, is effective on a metahistorical level in presenting historical figures in positions truer to their personalities and character than the recorded conversations we have from "real life." In fact, in using these techniques of fictional conversations and imagined encounters Fénelon may be said to have anticipated the sort of *mises-en-scène* many modern historians have adopted in their efforts to render history more vivid and believable to their readers.[74]

A representative example of the moral dialogues is dialogue L, in which we find the Roman emperor Marcus Aurelius being criticized by his father, Antoninus Pius, for the favoritism that he showed his son, Commodus, in assuring him the throne in spite of the young man's many obvious faults: "If you foresaw that the empire was going to corrupt him," Antoninus Pius says, "you should have abstained from making him emperor for the love of the empire that needed to be well governed and for the love of your son who would have been better off in a middling station of life."[75] Marcus Aurelius replies with a series of rationalizations. Antoninus Pius sees through them all, telling him that he alone was ultimately responsible for his moral decisions: "Oh, my son, stop trying to excuse yourself. Such an insane, wicked man could never have fooled a man as enlightened as you if tenderness had not weakened your prudence and your virtue."[76] This dialogue exemplifies two consistent tendencies in the *Dialogues of the Dead:* (1) the selection by Fénelon of one moral flaw for condemnation, here the paternal tenderness that blinded Marcus Aurelius to his son's vices, and (2) the ability to judge the faults of respected men of history, even when these faults were inspired by virtuous emotions such as love, honor, or hospitality.

Fénelon's role as preceptor to Louis XIV's grandchildren was never exclusively confined to overseeing academic work. He put an able staff in place to take most of this burden off of his shoulders, including well-known scholars such as the abbés Fleury and Langeron, published authors already. Nor was his role confined to the exposition of political ethics, although this was a role for which Fénelon felt an affinity and such theorizing is predominant in many of the dialogues. Fénelon's task was often, as Daniélou and Lemaître have pointed out, that of developing moral guidelines for daily situations in which the royal princes, like all children, find themselves.[77]

In the *Fables* Fénelon had initiated his program of teaching morality in an indirect and attractive way. The moral dialogues continue this pedagogical method and represent another facet of Fénelon's answer to the quotidian dilemmas he and his pupil faced. They also shed light on the increasingly close relationship between tutor and pupil. Each dialogue proposes a type of *cas de conscience*, in the wording of seventeenth-century France, that is to say, a moral dilemma forcing a decision on the person faced with the problem. These problems were doubtless legion for the young Louis. Could he ever give in to his passions? (Dialogue number L). Could he be defeated in battle by his weakness? (XXI). Should he put other people's good before his own? (XXXIV). The moral dialogues are Fénelon's attempt to address these moral questions faced by Louis and his brothers. And, although wrapped in fictional garb, they are informed by the purest of Christian ethics.

As interesting as both the pedagogical dialogues and the moral dialogues are, the former by giving insight into Fénelon's literary, aesthetic, and philosophical beliefs, and the latter by furnishing examples of the day-to-day moral instruction Fénelon was called on to provide, they pale in comparison with the number and importance of the third group of dialogues, whose goal was to inculcate the ethics of Christian politics. These political dialogues outnumber and overshadow the other two groups for the simple reason that, as Louis was growing older (he was fifteen to sixteen years old when the last dialogues were composed), he was becoming aware of his importance in the royal succession. Whereas traditional moral admonitions of the sort previously seen in the *Fables*—avoid laziness and gluttony, strive for patience and moderation, and so forth—are present to a greater or lesser extent in all three pedagogical works, they increasingly give way in importance to the teaching of political morality as Louis passed from adolescence into young adulthood.

Fénelon once wrote that he was an enemy of bloodshed: "I am a peace-loving priest, an enemy of bloodshed." The political dialogues show clearly that this horror of bloodshed, along with its concomitant love of justice and moderation, obsessed Fénelon's thoughts during the composition of these dialogues. Thus, the typical monarch of the political dialogues is egocentric, violent, and utterly devoid of moral scruples. Concerned only with his own self-gratification and self-aggrandizement, he searches to quench his lust for power and pleasures of the flesh in war and sensual dissipation. Having no sense of duty toward his people, he uses his power to live in ease at their expense rather than sacrificing himself for their benefit. This callous abuse of power, however, does not succeed in bringing happiness to the tyrants portrayed in Fénelon's fictional Underworld of retributive justice. The heartless, selfish ruler is seen not only to have been unhappy on earth, but now in the Underworld he is even more painfully conscious of the futility of his past misdeeds. The evil prince is presented in Hades as an impotent, pitiable creature who can only rail helplessly at his interlocutors, who, for their part, inevitably mock him by saying they have nothing to fear now from a "shadow."

There are many personal portraits in the political dialogues, ranging from ancient to contemporary history. We are shown Romulus arguing with Numa Pompilius in favor of the use of murder for political ends; we see Solon and Justinian debating the nature and purpose of laws; and Diogenes the philosopher tries to convince Dionysius the tyrant of the error of his despotism. In a foreshadowing of Sartre's existentialist motto "l'enfer, c'est les autres," these formerly all-powerful, sadistic persecutors now find themselves forced to undergo the harsh, judgmental gaze of their former victims. Reduced to impotence in Fénelon's stygian universe, they can only lash out verbally at their accusers and suffer the indignity of hearing the recurring refrain of the dialogues: "Hey, do you think you're still a tyrant down here?"

The political dialogues highlight the bleakness and cynicism of Fénelon's characterization of corrupt princes. Alexander the Great and Caesar may have conquered kingdoms and built empires, but they ultimately served to bring only suffering to their people due to their greed and lust for power. Justinian may be praised for his administration of Byzantium, but his elaborate code of laws was compiled to ensure his own glory and not to help his people live more virtuous lives. Even rulers traditionally seen as good, such as Marcus Aurelius, are shown in the *Dialogues* to have erred gravely by giving in to personal weakness and consequently bringing harm to the people for whose benefit they had been entrusted by God with authority.

Of all the black, cynical portraits of human nature that appear in the *Dialogues* the most execrable is that of Louis XI of France. He makes more appearances in the dialogues than any other character and seems to have embodied for Fénelon all the vices that the tutor wanted to teach Louis to avoid. All the dialogues involving Louis XI show him to be a sadistic, sarcastic, dissimulating tyrant concerned only with conquest and personal aggrandizement. Dialogue LVIII is representative of this portrayal of the man known to French history as the spider king. In it we find Louis XI confronted in Hades by Cardinal Balue, who had once been his ally but who later worked against him. Louis begins the dialogue by raging against his interlocutor (as do most of the tyrant-shades in the Dialogues before realizing that their rage is utterly useless in the static, immutable Underworld that has rendered them powerless). Cardinal Balue is quick to remind the king that they are no longer on earth and no longer in a position of social inequality. "We are all equals down here," he informs the wretched ghost of the former tyrant.[78] Louis and Balue debate the efficacy of Louis's political methods, which, according to the king, served to maintain his authority, but which, according to Balue, only served to create sycophants or enemies. Louis accuses the cardinal of the basest treachery and threatens him with *la cage*, Louis XI's notorious method of torture. This threat provokes only amusement on the part of Balue, who exclaims, "Ho! I've spent enough time there already. If you get me mad I won't say another word to you. Do you know that I hardly fear the ill humor of a king's ghost? What! Do you still think you're in Plessis-les-Tours with your hit men?"[79] Balue thereupon proceeds to justify his betrayal of Louis by reasoning that he was only following the example of the king himself, whose "fundamental precept" was to do everything for himself alone. After having listed Louis XI's various crimes, Balue concludes: "You never loved anyone. Whom did you expect to love you?" Louis can only bow to the force of the cardinal's logic and say in a manner typical of Fénelon's tyrants, who although not always repentant are always forced to concede the truth in their opponents' arguments, "I confess that your reasoning disconcerts me."[80]

From these examples the reader can easily detect the typical pattern of the political dialogues: a former tyrant meets with his former victim—now accuser—in the Underworld. Being powerless to inflict harm on his accuser, he can only suffer from the impotence of his state and bemoan his lack of virtue when alive. Thus Romulus (dialogues VIII, IX, and X) realizes that his conquests were, in the final analysis, worthless compared to the peaceful rule of Numa Pompilius. In dialogue XIII Justinian realizes that the majesty of his laws means nothing if not accompanied by a concern for the welfare of his people. The tyrant Dionysius in dialogue XXIII bemoans the futility of having brought misery to his subjects in the search for elusive pleasure, realizing that true happiness can only be found in a life of dedication to his people. Finally, Louis XI is forced to acknowledge that all his crimes and political machinations led to nothing but his condemnation by posterity and to realize that he will now spend eternity trying in vain to escape his victims' recriminations and the harsh stare of their constant witness to his failure as king while alive.

Dialogues of the dead as a genre never achieved lasting popularity in European literature, and Fénelon's dialogues are no exception. Many critics agree with Louis Cognet, who considers them dry and overly didactic. Yet, as manuals of morality they seem to have been successful in educating Louis to his duties as future king of France. Fénelon wanted to introduce the Duc de Bourgogne to a knowledge of political ethics. He was keenly aware, long before Lord Acton pronounced the words, that "power corrupts, and absolute power corrupts absolutely." He therefore sought to show Louis how such power had corrupted famous rulers throughout history. The goal, as always, was to teach the young prince how to avoid the mistakes of his predecessors while imitating their good qualities. For the author of the *Dialogues*, the ideal would have been, as Jules Lemaître states, "le retour à l'âge d'or," that is, a return to a golden age wherein a virtuous prince, uncorrupted by the vices of the court, would find his strength in this "moeurs simples" and "citoyens vertueux."[81]

Fénelon was painfully aware of how far removed the France of Louis XIV was from this idyllic realm. He trembled at the thought of sending his pupil alone into this world peopled with sycophants who would inflate his ego, wanton courtiers who would tempt him sexually, and militarists who would try to goad him into needless, bloody wars. Clearly it was to prepare his charge for the worldly, often sordid, court environment of Versailles that Fénelon composed the *Dialogues of the Dead*. They paint, it is true, a bleak picture of humanity. They portray, in fact, an environment wherein each character is propelled by self-interest and uses cruelty to achieve his ends. They reflect a society in which the virtuous are mocked and the wicked praised. The *dialogues* are Fénelon's moral response to that society and his indictment of it. The world may mock you, the dialogues teach, but God is not mocked. God reigns supreme and will ultimately judge human conduct.

The preceptor is not so doctrinaire or so naive as to suggest that the wicked always live miserable lives as a result of their sin. In the dialogues we see that the wicked may indeed enjoy an ephemeral prosperity while alive. But, as a faithful heir to the Baroque writers of the generation before him, Fénelon emphasizes the transitory and deceitful nature of this happiness. Life is a dream. It is ever changing, and happiness is ever elusive. The wise prince will realize the vanity of the world's pleasures. He will seek true happiness in the love of his people and the peace of mind achieved through his own moderation. Thus, the *Dialogues of the Dead* serves not only as a didactic work but also as an introduction to the more complex and more ambitious *Adventures of Telemachus*. In this celebrated work the Duc de Bourgogne's chief tutor will at last present to him a work specifically devoted to expounding the Fénelonian political ethic.

THE ADVENTURES OF TELEMACHUS

Most scholars agree that the novel commonly called the *Telemachus* was written sometime between 1694 and 1696. This work, by consensus considered Fénelon's fictional masterpiece, is a far more complex undertaking than either of the two pedagogical works discussed above. Fénelon's pupil, Louis, was now fourteen years old in an era when many young men were married and heads of household at his age. The young duke was being taken more seriously at court with each passing day, impressing even jaded courtiers with his precocious wit, wisdom beyond his years, and his remarkable and obviously sincere piety. It was well known at Versailles that his preceptor exerted a profound influence on the young prince's spiritual and intellectual development. Fénelon was indeed beginning to be considered far and wide as a new light on the horizon of French letters. Copies of his *Treatise on the Education of Daughters* were increasingly in demand as his role as chief tutor to the royal princes was appreciated.

It was therefore as a more mature and esteemed writer addressing a more mature and accomplished pupil that Fénelon set his pen to the task of composing a novel for the completion of Louis's moral education. Like the two preceding fictional works written for the young duke's instruction, the *Telemachus* is a textbook of ethics enclosed in a fictional framework. Unlike the previous two works, however, which were known only to Fénelon's inner circle at Versailles, a manuscript copy of the *Telemachus* was spirited off to a publisher in 1699. This publisher immediately saw the potential financial value of a novel by the preceptor of the royal grandchildren, who was by now not only the archbishop-duke of Cambrai but also famous throughout France because of role during the Quietist controversy. He therefore rushed into print several thousand copies of the novel within days of his receiving it. The novel's success was immediate and overwhelming. Coming as it did in the wake of Rome's condemnation of the *Maxims of the Saints*, which had brought about his definitive rupture with Bossuet and Madame de Maintenon, the novel was naturally assumed by the general public to be a roman à clef—a novel in which actual persons are depicted in fictional guise. What would be more natural, it was said, than that a courtier fallen from favor with his ecclesiastical patron, Bossuet, and his court patrons, Mme. de Maintenon and Louis XIV, should compose this venomous allegory with the intent of satirizing his adversaries. This practice was not unknown. Seventeenth-century France was a great age of pamphleteers and satirists, many of whom were vitriolic in their attacks against prominent figures of church and State. Figures at court were particularly targeted by the anonymous pamphlets that flooded the kingdom.

Fénelon's repeated denials of any satiric intent in writing the novel had, as might have been expected, no effect whatsoever on dissuading the throngs of readers. Nor did his protests that the manuscript had been given to the publisher only through the "indiscretion of a secretary" quell their interest. On the contrary, his denials only seemed to whet the literary appetite of the Parisian bourgeois, who were more convinced with each denial that the *Telemachus* was an attack on the people who had brought about Fénelon's disgrace and exile to Cambrai: Mme. de Maintenon and the king.

The book's popularity became such that it was reported that in Paris the bookstores selling the *Telemachus* were mobbed by frenzied crowds seeking copies of the novel at any price. Some prospective buyers were said to throw *Louis d'or* through the shop windows in hopes of thus obtaining a copy of the coveted book. As a result of this *succès de scandale*, the first printing of the novel was exhausted in a matter of days and the *Adventures of Telemachus* remained the most widely printed book of the first half of the eighteenth century in France. It was so popular and its author's prestige so great in the eighteenth century that it was used as the principal text by Cardinal Fleury's staff in the education of the future Louis XV. Rousseau is said to have always carried a copy of the *Telemachus* with him, and when asked once whom he would like to have been if he had not been Rousseau, he replied "Fénelon's valet de chambre" in order to have had the opportunity every day to converse with the archbishop.

But was the novel really intended as a satire of Louis XIV and his court, as so many assumed, or was it merely a fictional sequel to the *Odyssey*, enriched with Christian precepts for the moral education of the Duc de Bourgogne, as Fénelon claimed? It seems safe to say that if it was not entirely meant as satire, it certainly was not merely a work of fiction. Clearly, some of those who argued that the *Telemachus* was a roman à clef, carried away by their own enthusiasm, began to see court figures behind every rock of Calypso's grotto. On the other hand, in spite of the Homeric veneer of pagan antiquity in the novel, the objective reader can hardly analyze the novel without concluding that there is an allegorical element inherent in its structure and essential to its didactic aims.

This allegorical fiction need not surprise the reader familiar with Fénelon's methods. Long before he began composing the *Telemachus*, Fénelon had already clothed his pupil and himself in mythological garb to appear as characters in the *Fables*. Nor should the use of the Telemachus legend be considered an obstacle to an allegorical interpretation of the novel. In fact, the choice of Telemachus to teach morality and political ethics—and thereby to criticize Louis XIV's policies—was a natural one on the author's part for several reasons. First, it allowed him to continue teaching mythology and history to Louis. Louville, a courtier well placed at Versailles to observe the educational program of the young princes, wrote in his mémoires that these were both important subjects to Fénelon. For the *honnête homme* of the seventeenth century, knowledge of history and mythology was viewed as an essential component of a gentleman's *bagage culturel*. Second, as an admirer of the Alexandrian school of theology, Fénelon was well versed in the exegesis of Plotinus and Clement of Alexandria who saw in Homer's *Odyssey* an allegory: the flight of the seeker of the truth from sensual beauty to that of Ideal Beauty, which is God.[82] Therefore, by choosing to continue the *Odyssey* with further adventures of Telemachus, Fénelon was able to make use of the allegorical nature of the voyage motif as interpreted by the Alexandrian theologians. This interpretation was shared as well by recent mystics whom Fénelon admired, such as Saint John of the Cross. Moreover, a great deal of attraction of the legend for Fénelon, Goré maintains, undoubtedly lay in the fact that the classic poets had written relatively little about Ulysses' son. Thus, paucity of information gave Fénelon a freer hand than he might have had with other mythological figures; he could mold Telemachus to suit his allegorical and ultimately didactic ends. The fact that the Telemachus of Greek legend was a prince, son of a great king, and accompanied by his faithful adviser,

Mentor, only served to enhance the suitability in Fénelon's eyes of Telemachus as a choice for protagonist of his last great fictional work.

Thus, by the astute choice of the Telemachus legend, Fénelon is able to present a fictional cadre in which Louis, pampered and protected by the walls of Versailles, can vicariously undergo the trials of adversity suffered by Telemachus and learn from them. Considered in this light, the *Adventures of Telemachus* becomes quintessentially Christian in its content as well as its function, for the story of the hero who braves trials and tribulations in order to attain virtue and ultimately return home to be crowned in glory is none other than the archetype of the pilgrim's progress from sin to salvation. This same concept is found in seminal form in Saint Paul's description of the Christian as pilgrim,[83] in the French medieval Grail cycle, in Dante's *Divine Comedy*, in Bunyan's *Pilgrim's Progress*, and in many other works. What will differentiate the story of Telemachus from other allegories of Christian salvation is the identification of its hero so closely with one particular person, the young prince Louis. In the *Telemachus* Fénelon leaves little room for the reader to doubt that the protagonist of the novel, Telemachus, is to be identified with the Duc de Bourgogne and that the trials forced upon Telemachus in the novel are meant to serve as moral lessons for Louis so that he can learn from them to be a truly Christian king. The manner in which the author describes both Mentor and Telemachus further underlines this association in that the two fictional characters correspond—character trait for character trait—to contemporary accounts of the preceptor and his pupil. One has only to compare, for example, Saint-Simon's description of the Duc de Bourgogne with Fénelon's description of Telemachus in order to note the similarities between the two. Saint-Simon describes Louis in this way: "This prince was born terrible and his youth caused people to tremble; hard and angry to the point of tantrums even against inanimate objects, impetuous with a fury, incapable of putting up with even the least opposition...in short, given over to all sorts of passions."[84] Fénelon describes Telemachus as headstrong and sensual as well: "He followed his tastes without thinking...Anyone who would have seen him thus in his natural state would have judged him incapable of loving anything but himself...and his continual obsession with himself came from the constant tumults in which the violence of his passions cast him."[85]

If one then accepts the *Telemachus* as an allegory, the questions remain to what degree the novel is allegorical and to what end. Is the novel, for example, an allegory in the tradition of Bunyan's *Pilgrim's Progress*, in which Louis would represent in symbolic form the Christian seeking personal salvation? If this analysis is adopted, Mentor would then be seen as the symbolic representation of Divine Grace. Certain critics have tended toward this interpretation. Ely Carcassonne implies acceptance of this interpretation when he writes: "The mythology found in the *Telemachus* purified by a sort of gradual spirituality, ends up by joining Christian mysticism. The reason embodied by Minerva is the divine Word, the Logos. The theology of grace...is found in the *Telemachus*."[86] Or is the allegory more a political one, as both the public and the court believed in 1699? According to this analysis Telemachus would be seen as Louis, Duc de Bourgogne, and Mentor would represent Fénelon himself. The wicked king Adrastus, or perhaps the deluded Cretan prince Idomeneus, would, according to this allegorical interpretation, represent Louis XIV. Antoine Adam, for example, maintains that although Fénelon may be seen as part of a tradition in French ecclesiastical literature of criticizing the monarchy in general, it is impossible to take at face value Fénelon's claim that Louis XIV is not specifically represented allegorically in the novel.[87] Given Fénelon's attachment to the French School of Spirituality, whose leaders—especially Bérulle—consistently opposed the aggrandizement of the monarchy at the expense of the church, as well as his sincere pastoral desire for peace for war-torn France, it would have perhaps been impossible for Fénelon to write a textbook of political morality without having it contain either implicitly or explicitly a condemnation of Louis XIV. Indeed, the Sun King's profligate spending, his scandalous sexual morality, his policy of subjugation of the church and the nobility, and his bellicose foreign policy, whose disastrous effects Fénelon saw firsthand as archbishop of Cambrai, would lead him to write the famous "Letter to Louis XIV" at the same time that he was composing the *Telemachus*. This letter will be discussed in a separate section below.

The narrative of the *Adventures of Telemachus* begins, as do the classical epics that inspired it in the middle of Telemachus's story. Homer had recounted in the *Odyssey* Telemachus's love for his father and his search for him before their eventual reunion on Ithaca. Fénelon's novel pretends to supply additional material to this narrative by recounting adventures that Homer had not included in his poem. As Fénelon's novel opens, therefore, we find the young hero, Telemachus, on the island of the sea nymph Calypso, where he and his guardian, Mentor, had been washed ashore after a shipwreck. The reader steeped in classical mythology, as was Louis, would immediately recognize the literary allusion established by Fénelon between his novel and his literary inspiration, the *Odyssey.* Calypso, in Homer's epic, had already fallen in love with Telemachus's father, Ulysses, and now enduring her immortality with the greatest of difficulty, the nymph cannot console herself for the loss of Ulysses. "In her grief, she found herself unhappy at being immortal," Fénelon relates. She was still languishing when she saw the two castaways on her shore. Calypso recognizes Telemachus to be the son of her former lover and immediately becomes enamored of the youth. Offering the castaways every comfort of her island, Calypso hopes through her generosity to gain time to plan a stratagem to keep Telemachus permanently at her side. Thus Calypso, dissimulating her passion, feigns an interest in Telemachus's adventures in search of his father. Telemachus, unsuspecting the goddess's motives, agrees to relate the saga of his travels.

Telemachus's voyage had begun with his departure from Ithaca and his subsequent shipwreck off the coast of Sicily. There he had met Acestes, a Trojan who had become king of the island; Acestes aids him in continuing his travels. Once again on the seas, he is taken prisoner by Egyptian sailors and sold into slavery in Egypt. His suffering is not in vain, however, as Telemachus, aided constantly by Mentor's wise counsel, is given the chance to observe firsthand the workings of a prosperous kingdom ruled by the benevolent monarch Sesostris. This humane pharaoh was preparing to set Telemachus and Mentor free when he suddenly dies, leaving the throne of Egypt to his dissolute son Bochoris. Bochoris sends Telemachus off to herd sheep in the desert and later has him imprisoned. These trials serve as further lessons in Telemachus's moral instruction. Once, on the point of succumbing to despair, he hears a voice from within him, saying: "Son of the wise Ulysses, you must become like him great through your patience. Princes who have always been fortunate are not worthy of being so…How happy you will be if you surmount your misfortunes."[88] Thus from the novel's outset two of the most characteristic of Fénelonian themes are announced: (1) the need for patience in suffering the vicissitudes of fortune, and (2) the necessity of repressing human tendency to weakness, dissipation, and pride.

This message is further impressed on the young Telemachus when he meets Termosiris, a priest of Apollo, who in Fénelon's Christianized classical universe symbolically represents (as does Mentor) divine wisdom. Termosiris advises Telemachus to imitate the god Apollo who, when enduring captivity as a shepherd, used the time wisely to teach the uncivilized inhabitants of the region the art of music and an appreciation for the joys of their bucolic existence. Soon, the half-savage shepherds realized that they were in reality more fortunate in their simplicity than kings in their golden palaces. "My son," Termosiris said, "this story is meant to teach you…One day the pains and cruel worries that surround kings will make you, on your throne, miss the pastoral life."[89]

Termosiris, although a relatively minor character in the *Telemachus*, is significant in that he represents both the type of moral instruction Fénelon proposes throughout the novel by means of various fictional characters and also highlights the "pleasant" nature of the virtuous life he advocates. In the *Treatise on the Education of Daughters* Fénelon had already prescribed that moral teaching be done in a pleasant manner. He had warned the Beauvilliers against presenting as models to their daughters Christians whose morality was too ascetic or off-putting for a child. This concept of virtue as being not only pleasing to God but also pleasing in and of itself was one that, as mentioned above, Fénelon inherited from de Sales and de Paul, among others. It remains a constant throughout the pedagogical works and will indeed inform his moral direction as a whole. Therefore Termosiris, priest of Apollo and conduit of divine wisdom, is portrayed not as an emaciated anchorite but rather as a hale and hearty fellow, full of joy at God's goodness: "Even with his prudence, he was gay and easygoing." It may be noted in passing that these same adjectives (*gai* and *complaisant*) with which Fénelon describes Termosiris were often used by his contemporaries (such as Saint-Simon) to describe Fénelon himself.

In the Christian tradition redemption comes from suffering. This doctrine permeates the *Telemachus* and acts as its subtext. Therefore, similar to the biblical children of Israel freed from bondage, Telemachus is led by divine wisdom from the slavery of his passions to the Promised Land of salvation. Telemachus's freedom is brought about in this instance by an invasion of the Phoenicians, whom Telemachus accompanies to Tyre, where he learns of the oppressive rule of the tyrant Pygmalion, at whose hands he barely escapes death. Through the intervention of a favorite at court Telemachus is spared and winds his way eventually to Cyprus, the island associated with the cult worship of Venus. The virtuous Telemachus is repulsed by the weakness and dissipation that reign on Cyprus. As in the earlier *Fables* and the *Dialogues* Fénelon throughout the *Telemachus* associates simplicity and industry with virtue, whereas indolence and dissipation, which he groups under the French term *mollesse*, are always condemned as the most dangerous vices.

At this point in the narrative Mentor, who had been sold into slavery in Egypt and separated from Telemachus, is reunited with him through the generosity of his master, Hasael, a virtuous Phoenician travelling to Crete to study the laws of Minos. On Crete they observe the industrious and simple Cretans who, having lost their king, Idomeneus, are in the process of choosing another by means of an athletic contest. Telemachus engages in the games and, although victorious in all contests, declines the offer to become king, choosing instead to continue his odyssey. Telemachus and Mentor thereupon take to the sea again in hopes of finding Ulysses at last. It is during this voyage that they are wrecked upon the shores of Calypso's island.

Having finished the story of his travels, Telemachus is urged by Mentor to leave the island quickly lest he fall prey to Calypso's charms. "Take care," Mentor warns, "not to listen to the sweet, flattering words of Calypso."[90] Unknown to either of them, however, Calypso has already enlisted the aid of Venus to turn Telemachus's heart toward thoughts of love. Due to a mix up in love potions,

Telemachus ends up falling in love not with Calypso but with one of her nymphs, Eucharis. A contrast between the two nymphs, as well as the Olympians warring against each other, is indicative of Fénelon's allegorical technique in the novel.

Calypso, seconded by Venus and her mischievous son Cupid, is portrayed as beautiful, forever young, and charming. Yet, she is also languid, slothful, and obsessed with sensual pleasure. In attempting to win Telemachus's love she urges him to abandon himself to the pleasures of her island: "You have found here a deity ready to make you happy." To the reader acquainted with the mystical vocabulary of the French School, however, Telemachus's temptation to abandon himself to sensual pleasure can only seem a perverse reversal of the natural order, which requires Christians to abandon themselves to God and not to worldly, sinful lusts.

The spiritual battle that pits vice against virtue can also explain the allegory of the dream Telemachus has while on Calypso's island. In this dream he imagines Venus saying to him that he will soon be captive to her laws. He sees Cupid on the point of piercing him with an arrow, when, suddenly, Minerva appears and shields him with her aegis. Telemachus remarks that Minerva's countenance has nothing in common with that of Venus. Whereas Minerva is noble, strong, and simple in her appearance, Venus is effete, passionate, and "molle." Once again the Fénelonian contrast between simple virtue as opposed to dissipation *(mollesse)* asserts itself.

Telemachus falls so passionately in love with Eucharis that he is prepared to renounce his quest for his father (allegorically, the pilgrim's quest for salvation) and spend his life in sinful dissipation with her. This Mentor cannot allow. So, in what Adler termed one of the more "operatic" episodes in the novel, Mentor pushes his charge off a cliff into the ocean.[91] This gesture, forcing Telemachus to abandon himself to a greater power, works on several levels of meaning (as do many of the metaphors in the *Telemachus*). On the surface level, Telemachus, by being forced to cling to life in the midst of the raging sea, is physically snapped out of the magical spell cast on him by Cupid. On an allegorical level, however, this act calls to mind imagery of abandonment to God characteristic of the French School theologians. A familiar Salesian and Bérullian theme, found again in Mme. Guyon, is that a Christian is a drop of water that must lose itself in the ocean that is God. Mentor, by aiding Telemachus to cast off the sexual stupor in which he was wallowing metaphorically, is seen to be the incarnation of grace, strengthening him to resist temptation and seek salvation. Telemachus, as archetype of the hero (typical in this respect of other heroes of the quest genre, from Gilgamesh to Sir Percival) throws off temptation in order to continue on his quest for spiritual enlightenment.

The two swimmers are rescued by a ship whose commander, Adoam, promises to take them to Ithaca. Neptune, however, tricks the ship's pilot into steering a false course, and they arrive in Salentum, a kingdom newly founded by the exiled king of Crete, Idomeneus.[92] Their stay in Salentum gives Telemachus the opportunity to prove his courage by fighting against the Daunians, a people who, under their cruel leader Adrastus, have threatened several kingdoms of Hesperia. Mentor takes this time to reorganize Salentum in accordance with his principles of government. This he does by banning luxury items, such as silver and gold, and promoting farming and commerce. He particularly endeavors to reform Idomeneus's character. The king confesses to Mentor that he has allowed himself to become the victim of flattery and dreams of military glory, which have led him to wage countless unjust wars against his neighbors.

In the midst of the battle against the Daunians, Telemachus is convinced by a dream to search for his father in Hades. In the Underworld, in a setting similar to that seen in the *Dialogues of the Dead*, he witnesses the punishment of evil kings and the rewards in the Elysian fields accorded to virtuous rulers. It is here that he meets his grandfather, Arcesius, who tells him that Ulysses is still alive. Telemachus returns to earth to do battle with the Daunians and ends by slaying Adrastus and concluding a just peace.

Telemachus thereupon returns to Salentum to find it much changed from Mentor's reforms. He derives lessons of good government from this model kingdom. Although Telemachus has fallen in love with Antiope, Idomeneus's daughter, during his stay in Salentum, Mentor informs him that his destiny awaits him in Ithaca. They thus set sail once again and once again are shipwrecked. This time they find themselves on an island where

Telemachus encounters a mysterious stranger, the sight of whom moves him deeply, although he does not understand why. Mentor explains to him, after the stranger has departed, that he was Ulysses in disguise but that the gods want to test Telemachus's patience longer before reuniting father and son. When they finally arrive in Ithaca, Mentor insists that they offer sacrifice to Minerva. Telemachus willingly agrees and builds an altar. During the midst of the sacrificial holocaust Minerva sheds the disguise of Mentor and appears in her glory to give Telemachus final advice on how to live and govern virtuously.

Fénelon's description of the goddess in her metamorphosis offers a rich harvest for textual analysis. This passage is subject to allegorical interpretation on several levels, religious allegory being the most compelling. The goddess is described as being fragrant; Telemachus detects the fragrance of roses emanating from her person, doubtless an allusion to the Virgin Mary's title of Rose of Sharon. Moreover, in her epiphany Minerva incarnates divine wisdom, the Logos. The advice she gives from the altar may therefore be seen as a culmination and sanctification of the advice Telemachus has received from various sources (Termosiris, Sesostris, and others) throughout his peregrinations. The text lends support for such an interpretation in the physical reaction of Telemachus to the goddess's epiphany. He suffers from a fire piercing his heart. He cannot speak, so awed is he by the divine vision, yet he feels an indescribable sweetness amid his fear and trembling. There seems little doubt that Fénelon in this passage is alluding to the mystic's vision of God. One is reminded, for example, of Saint Teresa of Avila's mystical experiences—her ecstasies and visions (so vividly described by her in *The Life of Teresa of Avila* and represented by Bernini in sculptural form.) Often, in the midst of her contemplation, she describes "such a feeling of the presence of God as made it impossible for me to doubt that He was within me, or that I was totally engulfed in Him."[93]

In vocabulary reminiscent of Fénelon's favorite image of God as a loving father who leads his children by the hand, Minerva says: "I have instructed no mortal with as much care as you [...] I have led you by the hand through the shipwrecks."[94] Telemachus has thus been led from ignorance to knowledge, just as the Christian is led to knowledge of God by grace. And, as the Christian must suffer to gain redemption, Minerva reaffirms that Telemachus was destined to suffer in order to redeem himself in the eyes of his father and his people and thus become an enlightened ruler: "Because what man can rule wisely if he has never suffered."[95]

This final advice given by Minerva serves, like a coda in music, to reemphasize the advice given to Telemachus throughout the novel. The most important moral directives are twofold: (1) a virtuous king must love his subjects and work for their well being ("aimez les peuples" is repeated many times in the novel), and (2) a virtuous king must avoid dissipation and live simply ("fuyez la mollesse" and "mettez votre gloire dans la simplicité" are likewise frequent refrains). Above all, the virtuous king should never forget that he is a father to his people, the earthly image of God, the heavenly father, and only rules by divine commission to ensure their virtue and happiness.

The *Telemachus* is the most carefully crafted and most complex of the pedagogical works written for the Duc de Bourgogne. The novel's length and its form offered Fénelon a literary vehicle through which to express his mature views on political ethics and morality. This morality had been introduced in simpler form in the *Fables* and in more developed form in the *Dialogues of the Dead.* The *Telemachus*, however, is the culmination of Fénelon's theories of attractive education and indirect instruction.

These two means of moral instruction are found throughout the *Telemachus* and had been proposed by Fénelon years earlier in his *Treatise on the Education of Daughters.* They are perfected in the *Telemachus* through the use of Telemachus and Mentor as surrogates for Louis and his tutor. Putting Louis directly into the fictional universe of Greek mythology allows Fénelon liberty to place him in situations that he would never have experienced otherwise. The indirect moral instruction, although previously seen in both the *Fables* and the *Dialogues*, is more fully developed in this last pedagogical work. The models proposed in the fables had often been simplistic and one dimensional, focusing on one particular virtue to be taught. The models proposed in the dialogues, while more complex, were for the most part negative examples, focusing on vices to be avoided. In the *Telemachus*, however, there is a balance of positive and negative models. The wise Egyptian pharaoh Sesostris, for example, is described as a model of virtue and paternal solicitude for his people. Idomeneus, on the other hand, is rather an anti-hero, a tragic figure who had become prey to his weakness and passion, consequently neglecting the needs of his people.

Idomeneus is a figure whose analysis proves particularly enlightening, not only in understanding the author's didactic purpose in the novel but also in answer to the question of whether Fénelon's critics were correct in labeling the *Telemachus* a roman à clef. We recall that on reaching Salentum, Telemachus had found Idomeneus besieged in his capital city. He and Mentor learn that as a result of the king's belligerent policies he has made enemies of his neighbors. Mentor takes Idomeneus to task for having forgotten his vocation as father to his people. He condemns the evils of wars of conquest and preaches the virtues of peace among nations.

In one of the novel's most eloquent passages Mentor exclaims: "All of humanity is only one family dispersed over the face of the earth. All peoples are brothers and should love each other as such."[96] In a tone echoing the Old Testament prophets, Mentor cries, "Woe to those sinners who seek a cruel glory in the blood of their brothers!" Although Mentor admits, following Augustine's doctrine of just war, that warfare may sometimes become necessary, it is always an evil to which a Christian king should have recourse only as a last resort. "True glory can never be found outside of humanity," he concludes, "and whoever prefers his own glory to feelings of humanity is a monster of pride and not a man."[97]

This scene further accentuates the identification of Mentor as representative of the Divine both as avatar of Minerva and as fictional embodiment of Fénelon as *alter Christus*, the Paidagogus spoken of by Clement of Alexandria; he is the tutor par excellence who not only teaches earthly knowledge but also the path to salvation. As in the *Fables* and the *Dialogues*, moral instruction is drawn from fictional events. Whereas in the two previous works this function is served by a transcendent narrator, in the *Telemachus* this narrator takes concrete form as the Transcendent becomes Immanent. The divine Logos becomes incarnate in the dual forms of Mentor, the Paidagogus or Divine Teacher, and Minerva, the Hagia Sophia or Divine Wisdom. Each encomium or condemnation from the lips of

Mentor/Minerva serves both to comment on the action of the narrative and to put this action into a moral perspective for Louis.

The two fictional kings, Idomeneus and Sesostris, highlight the dual nature of monarchy in general and Louis XIV's rule in particular. The reader familiar with Louis XIV's temperament and physical appearance cannot but see similarities between Fénelon's description of Idomeneus and Louis XIV as a young man. Idomeneus is described as handsome and talented but corrupted by flatterers. His pride and the violence of his nature have led him into disastrous wars that have brought only suffering to his people. If the fictional portrait of Idomeneus is meant by implication as criticism of Louis XIV, the description of Sesostris is just as telling in what it implies by contrast. At the beginning of Telemachus's travels Mentor had praised Sesostris for the wisdom and benevolence of his rule. According to Mentor, Sesostris is a model of a virtuous king in that he rules as a father to his people, using his authority lovingly. He is conscientious and industrious, yet not rigid. The ideal king, indeed, is permitted to enjoy life's pleasures, provided that they are simple and virtuous. Sesostris is courageous and well versed in the arts of war, vigilant to protect his people from foreign aggression, yet, realizing the horrors of war, he is slow to anger and ever willing to work for peace and unity with his neighbors.

In both the *Fables* and the *Dialogues*, written for a younger child and more explicit in their morality, Fénelon presented stark portraits contrasting good and bad rulers. As a more complex work, the *Telemachus* offers no such moral dichotomy. There are no examples in the novel of totally evil kings; even Idomeneus has some excellent qualities and, having been converted by Mentor, redeems himself by renouncing his evil policies. Likewise, there are no examples of completely virtuous monarchs in the novel. Mentor makes it clear to Telemachus that even the best of men are imperfect. Although Christians, to borrow C. S. Lewis's phrase, "tend to glory," we cannot achieve absolute perfection in this world. "A king, however good and wise he may be, is still a man. His intellect is limited and his virtue as well," Mentor tells Telemachus.[98] Indeed, even good kings may err as a result of their weakness or ignorance. But, Mentor adds with insight reminiscent of Bérulle, if a man wills to good, then he is already in possession of the power to do good. If, therefore, men fall short of perfection, these same men have the free will to redeem themselves: "The most praiseworthy are those who have the courage to understand and redeem their misdeeds."[99]

We return, then, to the question posed above: Was the novel a moral allegory or a roman à clef meant to attack Louis XIV? Daniélou, expressing the consensus among historians, says that there is no doubt Fénelon intended the novel to criticize Louis XIV. She is doubtless correct in asserting that no one was fooled by Fénelon's claims to the contrary: "Personne ne s'y trompa."[100] At least on one level of interpretation, the *Telemachus* is indeed a roman à clef, an indictment of the personal morality and the foreign policy of Louis XIV. Yet Carcassonne is surely no less correct in seeing in Mentor a fictional representation of divine grace and in Telemachus an archetype of the Christian questing for salvation. The *Telemachus*, then, must be viewed as a complex literary work capable of being read on at least three distinct levels of meaning, apart from the obvious surface narrative. As a moral allegory, Telemachus is indeed the young hero who searches to find truth and wisdom. As a political allegory, Telemachus represents Louis, the royal student searching for means to rule justly, and Mentor is Fénelon, whose purpose is to teach political ethics. Finally, as a religious allegory, Telemachus is the Christian who chooses grace to lead him through life's tribulations in order to achieve salvation and mystical union with God. Therefore, inasmuch as the novel takes Telemachus on an odyssey from suffering to enlightenment and finally homecoming, these three levels of meaning may be seen to correspond to the mystic's traditional threefold quest for deification: the *via purgativa*, the *via illuminativa*, and the *via unitiva*.

Much of the Fénelonian morality presented in the *Telemachus* is traditional Christian morality clothed in mythological garb, so to speak. It is morality embellished and made "attractive" by its fictional trappings and made more effective (and *affective*) by the dramatic elements inherent in the fictional hero/quest genre. But if much of the morality proposed in the novel is traditional Christian morality, there is much in the work that is nevertheless quintessentially Fénelonian. Two examples may suffice to illustrate my point. Seventeenth-century France was called the century of saints, and many of Fénelon's contemporaries rivaled him in their piety. Many were active as teachers and spiritual directors and spoke on questions of public policy. Case in point: Fénelon in the *Telemachus* raises the question of the morality of war. One celebrated contemporary of his, Amand-Jean Bouthillier de Rancé, founder of the Trappists, was also opposed to war and spoke against it. Yet it is difficult to imagine Rancé condemning war with the emotional anguish of Mentor's "Woe to these sinners who seek glory in the blood of their brothers!" Another case: Antoine Arnauld and Pierre Nicole,[101] believed strongly in and taught the power of grace; yet it is nearly impossible, given their Jansenist theology, to imagine their describing the Christian as capable of opting for grace freely, consciously, and heroically as Fénelon has Telemachus do throughout the novel.

Indeed, in language very reminiscent of the Salesian injunctions to Philothée to choose grace and to battle heroically against sin, Mentor repeatedly tells his charge to believe in himself and God's power: "Be the worthy son of Ulysses; show a heart greater than all the evils that threaten you." This same counsel to Telemachus to find within himself the power to resist evil echoes the "heroic optimism" that Paul Bénichou associates with Corneille and the Jesuits.[102] We have seen this theological view of free will and grace to be an integral part of the spirituality of the French School authors. Fénelon is not simply rehashing timeworn clichés of Christian morality, nor is he merely limiting himself to Christian allegory of the type popularized by Jean-Pierre Camus earlier in the century.[103] In the *Telemachus* Fénelon boldly proposes the Salesian concept of heroic virtue and foresees a Christian "messianic" reign as being the only vocation worthy of his pupil, Louis.

Critical assessment of the *Adventures of Telemachus* has varied considerably over the years, from adulation to indifference and scorn. Voltaire and many of the eighteenth-century philosophers considered the *Telemachus* to be one of the finest novels ever written. The abbé Prévost thought it to be one of the few novels worth reading, and Rousseau believed it contained all political morality worth knowing. Bossuet, however, was representative of much contemporary French ecclesiastical opinion when he judged the novel to be "unworthy not only of a bishop but of a priest or even a Christian."[104] And, although used throughout the eighteenth century as a textbook in many Catholic schools, in the nineteenth century critics began to condemn the novel as being overly didactic and artificial. Gustave Lanson's assessment of the *Telemachus* is typical of many of his colleagues of the latter nineteenth and early twentieth centuries: "There is in this book an incoherent mixture of pagan fiction and Christian spirit. The constant allusions to the present diminish the warmth and the verisimilitude of the narrative. Too many adventures happen at the exact right moment to instruct Telemachus and, by ricochet, the Duc de Bourgogne."[105]

In the past forty years, however, there has been a reassessment of the *Telemachus*'s worth. René Pomeau speaks for many modern scholars in saying that the *Telemachus* "remains a great poem in spite of its faults."[106] We might echo this sentiment for, if Fénelon's style must be acknowledged to be at times sententious or melodramatic, these stylistic flaws were to a large degree the flaws of the age in which he lived, an age fascinated with Baroque theater and opera. Concessions should also be made to the didactic ends of the work. Fénelon, after all, did not set out to write a polished work of fiction; he set out, rather, to present his student with a clearly delineated program of political ethics and morality. In this, judging from its immense popularity as a textbook for princes throughout eighteenth-century Europe and especially from the influence it had on molding the character of the Duc de Bourgogne, it must be seen as having succeeded. Louis's contemporaries had no difficulty in seeing his portrait in that of Telemachus when they read the novel for the first time. And both contemporary and modern historians alike agree that the *Telemachus* helped shape the morality of the prince who, during the years he spent with his tutor, changed from a violent, willful child to the gentle, pious young adult who, in his own words, would always be for Fénelon "just little Louis."

Letters of Spiritual Direction

Fénelon gained respect as an intellectual early in his life especially for the innovative pedagogical theory of "attractive education" expounded in his *Treatise on the Education of Daughters* written for the Beauvillier family. He had also shown promise as a theologian with his *Refutation of Father Malebranche*, as a preacher with his sermons (such as the *Sermon on the Vocation of the Gentiles* included in this volume) and even as a poet. He gained notoriety for the *Telemachus*, which was widely considered to be a masterpiece of French prose. His popularity increased to international proportions when he published the *Maxims of the Saints*, his defense of the mystical doctrine of pure love, a work discussed widely throughout Europe and ultimately condemned by Rome.

None of these celebrated works however shows a more personal, intimate side of Fénelon's personality and spirituality than his letters of spiritual direction. Some of the most revealing letters with respect to Fénelon's maturing doctrine of pure love, especially as it was communicated to his disciples, were written in the years before 1697, the year of the publication of the *Maxims* and consequently the date after which he was increasingly embroiled in controversy over his mystical doctrine. Although he would continue to maintain an active correspondence with his friends and disciples right up to his death in 1715, after 1697 his letters took on a polemical tone and were often pervaded with questions relating to the Quietist debate in France and Rome, where his book was being judged. It is precisely because his letters prior to 1697 are more spontaneous and less self-consciously defensive than his correspondence after this date that the letters included in this volume all predate Fénelon's disgrace at court and exile to Cambrai.

Fénelon's spiritual correspondence breaks no new ground with respect to his theology. The vocabulary and themes of the French School of Spirituality previously encountered in the pedagogical works are all found here. If anything, they are more apparent in his letters of direction because the purpose of these works was to lead his friends along the path of pure love that he himself had trod. The reader already acquainted with Fénelon's work and the writings of his predecessors of the Salesian and Bérullian traditions would expect to find an insistence on the *néant* or nothingness of humanity, and it is indeed found throughout the letters of direction. We would expect to see reference to the Bérullian concept of radical dependence on God, and it is here. We would expect to see the Olierian necessity of abandonment to God's will and detachment *(désappropriation)* as well as de Sales's holy indifference *(sainte indifférence)*, and indeed these concepts are all found throughout the

Fénelonian correspondence. Weaving these various strains into his personal spiritual synthesis, we see Fénelon's conviction that man is nothing and God is everything. These themes are primordial and fundamental to Fénelonian spirituality. Nature is vanity—a great lie that would have us believe that life is more than a hollow dream. The only solution is in a childlike abandonment to God, hiding ourselves in God's embrace and trusting in divine love.

Much was made during Fénelon's lifetime, and subsequently, over the influence of Mme. Guyon on his spiritual formation. And—as will be discussed more fully below in the section dealing with Guyon and Quietism—it must be recognized that her vision of a new Eden under the messianic rule of the Duc de Bourgogne did inspire Fénelon. There is no doubt that the personal piety and the mystical fervor expressed in her visions, along with her sermons to the "little flock" at Versailles and her private letters to Fénelon, had an impact on the fervent quality and affective tone in the development of his personal spirituality. His mature mystical doctrine of pure love would also incorporate Guyonian themes and imagery—especially her emphasis on paternal/maternal metaphors. However, the danger lies (as has occurred ever since Bossuet's infamous coupling of Guyon and Fénelon as "Priscilla with her Montanus") in exaggerating Guyon's influence over Fénelon's spirituality and in depreciating the originality of his own synthesis. For if Fénelon incorporated Guyonian themes and images in his work, he no less incorporated those of the Alexandrian Fathers, the medieval mystics, and especially the French School authors.

As early as 1951 Jean Calvet, in a paper given in Cahors, France, for the tercentenary of Fénelon's birth, had urged that more research be done on Fénelon's intellectual and spiritual formation in his youth and young adulthood.[107] Calvet maintained that Fénelon's core spirituality was formed long before his meeting with Mme. Guyon, from his study of the mystic authors and his personal association with Tronson and others. A year later, in an article devoted to Fénelon's concept of self-annihilation *(anéantissement du moi)*, Jeanne Goré pointed in a similar direction by insisting on Fénelon's fidelity to Bérullian theocentrism and suggesting Guyon's influence on Fénelon was peripheral and not essential—more a question of form than of substance.

This may well be, since even Fénelon's earliest extant letters (dating from the late 1670s) show a concern for "simplicity" and "spiritual abandonment." Moreover, Fénelon, even in his earliest writings, identified himself as a proponent of Salesian interior mortification as opposed to the austerities in favor among the rigorist clergy, particularly the Jansenists. In his treatise on educating the Beauvillier daughters Fénelon had advised the duke and duchess to avoid presenting an example of austere piety to their children lest the girls associate true piety with exterior mortification. In the *Maxims of the Saints*, written nearly fifteen years later, he would still propose the Salesian model of eschewing pharisaical displays of piety in favor of an affective, interior piety so that the "outward appearance not be affected."

This preoccupation with inner mortification is a central one in Fénelon's letters of spiritual direction since most of his closest correspondents were active in secular life and often sought his opinion on whether they could live holy lives while participating in the court life at Versailles, for example, or the life of a soldier at war. Seventeenth-century France had no dearth of rigorist moralists who maintained that union with God was nigh impossible while living "in the world." Many of the leaders in this rigorist camp were among the lights of the church: Arnauld, Nicole, and Rancé, to name only three of the most famous.

Fénelon, however, in his correspondence will consistently return to the theme of interior discipline familiar to Salesian and Bérullian spirituality, saying in one letter that "austerities [...] are useful [...] however they do not serve to destroy the substance of self-love or cupidity, which is the root of all vices, nor do they unite the soul to God." What God expects of the faithful is not an exterior mortification of the flesh, but rather an interior destruction of "amour-propre," the egotistical, self-centered desires that resist our abandoning ourselves by an act of pure love to God's will. In language that foreshadows the more closely reasoned theological language of the *Maxims of the Saints*, Fénelon says that outward displays of piety are ultimately only "a justice according to the flesh" and not the spirit.

Although the extant collection of Fénelon's correspondence fills several volumes, the letters are linked together by recurring themes of self-annihilation and abandonment to pure love, as well as by a certain stylistic progression that is common to them all. And although, as mentioned above, the letters are not the polished works of theology or literature that the *Telemachus* is or even more so the *Maxims of the Saints,* they nevertheless have a beauty and grace of their own and provide their own interior cohesion. Indeed, in a sense they are sermons in miniature in that they share elements typical of the well-structured sermon: an introduction, or *entrée en matière;* a body consisting of one or more *points;* and a conclusion, often ending in a lyric crescendo of invocation to one of the Persons of the Trinity or an attribute of the divine Persons. Indeed, Abbé Gosselin, editor of the prestigious edition that bears his name,[108] saw several similarities between Fénelon's letters and his other spiritual writings. For this reason he included many letters by Fénelon under the rubric *Conversations and Advice on Various Points of Morality and Christian Perfection* together with works clearly not letters, such as short sermons, meditations, and so forth.

The typical letter of direction by Fénelon to one of his correspondents begins with a sober, cognitive appeal to reason. He often states the premise of the letter in the opening line, such as the following: "What men most lack is the knowledge of God," or "Madame, you seem to be troubled as to what occupations a Christian may legitimately engage in." After posing the problem, Fénelon suggests a remedy, developing his argument usually in several points by paragraph. Finally, he reaches his conclusion, usually ending his letter with an appeal to his correspondent to share in God's love. These conclusions often take the shape of short prayers or invocations, such as the following: "O Lord Jesus, fill us with your spirit and empty us of our own!" or "O Beauty! O Infinite Goodness! O Infinite Love! Burn; consume; carry away; annihilate my heart! Make it a perfect burnt offering!"

The themes of pure love and abandonment to God seen in these examples form a leitmotiv throughout the Fénelonian correspondence. His letters went out to those to whom he was closest and who had asked him to direct them. One such person in the 1680s was Françoise d'Aubigné, known in history as Mme. de Maintenon, the morganatic wife of Louis XIV and uncrowned queen of France. Although she would break publicly with Fénelon after 1697 in the midst of the Quietist controversy, during Fénelon's early years at court she was counted among his friends and protectors. Indeed, it was known in court circles that she had become a devoted disciple of this charismatic abbé who showed such genuine mystical fervor and such intellectual promise. She met with him alone or together with the *petit troupeau*, the little flock of Christians seeking spiritual perfection that had formed around Fénelon and Mme. Guyon. She often asked him to compose letters of spiritual direction for her as well. She seemed at this time to be genuinely attracted to the teachings of pure love and spiritual abandonment being preached by Fénelon. At his urging she would periodically go on spiritual retreats in her private apartments to meditate on his letters and other devotional works recommended by him.

In the extant correspondence the letters of direction from Fénelon to Maintenon make up an impressive percentage. They deal with various topics, ranging from her feelings of spiritual aridity or distress to practical questions dealing with her involvement in court life. Most, if not all, were written on an ad hoc basis as the need for counsel on these matters arose. Was Mme. de Maintenon troubled that she was not spending her time wisely enough? She asked Fénelon for a letter to direct her how better to occupy her time. Did she have scruples about the pleasures of Versailles in which she participated? She requested a letter to distinguish between a legitimate use of these amusements and a sinful one.

In one such letter of direction (entitled by Gosselin "On the Use of Time") Fénelon sets out to counsel Maintenon on the most holy use of her free time. She had been troubled that she was not using her time for the glory of God. Her director first compliments her for desiring to have such knowledge and realizing that her life is not her own but rather must be used for God's glory. He agrees with her that not one minute of life should be wasted, when that minute might be used in carrying out God's will: "God has not intended to leave us with any empty time [...] for us to waste."[109] Yet the best way to serve God, Fénelon continues, is to avoid anxiety and to submit with humility to God's will as it manifests itself in the counsel of her spiritual directors. She should, moreover, put into practice any advice given to her with a simple and docile spirit: "That simplicity that fights against all the duplicity of self-love."

Thus Fénelon establishes this letter's theme in the opening paragraph: the necessity of simplicity and humility in accepting God's will as our own.

Enlarging on this theme, Fénelon explains to Maintenon that all Christians are called to rid themselves of their selfish will in order to serve God, because it was God's will that literally created us out of nothingness. Indeed, our essence is incomprehensible without the divine essence, which puts all humanity in a radical dependence on God's being for our own. The proper use of time, therefore, is a continual reflection on our relationship to God. If we choose to lose ourselves in God and subordinate our will to the divine will, then we become as the children of whom Jesus speaks in the gospel, without whose childlike faith none can hope to enter the kingdom of heaven.

At this point in the letter, as if to dramatize the necessity of this submission to the divine will, Fénelon personifies Maintenon's soul and, using the rhetorical device of prosopopeia, stages a conversation between her soul and God. Convinced of the need for complete abandonment to God, Maintenon's soul cries out from the depths of her misery: "In whose hands, great God, would I be better off than in yours? [...] Walking blindly in the paths of my own heart [...] What could I accomplish in myself except a work of self-love, of sin and damnation?"[110]

Fénelon concludes that for time to be well spent, God only requires that Maintenon desire to lose her own will in order to conform to the divine will. She must do this by meekly submitting to God, as a child submits to his or her father. In opposition to spiritual direction of the rigorist camp, which would doubtless have counseled fasting and hairshirt, Fénelon counsels humility and self-sacrifice as the answer to Maintenon's question. And in spite of his fidelity to the French School of Spirituality and use of its vocabulary of annihilation and abandonment, this letter shows itself to be not simply an imitation of Bérulle or Olier. Fénelon's personality (so often described by his contemporaries as gentle and tolerant) shines through in every line. For not only does he expound the doctrine of radical dependence, he also adds that this dependence must lead to childlike simplicity and love, both of which are ubiquitous themes of the Fénelonian corpus.

In this letter we see Fénelon at his most original and most compelling. While other authors of the French School, particularly Bérulle, were great champions of the concept of the radical dependence of the creature to its maker; and while de Sales waxes eloquent in speaking of God as loving Father and good Prince, Fénelon creates an authentically original and personal tone when synthesizing these various elements of the Bérullian and Salesian tradition. By joining Bérulle's theocentrism and Olier's preoccupation with sacrifice to de Sales's vision of the loving Prince, Fénelon arrives at a conception of God that is both radical (in that God is indeed *all* and we, as creatures, *nothing*) and yet lovable (for God, as Father, desires nothing so much as our salvation.)

Fénelon was the first to acknowledge the intellectual and spiritual debt he owed his predecessors. His correspondence, no less than his theological works, is filled with references to mystical authors from the second century (Clement of Alexandria) to the seventeenth century. His veneration of Catherine of Sienna and Teresa of Avila is no less genuine than his veneration of de Sales or de Paul. Nevertheless, the author of such letters as "On the Use of Time," discussed above, is no slavish disciple of Clementine, Bernardine,[111] Carmelite, Salesian, or Bérullian spirituality. Although Fénelon's God demands a sacrifice of the ego as the only path from purgation to illumination and finally union, yet this command is not a cruel or inexorable decree of divine justice but rather a supreme manifestation of divine love. Fénelon's favorite passages of scripture—passages he references again and again in his letters of *spiritual direction*—are from the Gospel and Epistles of John. He frequently cites John 4:23 and 1 John 4:8: "Whoever does not love does not know God, for God is love." Another favorite scriptural text was Jeremiah 31:3: "I have loved you with an everlasting love." Whenever those under his spiritual direction felt discouraged or abandoned by God, he would console them with these and similar passages, reassuring them that "before all time" God loved them.

When confronted with the scruples experienced by Mme. de Maintenon on the subject of her engaging in court amusements, Fénelon returns to the theme of God's love and understanding. Louis XIV's spouse, we know from her own correspondence and contemporary accounts, was very troubled by her role at court. A sincere Christian, if at times anxious and overly scrupulous, she worried that moralists of rigorist bent—men such as Bossuet and Rancé whom she respected for their piety—were correct in condemning the royal entertainments she frequented, such as the ballet, the opera, and the theater. And if they were correct in so vehemently criticizing these entertainments as sinful, was she not endangering her soul's salvation by participating in them? These were the questions that Louis XIV's consort would ask Fénelon repeatedly throughout the decade of their intimacy between 1687 and 1697. Two letters from their correspondence especially touch upon this question.

In the letter entitled "To a Person of the Court" by Gosselin, but which might be more aptly entitled "Chains of Gold," Fénelon limits himself to one theme: the absolute necessity for Christians to accept God's will as their vocation. Mme. de Maintenon feels trapped in her "chains of gold" and is anxious that she might be incurring damnation. Fénelon agrees that her residence at Versailles is in its way no less onerous than captivity in a prison, for "chains of gold are no less chains than chains of iron."[112] There is, however, consolation for Christians in whatever prison they find themselves, literal or metaphorical; Christians have faith to accept captivity as God's will, even to the point of being thankful for the opportunity for suffering if that is God's will. "The only thing that ought to give you real consolation, Madame, is that God is taking away your freedom."

In an interesting use of paradox, Fénelon assures Maintenon that this realization of God's plan for her and the chains that bind her to Versailles, if they are borne with simplicity and docility, are in reality the means for freedom, true freedom from earthly affectations: "By it the chains of iron are changed [...] into happiness and freedom." Fénelon asks rhetorically: Of what use is the ability to satisfy carnal desires that people call freedom if we are not free from our passions to do God's will? Logically and methodically developing his arguments from point to point, Fénelon continues to pose questions to prove that freedom is only freedom when it allows us to do God's will, which is the only reason for our being.[113]

After having presented his argument, Fénelon moves to an appeal to Maintenon's emotions, describing her as blessed if she accepts humbly her station in life. "Blessed are those whom God tears from their own will to attach them to his own!"[114] For the Lord God is a jealous God. He is jealous of that ego that we pitifully put in opposition to the divine will. In a passage that rivals Olier's mystical vehemence, Fénelon urges his penitent to renounce her pride: the ego that stands in the way of her abandonment to God. She claims, for example, to want her freedom from Versailles in order to perform works of charity, yet she does not allow herself to realize that the work most pleasing to God is childlike acceptance of the divine will. This acceptance can only be achieved by Maintenon's crucifying her ego. And Fénelon further attacks the proposition that it is possible to find God through finding oneself. We can only find God in renouncing ourselves for "nothing is less conducive for belonging to God than to still want to belong to yourself."[115]

Though it is true, Fénelon states, that Christians legitimately require time to themselves for rest and relaxation, this time must be used judiciously and in accordance to each one's duties and obligations. Echoing de Sales's views in the *Devout Life*, he maintains that it would be ridiculous, if not sacrilegious, for a person engaged in the world, whose vocation is therefore in the world, to wish to not be part of society. "Que le torrent vous emporte malgré vous" (let the flood carry you away), Fénelon advises Maintenon. This flood is God's will, which will carry her along according to God's providential plan.

If she seems to suffer from the restrictions imposed on her at Versailles, this suffering in truth comes not from the Holy Spirit working within her, but rather from her ego urging her to set herself up as a model of virtue so that people will admire her more. And he returns repeatedly to his theme of the ego's insinuating, duplicitous nature. "You believe that you miss God, but actually it is yourself that you miss." The French word *moi* (ego) runs like a leitmotif throughout this letter. It is repeated five times in as many paragraphs. Fénelon strikes again and again at the source of Maintenon's real suffering, which, in his opinion, is her attachment to her own ego (even if unconscious on her part) and resistance to letting herself be led by God. He concludes by saying: "Let yourself be led! [...] You will go to pure love, to perfect renunciation, to total death of your own will while accomplishing that of God."[116]

Another letter touching upon similar themes is entitled by Gosselin "On Diversions." In this letter Fénelon is writing in response to a request by Maintenon to address the more specific question of court amusements such as gambling. Fénelon is unequivocal: "You should not be troubled about amusements in which you cannot avoid taking part." Provided that distractions are imposed upon them by their vocation in life, Christians may lawfully engage in them. There is nothing inherently evil about worldly amusements, Fénelon states. Unlike his rigorist opponents, who held that dancing, gambling, theater going, and so forth led to mortal sin, Fénelon maintains that such an excess of rigor is incomprehensible to Christians who have freedom in God's love. "There are many people," he says "who would have you moaning and groaning about everything and have you constantly upset." However, "I admit that I cannot get used to such rigidity. I prefer something simpler and I believe that God himself likes it much more."[117]

Each of us is called to a different station in life. What is appropriate for one station is not appropriate for another. The austerities enjoined upon a nun, for example, would be seen as scandalous displays of ostentatious piety at court. Such conduct would not edify but "would only serve to give a false idea of piety to people in the world." He admits that interior mortification is oftimes more painful than an outward display of devotion, but if Maintenon loves God she will take this path. Citing a passage from his favorite gospel (John 4:23) he reminds her that God does not seek exterior signs of piety but rather a pure and contrite heart, for "true worshipers shall worship the Father in spirit and truth." He continues by saying that when so-called devout Christians spend their time in flagellating themselves, fasting, and the rest, they delude themselves in believing such is God's will: "God is not pleased either with mere words...or any exterior ceremonies. What he asks is a will that is not shared between himself and any other thing."[118]

Fénelon urges his penitent, therefore, to suffer God's will. He uses the French verb *porter* (literally meaning "carry"), stylistically suggesting that this sacrifice of her ego will be her cross to bear. Yet if she carries her cross willingly, she will find that the burden is light and that even the vain amusements of court life will turn to good works when done with right intention to fulfill God's will.

He concludes this letter by empathizing with his penitent in her frustration and feelings of discouragement. It is often when we feel most abandoned by God, he says, that God is nearest to us. He closes with a Baroque image of floodwaters, also a favorite Guyonian image: "Our Father, far from abandoning us, only seeks to find our hearts open so that he might pour floodwaters of grace therein."[119]

One of the most poignant letters written by Fénelon to his royal penitent is on the subject of suffering. Entitled by Gosselin "Only Pure Love Knows How to Suffer," it is one of the most sympathetic of all Fénelon's letters to Maintenon. In this short letter he posits the perennial problem of human suffering that has challenged theologians from time immemorial. Why must the righteous suffer? "We know we must suffer and that we deserve it," Fénelon reminds his reader, yet he sympathizes with Maintenon's sufferings and acknowledges her struggle. Once again, however, he sees the cause of her struggle as her lingering attachment to her own self-will. Until she can abandon herself completely to God, he states, and crucify her will, this will remain as an obstacle between herself and God. Only an act of abandonment, an act of pure love, can relieve her pain, for only pure love understands the redemptive power of suffering.

Apart from Mme. de Maintenon, Fénelon's voluminous spiritual correspondence is directed in large measure to his closest friends at court, the Duc de Chevreuse and the Duc de Beauvillier and their wives, and various members of their respective families. In these letters of spiritual direction Fénelon often addresses the same sorts of concern found in his letters to Maintenon. Both duchesses, like Maintenon, were worried that their obligations at court would impede their path toward holiness. Fénelon's advice is similar to that given to Maintenon: childlike simplicity and abandonment to God's will. The warm, affectionate tone, however, is quite different from that found in his letters to Louis XIV's wife. For whatever reasons—and they were doubtless complex and multiple—Fénelon never felt the closeness to Maintenon that he would feel to the Chevreuse and Beauvillier families. Although Fénelon doubtless had genuine feelings of pastoral care for Mme. de Maintenon and certainly was sincere in his concern for her spiritual development and salvation, we cannot but notice in his correspondence with the royal consort an incompatibility between their divergent personalities that neither one of them ever completely overcame.

Many theories have been offered by historians to explain this mutual incomprehension. A common explanation is that they were only using each other for social and political advantage. In the 1680s Fénelon was already a close friend and spiritual adviser to the Beauvilliers and Chevreuses. These families were of ancient and respected nobility, and both had intermarried with the Colbert clan, which had further cemented their position with the king.[120] Both families, moreover, were well known as leaders of the *parti dévot* (devout group) at Versailles. They were highly respected for their piety and probity even by *libertins* (free thinkers). Mme. de Maintenon, according to this theory, sought the social acceptance that intimacy with these ducal families, in favor at court and with the king, could provide her. For although she was the uncrowned queen of France, she had nevertheless been born to minor nobility and had been married to the bourgeois author Paul Scarron in her youth, causes for her initial ostracism upon coming to Versailles. Similarly, Fénelon, as an up-and-coming young abbé at court looking to make his fortune (so this theory goes), could only benefit from the friendship and favor of the king's wife. Given such an unpropitious beginning for a relationship, based as it was on self-interest and power dynamics, it is not surprising that their relationship never developed into deep affection.

While this theory would go far in explaining the failure of Fénelon and Maintenon to develop a warm friendship, we should not discount the less cynical and equally compelling theory that Fénelon and Mme. de Maintenon were simply very different people. Maintenon, raised as a Calvinist and being by nature of practical mind set, could never resolve to abandon herself to spiritual effusions or mysticism. Fénelon, conversely, a product of the Catholic Counter-Reformation and increasingly influenced by his relationship with Mme. Guyon, was profoundly drawn toward mysticism. In a word, to quote Saint-Simon's famous description, Fénelon's sublime mystical spirituality "melded with" that of Mme. Guyon, while the hard pragmatism evidenced throughout Maintenon's climb to power was antithetical to his chivalrous personality.

Fénelon was often criticized by his enemies at court as being too slick, too "unctuous" in wishing to be accepted by all. He was not unaware of this criticism leveled at him but defended his manner by reference to Saint Paul, who himself had wished to be "all things to all men." Certainly one of the most salient features of his correspondence is Fénelon's ability to vary his style and his spiritual direction according to the age, gender, personality, and occupation of his addressee. His letters to Mme. de Maintenon are often harsh, relentlessly summoning her to renounce her vanity and self-love. His letters to the Beauvilliers and Chevreuses, while no less insistent on the necessity of spiritual abandonment, are much more compassionate and even playful in tone, giving free reign to the "débonnaireté" spoken of by de Sales.[121] It is this chivalrous "courtesy" that he emphasizes in letters to a member of the Colbert family in military service.

In a letter written to the Chevalier Colbert, dated September 1688, Fénelon addresses the spiritual needs of a young soldier who was far from advanced on the path of spiritual perfection. This young man, Antoine Martin Colbert, was the son of Louis XIV's former minister and was twenty-nine years old at the time of this letter. He was well known to Fénelon, being the brother of both duchesses Beauvillier and Chevreuse. Indeed, Fénelon seems to have held a special place in his heart for this young man who, judging from their correspondence, was indulging in all the indiscretions common to soldiers throughout history. Far from criticizing his behavior, Fénelon gently seeks to bring his friend to a greater realization of the need for a deeper spiritual life and more faithful participation in the sacraments. Apparently the chevalier had not been assiduous in his correspondence because Fénelon begins his letter by affectionately chiding his forgetfulness: "You have forgotten me; but it is not in my power to do as much to you. In the bottom of my heart I carry something that always speaks to me of you."[122]

In writing to his young friend, Fénelon takes upon himself the role of a shepherd calling back a lost sheep. He is conscious of the chasm that separates their two vocations. He acknowledges the exigencies of a military life. He realizes that the chevalier is surrounded by hard-bitten comrades and is not in a situation conducive to religious practice. The body of this letter is devoted to reminding Colbert, however, that if Fénelon's affection for him is great, God's love for him is infinitely greater. If he has forgotten both his spiritual director and God, neither has forgotten him.

Fénelon returns to one of the recurring themes of his writings, a typically Baroque one, and asks if this worldly life, "this miserable dream," has found luster in his eyes. In a series of questions forming the body of the letter Fénelon uses the stylistic devices of anaphora and repetition to pound home his argument that the glory of this world, whether military or other, is but a vain dream compared to the reality that is God. Has the "nothingness of this world" become more attractive to him since last they met? Has "the pure light of God's kingdom" become less bright to him? Has the "eternal beauty" no longer any charm for him? Has the source of God's heavenly mercies dried up? These questions are piled up one upon the other by Fénelon in a device known as accumulation, forming a rhetorical crescendo ending with the declarative statement: "No." No, Colbert cannot have forgotten either his spiritual adviser or God, because God has burdened Fénelon's heart with the "pressing desire" to call him back to the fold. Even if Colbert should ignore this letter, Fénelon says, he had to write it out of love for him, and even if he should not speak to him again, Fénelon will continue praying to God for him.

Fénelon concludes his letter by referencing the Christian freedom spoken of in the Gospels. "Do what you will, Monsieur, but love God." He urges Colbert to find time, even in the midst of the perils of war, to partake of the sacraments, particularly the Eucharist, whenever possible: "This is the delicious bread that we eat each day at the table of our Father." With such a powerful support it is impossible to fear anything on the battlefield. In a concluding sentence that betrays his tenderness for Colbert, Fénelon entreats him to "at least write" and not "flee from me."

In a second letter to Colbert, Fénelon addresses more directly the problem of leading a Christian life in the military. While acknowledging the difficulties, Fénelon again assures the soldier that he can "sanctify" his life in the military as in any other walk of life. In typical Fénelonian fashion, adapting his spiritual direction to the needs of his penitent, he advises Colbert to read not any mystic authors but rather the Old Testament. Joshua, Judges, the Book of

Kings—these are the scriptures that will instill a "manly" virtue in the young soldier and also lead him closer to the God of Battles. In this way, Fénelon tells him, he can "sanctify even war."[123]

In yet another letter to the Chevalier Colbert, Fénelon continues his theme of the God of Battles, an image in which he knows the soldier will "take pleasure." Using terminology that hearkens back to the Middle Ages, he assures Colbert that if he maintains his "fidelity" to God, God will maintain his fidelity to him.[124] And even though the field of battle might seem to be the farthest removed from God's grace, a soldier may still find divine support by turning to inner prayer. As to regular devotional reading, "we owe to God the fidelity of taking advantage of so great a support when he lets us have it; but when he removes it through some real necessity, he compensates for it by his mercy."[125] In short, Fénelon concludes, by keeping God in his heart and meditating inwardly on God's love and mercy, the chevalier sanctifies his profession and offers up to God a pleasing sacrifice.

Due to the chaotic nature of Fénelon's correspondence, many copies of letters were found after his death with no addressee or date. Although these letters obviously pose a problem for historians, many are stylistically among the most beautiful in the Fénelonian canon and indicative of his spiritual direction. The letter entitled by Gosselin "Fidelity in Small Matters" is an example of such an anonymous letter.[126] This letter, once again evincing Fénelon's indebtedness to Salesian spirituality, deals with the typical Fénelonian themes of pure love and sacrifice to God's will.

Fénelon distinguishes between great virtues and small acts of fidelity to God's will. While, he admits, heroic virtue is more impressive, it is rare. Conversely, small, everyday acts of faithfulness to God's will, while less impressive, are no less necessary to the Christian life. Borrowing a metaphor from Francis de Sales, he compares heroic and "small" virtues to sugar and salt. Sugar, the heroic virtue, is "more exquisite"; salt, however, "goes in all food necessary to life" and is just as important. Fénelon concludes his letter by warning his correspondent not to despise small acts of fidelity. In one of the most stylistically pleasing passages of all his correspondence, he uses anaphora and antithesis to underline his argument against minimizing or rationalizing small sins: "You say it's nothing, yet it is a *nothing* that is *everything* for you." He repeats: "It's nothing, yet it is a nothing that you love so much as to refuse giving it up to God." And he concludes: "It's a nothing that in the end you are saving for yourself—against God—and that will cause your destruction."[127]

As we have seen, Fénelon's correspondence is a collection of writings that vary greatly in imagery and tone according to his addressees, depending on their station in life and their spiritual needs. Molding each individual letter to address each case Fénelon is able to strike a tone as personal as that of a priest in the confessional, speaking directly to his penitent. What does not change in all his letters of spiritual direction, however, is the Fénelonian image of a loving, merciful God who can sanctify our lives if we are willing to give ourselves wholly to him. In opposition to spiritual direction of the rigorist camp, Fénelon does not require that his addressees leave their homes or occupations. He takes each person as he finds him or her and tailors his spiritual counsel to best fit that person's needs. Once, when speaking of a courtier who had converted under Jansenist influence and decided to leave Versailles and live the life of a solitary (similar to the Messieurs de Port-Royal),[128] Fénelon clearly states his opposition to such a life change, saying, "I cannot believe that it is God's wish that he suddenly leave his employ." God does not require "long faces" or visible displays of piety, he only requires that we sacrifice our ego to his will and walk simply in his ways.

LETTER TO LOUIS XIV

A letter that should perhaps be considered apart from Fénelon's spiritual correspondence, although in a real sense it is also a letter of spiritual direction, is his celebrated "Letter to Louis XIV." Among Fénelon's voluminous writings this one letter is today undoubtedly the most widely known by the general public. It is the most often anthologized of all his work and one that still generates lively debate among historians and literary critics.

Let me begin by stating what we know for certain about this famous letter. It was known of and talked about during Fénelon's lifetime, although it was not published until 1787 by d'Alembert.

The style of the letter seemed so harsh and the description of the Sun King so damning that doubts about the letter's authenticity remained until the Parisian publisher Renouard unearthed the original manuscript copy in Fénelon's own hand and published a facsimile along with a new edition of the letter in 1825. This publication put to rest any doubt that the letter was genuinely Fénelon's.

Since the letter was undated, the question of chronology has also generated debate among scholars for over two hundred years. However, internal evidence from the letter itself allows it to be dated in the 1690s, probably in 1693.[129] Several historical allusions in the letter provide these chronological parameters—the archbishop of Paris, Harlay de Champvallon, who died in 1695, was still living; famine devastated the countryside (the abundant harvest of June 1694 would therefore have deprived Fénelon of this argument); France was threatened by military defeat due to recent reversals—all these indications argue for a date no later than 1693.

The question that has been most hotly debated over the years, however, is doubtless Fénelon's intention in composing it. Did he actually intend for Louis XIV to read this letter? Or, as some have concluded, did he intend this letter for Mme. de Maintenon as a sort of aide-mémoire—talking points, as it were, in her private discussions with the king.[130] There are texts, including contemporary accounts, that bolster both arguments. In her correspondence Mme. de Maintenon speaks of a letter by Fénelon that was given to her for the king's direction. The Marquis de Fénelon, one of Fénelon's relatives, also stated that the letter was sent to the king "to whom it was delivered in the time of M. de Beauvillier."[131] On the other hand, other contemporary memorialists make no mention of the letter, an omission that would seem incredible given the vehement nature of the missive. As Morris Bishop has observed, "If the King had read it, his fury would have been beyond his powers of concealment."[132] Unless further scholarship unearths decisive proof in future, this question must remain unresolved.

What is not a matter of debate is the tone and theme of the letter. Its tone is brutal, almost caustic. Fénelon accuses Louis XIV of having turned France into "one great hospital" due to his constant, ruinous wars of aggression against his neighbors. This king, who was anointed by God to be a father to his people, has only impoverished his realm and caused innumerable deaths by disease and starvation. Instead of forming his privy counsel with wise ministers who would propose moderate policies both at home and abroad, Louis XIV has opted to surround himself with sycophants and flatterers who have accustomed the king "to incessantly receive exaggerated praise rising to the point of idolatry." Finally, this king who should live according to the gospel directive of simplicity and humility has "introduced a monstrous and incurable luxury to the court" in the magnificent but costly palace of Versailles.[133]

What moral should the reader derive from such an impassioned indictment of Louis XIV's rule? Should we conclude, as some eighteenth-century *philosophers* maintained, that Fénelon was one of their own: a *philosophe avant la lettre*? According to this interpretation, Fénelon would have been a precursor of the Enlightenment, and this letter would constitute one of the first attacks leveled against absolute monarchy in France. Other scholars maintain that Fénelon was firmly rooted in the medieval ethos of king as God's anointed, a ruler by divine right. Castex and Surer, for example, state that for Fénelon, "the king is a priest of God and father to his subjects."[134] Following this theory, Fénelon would have shared the belief of Saint-Simon and other frustrated nobles that Louis XIV, by his autocratic rule, had perverted France's traditional social structure of king, aristocracy, and commoners, all living in harmony according to their station. Lanson, for example, states in his classic study of French literature that Fénelon's letter was a "reaction against Louis XIV whom he truly hated. He could never forgive him, as a priest, his wars or as an aristocrat, his humiliation of the nobility."[135]

The truth lies perhaps between these two positions. There is little doubt that Fénelon believed in the divine right of kings to rule, and to rule absolutely. Both his public utterances and his private correspondence bear this out. However, there is equally no doubt that the author of the *Dialogues of the Dead* and the *Adventures of Telemachus* also believed that a king must first be a Christian and, as a Christian, held accountable for his actions based on the gospel imperatives of love, mercy, and justice for his people. One of the most frequent images in Fénelon's pedagogical work is that of the king as father to his people. As a father, the king on earth stands in place of our heavenly Father, who wishes only peace and salvation for us. Whenever a king chooses his own selfish gratification over the happiness and security of his subjects, he is to be condemned, and condemned in the harshest of terms, just as Nathan condemned David for his reckless rule of Israel.

Like the Old Testament prophet who dared to face the king, the anointed of God, and say to him "Tu es ille vir!" Fénelon in his "Letter to Louis XIV" does not hesitate to say to Louis as well: "You are that man!" It is doubtless because Fénelon showed such prophetic courage in standing up to the most powerful king of his time and such compassion for the suffering people of France that this letter remains the most celebrated of his works to this day.

The Quietist Controversy and the Maxims of the Saints

Now it is time to turn our gaze back to the Fénelon's early years at Versailles and his meeting with the woman who would exert such a powerful influence on his spirituality, Jeanne Guyon, in defense of whom he would be accused of Quietism and banished from court. Before entering into the detail of Fénelon's own struggle, let us begin by briefly discussing the spiritual movement labeled Quietism.[136]

Exploding on the religious scene in the second half of the seventeenth century, Quietism's adherents were found throughout Catholic Europe, from Italy to Spain. Even today, with the advantage of over three hundred years' hindsight and reflection, it is difficult to say exactly what Quietism was and was not. In broad terms—and at the risk of over simplification—Quietism may be defined as the mystical theology that encourages its disciples to ignore virtues and practices traditionally taught by the church in favor of entering into a passive state of quietude (from the Latin *quies*, meaning "rest") in which the soul communing with God is beyond the need for common "discursive" prayer or active acts of faith. In this passive, quiet state Christians were encouraged to suppress all mental images of Christ, all striving for perfection, all earthly considerations. Once Quietist disciples annihilated their own will, having emptied themselves completely and having passively accepted God's will in all things by means of a "single act" of abandonment, they were considered to have entered into a perfect union with God, a state of tranquility, of contemplation, of quietude. This state was deemed to be so perfect that acts, which would have been condemned in others, would not be considered sins if committed by Quietists. By the very nature of their newly acquired state of passivity and perfection, the disciples of Quietism were considered to be docile instruments of God's will and therefore immune to the possibility of sin.

Ronald Knox, in his penetrating study of heterodox Christian movements, including Quietism, rightly points out, however, that Quietism is less a heresy or school of thought than a "tendency," a "direction of the human mind" to exaggerate concepts that otherwise could be considered perfectly orthodox. He suggests that it is misleading to speak of a Quietist School, if by this we mean a well-thought-out set of beliefs that all members of a supposed Quietist heresy professed. Quietism, he maintains, is not a neat set of "conclusions." Rather, he asserts, Quietism, as it manifested itself in seventeenth-century Europe, ran the spectrum from almost completely orthodox teaching to extremely heterodox beliefs. "You can," he concludes, "be more or less of a Quietist."[137] The reader, therefore, should always bear in mind that many differences in style and emphasis (and in some cases even in rather essential beliefs) exist among the various mystics labeled Quietist. As Knox has shown, the teachings of Molinos are not necessarily synonymous with those of La Combe or Guyon, much less those of Fénelon. Keeping this caveat in mind, however, it is nevertheless incumbent upon us to indicate the major figures of Quietism (especially seen in relation to their influence on Fénelon) and attempt to delineate the broad outlines of Quietist belief as exemplified by their teaching. For our purposes three figures come to the fore as of preeminent importance: Miguel de Molinos, François La Combe, and Jeanne Guyon.

The leading figure of seventeenth-century Quietism (called the "Patriarch of Quietism" by Cardinal Bausset) was without a doubt Miguel de Molinos (1628–96).[138] Having been sent from Spain to Rome in 1663 by his superiors on an administrative assignment, Molinos ended up spending the rest of his life in that city. He became known as a spiritual director and published his *Guia espiritual (Spiritual Guide)* in 1675. Although Molinos gathered many disciples and was supported by several eminent churchmen, such as the Oratorian Pietro Matteo Petrucci (1636–1701), bishop of Jesi and later cardinal, he was vehemently attacked by others (especially the Jesuit Paolo Segneri) for both his teachings and his dissolute morals. Investigated by the Roman Inquisition, sixty-eight propositions taken from the *Spiritual Guide*, his correspondence, and his oral teaching as testified to by witnesses to the Inquisition were condemned by the Inquisition as heretical. Molinos was sentenced to life imprisonment and died imprisoned in Rome, repenting—it is said—of his errors.

According to Cardinal Bausset there are three principal distinguishing characteristics of Quietism that can be derived from Molinos's writings:

1. Perfect contemplation—a permanent state of the soul in which there is no longer any reasoning or thought either about God or oneself. The soul passively receives the imprint of divine love and light without having the necessity of performing any act of love or adoration or indeed any act of discursive prayer or Christian piety as commonly understood.
2. Apatheia (lack of desire)—In this state of perfect contemplation the soul no longer desires anything for itself, not even its own salvation. There is a total absence of fear of damnation as the soul only seeks to abandon itself totally to God's will. In the *Spiritual Guide* Molinos states: "The soul must not think either of its own reward, nor punishment; neither of heaven nor of hell."[139]
3. Dispensation of Christian obligation—The Christian mystic who by the "single act" of abandonment to God's will has attained to this state of perfect contemplation no longer has the need for the sacraments of the church or the practice of good deeds that bind ordinary Christians. These acts all become indifferent. And even though the lower part of the soul may become tainted by sinful thoughts and desires, the higher part of the soul (in which intelligence and will reside) is not soiled by these sinful desires. As Molinos explains in the

Spiritual Guide: "Perfection consists in a continual act of love of God containing to a superior degree the acts of all other virtues that renders them useless."[140]

Knox, in *Enthusiasm*, goes further than Bausset, offering a slightly longer and more nuanced list of Quietism's essential characteristics. According to him, Quietism may be defined not only by the concepts of passive contemplation, lack of concern for one's salvation, and disengagement from normative Christian morality, but also by an instinctive rejection of "reflection" or intellectual considerations in prayer and the tendency to de-emphasize devotion to Christ's sacred humanity. Since Quietists aimed for intimate, direct union with God, any mental images, even those of Christ's infancy or passion, were considered distractions to the purest forms of contemplation. These sorts of antinomian doctrines of which the Quietists were accused had previously appeared under different names through the history of Christianity. For example, the Spanish Alumbrados of the early seventeenth century, seen by many as precursors of Quietism, were accused of holding similar beliefs.

The practical result of Molinos's teaching was that many of his disciples neglected the time-honored devotional practices of the church. Many even abandoned the confessional as well, judging that since they were in a state of permanent union with God they no longer had need of absolution. Some of his more hedonistic disciples were accused by the Roman Inquisition of engaging in acts of sexual license and criminality, believing that their bodies (and the physical acts they performed) were no longer of any importance because their soul was intimately and permanently united with God.

In France two mystics, Père François La Combe (1640–1715) and Mme. Jeanne Guyon (1648–1717), were teaching and gathering disciples to their concept of disinterested love at roughly the same time as Molinos was active in Rome.[141] Although neither La Combe nor Guyon ever admitted to having more than a passing acquaintance with Molinos's doctrine, both were seen by their enemies as being tainted with the Spanish mystic's errors. Guyon would be attacked repeatedly for intemperate language used especially in three of her writings: *Moyen Court (Easy and Short Method of Prayer That Everyone Can Easily Practice)*, *Torrents spirituels (Spiritual*

Torrents), and her commentary on the Song of Songs. Whether rightly or wrongly, her critics saw her doctrine as reminiscent of and, they suspected, inspired by Molinos.[142]

In fact, many examples could be given of similarities—whether deliberate or coincidental—between the Quietist teachings of Molinos and Guyon's own teaching. From belief in "silent communications" to the "single act," Guyon in her writings echoes Falconi, Malaval, Molinos, and other celebrated Quietists.[143] One teaching of Guyon's that was to trouble Bossuet perhaps above all others, for example, was her willingness to accept damnation if it were God's will—the so-called impossible demand that had been discussed previously by de Sales and other mystics. In common with Molinos, Guyon took this concept to its logical conclusion, maintaining that Christians seeking perfection and union with God should not only be willing to accept the sacrifice of personal salvation but also to glory in this acceptance as proof of their total love of God and indifference to their own fate. Knox points out that Guyon indeed seems to "harp on the matter of damnation," as if it were a matter of "standing or falling to her *petite église*."[144] Guyon apparently felt that complete abandonment to God's will necessarily entailed the willingness—indeed eagerness—to undergo this ultimate sacrifice of one's personal salvation. In one passage of the *Torrents spirituels* she exclaims: "It matters not whether I am in the pit of Hell with the demons, provided that I'm not sinning."[145] In another celebrated passage, she asks God: "Damn me, so that I may stop sinning."[146]

Up to the time when Mme. Guyon became known to the general public in France in the 1690s, her life had been a tumultuous one. After an unhappy marriage she was left a widow in 1676, at which time she decided to wander throughout France, Savoy, and Italy preaching her "short and easy" method of passive prayer that would allow her disciples to die to themselves *(s'anéantir)* and meld themselves into mystical union with God. During a sojourn in Savoy she met with Père La Combe, a Barnabite priest of similar mystical leanings, who became her confessor and spiritual director. It is difficult to qualify Guyon and La Combe's association as anything other than unfortunate for both of them. Instead of being the steadying influence—the moderating force—that each needed to calm his or her exalted nature, they acted on each other in the opposite sense. Père La Combe has been described by one biographer as "hyper-nervous and hyper-emotional: a man given to visions, celestial communications and imprudent exaltation."[147] Another historian has called him simply "unbalanced."[148] These two nervous, exalted personalities seem to have encouraged one another in the expression of the most extravagant forms of mystical experience. They seem to have, moreover, fostered in each other the belief that they were both privileged beings, predestined by God for a special ministry: the apostolate of pure love experienced in silence and quietude.

If La Combe's and Guyon's apostolate were destined for greatness, it was still not free from difficulties and even suffering. Both Jeanne Guyon and her confessor would be calumnied wherever they sojourned. They would both spend years in prison; La Combe, in fact, died in prison, and Guyon spent her last years under a sort of house arrest. Being of delicate constitutions, both would suffer from chronic pain and illness. None of these trials, however, discouraged Guyon. In her *Autobiography* she describes the suffering she endured in achieving union with God as a divine gift. "I suffered gaily," she says, "like a child," learning all the while to communicate with God in "an ineffable silence, the language of the angels."[149]

It was during her travels with La Combe, amid their alternating periods of suffering and exaltation, that Guyon deepened her knowledge of the mystical tradition. Although she never pretended to be a professional theologian, her reading of the mystical authors would eventually be voracious and wide, encompassing patristic and medieval authors such as the Pseudo-Areopagite and Tauler as well as more modern mystics such as Francis de Sales and Teresa of Avila. In her writings she consequently borrows from this rich tradition of mystical imagery, describing herself variously as "a little fish in the ocean" of divine union and as a "child" in the "state of childish simplicity."[150]

Whereas these sorts of metaphor were often found in approved mystical writings, Guyon would furnish ammunition for her later detractors when she went beyond such commonly accepted images and began to speak of her unique "apostolic motherhood." It was given to her to understand, for example (in her "silent communications" with God) that she was to become a "shepherdess" to a "little flock" of contemplatives seeking to worship God in spirit and truth. She saw herself, moreover, as the crowned Woman of the Apocalypse (an identification that incensed Bossuet no end). She told her disciples that they should think of her as their spiritual mother (and call her *ma mère*), because she had suffered pains of childbirth when they became her spiritual offspring. It would be her maternal mission to guide them in the way of pure, disinterested love, showering them with the overabundance of the gifts granted to her by God. She saw herself as a means of grace for her disciples, being so filled with grace that—at least in one instance—she had to have her corset unlaced to give her relief.[151] "Oh! My Lord," she exclaims in one passage, "Give me hearts on which to pour out my plenitude!"[152] It would be Mme. Guyon's greatest reward (as well as, eventually, her greatest trial) to have her prayer answered throughout the years following her travels with La Combe in the 1680s. From Gex and Geneva to Grenoble, Lyon, Turin, and finally Paris she would gather disciples to her bosom wherever she preached and taught her doctrine. The greatest and most brilliant of these fellow travelers to pure love would, of course, be Fénelon, whom she would meet upon her return to France.

Having embarked together on a spiritual odyssey throughout southeastern France, preaching and teaching her doctrine as best they could with the forbearance of ecclesiastical authorities,[153] La Combe and Guyon finally ended up in Paris in 1686, where they endeavored to continue their ministry but found the climate uncongenial. Harlay de Champvallon, archbishop of Paris (a dissolute and vain prelate) was hostile to their teachings and had La Combe imprisoned in 1687 and Guyon in 1688. Benefiting from her family's connections, Mme. Guyon was quickly released and returned to Paris, where she became friends with the Colbert clan, the two daughters of Louis XIV's former finance minister, at this time both duchesses (one married to the Duc de Beauvillier and the other to the Duc de Chevreuse). All of these personages were of the highest aristocracy and wielded enormous influence at court. Indeed, the fascination with Quietism in seventeenth-century France among the literate public has as much to do with the celebrity and high social standing of those associated with the movement as it does with theology. Add to this fascination with celebrity the intellectual brilliance of Fénelon; the renown of those vehemently opposing Quietism, such as Bossuet, Rancé, Nicole, and Noailles (all scholars with an international reputation); and the personal intervention of Louis XIV and Mme. de Maintenon—and all the elements are present for a confrontation of the most dramatic sort. In fact, no other theological dispute had so gripped the imagination of the French reading public since Pascal had so brilliantly sparred with the Jesuit Casuists more than fifty years previously in his *Provincial Letters.*

At the time that Mme. Guyon returned to Paris, the Beauvillier and Chevreuse families were already under the spiritual direction of Fénelon, who had recently been appointed chief tutor of Louis XIV's grandsons, the little dukes of Bourgogne, Anjou, and Berry. Although Guyon had already met and charmed the Colbert clan and Mme. de Maintenon, in the beginning Fénelon's relationship with Mme. Guyon was reserved. He was careful to maintain his distance, being somewhat taken aback by the extravagance of her mystical effusions. Nor did he wish to do anything to compromise his position with Mme. de Maintenon, whose spiritual director he had become, or to endanger his growing reputation as a solidly orthodox theologian and protégé of France's preeminent churchman Bossuet. In the summer and autumn of 1689, however, their friendship grew and Fénelon's reticence waned. He came to appreciate the sincerity of Guyon's spiritual ardor. Much more, perhaps, he came to admire the depth of her spiritual experiences and mystical union with God. He had always yearned to experience such spiritual ecstasy and closeness to God, experiences that had heretofore been denied him. He seems to have seen in Jeanne Guyon not only a friend and deeply committed Christian, but also a mentor to the inner paths of the spiritual life analogous to the role that Teresa of Avila had played as friend, confidante, and mentor to John of the Cross or Madame Acarie to Bérulle a century earlier. For nearly five years the little flock, as she called them, of the Beauvilliers, the Chevreuses, Fénelon, and Maintenon met together, prayed together, and discussed means of living out the gospel together. Fénelon acted as confessor to them all and undertook during these years a correspondence with each of them that would eventually produce hundreds of letters of spiritual direction.

This harmonious situation was not to last, however. By the spring of 1693 Mme. de Maintenon had begun to become anxious at the influence that Guyon was exerting on Fénelon and the two ducal families, the Beauvilliers and the Chevreuses. She was disturbed by the language Guyon used to describe herself and her apostolate. Not herself experienced in the vocabulary of mysticism, Maintenon was at a loss as to how to understand Guyon's referring to herself as the "building stone" and the "shepherdess" and "mother."[154] On May 2, 1693, Maintenon ordered Guyon to not return to Saint-Cyr. A convert to Catholicism, and always fearful of having her personal orthodoxy called into question or being found guilty by association, Maintenon finally asked Bossuet to investigate Mme. Guyon's doctrine and writings. After consultation with Beauvillier and Chevreuse, it was decided that Bossuet would be seconded in his deliberations by Noailles, bishop of Châlons, and M. Tronson, director of Fénelon's former seminary of Saint Sulpice. The composition of this commission was, therefore, decidedly favorable to Fénelon.[155] Mme. de Maintenon was doubtless hoping—as Cardinal Bausset would later relate—"that the opinion of the commissioners would contribute in disabusing Fénelon and M. de Beauvillier of the illusions they had concerning Mme. Guyon."[156]

During this spring and summer of 1693, Fénelon, as intuitive as ever, had sensed the growing disquiet over Guyon's teaching at Saint-Cyr and Versailles. He knew Maintenon well enough to divine her growing panic at association with a possible heretic. It was time to act. He therefore encouraged Mme. Guyon to allow herself and her writings to be judged by this panel of competent ecclesiastical judges. At this time he still trusted in Bossuet's intellectual ability to discern heresy from the mere intemperate, extravagant language that Guyon had used. He doubtless also still trusted in the bonds of affection that had been forged between his mentor, Bossuet, and himself during the previous decade.

By March 1694 Bossuet had finished his initial examination of Guyon's writings and addressed a long letter to her in which he made clear that he was very concerned about what he termed "false maxims concerning prayer." He mentioned several examples of the "errors" and "illusions" into which he believed that Guyon had fallen. Guyon had used symbolism and metaphor in her writings reminiscent of the imagery used by mystics before her, many of whom were approved by the Catholic Church. These images evoking mystical marriage and divine union, although part and parcel of mystical tradition, were new and shocking to Bossuet, a commonsense, practical prelate descended from a family of middle-class lawyers, who had been trained in the precise terminology of Scholasticism. Fénelon would repeatedly claim that Bossuet had never even read the mystical authors before his participation in the Conferences of Issy and, while this is no doubt an exaggeration, it is true that Bossuet himself spoke of his incomprehension—antipathy even—for the mystical tradition. In one letter to a friend, written at the very time he was examining Mme. Guyon's doctrine, he states: "I have never heard so much talk of [contemplative] prayer before and, in spite of myself, I can't shake a certain disgust I feel for these mystics."[157] To Guyon herself he admitted in a letter that he did not understand all that she said about mystical unions and her role as mother and shepherdess to her sheep, of binding and loosing their sins, and so forth. "Here where you write," he says in a letter to her, "that 'whatever I bind, will be bound and whatever I loose shall be loosed' is excessive and unbearable." He goes on to say that he fears that she had conferred apostolic sanction upon herself in a way "of which there is no example in the whole church." He ends his letter, however, with an irenic tone, saying that he approves of her docility by agreeing to submit to his judgment and he is prepared for her to "explain" herself "more fully" at a later date.[158] This date would come that summer, beginning in June, when, along with M. de Noailles and M. Tronson, he would meet in the village of Issy, outside of Paris, to debate once again Guyon's doctrine and issue a final opinion as to her orthodoxy.

Fénelon's reactions to the conference were mixed: anxiety that the commissioners would condemn Guyon alternated with relief that the matter would be at least resolved. At this stage of the proceedings he seemed hopeful that the commissioners would either find in favor of Guyonian mysticism or at least not assail the basic tenets of the mystical tradition. In June 1694 Fénelon wrote that he would accept whatever decision the commissioners reached: "I declare before God [...] that I will subscribe without any equivocation or restriction to all that M. Tronson along with Messieurs de

Meaux [Bossuet] and de Châlons [de Noailles] decide concerning questions of spirituality in order to anticipate any errors or illusions of Quietism and the like."[159]

The Conference of Issy (often called conferences because the commissioners met at different intervals) lasted from mid July 1694 to March 10, 1695. According to Bossuet:

> We read entire books...It was a question of absolute importance for the church since it was about nothing less than preventing the rebirth of Quietism that we saw beginning again in the kingdom in the writings of Madame Guyon. And we regarded as the greatest of all misfortunes that she had for advocate Monsieur the abbé de Fénelon. His intellect, his eloquence, his virtue, the position he occupied and those that were destined for him caused us to make every effort to bring him back to reason.[160]

Fénelon, for his part, saw Bossuet as the one who needed enlightenment. He would write later that "this prelate admitted at the beginning of the conferences that he had never read either Saint Francis de Sales or the Blessed John of the Cross or most of the mystical authors."[161] He saw not only Mme. Guyon and himself as being under attack, but also mystical doctrine itself. Under such circumstances it was almost inevitable that there would be misunderstanding among the various parties involved in the conferences.

In September 1694 the Duc de Beauvillier asked M. Tronson personally to interview Mme. Guyon and question her about her doctrine. It is not known whether the superior of Saint Sulpice was actually able to fulfill his request, being nearly bedridden during this time from the gout. However, in November 1694 Fénelon attempted once more to persuade Tronson to engage his authority on Guyon's behalf by sending a copy of his letters to Mme. de Maintenon to Tronson, asking him to judge whether he finds any hint of Quietist heresy in them.

The commissioners turned directly to Mme. Guyon in October 1694, receiving a written apologia of her writings in which she tried to explain away confusion over her mystical terminology. Two months later, on December 6, 1694, Bossuet and Noailles interviewed Mme. de Guyon for several hours, questioning her at length about her doctrine. Throughout these months Fénelon had been sending letters to Bossuet, trying to defend Guyon's mysticism to him, mysticism that Fénelon believed to be in agreement with approved mystical doctrine of the church. He doubtless sincerely hoped to bring Bossuet around to his views on "pure love" and the "interior life" by deluging him with these written explanations and citations from mystical authors.

Bossuet remained unmoved. Indeed, he became increasingly suspicious of Fénelon's role in defending mystical doctrine, a role he sees more and more as a defense of Guyon herself. "Without naming Mme. Guyon or her books, everything tended to support them or excuse them."[162] In January 1695 Fénelon, hoping to break the impasse and appeal directly to Bossuet, composed an apologia of his own life and views of mystical doctrine, which he sent to Bossuet.

An event now occurred to somewhat change the balance between Fénelon and the three commissioners. On February 4,1695, Fénelon was nominated to be archbishop of Cambrai by Louis XIV. Thus he was no longer simply a priest, inferior in degree to Bossuet and Noailles. Up to this point he had been treated courteously but somewhat condescendingly, especially by Bossuet. He would henceforth be anointed with the same sacred oil as the other bishops, a successor of the apostles as they are. From this date, therefore, the commissioners agreed that they should allow Fénelon to join their group as an equal and take part fully in their discussions.

No radical change of heart was observed in Fénelon, however. He still maintained an attitude of deference and respect toward his colleagues. In spite of his newfound position as an equal member of the commission on February 8, 1695, Fénelon agreed voluntarily to sign the "Act of Adhesion to Cardinal de Bérulle's Doctrine," in which he declared that he had never believed any other doctrine concerning "the interior paths" than that held by Bérulle "in the precise sense that he himself gave to his words." And although he continued to defend Mme. Guyon, saying that he still believed her doctrine to be that of Saint John of the Cross and Saint Francis de Sales, he stated, "I am ready to condemn it if it is required of me."[163]

At this point the commissioners had interviewed Mme. Guyon and poured over thousands of pages of documents relating to her doctrine and the works of mystical authors stretching back to Clement of Alexandria in the second century. They had received manuscript after manuscript from Fénelon himself, defending his interpretation of pure love. As Bossuet would later write in the *Relation*, "He had explained himself in such detail that we perfectly understood all his thoughts."[164] They had drafted a list of propositions concerning mystical doctrine that they all agreed was a compromise allowing Fénelon honorably to hold to the doctrine of approved mystics such as de Sales and Saint Teresa while condemning what they saw as excesses in Mme. Guyon's mystical works. There seemed to be no point in dragging out the discussions any longer. By February 1695, therefore, the discussions were clearly nearing an end. Bossuet wrote Tronson that he was ready to "put an end to this business between us." It appears that right up to the close of the conference Bossuet held to the hope that he could separate Fénelon from Guyon and "lead him gently back" to Bossuet's own views of Catholic orthodoxy.[165]

Ultimately, thirty-four propositions came out of these conferences at Issy. At first Fénelon was not satisfied with the final document. He apparently quibbled with his fellow commissioners over the exact wording of the propositions concerning pure love, points that we know were dear to his heart and would continue to be recurring themes in all his writings until his death. The crux of the problem seems to have been this: Fénelon firmly believed in the doctrine of a pure, disinterested love of God in the sense that a Christian could and should love God without any selfish thought of personal salvation. Bossuet, on the contrary, believed this opinion to be erroneous at best and heretical at worst. In spite of all the copies of works and quotations from a multitude of Christian mystics asserting this doctrine, he could never bring himself to believe that love of God could exclude a personal interest in salvation. He would go so far as admit that many approved Catholic saints seemed to speak of pure love as Fénelon understood it, but he could never wholeheartedly accept that this was anything other than an "extravagant" (his word) and dangerous doctrine.

Nevertheless, on March 10, 1695, after some tweaking of various propositions in an effort to satisfy Fénelon's objections (what Bossuet called "the delicateness of his spirit"), the commissioners met and signed the final document, the "Articles of the Conferences of Issy," as they would be known. Thereupon (to quote Knox), each commissioner—fervently believing that he was in the right—"proceeded to interpret the articles in opposite senses."[166] On the completion of the conferences the commissioners returned to their respective dioceses, and both Bossuet and Noailles published ordinances in which they reproduced the articles agreed upon at Issy and also condemned various Quietist writings. Bossuet's ordinance, for example, condemned not only Mme. de Guyon's *Short Method* and her *Explanation of the Song of Solomon*, but also Molinos's *Spiritual Guide* and Malaval's *Easy Practice*, both of which had previously been condemned by the Holy See for their Quietist doctrine.

Since the proceedings surrounding the conferences at Issy would in following years be the subject of so much acrimonious debate between the various signatories, we would do well at this point to consider some of the actual articles to which Fénelon set his signature. Let us particularly consider those articles that would later lend themselves to the most heated debate. These are the essential articles:

1. Each Christian, no matter what state he is in, although not necessarily in every moment, is obliged to conserve the exercise of faith, hope, and charity, and to produce acts thereof, as three distinct virtues.

5. Each Christian, in every state, although not at every moment, is obliged to want, desire, and ask explicitly for his eternal salvation, as a thing that God wants and that he desires that we should want as well, for his glory.

9. It is not permitted for a Christian to be indifferent concerning his salvation, nor for the things that have a relation to it. Holy Christian indifference concerns events in this life (excepting sin) and the dispensation of consolation during time of spiritual aridity.

19. Perpetual prayer does not consist in a perpetual and unique act that is presumed to be without interruption and that must never be repeated, but rather in a habitual preparation and disposition to do nothing that might displease God and to do

everything to please him. The contrary proposition that would exclude in any conceivable state—even perfect—all plurality or succession of acts would be erroneous and opposed to the tradition of all the saints.

20. There are no apostolic traditions except those that are recognized by the entire church and whose authority was decided by the Council of Trent; the contrary proposition is erroneous and supposed secret apostolic traditions would be a trap for the faithful and a means of introducing all sorts of bad doctrines in the church.

25. It is not permitted for a Christian, under any pretext of passive prayer *(oraison passive)* or another extraordinary sort, to wait in the conduct of his life, either spiritual or temporal, for God to decide each action for him by a special means or inspiration; the contrary leads to testing of God, to illusion, and to lethargy.

28. The extraordinary paths *(voies extraordinaires)*, with the signs that the approved mystics have given of them, according to the mystics themselves, are very rare and are subject to the oversight of bishops, ecclesiastical superiors, and doctors who must judge them, not so much according to the experiences themselves, but rather according to the immutable laws of scripture and of Tradition. To teach or practice the contrary is to attempt to cast off the yoke of obedience that we owe to the church.

After the signing of these articles, life seemed to calm down for Fénelon. He continued to be tutor to the king's grandchildren. In what was seen as a sign of reconciliation, he was consecrated archbishop of Cambrai by Bossuet himself in July 1695 in the presence of Mme. de Maintenon at Saint-Cyr, the private school she had founded for impoverished girls of noble birth outside of Paris.

As for Mme. Guyon, since January 1695 she had been in self-imposed seclusion in the Convent of the Visitation in Bossuet's diocese of Meaux. It was at this point that the waters of discord became agitated again, mostly because of the rash conduct of Guyon herself. After promising adhesion to the formularies of Issy and assuring Bossuet of her personal devotion to him and her "pure and simple submission," she had requested a certificate attesting to her submission to the Catholic faith and opposition to Quietism as articulated in the Articles of Issy. Bossuet granted this document, unsuspecting of the woman he would later term "the cause of the divisions of the church."[167] Guyon, thereupon, pretended to go to Bourbon to take the waters for her health. In actuality, however, she headed for Paris, where she hid under various assumed names and began spreading about the tale that the Issy commissioners, with Bossuet in the lead, had absolved her from any suspicion of heresy.

Bossuet was chagrined upon hearing this, accusing her of bad faith and hypocrisy. Mme. de Maintenon too was alarmed that Guyon seemed to be gathering around her once again the members of her "little flock." She determined to put a stop to this and finish the matter once and for all, since the conferences at Issy apparently had not been able to do so. She persuaded the king to issue a warrant for Guyon's arrest. The unfortunate mystic was subsequently imprisoned in the Château de Vincennes on December 24, 1695. In spite of requests by her friends for royal clemency, she would spend most of her remaining life either in prison or under house arrest.[168]

It was now Fénelon's turn to suffer the consequences of his association with Mme. Guyon. Once Louis XIV learned, from Bossuet and Maintenon, the extent of Guyon's influence over both the governor of his grandchildren's education (Beauvillier) and their tutor, he began to take steps to remove his patronage from Fénelon. Not only did Maintenon whisper doubts about Fénelon's trustworthiness in the king's ear, but Bossuet in a melodramatic gesture literally threw himself to his knees in front of the king to denounce the viper that he had nourished in his bosom. Moreover, as Louis delved into Fénelon's writings, he became more suspicious of this cleric who was being denounced as unorthodox and was perhaps seditious as well.

The two works that more than any others led both to Fénelon's theological and literary reputation and to his political disgrace were the *Maxims of the Saints* and the *Adventures of Telemachus*. The pedagogical tale of Ulysses' son, Telemachus, has already been discussed. Let us now consider the *Maxims*, the book that Fénelon began to write during the deliberations of the conferences at Issy and that he published in January 1697, a year and a half after he had signed the Articles of Issy, pledging his conformity to the doctrine articulated therein.

What is this book, the *Explanation of the Maxims of the Saints on the Interior Life*, to give its full title, and why did it cause such a furor in both ecclesiastical and court circles of its time? Why did it lead to the breakup of a twenty-year friendship between its author and Bossuet, whom Fénelon had considered his mentor and protector? Why was it debated and criticized throughout theologically literate French circles and ultimately condemned by the pope? The answers to these questions lie both in the nature of the book itself and, perhaps more important, in the personality of its author.

After solemnly professing in a letter to Bossuet earlier that year, in 1696, to "obey" the man whom he described as not only a "very great theologian" but the image of God,[169] Fénelon refused to approve Bossuet's *Instruction sur les états d'oraison*, published the same year. This was scandalous in Bossuet's eyes, being an act that now publicly distanced Fénelon from a man who had been associated in the public mind with him for so many years: his friend and his patron. Moreover, as Bossuet noted, Fénelon was now putting himself forth publicly as the defender of this misguided, heretical woman whom he and his fellow commissioners had just formally condemned in both the Articles of Issy and in their respective pastoral ordinances. The Eagle of Meaux prepared to unsheathe his talons against Fénelon; they would not be retracted again during his lifetime. Fénelon would not be moved, however, from his position. As he stated in a letter that year to Mme. de Maintenon, one of the last he would write her: "I can be mistaken about a person whom I believe to be a saint [...] but I have seen close up definite acts of hers that have infinitely edified me; why would people now want me to condemn her regarding other facts that I have not seen?"[170]

Moreover, the book that he composed was not in reality an effort to defend the reputation of his friend, Jeanne Guyon. Fénelon was politically astute, and he realized by this time that Guyon was irremediably discredited and beyond his powers to help. Indeed, after her imprisonment they would never see each other again. No, what Fénelon had undertaken to accomplish in writing the *Maxims of the Saints* was not a defense of Jeanne Guyon but an apologia of the doctrine he held as his own, that of disinterested pure love. The book would be nothing less than a defense of the mystical tradition of the Catholic Church, a tradition he felt to be in danger and under attack. This tradition he believed was at the heart of the purest and most perfect expression of Christianity and must be defended at all costs, whatever the repercussions to his reputation or political future at Versailles. Although he realized that Guyon had been guilty of flights of fancy and verbal exaggeration in her books, he was no less convinced of the reality of the mystical experience hidden underneath her exaggerations. It was this reality that he intended to defend.

The *Maxims* is composed of forty-five articles presented in a thesis-antithesis form that stretches back to classic models of Antiquity and that had found expression in many medieval theological works. This structure allowed Fénelon to present quotations from approved mystics expounding their doctrine and to juxtapose them with passages from heretical sources that seem to be asserting similar positions but that actually fall into error and should be condemned by the church.[171]

In his introduction to the *Maxims*, Fénelon is at pains to strike a balance between what he firmly believed to be approved mystical doctrines of "pure love," "detachment from oneself," "spiritual abandon," and "holy indifference," on the one hand, and the misinterpretations and excesses of these doctrines that had already been condemned as Quietist by Rome and so recently by his colleagues at Issy, on the other. "It is of the utmost importance," he writes "to explain the doctrine of pure love and to mark clearly the limits beyond which a Christian's detachment cannot go." This detachment, for example, can never exclude the love of God or conformity to God's will, which always desires our salvation, a doctrine that Bossuet and others had found in Guyon's writings. Pure love and holy indifference cannot mean that a Christian is no longer under an obligation to obey the church's laws because "this selfless love *[amour désintéressé]* is always inviolably attached to the written law…and provokes all the distinct virtues as selfish love *[amour intéressé]*."

The *Maxims*, therefore, provides a blueprint for the mystical journey from selfish love of God to selfless love of God, passing through stages of love mingled with vestiges of self-interest, called by Fénelon "amour mélangé." According to Fénelon, the mystic is hindered in the spiritual journey by what he terms "propriété," or self-love, and "cupidité," the "root of all vices." Only by passing through spiritual trials ("les épreuves") can the mystic eventually succeed in detaching himself or herself ("désapproprier") from this love of self. These trials are characterized by experiences of spiritual aridity and feelings of abandonment by God, the dark night spoken of by Saint John of the Cross and others. The mystic endures these trials by recourse to prayer and contemplation. The further along the inner paths the mystic advances, the more passive the mystic's prayer will be, contemplating God continually and passively. If successful, the mystic will achieve pure love, a love purified by these mystical trials from any self-interest. In a state of pure love, the mystic loves "God's sovereign beauty in itself and only for itself."

The culmination of pure love is union with God, the supreme degree of the spiritual life. Fénelon describes this union as a passive state ("état passif") in which spiritual childhood ("enfance") reigns supreme. This state is simple, humble, peaceful, and led by actual grace in the present moment. In this state of "transformation" God imprints himself on the soul and consumes it in a spiritual union, often described by mystics as spiritual wedding, the "noces spirituelles" that, without being a hypostatic union such as Christ had,[172] is nevertheless a complete union of will to will and is a foreshadowing of heavenly beatitude, permitting the soul on earth to remain in a state of purity ("pureté entière").

In his attempt to understand the concepts of the inner paths, the trials, and selfless love that compose the mystical experience, Fénelon has recourse to the doctrine of two levels of the soul. This concept had previously been championed by many mystics, including de Sales, and was accepted by the church as an explanation of the mystical state.[173] According to this doctrine, the soul is composed of a "superior" and an "inferior" level. The former is capable of will and intelligence; the latter, feeling and emotion. Thus, underneath the "empirical personality" that is capable of reasoning and making conscious decisions, there is a "mystical personality" whose acts are "so simple, so direct, so peaceful and so uniform that they seem to form only one sole act, or even that they seem to be no act at all but rather the tranquil repose of pure union" (Art. XXIX).[174]

In this state our conscious being, the ego, which as Fénelon states repeatedly in his correspondence is only an illusion, is absorbed into the reality of God's being. Mystical knowledge is, therefore, in a sense, a knowledge more pure and more real in its intuition than "discursive" logic. The mystic's sensibility seeks to meld into a loving, peaceful "quietude"; the mystical will into a nonresistance to divine operation, being moved as God wills. In this mystical state the soul unites to the reality that is God, like "a drop of water in the ocean," to use Fénelon's term, in perfect passivity. This perfectly passive and "transformed" state is that of pure love, in which the individual will can no longer be distinguished from the divine will. This is the love of which the author of the *Maxims* speaks when he defines the highest degree of love as the "love born of pure charity, without any mingling of motive of self-interest."

No matter how subtle Fénelon's arguments are, however, or how painstakingly nuanced his distinctions between the orthodox and heretical variations of mystical doctrine, he could not avoid the appearance of being too clever, too hair-splitting in his argument. The old cry of "casuist" that had been used so effectively against the Jesuits by Pascal and others throughout the seventeenth century was heard again. Even M. Tronson, Fénelon's friend and mentor, widely considered one of the most eminent theologians of his time, wrote after reading the *Maxims:* "I can only esteem what I understand of it and admire what I don't understand."[175] Saint-Simon quipped sarcastically "no one but theologians could pretend to understand it and even among them only after three or four readings."[176] In spite of its esoteric nature, however, the book took on a life of its own. Calvet says, "No one read it but they kept talking about it." It was said that Monsieur de Cambrai was supporting unheard of doctrines. No one understood them but everyone knew they were dangerous.[177]

In spite of a valiant attempt to establish subtle distinctions between his own doctrine and that condemned by the Articles, Fénelon could not reconcile the obvious sense of the formularies that he had signed at Issy with the logical interpretation of the doctrines that he defends in the *Maxims.* One or two examples of this disconnect should suffice. Article IX of the Articles of Issy clearly states that "it is not permitted for a Christian to be indifferent concerning his salvation, nor for the things that have a relation to it." And yet in the *Maxims of the Saints* Fénelon writes that "one can love God with a love that is pure love, without any mixture of the motive of self-interest." Here "self-interest" ("l'intérêt propre") must logically include an interest in eternal salvation. Another example is Article XX, which states: "There are no apostolic traditions except those that are recognized by the entire church and whose authority was decided by the Council of Trent. The contrary proposition is erroneous and supposed secret apostolic traditions would be a trap for the faithful and a means of introducing all sorts of bad doctrines in the church." And yet in the Introduction to the *Maxims* we read that a discussion of the mystical paths "demands a type of secret," and that "pastors and saints throughout the ages had a sort of economy and secret in talking about pure love only to those souls to whom God had given the attraction and the understanding."

The list of examples could be multiplied many fold. The inconsistencies are apparent, and they raise an obvious question: why was Fénelon signatory to a document whose doctrine was not his own and to which, ultimately, he could not agree? We will perhaps never know the complete answer, since it lies in the innermost recesses of Fénelon's complex psychological makeup. There is little doubt that he felt pressured to sign the Articles of Issy by Bossuet, by Mme. de Maintenon, by his friends at court, and doubtless by his family as well. It must be remembered also that at the time he signed the Articles he was still technically a parish priest. A year and a half later, when he published the *Maxims*, he was the consecrated archbishop of Cambrai and a duke of the Holy Roman Empire, residing in his own arch-episcopal palace in lands theoretically out of the control of Louis XIV.

There are doubtless other reasons Fénelon took the fatal step of braving the wrath of the leading churchman in France, Bossuet, and the king himself. He perhaps felt a chivalrous impulse to defend, as far as possible, his friend Mme. Guyon, who was a free woman at the time of the Conferences of Issy but in prison by the time Fénelon published the *Maxims of the Saints*. More important, he felt a duty, especially now as bishop and pastor of the church, to defend what he sincerely believed to be true Christian doctrine from the attacks of those who either could not or would not understand the "inner paths" of mysticism. Ultimately, he must in his own mind have rationalized his signing the Articles of Issy as understanding them in a sense that Bossuet and the other commissioners did not.

The storm clouds that had been forming over Fénelon's head ever since his falling under the influence of Mme. Guyon at Versailles in the early 1690s were now to break open and rain down on the unfortunate archbishop of Cambrai. Mme. de Maintenon was not mollified by the letters she received from her former spiritual director and erstwhile friend. She was by now too afraid of both his doctrine, which she considered suspect, and his conduct, which she considered dangerous and even unstable. She had in any event now found a new confessor and spiritual director in the person of Godet des Marais, bishop of Chartres, in whose diocese Saint-Cyr was located and whose director he had become. Whereas earlier she had encouraged Louis XIV to give favor to Fénelon, now she encouraged the king to distance himself from him. Indeed, if we are to believe Bremond's argument in his *Apologie pour Fénelon*, she provoked her royal spouse to actually weigh in against Fénelon in the proceedings, which would now shift to Rome.

THE CONDEMNATION OF THE *MAXIMS OF THE SAINTS*

Fénelon had rushed the *Maxims* to publication in January 1697. By July of that year—astute political observer that he was—he realized that Maintenon and Louis XIV had turned against him in their support of Bossuet. Feeling cornered, he wrote in a letter to his close friend—later his designated representative in Rome—the Abbé de Chanterac that "the intensity of our adversaries only grows stronger," describing Bossuet's, Marais's, and Noailles's conduct as "ignoble."[178] Despairing of obtaining justice in a France dominated now by his enemies, he decided he had no other option than to appeal his case to Rome. In a letter to the king, dated July 25, he requested permission to be allowed to go to Rome to defend personally his writings before the Holy See. Louis XIV, however, refused to allow Fénelon to leave his diocese. Indeed, the day after receiving Fénelon's letter the king intervened directly in the affair by formally requesting that Pope

Innocent XII appoint a commission to judge Fénelon's doctrine as expounded in the *Maxims*, leaving little doubt in his letter of what he thought the ultimate verdict should be.

For the next year and a half a veritable war of pamphlets ensued between Fénelon and Bossuet and their respective allies, with titles such as "Difficulties" by Godet des Marais followed by Fénelon's "Response to the Difficulties"; Bossuet's "Four Questions" countered by Fénelon's "Response to the Four Questions"; and so on. The exchange continued incessantly from one month to the next. This pamphlet war culminated in Bossuet's publication (June 1698) of his *Relation sur le quiétisme*, giving his own viewpoint of the history of his dealings with Guyon and Fénelon over Quietism. Fénelon answered one month later with his *Réponse de Monseigneur l'Archévêque de Cambrai à la Relation sur le quiétisme*.

By this point in the game Fénelon and Bossuet were each convinced that the other was not only mistaken about doctrinal matters regarding the mystical tradition but was actually acting in bad faith, endeavoring maliciously to destroy his reputation. Fénelon wrote to the papal nuncio in 1698, at the height of this propaganda war with Bossuet, that he was utterly persuaded that Bossuet purposely was misconstruing Fénelon's writings for polemical purposes: "He seems to me full of all imaginable artifice to take all my words in a sense counter to their meaning in order to give them impious meanings."[179]

Throughout 1698 the king (who had shown his bias against Fénelon the previous year by refusing to allow him to go to Rome to defend himself) grew increasingly hostile to the archbishop of Cambrai. In June 1698 Louis XIV ordered all Fénelon's friends and relatives to leave the court. In a France centered both politically and culturally on Versailles, being banished from court was seen as the ultimate disgrace. Louis XIV followed the banishment of Fénelon's relatives by depriving the archbishop of the title and pension of tutor in January 1699. Fénelon had doubtless seen this signal humiliation coming. He well knew what position the king had taken with respect to him and his friends. He well knew that his three principal adversaries among the bishops (Bossuet, Godet des Marais, and Noailles) would never have attacked him so viciously without the king's express consent and support. In September 1698, only four months before Louis XIV removed him as tutor, Fénelon had presciently written to the Abbé de Chanterac about how tenuous his position was with respect to his opponents. "I cannot do everything at once," he laments. "There are three of them; they have inexhaustible and infinite support and means. I am alone, without resource, in poor health, and exhausted more from the pain in my soul than by work."[180]

At the same time that the king was punishing Fénelon and his friends and relatives, he was supporting (morally, politically, and financially) Bossuet and his nephew in Rome in their efforts to convince (and—when persuasion was not successful—to exert pressure on) the members of the papal commission to rule against Fénelon. Indeed, it would not be too extreme to say that, through his agents in Rome, the king was attempting to strong arm Innocent into condemning "the wildest, most fanciful churchman in all my realm," as he had begun calling the archbishop. No tactic seems to have been too base for the Abbé Bossuet to use to further the king's and his uncle's cause. From expensive Christmas gifts to the commissioners to the dissemination of (mostly untrue) gossip about Mme. Guyon's relations with La Combe and Fénelon—all became legitimate weapons to be used against this new "Montanus" and his "Priscilla." Knox calls the Abbé Bossuet nothing more than a "wretch" and maintains that "the saddest memory you can carry away from reading this correspondence [between Bossuet and his uncle] is that of his uncle, the Eagle of Meaux, feeding this carrion-bird with scraps of gossip about Madame Guyon and her guilty relations."[181]

Exiled to his diocese in Cambrai, Fénelon could only follow the seemingly interminable process in Rome by correspondence with his friends in the Vatican, especially his representative the Abbé de Chanterac, who was pleading his cause before the commission. No one seemed to know exactly which way the commission would rule. Indeed, contemporary witnesses to the scene saw Pope Innocent as being clearly inclined to acquit Fénelon of suspicion of heresy. The commissioners themselves, however, many of whom were being bribed and coerced by Louis XIV, seemed split evenly: five in favor and five opposed to condemning Fénelon. The commission was to meet over fifty times between September 1698 and March 1699, attempting to break this impasse.

Fénelon in Cambrai continued to wait and worry. In one particularly poignant passage to Chanterac, written in September 1698, he asked: "Will Rome allow this horrible scandal to go on forever?"[182] Finally, on March 12, 1699, Pope Innocent gave in to the Sun King's unbearable pressure and issued the apostolic brief *Cum alias* by which he condemned twenty-three propositions taken from the *Maxims of the Saints.*

The brief, too lengthy to be cited in its entirety, is composed in the legalistic Latin characteristic of papal pronouncements. The pope maintains in *Cum alias* that certain of Fénelon's teachings on pure love contained in the *Maxims* are pernicious to sound doctrine and scandalous to the faithful. "There had arisen throughout France," the brief declares, "so great a cry and hue about the bad doctrine of this book that [...] we gave the same book to some of our venerable brother cardinals of the Holy Roman Church and certain other doctors of theology to be examined by them with all the consideration that such an important matter requires."[183]

As Bossuet had early noticed and had repeatedly attacked during his controversy with Fénelon, the weak point in the *Maxims* had always seemed to be the question of whether Fénelonian pure love at its purest did not exclude Christian hope in eternal happiness and salvation. And, although Fénelon had always tried to distinguish himself from Molinos's "single act" by which the soul remains in a state of quietude obeying God's will passively without the necessity of hoping for its own salvation, remnants of this Quietist doctrine still seemed to reside in the book. Of the twenty-three propositions condemned by the papal brief, nearly two-thirds ultimately have to do with this question. Indeed, the condemned proposition on which the brief seems to place most emphasis (by including it last in the condemnation) was proposition XXIII, which accuses Fénelon in the *Maxims* of exalting pure love so much that Christian hope is eliminated as a part of the inner life. The article condemns the tenet: "Pure love can by itself encompass the inner life, and becomes therefore the unique principle and only motive of all deliberate and meritorious acts."

Cum alias was a severe blow to Fénelon and his friends, both in Rome and in France. Bossuet's nephew and representative to the papal commission wrote his uncle as soon as he learned of the brief, calling it a miracle. Bossuet exulted in his triumph along with the king and Mme. de Maintenon. They were all certain that they had done their duty in both humiliating a rebellious prelate and extirpating his dangerous doctrine. The king was actually smug in his victory over his archbishop.[184] Saint-Simon, for example, relates that upon meeting with Fénelon's friend the Duc de Beauvillier in the counsel chamber, Louis asked: "Well, Monsieur de Beauvillier, what do you think of things now? Monsieur de Cambrai has been condemned in all shapes and forms." Whereupon, Beauvillier, showing his typical greatness of spirit, replied: "Sire, I have been a special friend of M. de Cambrai's and I always shall be. Nevertheless, if he does not submit to the pope, I will no longer have any contact with him."[185]

Fénelon, however, did submit. As soon as *Cum alias* was known in Paris, Fénelon's brother left for Cambrai to apprize the archbishop of its contents. News of the condemnation found Fénelon in his cathedral church in Cambrai at the very moment in which he was preparing to climb into the pulpit to preach a sermon in commemoration of the day. (It was March 25—feast of the Assumption.) Upon hearing this news—doubtless one of the saddest moments of his life—Fénelon nevertheless found the courage to put aside his prepared sermon and instead delivered an extemporaneous sermon on the necessity for faithful Catholics to submit to the pronouncements of the church. *Roma locuta est; causa finita est*—Rome has spoken; the matter is concluded.

On March 29, only four days after being informed of the papal condemnation, Fénelon wrote Beauvillier a letter in which he demonstrated his complete docility in the face of the papal decision. This letter is so revealing as to Fénelon's personality—his courage in the midst of adversity, and his humility to the church's magisterium—that it bears citing at some length. After having thanked Beauvillier for his support and friendship, Fénelon speaks of his own attitude toward the condemnation:

> As for me, I try to carry my cross with humility and patience. God is giving me the grace to be at peace in the midst of this bitterness and pain [...] This is because my conduct is already decided, and I have no reason to

> deliberate further. It only remains for me to submit and to be silent. This is all that I have ever wished and I have only now to choose the terms of my submission.

Fénelon expresses both his relief that the matter has finally come to a conclusion and his surprise at certain circles who believed he would contest the condemnation:

> Sometimes I feel like laughing at the fear that certain zealous folks show me, thinking that I will not be able to make up my mind to submit. Sometimes, too, I am irritated with those who write me long exhortations to convince me to submit. They speak to me of the glory that is to be found in this humiliation and of the heroic act that I will be undertaking. All of this fatigues me a little, and I'm tempted to say to myself: "What have I ever done to those people for them to think that I would have so much difficulty in preferring the Holy See's authority to my own feeble understanding—or the peace of the church to my book?"[186]

Indeed Fénelon's conduct in submitting to the apostolic brief was seen by all disinterested parties as a pure example of Christian humility. Bossuet and his allies naturally saw Fénelon's submission as contrived and even hypocritical. They could deservedly congratulate themselves, however, because to a great extent they had accomplished their aims. Not only had the *Maxims* been condemned and put on the Index, but Fénelon's reputation would remain damaged right up to the twentieth century, when his rehabilitation was undertaken by Abbé Bremond in his magisterial *Apologie pour Fénelon.* Indeed, one could argue that the condemnation was a blow from which Fénelon's reputation in Catholic circles would never totally recover. Even today, out of consideration of the papal condemnation, the *Maxims of the Saints* do not appear in any approved Catholic editions of Fénelon's complete works, and his doctrine of pure love is still under a cloud of suspicion among many.

Yet a careful study of the process leading to the brief reveals that the condemnation had as much—or more—to do with political intrigue and royal pressure tactics by Louis XIV than it did with any inherently unorthodox doctrine propounded by Fénelon. Fénelon himself saw (as have modern historians of Quietism such as Leszek Kolakowski)[187] that his writings could as easily be understood in an orthodox as in an unorthodox sense, depending on the reader's bias. Even Bossuet's nephew and representative, the Abbé Bossuet, admitted in a letter to his uncle following the condemnation that it had taken "no less than the bolts of lightning that came from France [the pressure from Louis XIV] to shake the pope to his senses who, within a few days, would fall back into his original prejudice and resolve to save M. de Cambrai's reputation."[188]

Ronald Knox had said much the same in *Enthusiasm;* he argues that Pope Innocent had chosen the most lenient course possible in condemning the *Maxims.* "Through the direct influence of the pope none of the propositions was stigmatized as 'heretical,' or even as 'bordering on heresy."[189] Knox concludes, in his felicitous turn of phrase, "After all the royal letters and the Christmas-boxes, Rome had pronounced on the doctrine without chastising the delinquent."[190]

Even one of the Louis XIV's most recent and respected biographers has written in a similar vein, saying that by the pope's choosing to issue a brief—instead of the more formal bull—and by condemning the propositions in a global sense, *Cum alias* is not really so much a condemnation at all but rather becomes "a mere admonition with nothing precise condemned at all, and by using the mildest possible theological qualifications, coming nowhere near heresy, blasphemy, impiety or even 'offensive.'"[191]

THE AFTERMATH

The handwriting of Fénelon's disgrace had been on the wall ever since 1695 at the close of the Conference of Issy. Most well-placed observers at court saw even his elevation to the archbishopric of Cambrai as a signal of royal disfavor. After all, had not Fénelon's friends at court been as much as assured that the archbishopric of Paris would be his? Instead, upon the death of Harlay de Champavallon in 1695, this most prestigious and powerful see in France was awarded to his former classmate, Noailles. From this date on, Fénelon's political and ecclesiastical career would lurch from one humiliation to the next. In the space of four years he would suffer the indignity of having all of his livings (apart from the archbishopric of Cambrai itself) removed from him. These deprivations finally culminated, after the controversy over the *Maxims of the Saints* and as the *Telemachus* was beginning to appear in pirated copies at court, in his removal in 1699 from his post of tutor of the *enfants de France* and banishment to his diocese of Cambrai.

If by exiling Fénelon to his diocese and by removing him from lucrative positions at court Louis XIV thought to crush the rebellious archbishop's spirit, however, he was very much mistaken. These marks of royal disgrace and even banishment to his diocese did not mean the end of Fénelon's life. Indeed, in the years from 1699 to his death in 1715 he would become one of the most active diocesans in France, earning by his pastoral care the enduring love of his flock and the grudging respect of even some of his former adversaries in the Quietist controversy. During these first two decades of the eighteenth century he would go on to wage a ferocious battle against the Jansenists in the form of treatises, letters, sermons, and books running the length of many hundreds of pages of closely reasoned theological argument. His literary reputation had been assured with the publication of the *Telemachus*, still considered by many critics to be the finest prose poem written in French. In the year before his death his *Letter to the French Academy* would be read to general acclaim, assuring him a place in the realm of literary criticism as well. In reality not a letter but a treatise dealing with questions ranging from drama and poetry to stylistics and hermeneutics, this *Lettre à l'Académie française*, would be his last major work of literature. In fact, it is the only one of all the works he composed after his banishment to Cambrai that is still widely read today.

He would never meet with the king again. He would never see Mme. de Maintenon again. He would enjoy only one brief visit with Louis, Duc de Bourgogne, made Dauphin by the death of his father in 1711. Fearing for their reputation and fortune, he urged his close friends the Beauvilliers and the Chevreuses to maintain a prudent distance from him, and they complied with his wishes. In time they too died, leaving him surrounded by only a handful of friends and family in the last five years of his life.[192]

Death came quickly and quietly for the archbishop of Cambrai. After his carriage overturned in a creek while he was returning to his palace from a pastoral visit, he was drenched and caught cold. The cold rapidly developed into fever, and within seven days the archbishop was dying. He accepted his sufferings calmly, with Christian resignation and hope. On January 7, 1715, the archbishop-duke of Cambrai, Prince of the Empire, known as "the Swan" by his admirers for the gentleness of his disposition and the gracefulness of his style, passed into history. He preceded his monarch, Louis XIV, in death by only a few months. He was loved and mourned by many, and respected by many more who did not love him. Saint-Simon, the famous memorialist, neither friend nor admirer of Fénelon, nevertheless summed up the feelings of many when he said of the archbishop: "Take him for all in all, he was a great man and a beautiful mind."

Sermon for the Feast of Epiphany on the Vocation of the Gentiles[1]

Surge, illuminare, Jerusalem, quia venit lumen tuum, et gloria Domini super te orta est.

—Isaiah LX[2]

Blessed be God, my brothers, since today he puts his word into my mouth to bless and praise the work that he is accomplishing by this house![3] I have been wishing for a long time, I admit, to open up my heart before these altars and to say in praise of grace all that it works in these apostolic men to enlighten the Orient. It is therefore in a state of joy that I speak today of the vocation of the Gentiles in this house whence men from whom the remainder of the Gentiles hear the good news go out.

Hardly was Jesus born, the hope and desire of nations, than the Magi, worthy pioneers among the Gentiles, who were guided by the star, came to recognize him. Soon the startled nations will come en masse after them. Idols will be crushed and the knowledge of the true God will be as abundant as the waters of the oceans that cover the earth. I see the peoples, I see princes throughout the course of history worshiping him whom the Magi come to worship today.[4] Nations of the East, you will come to Bethlehem in turn; a light (compared with which that of the star is only a shadow) will astound your eyes and dissipate your darkness.[5] Come, come, make haste to come to the house of the God of Jacob.[6] O church! O Jerusalem! Rejoice. Let out your cries of joy. You who were barren in these lands, you who could not give birth, you will have at the ends of the earth innumerable children. May your fecundity amaze you. Look about you and see. Let your eyes be filled with your glory. Let your heart admire and overflow. The multitudes are turning toward you. The islands too are coming. The strength of the nations has been given to you. New Magi, who have seen Christ's star in the East, are coming from the depths of the Indies to seek him.[7] Arise, O Jerusalem! *Surge, illuminare,* etc.

But I feel my heart moved inside me. It is torn between joy and pain. The ministry of these apostolic men and the vocation of these people is the triumph of religion. But it is also perhaps the effect of some hidden condemnation that hovers over our heads. Perhaps it will be on our ruins that these people will rise up, like the Gentiles rose up on those of the Jews at the church's birth. Here is a work of God made to glorify his gospel, but is it not also to transfer it! We would have to not love the Lord Jesus at all to not love his work, but we would have to forget ourselves not to tremble because of it. Let us rejoice therefore in the Lord, my brethren, in the Lord who gives glory to his name; let us rejoice with fear and trembling. These are the two thoughts that will fill this speech.

Spirit promised by truth itself to those who seek you: may my heart only breathe to attract you within it; may my mouth remain mute rather than to open except to your word![8] May my eyes close themselves to any light other than that which you shine from on high! O Holy Spirit, be everything in everyone: in those who listen to me, intelligence, wisdom, sentiment; in me, strength, unction, light! Mary, pray for us. *Ave Maria*...[9]

First Point

My brothers, what is this Jerusalem of which the Prophet speaks,[10] this peaceful city whose gates are closed neither by day nor by night, this city that sucks the milk of the nations and whose nursemaids are the kings of the earth, who themselves come to adore her sacred remains? She is so powerful that any kingdom that will not submit to her will perishes, and so blessed that she will have no other sun except God who will make eternal day shine upon her. Who cannot see that this cannot be that Jerusalem rebuilt by the Jews brought back from Babylon, a weak, unhappy city, often at war, always in bondage under the Persians, the Greeks, the Romans, and finally under those last conquerors reduced to ashes with a universal scattering of her children—a diaspora that still endures after sixteen centuries?[11] It is manifestly, therefore, outside of the Jewish people that we must seek the fulfillment of the promises from which they have fallen short.[12]

There is no other Jerusalem save that on high who is our mother, according to Saint Paul: she comes from heaven and gives birth on earth.[13]

How beautiful it is, my brothers, to see how the promises have been fulfilled in her! The Messiah's nature was such that he was to subjugate not by arms, like the carnal Jews crudely claimed, but—something infinitely more noble and worthy of the magnificence of the promises—to attract by his power over human hearts all idolatrous nations under his reign of love and truth.

Jesus Christ is born, and the face of the world is renewed. The Law of Moses, his miracles, and those of the prophets had not served as a dike against the flood of idolatry and preserved the cult of the true God among a single people huddled in a corner of the world, but he who comes from on high is above everything. It has been reserved to Jesus to possess all nations as his birthright. He possesses them, you see. Since he was raised on the cross he has attracted everything to himself. Even at the origin of Christianity Saint Irenaeus and Tertullian showed that the church was already more vast than that empire which boasted of being itself alone the entire universe. The savage and inaccessible northern regions that the sun hardly brightens have seen the heavenly light. The burning beaches of Africa have been inundated with floods of grace. Even emperors have become worshipers of the name that they formerly blasphemed and supporters of the church whose blood they used to shed. But the virtue of the gospel must not dry up after these initial efforts. Time can do nothing against the gospel. Jesus Christ, who is its source, is from all time: he was yesterday; he is today; and he will be everlasting. Thus I see this fecundity that is forever renewed; the power of the cross does not cease to attract everything to her.

Look at these barbarous peoples who caused the Roman Empire to fall. God has multiplied them and held them in reserve under frozen skies to punish pagan Rome drunk with the blood of the martyrs. He unleashed the bridle and they inundated the world. But, in overthrowing that empire, they submitted themselves to the Savior's empire, being all at once ministers of vengeance and objects of mercy without knowing it. They were led, as if by the hand,[14] before the gospel; it is of them that we can literally say that they found the God that they were not seeking.[15]

To how many peoples have we seen the church give birth since the eighth century, in even that most wretched age, when her rebellious children had no more shame than to reproach her for being barren and repudiated by her husband! In the tenth century, that century whose misfortunes we exaggerate, nations fell over themselves running to the church en masse: from the German, transformed from a ravaging wolf to a lamb; the Pole, the Pomeranian, the Bohemian, and the Hungarian led to the apostles' feet by his first king, Saint Stephen. No, no, you see that the source of heavenly blessings does not dry up. So the Bridegroom gave new children to his spouse to justify her and to show that she never ceases to be his only Beloved.[16]

But what have I seen for the past two centuries? Immense regions suddenly opening up—a New World unknown to and greater than the Old.[17] Do not believe that such a prodigious discovery is due only to man's audacity. Even when human passions seem to be decisive, God only gives them what is necessary to be the instruments of his plans. Thus man becomes excited, but God is actually leading him.[18] The faith planted in America, in spite of so many storms, has not ceased bearing fruit.

So who is left? People of the Far East, your time has come. Alexander, that rapid conqueror, whom Daniel portrays as not letting his feet touch the ground[19]—even he who was so jealous to subjugate the whole world stopped far short of you. But then, charity goes farther than pride.[20] Neither burning sands nor deserts, nor mountains, nor distances between places, nor tempests, nor the oceans' many reefs, nor intemperate climes, nor the fatal line of the Equator where one discovers a new sky, nor the hostile waves, nor the barbarous coasts can stop those whom God sends. Who are they who fly like the clouds? Winds, carry them on your wings. May the South, the East, and the unknown Isles await them and watch in silence as they come from afar. How beauteous are the feet of these men that are seen coming from the mountaintops bringing peace, announcing everlasting possessions, preaching salvation, and saying, "O Zion, your God will reign over you!"[21] Here they are, these new conquerors who come without weapons except for the Savior's cross. They come not to steal the riches or shed the blood of the vanquished but rather to offer their own blood and hand over heavenly treasure.[22]

You nations who saw them coming, what could your surprise have been at first, and who could describe it? Men coming to you without being attracted by any motive either of commerce or ambition or curiosity; men who, without having ever seen you, without even knowing who you are, love you tenderly, leave everything behind for your sake, and seek you out beyond the seas through so many perils and fatigue to announce to you the eternal life that they have found! Nations buried in the shadow of death, what a light above your heads![23]

My brothers, to whom do we owe this glory and this blessing in our days? To the Society of Jesus who, from its birth and with the support of the Portuguese, opened up a new path for the gospel in the Indies. Was it not she who lit the first sparks of fire of their apostolate in the bosom of these men who gave themselves over to grace? The name of this child of Ignatius[24] will never be erased from the memory of the righteous, who with the same hand with which he rejected positions of the most brilliant sort, formed a little society of priests, the blessed kernel of this community.[25]

O heaven, preserve forever the source of such abundant grace and let these two bodies carry together the name of the Lord Jesus to all the nations who do not yet know him!

Among these different kingdoms where grace takes many shapes according to the diversity of the natives, their mores, and governments, I see one of them who is the channel of the gospel for the others. It is in Siam that these men of God are to assemble. It is there that a clergy composed of so many languages and peoples is being formed, from whom the word of life will flow. It is there that are beginning to be built up to the clouds temples that will resound with sacred hymns.

Great king,[26] whose hand raises them up, why are you waiting to build the most agreeable and the most august temple for the true God of your heart? Perspicacious and attentive observers, who show us such exquisite taste, faithful ministers whom he has sent from the land where the sun rises to that where the sun sets to see Louis,[27] take back to him what your eyes have seen: this kingdom closed, not as in China by a simple wall, but by a chain of fortified places that render our frontiers inaccessible; this gentle and pacific majesty who reigns within; but especially this piety that seeks to have God reign rather than man. May the most distant posterity learn from our histories that the Indian[28] came to put at the feet of Louis the riches of the dawn in gratitude for the gospel received by them due to his efforts! Yet it is not a question simply of our history. One day, God willing, among these people may fathers, touched by gratitude, say to their children in order to instruct them: "In past times, in a century favored by God, a king named Louis, zealous to spread the conquests of Jesus Christ far beyond his own, had new apostles sent to the Indies. It is because of this that we are Christians and for this our ancestors ran from one end of the world to the other to find the wisdom, glory, and piety that were in that mortal man!"

Under his protection, that distance of place cannot weaken, or rather (because God forbid that we should put our hope elsewhere than in the cross!) by the almighty power of the name of Jesus Christ, bishops, priests, go announce the gospel to all creatures. I hear the voice of Peter sending you and inspiring you.[29] He lives; he speaks through his successor. His zeal and his authority never cease to support his brothers. It is from the principal See; it is from the center of Christian unity that the rays of the purest and most fecund faith emanate to pierce the shadows of the lands of the Gentiles.[30] Go, therefore, quick and lively angels. May the mountains descend under your steps; may the valleys fill in; may all flesh see the salvation of God.[31]

Lash out, cruel Japan. The blood of these apostolic men only seeks to flow from their veins, to wash you in the blood of the Savior whom you do not know. Empire of China, you will not be able to close your doors. Already a holy pontiff, following in the footsteps of Francis Xavier, has blessed that earth by his last sighs.[32] We have seen him, this magnanimous and simple man, who came back tranquilly from making a tour of the entire globe. We have seen this premature old age, so moving, and this venerable body, bent down not under the weight of years but under the weight of penitence and his labors, and he seemed to say to us all, in the midst of whom he spent his life, to us all who could not get enough of seeing him, of hearing him, of blessing him, of savoring the unction and smelling the sweet fragrance of Jesus Christ who was in him: Now here I am, I know that you will never again see my face. We saw him who had just traversed the entire world but his heart, larger than the world, was still in those far-off regions. The Spirit called him to China and the gospel, which he owed to that vast empire, was like a consuming fire in the depth of his bowels that he could no longer restrain.

Therefore, go forth, holy elder, and traverse once more the astonished and submissive ocean. Go in the name of God. You will see the Promised Land. You will be permitted to enter therein, because you have hoped against hope itself. The storm that was meant to cause a shipwreck will instead throw you upon the longed-for shore. For eight months your dying voice will cause China's coasts to resound with the name of Jesus Christ. Oh, precipitate death! Oh, precious life, that should have lasted longer! Oh, sweet hopes so sadly snatched away! But let us adore God and be silent.

So, my brothers, here is what God has done in our time, to close profane and impious mouths. Who other than Jesus Christ, Son of the living God, could have dared promise that after his torture all nations would come to him and would believe in his name? Nearly seventeen centuries after his death, his word is still alive and fruitful in all the ends of the earth. By the fulfillment of an unheard-of promise so vast, Jesus Christ shows that he holds in his immortal hands the hearts of all nations and all ages.

By this we show again the true church to our erring brothers, as Saint Augustine showed her to the sects of his age.[33] How beautiful it is, my brothers, and how reassuring to speak the same language and to give precisely the same marks of the church that this church father gave thirteen hundred years ago! It is this city situated on the summit of the mountain, which is seen from afar by all the peoples of the earth.[34] It is this kingdom of Jesus Christ, which possesses all nations. It is this society, the most widespread, that alone has the glory of announcing Jesus Christ to the idolatrous peoples. It is this church that not only must be always visible but always the most visible and the most brilliant, because it is necessary that the greatest exterior, living authority that exists among Christians lead the simple folk surely and without discussion to the truth.[35] Otherwise, Providence would be unfaithful to herself. She would make religion impracticable for simple folk. She would cast the ignorant into an abyss of debate and the uncertainties of philosophers. She would have given the text of the scriptures (so obviously subject to many different interpretations) only in order to nourish pride and division. What would become of those souls, docile toward others and mistrustful of themselves, who would be horrified at having to choose their own meaning over that of the assembly more worthy of being believed than any other that exists on earth? What would become of the humble who would fear—and rightly so—being deceived on their own rather than being misled by the church? It is for this reason that God sent the uninterrupted succession of the pastors, naturally so suited to transmitting truth from hand to hand in the course of the centuries. It is for this reason that he put this unique and vast fertility in the true church to differentiate her from all congregations cut off from her—those languishing obscurely, barren, and huddled in a single corner of the world. How do these new sects dare say that idolatry reigned everywhere before their Reformation? All nations having been given by the Father to the Son, has Jesus Christ allowed his inheritance to be lost? What hand more powerful than his own has snatched it away from him? What! Has his light been extinguished throughout the universe? Perhaps you believe, my brothers, that this is from me. No, it is Saint Augustine who speaks this way to the Donatists, to the Manicheans, and, only changing the names, to our Protestants.[36]

This vastness of the church, this fertility of our mother in all parts of the world, this apostolic zeal that shines forth in our pastors alone and that the new sects have not even undertaken to imitate put the most famous defenders of schism in an awkward position. I have read it in their recent books; they cannot hide it. I have even seen some of the most sensible and upright persons of that party admit that this brilliance, in spite of all the cleverness with which they try to dim it, strikes them in their very hearts and attracts them to us.

How great, therefore, is this work that consoles the church; that increases her; that repairs her losses; that renders God understandable to men; that shows forth Jesus Christ always alive and reigning in our hearts by faith according to his word (in the midst even of his enemies); that spreads his church in all lands so that all nations may listen to her; that puts in her this brilliant sign that every eye can see and by which the simple folk are reassured, without debates, that the truth of doctrine is attached to her? How great is this work? But where are the workers capable of sustaining it? But where are the hands capable of gathering the rich harvests that already whiten the fields of the Orient? Never has France, it is true, had more pressing needs for herself than today. Pastors, assemble your counsel and your strength to finish felling this great tree whose haughty branches reached to the sky and who is already weakened down to its deepest roots. Do not let any hidden spark of heresy's fire ignite; stir up your discipline; hasten to uproot scandal and abuses by the vigor of your canons; feed to your children the chaste delights of holy letters; form men who will uphold the majesty of the gospel and whose lips will harbor knowledge. O mother, have your children suckle on the two breasts of knowledge and charity. May the truth shine on the earth through you. Show that it is not in vain that Jesus Christ pronounced this oracle for all time without equivocation: "He who hears you hears me."[37] But let not interior needs make us abandon exterior ones. Church of France, do not lose your crown. With one hand, give the breast to your own children to suckle; hold out the other to that far corner of the earth where so many newly born, still tender in Jesus Christ, emit feeble cries to you and wait for you to have the feelings of a mother for them.

Oh, you, who said to God, "You are my lot and my inheritance."[38] Ministers of the Lord, who are also his inheritance and his portion, crush beneath your feet both flesh and blood. Say to your parents, "I do not know you." Know only God; listen only to him. May those who are already attached here in a regulated job persevere in it, for gifts are diverse and it suffices that each one follow his own; but let them give at least their wishes and prayers to this nascent work of faith. May each of those who are free say to himself, "Woe to me if I do not preach the gospel." Alas! Perhaps all the kingdoms of the Orient put together do not have as many priests as one parish of a single city. Paris, you enrich yourself with the poverty of nations or, rather, through some wretched enchantment, you lose for yourself what you take from others. You deprive the Lord's field of its cultivation; briars and thorns cover it over. You are depriving the workers of the reward due their work. My brothers, shall I not cry out today like Moses at the gates of Israel's camp: "If someone is on the Lord's side, let him come to me."[39] God is my witness, God before whom I speak, God before whose face I serve each day, God who tests the mind and searches the heart.[40] Lord, you know that it is with embarrassment and pain that, admiring your work, I feel neither the strength nor the courage to go accomplish it. Blessed are they to whom you grant the strength to do it! And I myself am blessed, in spite of my weakness and my unworthiness, if my words might light that heavenly fire in the heart of some holy priest, a fire with which a sinner such as I does not deserve to burn.

Through these men weighed down with riches of the gospel, grace increases and the number of believers multiplies from day to day. The church blossoms once more and her entire ancient beauty is renewed. Over there, they run to kiss the feet of a priest when he passes by. Over there they carefully gather, with famished and yearning hearts, even the least morsels of God's word that come out of his mouth. Over there they wait impatiently all week for the Lord's day, when all brothers, in holy quiet, tenderly give one another the kiss of peace, being all together of one heart and one soul. Over there they sigh for the joy of assemblies, for the hymns and praises of God and the sacred feast of the Lamb. Over there they yet see the labors, the voyages, and the dangers of apostles with the fervor of nascent churches. Among these churches, blessed are they whom persecution's fire is testing to make them more pure! Blessed are these churches that we cannot prevent ourselves from looking upon with jealous eyes! We see in them catechumens who desire to plunge not only into salvific waters but also into the flames of the Holy Spirit and to whiten their garments in the blood of the Lamb. We see catechumens who await martyrdom along with their baptism. When will *we* have such Christians, whose delight is in nourishing themselves with the word of faith and tasting the virtues of a future age and conversing only of that blessed hope?[41] Over there, that which is seen as excessive and impracticable, that which we cannot believe possible about the faith in histories of the church's earliest times, is the actual practice of these churches. Over there, being Christian and not being bound to this world is the same thing. Over there, they do not dare show our lukewarm European Christians to these faithful who are on fire, for fear that our contagious example teach them to love life and open their hearts to the poisoned joys of this age. The gospel in its integrity is yet etching on them its natural imprint. It is forming the blessed poor, and those who mourn yet find joy in their tears, and rich folk who fear having their consolation in this world.[42] All middle ground between this age and Jesus Christ is ignored; they only know how to pray, to hide, to suffer, to hope. Oh, dearest simplicity! Oh, virgin faith! Oh, pure joy of God's children! Oh, beauty of ancient days that God has brought back to earth and of which only a sad and shameful memory remains among us! Alas! Woe to us! Because we have sinned our glory has left us.[43] It flies beyond the seas; a new people are taking it from us. My brothers, this is what should make us tremble.

Second Point

If God, terrible in his counsel for the children of men, has not even spared the natural branches of the olive tree, how could we dare hope that he will spare us—us, my brothers, wild grafted branches that we are, dead branches incapable of bearing fruit?[44] God smites his ancient people mercilessly, this people who was heir to the promise, this people who was the blessed race of Abraham, for whom God declared himself for all time. He smites them blindly; he pushes them out from his face; he scatters them like ashes to the wind. They are no longer his people, and God is no longer their God, and this reprobate nation no longer serves any function other than showing to all other nations under heaven the divine curse and vengeance that falls upon it drop after drop and that will remain with it until the end time.

How is it that the Jewish nation has fallen from the covenant of its fathers and the consolation of Israel? Here is how, my brothers. They hardened themselves even in the midst of grace. They resisted the Holy Spirit. They would not recognize the One sent by God. Full of the desires of the age, they rejected a redemption that, instead of flattering their pride and carnal passions, was to deliver them from their pride and passions. This is what closed their hearts to the truth. This is what snuffed out their faith. This is what caused the light to shine in the darkness, and the darkness to not comprehend it.[45] Did the reprobation of this people wipe out the promises? God forbid. The Almighty is pleased to show that he is jealous of owing his works only to himself. He rejects what was his people in order to call those who were not his people, that is to say, the scattered nations who had never formed a body or a state or a religion.

These nations who were living sunk down in a brutal idolatry now come together and suddenly are a beloved people. Nevertheless the Jews, deprived of the knowledge of God (hereditary among them up to that point), enrich all nations with their ruin. Thus God transfers the gift of faith according to his good pleasure and according to the profound mystery of his will.

What caused the reprobation of the Jews (let us pronounce our judgment here, my brothers, to anticipate that of God); what caused their reprobation; must it not also lead to ours? This people, when God smote them, were they more attached to the world than we are? Were they more immersed in the flesh, more drunk from worldly passions, more blinded by their presumption, more full of themselves, more empty of God's love? No, no, my brothers; their iniquities had not yet risen at all to the level of our own. The crime of crucifying Jesus Christ anew—Jesus Christ recognized, Jesus Christ appreciated, Jesus Christ reigning among us—the crime of purposefully crushing underfoot our only sacrificial victim of propitiation and the blood of the covenant—is this all not more enormous and more unforgivable than that of shedding that blood, as did the Jews, without knowing it?

Is this people the only one that God has punished? Let us hasten to come down to examples of the new faith; they are more frightening still. My brothers, cast your tear-soaked eyes on those vast countries whence our faith rose above our heads like the sun. What have they become, the famous churches of Alexandria, of Antioch, of Jerusalem, of Constantinople, which had innumerable churches under them? It was there that, for so many centuries, the assembled councils snuffed out the blackest errors and issued oracles that will live eternally.[46] It was there that holy discipline, that model for which we yearn in vain, reigned in majesty. That land was watered with the blood of the martyrs; it exuded the fragrance of the virgins; the desert itself flourished because of the hermits. But all now is desolation on those mountains flowing with milk and honey, where the flocks of Israel used to pass without fear. Now, there are only inaccessible caves over there full of serpents and lizards.[47]

What remains on the coasts of Africa, where assemblies of bishops used to be as numerous as the ecumenical councils and where God's law awaited explanation from the mouth of

Augustine?[48] I no longer see anything but a land still smoldering from the lightning with which God struck it.

But what terrible word of retrenchment has God not caused us to hear on earth within this past century! England, breaking the sacred bond of unity that alone can restrain minds, has given herself over to all possible illusions of her heart. A part of the Low Countries, Germany, Denmark, Sweden, are like so many reeds that a vengeful blade has cut off and thus are no longer attached to any stalk.[49]

The church, it is true, is making up for these losses. New children born beyond the seas wipe her tears for those whom she has lost. But the church has the promise of eternity; and we, my brothers, what do we have except the dangers that show us with each step the abyss opening up beneath our feet? The river of grace never dries up, it is true, but often, in order to water new lands, its course is turned and it leaves only dry sand in its former channel. Faith will never die, I admit, but it is not attached to any of the lands to which it gives light. It leaves behind itself a hideous night to those who scorned the day and carries its rays to purer eyes.

What would faith do any longer with people corrupt down to the root, who wear the name of faithful only to blacken and profane it? Cowardly and unworthy Christians, because of you Christianity is debased and misunderstood. Because of you, the name of God is blasphemed among the Gentiles. You are no longer any more than a stone of scandal at the door of God's house, causing those who go there seeking Jesus Christ to stumble.

But who can repair the misfortunes of our churches and raise up truth, which is trampled underfoot in public squares? Pride has broken down its dikes and flooded the earth. All conditions are mixed up. Opulence is now called politeness; the most senseless vanity, propriety; the insane are now leading the wise, and making them to be like them. Fashion, so ruinous due to its fickleness and its capricious excesses, is a tyrannical law to which people sacrifice all other considerations. The last of duties is paying ones debts. Preachers no longer dare to stand up for the poor in the sight of a crowd of creditors whose clamor rises up to the heavens. Thus justice silences charity, but justice itself is no longer heeded. Rather than moderate superfluous expenses, people cruelly refuse what is necessary to their creditors. Simplicity, modesty, frugality, that rigorous integrity of our ancestors, their frankness, their modesty are seen as rigid and austere virtues now in an overly crass age. On the pretext of making themselves refined, people have become soft—soft for voluptuousness and hardened against virtue and honor. Every day ad infinitum they make up new "needs" in order to justify the most odious passions. What was considered scandalous opulence in the highest social strata forty years ago has become "decorum" now for even the most middling social class. Hateful refinement of our time! Monster of our customs! Both poverty and luxury grow as if in tandem. People are profligate with their own possessions and greedy for those of others. The first step to fortune is to ruin oneself. Who could bear the insane haughtiness that pride affects and the ignominious baseness that self-interest causes people to have? We no longer know any other prudence than dissimulation, any other rule of friendship than self-interest, any other benefit that can be attached to a person once we have discovered that that person is useless or boring. Men, made rotten down to the marrow of their bones by pleasure's convulsions and violent and refined enchantment, no longer find any but an insipid charm in the consolations of an innocent life. They fall into fatal languishing of boredom as soon as they are no longer driven by the fury of some passion. Is this what it is to be a Christian? Let us leave from here. Let us go into other lands where we would not be reduced to seeing such disciples of Jesus Christ. O gospel! Is this what you teach? O Christian faith! Avenge yourself; send eternal night over the face of the earth—this earth covered with the flood of iniquity.

But, once again, let us look at our resources without deluding ourselves. What authority can set right such depraved morals? A vain and intemperate wisdom, an arrogant and unbridled curiosity drags minds along with it. The North keeps giving birth to new monsters of error. Among this ruins of the former faith everything is falling; everything is crumbling bit by bit. The rest of the Christian nations feel the shock from it. They see the mysteries of Jesus Christ shaken down to their foundation. Profane and reckless men have gone beyond the pale and learned how to doubt everything. This is what we hear everyday; the sound of ungodliness, like a distant thud, strikes our ears and tears at our hearts. After corrupting themselves in what they know, they blaspheme what they don't know, an amazing phenomenon reserved for our age. Education increases and faith decreases. The word of God, in former times so fertile, would become barren if impiety dared. But impiety is crumbling under Louis and, like Solomon, he scatters this wickedness with a look.[50] Nevertheless, of all the vices we no longer fear any but scandal. What am I saying? Scandal itself is at its height because incredulity, although timid, is not mute. It knows how to insinuate itself into conversations, even if it is sometimes clothed in venomous mockery, and sometimes in questions where people try to tempt Jesus Christ like the Pharisees.[51] At the same time, the blind wisdom of the flesh, which claims to have the right to moderate religion as it desires, dishonors and weakens what remains of faith among us. Each one walks in the path of his own choosing; each one, ingenious in deceiving himself, develops a false conscience. Pastors no longer have any authority; there is no longer any uniformity in discipline. This dissolute abnormality is no longer content with being tolerated; it wants itself to be the norm and calls excessive anything that opposes it. The wise dove whose lot here on earth is to moan redoubles her cries. Sin abounds; charity grows cold; darkness thickens; the mystery of iniquity takes shape. In these days of blindness and sin, the elect themselves would be seduced if they were capable of it.[52] The torch of the gospel, which must go around the globe, is nearing the completion of its race. O God! What do I see? Where are we? The day of ruin is near, and the time hastens to arrive. But let us adore God's inscrutable secret in silence and with trembling.

Contemplative souls, ardent souls, hasten to retain the faith on the verge of escaping us. You know that ten righteous men would have saved the abominable city of Sodom that the heavenly fire consumed. It is up to you to cry plaintively without ceasing at the feet of the altars for those who do not bemoan their own misery. Oppose yourself. Be Israel's shield against the arrows of the Lord's wrath. Do violence to God; he desires it. With your innocent hand stop the sword already raised.

Lord, you who say in your scriptures, "Even if a mother could forget her own son, the fruit of her womb, I will never forget you,"[53] do not turn your face against us. May your word grow in those kingdoms where you send it, but do not forget the ancient churches whose hand you have so happily guided to plant the faith among these new nations. Remember Peter's See, immutable foundation of your promises. Remember the church of France, mother of that of the Orient, on whom your grace shines. Remember this house, which is your own; the workers that she forms; their tears, their prayers, their labors. What can I say to you, Lord, for ourselves? Remember our misery and your mercy. Remember the blood of your Son, which flows on us, which speaks to you in our behalf, and to which alone we entrust ourselves. Instead of tearing away from us this little bit of faith that remains with us, according to your justice, increase it; purify it; vivify it; cause it to pierce all our shadows; cause it to snuff out all our passions; cause it to rectify our judgments so that, after having believed here on earth, we may be permitted to see eternally in your bosom what we have believed. Amen.

FABLES

Number I—An Old Queen and a Young Peasant

Once upon a time there was a queen so old that she no longer had any teeth or hair. Her head shook like wind-blown leaves. She could no longer see anything, even with her glasses. The tip of her nose and her chin touched each other. She was shriveled by half and bent over like a ball, with her back so curved that you might have thought her always to have been deformed. A fairy, who had helped with her birth, came up to her and said, "Do you want to be young again?" "Of course," the queen answered. "I would give all of my jewels to be twenty again." The fairy continued, "Well, you will have to give your old age to someone whose youth and good health you will take. To whom shall we give your hundred years?"

The queen had a search made all around for someone who would agree to be old so that she might become young again. Many paupers wanting to be rich came, but, when they had seen the queen cough, spit, moan, eat her gruel, be dirty, hideous, stinking, suffering, and somewhat senile, they no longer wished to take up her age. They preferred to beg and wear rags. Ambitious folk also came to whom she promised great titles and honors. "But what can we do with these titles," they would say after having seen her; "we would not dare show ourselves in such a disgusting and horrible state."

Finally a young village girl showed up, beautiful as the day was long, who asked for the crown as her prize in exchange for her youth. She was named Peronelle. At first the queen became angry, but what was there to do about it? What was the point in being irate? She wanted to be young again. "Let us share my kingdom," she said to Peronelle. "You will have half and I half; this is enough for a little peasant like you." "No," the girl answered, "it is not enough for me. I want it all. Leave me my peasant bonnet and my rosy complexion, and I'll leave you your hundred years, your wrinkles, and death nipping at your heels." "But," the queen answered, "what will I do if I no longer have a kingdom?" "You will laugh and dance and sing like me," said the girl. And thus saying, she began to laugh and dance and sing. The queen, who was far from being able to do as much, said to her: "What would you do in my place? You are not used to old age." "I don't know what I would do," said the peasant, "but I would like to try it out because I have always heard it said that it's great being a queen."

While they were negotiating, the fairy appeared and said to the peasant, "Do you want to try out being an old queen to see if this job would suit you?" "Why not?" said the girl. At that very instant wrinkles covered her forehead; her hair turned gray; she became grumbling and senile; her head began to shake and all her teeth to clatter. She was a hundred years old now. The fairy opened a small box and took out of it a crowd of officers and courtiers, richly appareled, who grew in size as they left the box and who paid their respects to the new queen. A great feast was served to her, but she was disgusted by it because she could not chew the food. She was amazed and ashamed. She did not know what to say or do. She nearly coughed up a lung.[1] She dribbled on her chin. She had a drop of snot that she wiped with her sleeve. She looked at herself in the mirror and found herself to be uglier than an ape.[2]

Meanwhile, the real queen was sitting in a corner, laughing and becoming prettier by the minute. Her hair was coming back and her teeth as well. She was getting her rosy, healthy complexion back. She was getting her youthful appearance back in a thousand ways. But she was filthy, unkempt, and looking like a rag that had been dragged through ashes. She was not accustomed to this appearance. The guards, taking her for some kitchen servant, tried to chase her out of the palace.

At this point Peronelle said to her: "You are obviously very upset at no longer being queen and I even more so for being queen. Here, take back your crown. Give me back my gray overalls." The exchange was made then and there. The queen was old again, and the peasant became young again. Hardly had the change been effected than both were sorry for it. But the time for changes had passed. The fairy condemned them to remain each in her station. The queen cried every day. As soon as she had a pain at the end of her finger she would say: "Alas! If only I were Peronelle, right now as I'm speaking I would be lodged in a hut and living off of chestnuts. But I would be dancing under the elm tree with the shepherd boys to the sound of the flute. What good is it to me to have a beautiful bed where all I do is suffer and so many people around who cannot relieve me?"

This pain of remorse only served to increase her sorrows. The doctors, who were constantly around her (at least twelve of them), exacerbated her pains as well. Finally, at the end of two months, she died.

Peronelle was dancing along a clear stream with her friends when she learned of the queen's death. Then she realized that she had been happier, if not wiser, in having lost royalty. The fairy came to see her and gave her the choice of three husbands. One was old, disagreeable, ill humored, jealous, and cruel, but rich, powerful, and a great lord who could not bear having her away from him day or night. The second was good looking, gentle, easygoing, likable, and of noble birth, but poor and unlucky in everything. The third was a peasant, like her, who was neither handsome nor homely, who would love her neither too much nor too little, and who would never be either rich or poor. She did not know which one to choose because, naturally, she really liked beautiful clothes, fine appointments, and great honors. But the fairy said to her: "Go on with you! You are a silly girl. Do you see that peasant over there? He's the husband you need. You would love the second suitor too much, you would be loved too much by the first suitor, and both would end up driving you crazy. It is enough that the third suitor not beat you. It is better to dance on the grass or the heather than in a palace, and to be Peronelle in the village than an unhappy lady in wealthy society.[3] Provided that you have no regrets for your former greatness, you will be happy with your farmer the rest of your life."

Number IX—Patience and Education

A mama bear had a baby bear that had just been born. He was horribly ugly. You could not recognize in him any semblance of an animal. He was just a misshapen and hideous mass. The mama bear, all ashamed of having such a son, goes to find her neighbor the crow, who was making a loud noise by cackling in a tree. "My good friend," she says, "what will I do with this little monster? I want to strangle him." "Take good care not to do this," says the chatty neighbor. "I have seen other mama bears in the same situation as you. Go home; gently lick your son.[4] Soon, he will be handsome and will do you proud." The mother easily accepted what had been said to her in favor of her son. She had the patience to lick him a long time. Finally, he began to be less deformed, and she went to thank the crow with these words, "If you had not moderated my impatience, I would have cruelly torn my son apart, he who now is all the pleasure of my life."

Oh! How easily impatience blocks good things and causes great evils![5]

Number XXIV—Nightingale and Warbler

On the evergreen banks of the Alpheus River[6] there is a sacred copse of trees where three nymphs bring forth their clear springs with great noise and water the budding flowers. The Graces go there often to bathe.[7] The trees of this copse are never agitated by the wind, which respects them; they are only caressed by the breath of the gentle zephyrs. The nymphs and the fauns dance here in the evenings to the music of Pan's flute.[8] The sun cannot pierce with his rays the dense shadow that the interlaced branches form in these woods.

Silence, darkness, and a delicious coolness reign here both night and day. Underneath this foliage you can hear Philomela,[9] who sings with a plaintive and melodious voice of her ancient misfortunes, from which she is still not consoled. A young warbler, however, here sings of her pleasures and announces springtime to all the shepherds of the neighborhood. Even Philomela is jealous of her friend's tender songs. One day they see a young shepherd whom they had never seen before in these woods.[10] He appeared handsome to them, noble and a lover of the Muses and music.[11] They thought he might be Apollo[12] as he had appeared before at the palace of King Admetos,[13] or at least some young hero of divine blood. The two birds, inspired by the Muses, began immediately to sing these words: "Who is this shepherd, or this unknown god who comes to grace our copse? He is attentive to our songs. He loves poetry and it will soften his heart and make him as loveable as he is proud."

And Philomela continued alone: "How this young hero grows in virtue like a flower blooming in the springtime. How he loves the gentle games of the intellect. May the Graces forever be on his lips. May the wisdom of Minerva[14] reign in his heart!"

The warbler replied: "May he equal Orpheus[15] by the charm of his voice and Hercules[16] by his great deeds! May he carry the audacity of Achilles[17] in his heart without his ferocity! May he be good and wise, beneficent, tender toward men and beloved of them! May the Muses give rise in him of all the virtues!"

Thereupon the two inspired birds took up together their song: "He loves our pleasant songs; they enter in his heart like the dew falling on our sunburned lawns. May the gods calm him down and make him ever fortunate. May he hold in his hand the cornucopia.[18] May the golden age return through him.[19] May wisdom flow from his heart onto all mortals, and may flowers be born under his footstep!"[20]

While they sang the zephyrs held back their breath. All the flowers of the woods opened up. The streams formed by three fountains suspended their course. The satyrs and the fauns[21] pricked up their ears to hear better. Echo[22] repeated his sweet words to all the rocks around. All the dryads[23] came out of the bosom of their green trees to admire him of whom Philomela and her friend had just sung.

Number XXI—Young Bacchus and the Faun

One day the young Bacchus,[24] whom Silenus[25] was instructing, was looking for the Muses in a forest whose silence was only broken by the sound of the fountains and the song of the birds. The sun could not pierce this dense vegetation with its rays. Semele's child sat down at the foot of an old oak tree, from whose trunk several men of the golden age had been born, in order to study the language of the gods. This tree had even given oracles in former times, and Father Time with his cutting scythe had not dared to fell it. A young faun was hiding beside this sacred and ancient oak. He lent his ear to the verses that the child [Bacchus] was singing and whose faults Silenus was noting with a mocking smile. At the same time the naiads and the other nymphs of the woods were smiling as well.

Now, this critic [the faun] was young, gracious, and full of mirth.[26] His head was crowned with ivy and grapevine. His temples were decorated with bunches of grapes. A bough of ivy hung from his left shoulder to his right side like a scarf, and the young Bacchus was pleased to see these leaves that were sacred to his cult.[27] The faun was wrapped around his waist with the frightful, bristling[28] skin of a young lion that had been killed in the forest. He held a curved and knotty staff in his hand. His tail peeked out from behind him as if it were playing on his back.

But as Bacchus could not put up with a mocking jokester, always eager to make fun of his expressions if they were not pure and elegant, he told him in a proud and impatient tone of voice: "How do you dare mock the son of Zeus?" The faun replied nonchalantly: "He! How can the son of Zeus dare commit an error?"

Number XXXII—
Indiscreet Prayer of Neleus

Among all the mortals who had been loved by the gods, none had been more dear to them than Nestor.[29] They had showered their most precious gifts on him: wisdom, a profound knowledge of mankind, and a pleasing, engaging eloquence. All the Greeks listened to him in admiration, and, in his old age, he had an absolute power over their hearts and minds. Before the end of his days, the gods wished to grant him yet one more favor, which was to see the son of Pisistratus.[30] When he came into the world Nestor put him on his lap and, raising his eyes to heaven, exclaimed: "O Pallas![31] You have filled your favors to overflowing. I have nothing more to wish for on earth, except that you fill with your spirit[32] this child that you have allowed me to see. O powerful Goddess, I am sure you will add this favor to all these others that I have received from you. I do not ask to see the time when my prayer will be fulfilled. The earth has already suffered me long enough. Daughter of Zeus, cut the thread of my days."[33] Having pronounced these words a sweet sleep overcame his eyes. He was united with the sleep of death and, effortlessly, painlessly, his soul left his body—cold and almost withered away by the three ages of man that he had lived through.

This grandson of Nestor was named Neleus. Nestor, for whom the name of his father had always been dear, wanted his grandson to carry this name.[34] When Neleus had outgrown his childhood, he went to make a sacrifice to Athena in a woods near the city of Pylos, which was sacred to this goddess. After the flower-crowned victims had been slaughtered and while those who had accompanied him were taking care of the ceremonies that follow the immolation (while some were chopping wood and others were making fire from rocks; while some were skinning the victims and cutting them up into several pieces and while all were distant) Neleus remained beside the altar.

Suddenly, he felt the earth shake. From the depths of the trees groans were heard. The altar appeared to be ablaze, and at the top of the flames a woman of such a majestic and venerable mien appeared that Neleus was awestruck by the sight.[35] Her face was above that of any human form. Her eyes were more piercing than lightning bolts. Her beauty had nothing of the effeminate or the weak about it.[36] She was full of graces and gave the appearance of strength and vigor. Neleus, feeling the impression of the deity, prostrated himself on the ground. All his limbs trembled violently. His blood turned to ice in his veins. His tongue became stuck to his palate, and he could not utter any word.[37] He remained speechless, immobile, and almost lifeless. Then Pallas gave the strength back to him that had failed him: "Fear not," said the goddess, "I am come from the heights of Olympus to show you the same love that I gave to your ancestor, Nestor. I put your happiness in your own hands. I will grant all your prayers, but reflect attentively before asking me." So Neleus, recovered from his astonishment, and charmed by the gentleness of the goddess's words, felt inside himself the same assurance that he would have felt in front of a mortal person. He was in the first flush of youth, at the age when pleasures that are begun to be felt can preoccupy and taint the soul. At this age one has not known bitterness, the inevitable consequence of pleasures; one has not yet been instructed by experience. "O Goddess!" he cried out, "if I can always experience the pleasures of the flesh, all my dreams will be fulfilled."

The goddess had seemed affable and extraverted before, but on hearing these words she became cold and stern: "You are only thinking about what pleases the senses. All right, you will be satiated with the pleasures your heart desires." The goddess thereupon disappeared. Neleus left the altar and undertook the path to Pylos. He saw flowers of such precious fragrance that none had ever smelled before bloom under his feet. The countryside became more beautiful and took an appearance that charmed Neleus's eyes. The beauty of the Graces, Venus's companions, spread over all the women who appeared before him. All that he drank turned to nectar; all that he ate became ambrosia.[38] His soul was inundated in an ocean of pleasures.[39] Dissipation took over Neleus's heart and soul. He no longer lived except for it; he was no longer preoccupied except by one sole care, which was that pleasures should come his way one after another and that he not have a single moment in which his senses were not stimulated. The more he tasted pleasures, the more ardently he desired them. His spirit became weak, and he lost his former vigor. His daily business became a horrible weight to bear. Anything serious became painfully boring to him. He cast from his sight the wise counselors who had been formed by Nestor and who were regarded as the most precious inheritance that that prince had left his grandson. Both reason and pleadings were useless and became the object of his most lively aversion. He shuddered if someone opened his mouth to give him some sage advice.

He had a magnificent palace[40] built in which were seen shining gold, silver, and marble; everything was lavish to please the eye and invoke pleasure. The fruit of so many efforts at self-gratification is boredom and distress. He hardly had acquired what he wished for when he became tired of it. It became necessary for him to often change dwellings and so he ran from one palace to the next—palaces that he would have built then torn down. True beauty and grace no longer appealed to him. He now needed the bizarre, the uncommon, and the extraordinary. Anything natural and simple seemed insipid to him, and he fell into such lethargy that he no longer really lived. He only was aroused by fits and starts.

Pylos, his capital, changed appearance. Before, people in this city loved to work; they honored the gods; honesty reigned in their business transactions; everything was in good order; and even the common folk found peace and comfort in their daily occupations,[41] which they did day after day without being overburdened. An unbridled luxury took the place of decency and true wealth. Everything became a question of vain ornamentation and sought-after amenities. The houses, gardens, and public buildings changed their appearance. Everything became strange looking. The truly great and majestic, which are always simple, disappeared. But what was worse, the inhabitants, following Neleus's example, now only liked, only prized, only sought after dissipation and voluptuousness. They ran after these things at the expense of innocence and virtue. They became agitated, tortured even, in grasping at the vain, chimerical illusion of happiness, and they ended up losing both their tranquility and peace of mind. They were all unhappy because they wanted too much and because they did not know how to put up with anything or wait for anything. Agriculture and the other useful arts became almost disdained. Only those arts that weakness and effeminacy invented were honored; only those that lead to riches were encouraged. The treasures that Nestor and Pisistratus had amassed were soon spent. The state revenue became prey to cupidity and stupidity. The common folk began to murmur and the nobility complain. Only the wise kept silent for a while, but finally they too spoke and their respected voice was heard by Neleus. His eyes were opened; his heart was melted. He once again had recourse to Minerva. He taxed the goddess with having granted his reckless prayer so quickly. He begged her to remove her perfidious gift. He asked for wisdom and justice.[42] "How blind I was!" he exclaimed. "I realize the error of my ways. I hate the fault that I have committed.[43] I want to make it good and to seek in applying myself to my duties—in the care of succoring my people and in innocence and purity of life—the tranquility and happiness that I so vainly sought in sensual pleasures!"

The Dialogues of the Dead

Dialogue XXVIII—Dionysius and Diogenes

Dionysius:[1] I am delighted to see a man of your reputation. Alexander had told me about you ever since he came down here.

Diogenes:[2] As for me, I had heard only too much about you on earth. You made noise like storms that ravaged everything.

Dionysius: Is it true that you were happy in your barrel?

Diogenes: A sure sign that I was happy is that I never sought anything else and that I scorned even the offers of that young Macedonian of whom you speak.[3] But isn't it true that *you* were not happy even while possessing Syracuse and Sicily, since you still wanted to enter through Rhegium to conquer all of Italy?[4]

Dionysius: Your moderation was only vanity and affectation of virtue.

Diogenes: Your ambition was only folly, an insane pride that cannot do justice either to yourself or to others.

Dionysius: You speak very boldly.

Diogenes: And you, do you think you're still tyrant here?

Dionysius: Alas, I feel only too well that I am no longer master. I held the Syracusians, as I have boasted many times, in chains of diamonds. But the Fates' scissors cut those chains along with the thread of my days.[5]

Diogenes: I hear you sigh, and I am sure that you sighed just like that even during your days of glory. As for me, I did not sigh at all in my barrel, and I have no need to sigh down here either because I didn't leave anything worth pining over when I died. Oh, my poor tyrant, how much you have lost in being so rich and how much Diogenes has gained by possessing nothing!

Dionysius: All sorts of pleasures used to flood down on me. My music was admirable. I always had an exquisite table prepared, slaves without number, perfumes, furniture of gold and silver, paintings, statues, spectacles of all sorts, witty people around me to talk with me and praise me, armies to conquer all my enemies.

Diogenes: And above all that, suspicion, fears, and anger that prevented you from enjoying all your worldly goods.

Dionysius: I admit it. But what a way of life is living in a barrel?

Diogenes: Hey! Who was keeping you from living peacefully like any other man in his house and taking up a gentle philosophy? But is it true that you always believed you saw a sword suspended above your head even in the midst of your revels?[6]

Dionysius: Let's not talk about that anymore. You want to insult me.

Diogenes: Will you permit me to ask you another question as hard as that one?

Dionysius: I'll have to put up with it. I have only threats now to prevent you from it. I am totally disarmed down here.[7]

Diogenes: Did you promise rewards to all those who could come up with new pleasures? That was a strange lust for voluptuous pleasure. Oh, how you deluded yourself! To have overthrown everything in your country to be happy and to end up being so miserable and so hungry for pleasures.

Dionysius: I had to try to have new pleasures invented since I was jaded to all ordinary pleasures.

Diogenes: All of nature was not sufficient for you, then? Hey! What could have quenched your furious desires? But these new pleasures, could they have cured your suspicions and snuffed out the remorse you felt for your crimes?

Dionysius: No, but sick folk search for whatever they can find to relieve their pain. They try novel remedies to cure themselves and new dishes to pique their appetite.

Diogenes: You were so jaded, so satiated with everything you had and hungry for everything you couldn't have. Now, there's a pretty situation to be in. And to think that this situation was the one you took so many pains to acquire and to preserve! There's a nice recipe for making oneself happy. How ironic of you to make fun of my barrel where a little water, bread, and sunshine made me happy. When a person knows how to appreciate these simple pleasures of nature, he never becomes insipid and never lacks for anything. But when he scorns them, in vain can he be rich or powerful; he lacks for everything because he cannot enjoy anything.

Dionysius: These truths that you speak afflict me because I'm thinking about my son whom I left as tyrant after me. He would be happier if I had left him as a poor artisan accustomed to moderation and instructed by bad fortune. At least he would have a few real pleasures that nature does not refuse to those in common conditions.

Diogenes: To give him an appetite, you would have to make him feel hunger, and to take away boredom from his golden palace, you'd have to put him in the barrel that I left vacant with my death.

Dionysius: I wonder if he'll be able to maintain himself in the power that I had so much difficulty in preparing for him.

Diogenes: Eh! What do you expect a man born in luxury and the indolence of too much prosperity to know? He hardly knows how to take pleasure when it comes right up to him. Everyone is going to have to suffer to find ways to amuse him.

Dialogue L—
Marcus Aurelius and Antoninus Pius

Marcus Aurelius:[8] O Father, I need to come console myself with you. I would never have believed that I could feel such sharp pain, having been raised in the hardened virtue of the Stoics,[9] and having descended in these blessed lodgings where all is peaceful.

Antoninus:[10] Alas, my dear son. What misfortune has cast you into this anxiety? Your tears are indecent for a Stoic. What is the matter?

Marcus Aurelius: Ah! It is that I've just seen my son, Commodus.[11] A debauched woman had him assassinated to beat him to the punch since he had put her name on a list of people whom he intended to have killed.

Antoninus: I knew that he led a depraved life. But why did you neglect his upbringing? You are the cause of his misfortune. He can well complain more of your negligence, which caused his ruin, than you complain of his debaucheries.

Marcus Aurelius: I did not have the time to think about a child. I was always overwhelmed by a multitude of political affairs and the foreign wars of such a great empire. I nevertheless did not neglect taking some care of him. Alas, if I had been a private citizen I could have educated him and brought him up myself. I would have made an honest, virtuous man out of him.[12] But I left him too much power to ensure virtue or moderation in him.

Antoninus: If you foresaw that the empire was going to corrupt him, you should have abstained from making him emperor,[13] both for the love of the empire, which needed to be well governed, and for the love of your son, who would have been better off in a middling station of life.

Marcus Aurelius: I never foresaw that he would become so corrupted.

Antoninus: But should you not have foreseen it? Was it your paternal tenderness that blinded you? As for myself, I chose in you a stranger, crushing underfoot all my family's interests. If you had done the same, you would not now have so much displeasure. Your son, however, causes you as much shame as you gave me honor. Tell me the truth. Did you never see anything wrong in the young man?

Marcus Aurelius: I saw enough serious character flaws but I kept hoping that he would reform.

Antoninus: That is to say, you wanted to experiment at the expense of the empire. If you had sincerely loved the Fatherland more than your family, you would not have wanted to put the public welfare at risk in order to maintain the greatness of your particular house.

Marcus Aurelius: To be frank with you, I never had any other intention save that of putting the empire over my son. But the love that I had for my son prevented me from observing him closely enough. In doubt, I deluded myself and hope seduced my heart.

Antoninus: Oh, what misfortune that even the best of men are so imperfect and, having so much difficulty in doing good, they often unwillingly cause so many evils!

Marcus Aurelius: I considered him well built, adroit in all physical exercises, surrounded by wise counselors who had my confidence and who could moderate his youth. It is true that his natural inclination was frivolous, violent, hedonistic.

Antoninus: Did you not know any man in Rome more worthy of the empire of the world?

Marcus Aurelius: I admit that there were several, but I thought myself right in giving preference to my son, provided that he had some good qualities.

Antoninus: What, then, did that language of heroic virtue mean when you wrote to Faustina[14] that if Avidius Cassius were worthier of the empire than yourself and your family, she would have to consent to his prevailing and that your family should perish with you?[15] Why not follow these grand precepts when it came to choosing a successor? Did you not owe it to the Fatherland to give preference to the worthiest choice?

Marcus Aurelius: I confess my fault. But the wife that you gave me along with the empire, and whose running around I put up with out of respect for you, never let me follow the purity of those precepts. By giving me that wife with the empire you committed two mistakes. By giving me your daughter, you made the first mistake, and mine was the consequence of it. You gave me two gifts, one of which ruined the other and prevented me from making good use of the other. It pains me to have to justify myself by blaming you, but you are coming down too hard on me. Did you not do for your daughter what you are reproaching me for having done for my son?

Antoninus: In criticizing your mistake, I'm not disavowing my own. But I had given you a wife who had no authority; she only had the name of empress. You both *could* have and *should* have divorced her—according to the law—when she behaved badly. At least you should have risen above a woman's nagging. Moreover, she was dead and you were free when you left the empire to your son. You recognized in your son his frivolous and reckless nature. He only dreamed of giving spectacles; shooting arrows; stabbing wild beasts, making himself as wild as they; becoming a gladiator; indulging his imagination; going nude (dressed only in a lion's skin as if he were Hercules); wallowing in heinous, frightful vices; and giving in to his paranoid suspicions with monstrous cruelty.[16] Oh, my son, stop trying to excuse yourself. Such an insane, wicked man could never have fooled a man as enlightened as you if tenderness had not weakened your prudence and your virtue.

Dialogue LVIII— Louis XI and Cardinal Balue

Louis XI:[17] Miscreant, how do you dare come before me after so many of your betrayals?

Balue:[18] Where do want me to go hide myself? Am I not hidden well enough in the crowd of the shades? We are all equal down here.[19]

Louis XI: It's certainly appropriate for you to talk like that, you who were only the son of a miller in Verdun!

Balue: Hey! It was a good quality to be of lowly birth according to you.[20] Your buddy, the provost Tristan, your doctor Coctier, your barber Olivier le Diable were your favorites and your ministers. Janfredy, before me, had obtained the purple by your favor.[21] My birth was roughly worth as much as theirs was.

Louis XI: None of them had committed such black treason as you did.

Balue: I don't believe a word of it. If they had not been corrupt you would neither have treated them well nor employed them.

Louis XI: Why would you want me not to choose them on their merit?

Balue: Because merit was always suspect and odious to you, because virtue scared you, because you didn't know how to take advantage of it, because you only wanted to be served by base and venal folk, ready to enter in your intrigues, in your deceits, in your cruelty. A decent man, who would have been horrified to deceive and do evil, would have been good for nothing to you—you who wanted only to deceive and hurt to satisfy your unlimited ambition. Since I must speak frankly in this country of truth, I admit that I was a dishonest man, but it was because of that that you preferred me to others. Did I not serve you adroitly and well in getting the best of both nobles and commoners? Did you find a scoundrel more artful than I in working with all classes of people?

Louis XI: It's true, but in deceiving others to obey me, you weren't supposed to deceive me as well. You were working in concert with the pope to have me abolish the Pragmatic Sanction against the true interests of France.[22]

Balue: Ho! Ho! Did *you* ever care about France or her true interests? You never looked to any interest but your own. You wanted to use the pope and have him sacrifice ecclesiastical canons for your sake. I only served you after your own example.

Louis XI: But you put all these ideas in my head, even when contrary to the real interests of my crown, to which my greatness was attached.

Balue: Not at all. I wanted you to sell that filthy parchment to Rome at a good price. But let's go on to another subject. Even if I had deceived you, what could you have to say about it?

Louis XI: How's that? What could I have to say to you? I find that amusing. If we were still alive I'd have you put in the cage pronto.[23]

Balue: Ho! Ho! I've spent enough time there already. If you get me mad I won't say another word to you. Do you know that I hardly fear the ill humor of a king's ghost? What! Do you think you're still in Plessis-les-Tours with your hit men?[24]

Louis XI: No, I know that I'm not there, and that's all the better for you. But I want to listen to you just for the novelty of it. So, prove to me by lively reasoning that you had to betray your master.

Balue: This paradox surprises you, but I'm going to show the truth of it.

Louis XI: Let's see what he means.

Balue: Is it not true that a poor son of a miller, who never had any education except that of a great king's court, had to follow the precepts that were accepted by consensus there as the most useful precepts and the best?

Louis XI: What you say does have some plausibility to it.

Balue: So, answer me yes or no without getting angry.

Louis XI: I dare not deny something that seems so well founded or admit something that might embarrass me by its consequences.

Balue: I see that I must take your silence for a forced confession. The fundamental precept of all your counsels, that you had spread throughout your court, was to do everything for yourself alone. You counted for nothing either the princes of your blood or the queen whom you held captive and distant, or the Dauphin whom you raised ignorant and in prison or the kingdom that you ravaged by your harsh and cruel policies in the interests of which you preferred your jealous desire for tyrannical authority. Even your favorites and your trusted ministers whom you used to deceive others meant nothing to you. You never loved any of them. You never confided in any of them except by necessity. You sought to deceive them when their turn came like everyone else. You were ready to sacrifice them at the slightest whim or for the least advantage. No one was ever secure for a minute around you. You played with men's lives. You loved no one. Whom did you expect would love you? You wanted to deceive everyone. Whom did you expect to give you selfless friendship and trust?

This disinterested faithfulness, where would we have learned it? Did you deserve it? Were you expecting it? Could one practice it around you and at your court? Could anyone have lasted a week around you with a sincere and honest heart? Were we not forced to be scoundrels as soon as we got near you? Were we not declared criminals as soon as we attained your royal favor since no one could attain it without criminality? Didn't you take that for granted? If anyone had wanted to preserve a conscience or some sense of honor, he would have been careful to have never met you. He would have gone to the ends of the earth rather than live in your service. How could you expect that any soul that you corrupted and in whom you inspired only criminality toward the human race retain any disinterested or heroic fidelity to you alone? Were you deluded enough to think it?

Did you not think all men would act toward you as you did toward them? Even if anyone could have been good and sincere toward other men, he would have had to be duplicitous and wicked with you. By betraying you I only followed your lessons. I only walked in your footsteps. I only gave back to you what you used to give every day. I only did what you expected of me; I only took as the principle of my conduct the principle that you looked upon as the only one that should motivate anyone. You would have despised a man who knew any other motive except his own self interest. I did not want to deserve your scorn, and I preferred to deceive you rather than to be a simpleton—in accordance to your own principles.

Louis XI: I confess that your reasoning disconcerts me and weighs heavily on me. But why did you plot with my brother, the Duke de Guyenne, and with the Duke of Burgundy, my cruelest enemy?

Balue: It is precisely because they *were* your most dangerous enemies that I allied myself with them in order to have some protection against you, in case your tempestuous jealousy influenced you to destroy me. I knew that you would count on my betrayal and you could believe it without any foundation. I preferred to betray you to save myself from your hands rather than to perish at your hand based on mere suspicion without having betrayed you. Finally, I was content, following your own precepts, to increase my own value to both factions and to get a reward from you for my services in the midst of the brouhaha of this conflict—a reward that you never would have accorded me willingly in a time of peace. This is what an ungrateful, suspicious, duplicitous prince who loves only himself should expect of his ministers.

Louis XI: But here's what a traitor who sells his king should expect: you don't have him put to death when he is a cardinal but you keep him in prison eleven years; you deprive him of all his great treasure.

Balue: I admit my only mistake; it was in not deceiving you with enough prudence and allowing my letters to be intercepted. Give me the chance again and I'll betray you again according to your just deserts, but I'll deceive you more subtly for fear of being discovered.

The Adventures of Telemachus

Chapter One

Calypso[1] could not get over Ulysses' departure.[2] In her grief she found herself unhappy at being immortal. Her cave no longer resounded with the sound of her song. The nymphs who waited upon her no longer dared to speak to her. She often took walks alone in the flower-strewn parks whose eternal spring bordered her island. But these beautiful spots, far from calming her pain, only reminded her of the sad memory of Ulysses, whom she had seen there with herself so many times. Often she stood, immobile, on the seashore that she watered with her tears, and she constantly turned toward the coast where Ulysses' vessel—plowing the waves—had disappeared from her eyes.

Suddenly, she noticed the debris of a ship that had just wrecked: rowers' benches in pieces, paddles scattered here and there on the sand, a rudder, a mast, ropes floating near the shore. Then she saw two men far off, one of whom appeared old, the other—although young—resembled Ulysses. He had his gentleness and his proud countenance, with his size and his majestic bearing. The goddess realized that this was Telemachus,[3] son of that hero. But, although the gods far surpass men in knowledge, she could not fathom who the venerable old man accompanying Telemachus was. That was because the higher gods hide from the inferior deities whatever they want, and Minerva,[4] who was accompanying Telemachus under the form of Mentor, did not wish to be recognized by Calypso. Nevertheless, Calypso rejoiced at this shipwreck, which put on her island the son of Ulysses, so like his father. She went toward him and, pretending not to know who he was, said: "Whence comes to you the rashness to land on my island? Know, young stranger, that no one comes into my empire with impunity."

She attempted to hide the joy in her heart with these menacing words. Her joy, however, burst out on her face in spite of her. Telemachus answered her: "Oh, you, whoever you are, mortal or goddess (although looking at you, I can only take you for a deity), can you be insensitive to the misfortune of a son who, looking for his father and at the mercy of wind and wave, saw his ship break apart against your reefs?

"Who is your father whom you are seeking?" responded the goddess.

"His name is Ulysses," said Telemachus. "He is one of the kings who, after a siege of ten years, overthrew the celebrated Troy. His name was famous in all of Greece and in all of Asia by his valor in combat and even more so by the wisdom of his counsel. Now, wandering in the vast expanse of the seas, he runs every terrible risk. His homeland seems to flee before him. Penelope, his wife, and I, who am his son, have lost hope of ever seeing him again. I wander, facing the same dangers as he, in order to find out where he is. But, what am I saying? Perhaps he is even now buried in the deep abyss of the sea. Have pity on our misfortune and, if you know, O Goddess, what the Fates have done either to save or to destroy Ulysses, please deign to instruct his son Telemachus."

Calypso, amazed and moved at seeing so much wisdom and eloquence in such a lively youth, could not get her eyes full enough of looking at him, and she remained silent. Finally she said to him: "Telemachus, we will tell you what happened to your father. But the story is long. It is time for you to rest from your labors. Come into my dwelling where I will receive you like my son. Come; you will be my consolation in this loneliness, and I will be your happiness, provided that you know how to appreciate it."

Telemachus followed the goddess surrounded by a crowd of young nymphs, above whose heads she strode like a great oak that in the forest raises its thick branches above all the trees that surround it. He admired the splendor of her beauty, the rich purple of her long, flowing dress, her hair tied up in the back casually but gracefully, the fire that seemed to dart out of her eyes, and the gentleness that tempered this liveliness. Mentor, his eyes lowered, keeping a modest silence, followed Telemachus.

They arrived at the door of Calypso's cave, where Telemachus was surprised to see, with apparent rustic simplicity, all that might charm the eyes. Gold was not seen, nor was silver, nor marble, nor columns, nor paintings, nor statues. This cave was hewn from the rock, with a vaulted ceiling full of sea shells. It was carpeted with a young vine that stretched its tender branches equally on all sides.

The gentle breezes preserved a delicious coolness in this place in spite of the sun's heat.

Fountains, flowing with a soft babble onto fields strewn with amaranth and violets, formed baths in various spots as pure and clear as crystal. The green grass in which the cave was surrounded was spangled with a thousand budding flowers. Woods of thick trees bearing golden apples were there also, whose blooms renewing themselves in all seasons gave off the sweetest of perfumes. These woods seemed to crown the beautiful prairies, making a night that the sun's rays could not pierce. There, only the song of birds was heard, and the sound of the brooks, whose water falling down from a rock up above formed large foaming bubbles, then fled across the prairie.

The goddess's cave was on the incline of a hill. From there one could see the sea, sometimes clear and uniform like ice, other times ebullient and crashing against the rocks where its waves broke and groaned, rising up like mountains. On the other side one could see a river where islands formed bordered with flowering linden trees and tall poplars, which raised their proud heads up to the clouds. The various canals that formed these islands seemed to play in the countryside: some sent their clear waters rolling down rapidly; others had peaceful, dormant water; still others turned back on themselves in long detours as if trying to go back to their source and seemed incapable of leaving these enchanted shores. Hills and mountains could be seen off at a distance, losing themselves in the clouds, whose bizarre shape formed a horizon tailor made for the eyes' pleasure. The neighboring mountains were covered with green vines, which hung down in clusters; grapes whose color was finer than the finest purple could not be hidden under the leaves, and the vines were weighed down with their fruit. The fig tree, the olive tree, the pomegranate, and all the other trees covered the countryside and made up one great garden.

Calypso, having shown Telemachus all this natural beauty, said to him: "Go rest. Your garments are wet. It is time that you changed them. Afterward we shall see each other again, and I will recount to you stories that will touch your heart." At the same time, she showed him, along with Mentor, into the most secret and most remote spot in a cave located beside the one in which the goddess dwelt. In this cave the nymphs had taken care to light a big fire of cedar wood whose fragrant smell spread out on all sides. They had also left clothing there for the new guests. Telemachus, seeing laid out for him a fine woolen tunic, whose whiteness outshone the snow's, and a gown of purple with golden trim, took the pleasure that is natural in a young man considering all this magnificence.[5]

Mentor said to him in a grave tone of voice: "O Telemachus, are these the thoughts that should occupy the heart of Ulysses' son?"[6] Think, rather, of upholding the reputation of your father and of conquering the destiny that persecutes you. A young man who vainly loves dressing up like a woman is unworthy of wisdom and glory; glory is reserved only to the heart that knows how to suffer pain and crush pleasures underfoot."

Telemachus responded, sighing: "May the gods cause me to perish rather than to suffer from weakness[7] and voluptuousness taking control of my heart and soul![8] No, no, the son of Ulysses will never be vanquished by the charms of an effeminate, pusillanimous life. But what heavenly favor has allowed us to find, after our shipwreck, this goddess or mortal who overwhelms us with good things?"

Mentor responded: "Be afraid, rather, that she not overwhelm you with misfortunes. Fear her deceitful sweetness more than the reefs that shattered your ship; shipwreck and death are less frightful than pleasures that attack your virtue. Be careful in believing what she tells you. Youth is presumptuous. Young people believe themselves capable of anything. Although fragile, they never believe themselves to have anything to fear. They confide easily and imprudently in others. Take heed that you not listen to the sweet, flattering words of Calypso, which will slither like a snake among flowers. Be afraid of the hidden poison; be mistrustful of yourself and always wait to hear my counsel."

Afterward, they returned to Calypso, who was waiting for them. The nymphs, with their braided hair and white garments, first served a simple, yet exquisite, meal both in its taste and presentation. No other meat was seen except that of the birds that they had pierced with their arrows, while hunting, or trapped in their nets. A wine, sweeter than nectar, flowed from great silver vases into cups of gold crowned with flowers. All the fruits that springtime promises and that autumn delivers on earth were brought in baskets. At the same time, four young nymphs began to sing. At first they sang of the combats of the gods against the giants,[9] then the loves of Jupiter and Semele,[10] the birth of Bacchus and his upbringing conducted by old Silenus,[11] the foot race between Atalanta and Hippomenes,[12] who beat her by means of golden apples taken from the gardens of the Hesperides.[13] Finally they sang of the Trojan War; the combats of Ulysses and his wisdom were praised to the skies. The first of the nymphs, who was named Leucothoé, joined the strains of her lyre with these sweet voices. When Telemachus heard his father's name, tears falling along his cheeks gave new luster to his beauty. But since Calypso saw that he could not eat and that he was racked with pain, she gave a sign to the nymphs. Immediately, they began to sing of the combat between the centaurs and the Lapiths[14] and the descent of Orpheus into Hades to bring back Eurydice.[15]

When the meal had ended the goddess took Telemachus and spoke to him thusly: "You see, son of the great Ulysses, with what favor I receive you. I am immortal; no mortal can come onto this island without being punished for his rashness, and even your shipwreck would not save you from my indignation if I did not love you. Your father had the same good fortune[16] as you; but alas, he was incapable of taking advantage of it. I kept him for a longtime on this island. He only had to live here with me as an immortal but his blind passion to see his wretched country again made him reject all these advantages. You see all that he lost just to see Ithaca again—which he has yet to see.[17] He insisted on leaving me. He left, and I have been avenged by the storm. His vessel, after having been the winds' play thing, was buried under the waves.[18] Profit by his sad example. After his shipwreck you have nothing more to hope for, neither to see him again nor to reign over the island of Ithaca after him. Take consolation from having lost him, since you have found here a deity ready to make you happy and a realm that she offers you."

Letters of Spiritual Direction

Letter XL—On Character

Circa 1689–90

Madame,[1]

I can only speak to you of your character flaws hesitantly, doubtfully, and almost without rhyme or reason. You have never acted consistently with me, and I give little credence to what others have told me about you. But, regardless, I will tell you what I think, and God will make whatever use of it he sees fit.

You are natural and artless; it flows from this that you do good without even needing to think about it to those whom you like and for whom you have esteem. But, as soon as the attraction is gone, you can act too coldly. When you are harsh, your harshness can go far. I imagine that there is down deep inside you both haste and slowness. Whatever wounds you, wounds you deeply.

You were born with pride in your reputation, that is to say, that sense of self-worth that is all the worse since one is not ashamed of thinking that this is good. One would more easily get over some stupid vanity. You still have a lot of this pride in your reputation left in you, without your even noticing it.[2] Your being thin-skinned about matters that can still cut to the quick shows how far your pride is from being extinguished. It is still essential for you to have the esteem of honest, decent folk[3] and the approbation of people of quality. You hold dear the pleasure of maintaining your prosperity with moderation. Finally, it is essential for you to appear to be above your station by virtue of your virtues.

Your ego, of which I have spoken to you so many times, is still an idol that you have not broken. You want to go to God with all your heart, but not if it means the loss of your ego. On the contrary, you seek your ego in God. The palpable sense of God's presence that you find in prayer supports you; if this sense were to be lacking, however, the attachment that you have to yourself and to the reputation of your own virtue would cast you into a dangerous trial and tribulation. I hope that God will pour the purest milk until the time that he deigns to wean you and feed you with the bread of the strong.[4]

But be assured that the least attachment to the best things, with respect to you, will hinder you more than all the imperfections that you could fear. I hope that God will show you the light to understand this better than I have explained it.

You are naturally good and inclined to be trusting, even perhaps a little too much with people of quality whose prudence you have not tested enough. But when you begin to mistrust, I imagine that your heart closes up too much; guileless and trusting folk are usually this way, when they are forced to be mistrustful. There is a medium between excessive confidence that surrenders itself and suspicion that doesn't know anymore what to trust when it feels that what it held close is in actuality escaping. Your good mind will enable you to see that, if honest folk have character flaws that you cannot allow yourself to go blindly along with, they also have a certain conduct that is simple and upright by which we can surely recognize them for what they are.

The character of the gentleman is not doubtful to him who well knows how to be observant in all circumstances. The most profound and the best disguised hypocrisy never attains the appearance of that guileless virtue, but you must remember that virtue, even the most guileless, reflects on its own conduct and seeks, to a certain degree, its own interest without being aware of it. You must, therefore, equally avoid being suspicious of tried and true people of merit as well as abandoning yourself entirely to their way of living.

I tell you all of this, Madame, because in the position you are in one discovers so many disgraceful things and one hears so often things made up by slander that one no longer knows what to believe. The more one is inclined to love virtue and to trust in it, the more one is embarrassed and troubled in these occasions. There is only the love of virtue and a certain discernment of sincere virtue that can prevent us from falling into the disadvantage of mistrusting everyone, which would be a very bad thing.

I have said, Madame, that you mustn't surrender yourself to anyone. I believe, however, as a question of Christian principle and through sacrifice of your belief in your own reason,[5] that you must submit yourself to the counsel of a single person that you have chosen for spiritual direction. If I specify one person alone, it is that it seems to me that you should not keep adding on to the number of spiritual directors or change them without serious cause. Because these changes and shuffling around can produce uncertainty and often dangerous differences. At the very least, you are held back, instead of advancing, by all these different opinions. It usually happens that, when you have so many different opinions, you end up following your own opinion by the very necessity in which you find yourself of having to choose among all those that you have received from everyone.

I do agree that, apart from the advice of a wise director, you can on occasion take other counsel with respect to temporal affairs, which another might be able to see more clearly than the spiritual director. But I come back to this: except for spiritual direction, for which you should submit yourself to a good director, for all the rest that is outside of spirituality you should not surrender yourself to anyone.

People believe in society that you sincerely love goodness. Many people have believed for some time that a laudable sense of your reputation made you take this tack. But it seems to me that the public is cynical and that it should give due respect to the purity of your motives. They say too, however, that you are (and according to all appearance this is true) harsh and severe, that it is not permitted to have character flaws around you, and that being so harsh with yourself, you are as harsh with others. They say that when you start to find some weakness in people whom you had hoped to find perfect, you become too quickly disenchanted with them and that you push your distaste beyond the pale. If it is true that you really are as people describe you, this flaw will only be removed by long and deep study of yourself.

The more you die to yourself by abandoning yourself totally to God's will, the more your heart will grow to tolerate the flaws of others and to empathize with them unconditionally. You will see around you, then, only misery; your eyes will be more observant and will discover more than you can see today. But nothing will then be able to scandalize you or surprise you or harden you. You will see corruption in mankind like water in the ocean.

The world is lax and yet without pity in its severity. You will not look like the secular world; you will be faithful and exact, yet compassionate and gentle, just as Jesus Christ was for sinners while he exposed the Pharisees whose outward virtues were so gaudy.

They say that you involve yourself too little in court business. Those who say this are moved by anxiety, by the desire they have of being involved in government, and by the spite they have against those who give out favors or by the hope of obtaining favors from you. As for you, Madame, it is not appropriate for you to redress a situation that is not in your power.[6]

Zeal for the king's salvation must not make you go beyond the bounds that Providence seems to have marked out for you. There are a thousand deplorable things, but you must wait for the time that God alone knows and that he holds in his power.

It is not falseness that you have to fear as much as you fear it. Duplicitous people never believe that they are false. The upright always fear not being so. Your piety is true; you have never had the vices of this world, and for a long time you have even renounced the world's errors.

The real means of bestowing grace on the king and the state is not to cry out or to tire out the king; it is to edify him, to die incessantly to yourself. It is to open the heart of this prince little by little by your guileless, open, warm, and patient behavior—conduct that is both free and childlike in its patience. But to speak heatedly and harshly, always to come back to the charge, to build up your battlements secretly, to make plans based on human wisdom to reform what has need of reform—this is to wish to do good by means of a bad path. Your solid piety rejects such means, and you have only to follow simply the dictates of your piety.

What appears to me true with respect to political affairs is that your mind is more capable than you think. You underestimate yourself too much or perhaps you are too afraid of entering into discussions contrary to the desire you have for a peaceful and reflective life. Moreover, I imagine that you fear the character of those whom you find on your path when you become involved in some political business. Ultimately, it seems to me, your natural intelligence and your experience are capable of more than you give them credit for.

I persist in believing that you should never insinuate yourself into affairs of state. But you should learn about them, commensurate with your natural abilities. And when Providence offers you opportunities to do good without pushing the king beyond his limit, you should never shirk these opportunities.

I have gone into detail listing what people say about you. Here, Madame, is what I personally have to say: It seems to me that you still have too natural an affinity for friendship, for goodness of heart, and for all that ties you to good society. This is without doubt all for the best, according to reason and human virtue, but it is for that very reason that you must renounce it.

Those who have a hard and even cold heart certainly have a very great natural character flaw. It is even a great imperfection that remains in their piety, for if their piety were more advanced it would furnish them what they lack in this area. But we must allow that real goodness of heart consists in faithfulness to God and in pure love. All generosity, all natural tenderness is only a more seductive, more refined, more flattering, more pleasant, and, consequently, more diabolical form of self-love.

I tell you all this without any personal interest, because I am rather off-putting in my behavior and cold in the beginning but warm and tender at heart. Nothing of all this has anything to do with the man to whom you have duties of a different type;[7] the strengthening of grace, which has already made so much progress in him, will end up making another man out of him. But I speak to you for the sole interests of God in you. You must sacrifice without any reservations all affection.[8]

If you weren't still so attached to yourself, you would no longer have the desire to see your friends attached to you than to see them attached to the king of China. You would love them with the pure love of God, that is to say, with a perfect love, infinite, generous, active, compassionate, consoling, consistent, well-meaning, and tender like God himself. God's heart would be poured into yours. Your friendship would not be any more capable of fault than he who would love in you. You would not want anything from others, save that which God would want from them and only for himself. You would be jealous for him against yourself; and if you demanded from others a warmer, more cordial behavior, it would only be for their own perfection, and for the perfecting of God's designs for them.

What hurts you, therefore, in hardened hearts only hurts you because your own is still too hardened inside of itself. Only self-love can wound self-love. The love of God suffers indulgently the infirmity of love of self and waits peacefully for God to destroy it. In a word, Madame, the fault of desiring friendship is not less before God than that of being without friendship. The true love of God would have you generously love your neighbor without hope of anything in return.

Moreover, it is so necessary to sacrifice to God your ego, of which we have already spoken so often, that you no longer seek it either for your reputation or for the reassurance that it gives you in witnessing your own good qualities and good intentions. You must die to all of this without any reservation and not even keep your virtue, in that it relates to you. This is not an absolute obligation for all Christians, but I believe that it is the perfection of a soul that God has prepared as much as he has your own by his mercies.

You must be prepared to be scorned, hated, slandered, and condemned by others. You must be prepared to find in yourself only confusion and condemnation in order to sacrifice yourself, without any leniency, to the sovereign kingdom of God, who disposes of his creatures according to his good pleasure. This is a hard saying to whomever desires to live in himself and content himself with his own virtue, but this saying is pleasant and consoling for a soul who loves God so much that she would, on her own, give up loving herself![9]

You will see one day how great the friendship is of those who are so disposed. Their heart is immense because it shares in the immensity of God, who possesses them. Those who enter into the ways of pure love, in spite of their natural inclination toward being harsh and curt, are always growing and opening themselves more and more. Finally, God gives them a heart similar to his own, and a mother's bosom for all whom he unites to them. Thus real and pure piety, far from making us hard or indifferent, actually draws us away from indifference, from coldness, from the harshness of self-love that wraps itself up in itself in order to center everything on itself.

[Fénelon addresses again the issue of Mme. de Maintenon's influence in court affairs and urges caution and prudence.]

You have at court persons who appear well intentioned. They deserve to be treated well and encouraged by you, but you must be cautious because a thousand people would pretend to be devout just to please you. They would appear to be touched by those who approach you and would attain their goal by this means. This would only be to encourage hypocrisy and expose yourself to being seen as naive and gullible. So, you must learn to discern the rectitude and selflessness of those who seem to turn to God before showing them that you have noticed their virtue. If they are women who need to be encouraged and supported, have them helped by persons in whom you have confidence without showing yourself in it.

I believe that you should admit only a few to your pious conversations in which you seek to speak freely. What is good is not always appropriate for others' needs. Jesus Christ said: "I have yet many things to say to you, but you cannot hear them now."[10] The church fathers only unveiled the mysteries of Christianity to those who wanted to become Christians, and only inasmuch as they found them willing to believe in the mysteries.

While waiting to be able to do good by the choice of pastors, try to lessen evil. For your family, give them that care which depends on you, according to the rules of moderation that you have in your heart. But avoid equally two things: one, refusing to speak in favor of your relatives when it is reasonable to do so; the other, becoming angry when your recommendations do not succeed. You must simply do your duty and accept failures in peace and in humility. Pride would prefer your being spiteful. It would take the course of refusing to speak, or again, it would have you explode in order to take by force whatever is refused. It appears that you love your family members, as you should, without being blind to their faults and without losing sight of their good qualities.

Finally, Madame, be assured that for the correction of your character flaws and for the accomplishment of your duties, the most important thing is to work at this inside yourself and not just on the outside.[11]

This outward detail, even if you should give yourself entirely to accomplishing it, will always be beyond your ability. But, if you let God's Spirit do what is necessary for you in order that you might die to yourself and cut off your ego at its very root, your flaws will fall off little by little by themselves. God will enlarge your heart to the point that you will not be daunted by the extent of any of your duties to him. Then the scope of your duties will grow with the scope of your virtues and with the capability of what will be inside you, for God will give you other good things to accomplish proportionate to the new breadth that he will have given you inside of you.

All of our faults only come from being still attached to and centered on ourselves. It is our ego that wants to use our virtues to its own end. Renounce, therefore, without ever hesitating this miserable ego even in the most minor things where the spirit of grace would have you understand that you are still looking for satisfaction of ego. Here is total and true crucifixion; all the rest is only superficial and touches the surface of the soul. All those who seek to die to their old selves by any other means only end up leaving their life on one hand and then picking it back up with the other. It is never successful.

You will find through experience that when—in order to die to yourself—you take the path that I've proposed to you, God leaves nothing to the soul. He pursues your soul relentlessly until he has removed the very last breath of its own life therein, in order to have your soul live in him in an infinite spirit of peace and freedom.[12]

Letter I—On the Use of Time

Madame,[13]

I understand that what you desire from me is not only to establish the great principles to prove the necessity of using your time well; grace persuaded you of the need long ago. One is always happy when one finds souls with whom more than half the path has already been traveled, so to speak.[14] But don't let this comment flatter you; there remains much yet to do, and there is a great distance between the spirit's willingness and even the heart's good disposition, and an exact and faithful practice.

Nothing has been more common in all ages, and nothing is more common today, than to meet perfect and holy Christians in theory. "You will know them by their works and by their behavior," says the Savior of the world.[15] And it is the only rule that never deceives, provided that it is properly developed. And it is thereby that we must judge ourselves.

There are several time periods to distinguish in your life, but the maxim that should apply universally in all of them is that there must be none that is useless. They must all enter into the order and in the interconnections of our salvation. They must all be filled with the duties that God has attached to them with his own hand and of which he will demand an accounting from us. For, from the earliest instant of our being up to the last moment of our life, God has not intended to leave us with any empty time, any time that we could say that he has given up to our discretion, or for us to waste. The important thing is to know what he desires that we do with it. And that we manage to accomplish this, not by an anxious and hectic ardor, which would be more apt to cloud things up in our mind than to enlighten us as to our duties, but by a sincere submission to those who take the place of God for us.[16] We accomplish this, secondly, by a pure and upright heart that seeks God in simplicity and that sincerely fights against all the duplicity and lies of our ego as it finds them. We not only waste time by doing nothing or doing wrong, but we also waste it by doing other than that which we should be doing, even if what we are doing is good.[17] We are strangely ingenious in constantly attempting to find ourselves. And what worldly folk do obviously and without trying to hide it, people who have the desire to belong to God often do more subtly in light of some pretext, which serves as a cover for them, preventing them from seeing the deformity of their conduct.

A general way to use time well is to accustom yourself to living in a continual dependence on God's Spirit, receiving from moment to moment whatever pleases him to give us, consulting him when in doubt in occasions where we have to make a decision on the spot, having recourse to him in weakness when virtue falls as in a faint, invoking him and raising ourselves up to him when our heart, being led on by material objects, sees itself imperceptibly conducted off of its path, and being caught in a state of forgetfulness and remoteness from God.

Happy is that Christian who, through a sincere renouncing of himself, holds himself in the hands of his Creator, ready to do anything that he would wish and who would never tire of saying to him a hundred times a day: "Lord, what would you have me do?"[18] "Teach me to do thy will for thou art my God."[19] You will show that you are my God by teaching me, and that I am your creation by obeying you. In whose hands, great God, would I be better off than in yours? Outside of them, my soul is always exposed to attacks of her enemies and my salvation always in danger. I am nothing but ignorance and weakness; I would hold my ruin as certain if you left me to my own devices, using as I wished this precious time that you give me to make myself holy and walking blindly in the paths of my own heart. In this state what could I make at any moment except a bad choice? And what would I be capable of effecting in myself except a work of self-love, of sin, and of damnation? Send therefore, Lord, your light to guide my steps. Hand out to me your grace in each and every occasion according to my needs, as we give food to children according to their age and their weakness. Teach me, by a holy use of the time that you give me now, to restore the past and never foolishly to count on the future.

The time for business and exterior occupations only needs—in order to be well used—a simple attention to the orders of divine Providence. Since it is he who prepares them for us and who presents them to us, we only need to follow his orders with docility and submit our moods, our will, our scruples, our anxiety, our obsessions with ourselves, and even our outpourings, our manic moods, our vain joy, and the other passions that come in opposition according to whether the things we have to deal with are agreeable or unpleasant. We must take care not to let ourselves be overwhelmed by that which comes from the outside and not to be drowned in the multitude of exterior activities, whatever they might be.

We must try to begin all our undertakings with the view of God's pure glory, continuing them without dissipation and finishing them without hurry and without impatience.

The times for chitchat and amusements are the most dangerous for us and perhaps the most useful for the others. We must be on our guard, that is, more faithful in the presence of God. The practice of Christian vigilance—so recommended by our Lord—the aspirations and the elevations of mind and heart toward God (not only habitual but actual, inasmuch as is possible) by the simple understanding that faith gives us, the sweet and peaceful dependence that the soul maintains toward grace, that the soul recognizes for its only principle of security and of its strength—all this must be put into practice to preserve us from the insidious poison that is often hidden inside chats and pleasures and in order to know how to state with wisdom that which can instruct and edify others and especially those who have in their hands great power and whose will can achieve so much good or so much evil.

Free time is usually most pleasant and most useful for us. We can hardly make better use of it than to devote it to restoring our strength (I mean here our physical strength) in a more secret and intimate communing with God. Prayer is necessary; it is the source of so many blessings that the Christian who has discovered this treasure cannot prevent himself from coming back to it as soon as he has time to himself.

There would be other things to tell you concerning these three times. Perhaps I could tell you still something more about them if the insights that occur to me now are not lost. In any case, it is a small loss. God gives other insights when it pleases him; if he doesn't give any, it is a sign that they are not necessary and as soon as they are not necessary for our well being we should be content that they are lost.

Letter II—On Diversions

Madame,

It seems to me that you should not be troubled about amusements in which you cannot avoid taking part.[20] There are many people who would have you moaning and groaning about everything and have you constantly upset by arousing in you a disgust for the diversions to which you are subjected.[21] As for myself, I admit that I cannot get used to such rigidity. I prefer something simpler, and I believe that God himself likes it a lot more.[22] When amusements that are innocent in themselves and in which you take part through the rules of behavior of the position in which Providence has put you, then I believe that it is sufficient to take part in them in moderation and in the sight of God. Behavior that is harsher, more reserved, less obliging, and less open would only serve to give a false idea of piety to people in the world who are already only too prejudiced against it and who would believe that you cannot serve God except by lugubrious and morose conduct.

I conclude therefore, Madame, that when God puts us in certain places that force us to be all things, such as the position you are in now, the only thing to do is to stay there peacefully without beating up on yourself constantly about the insidious motives that might imperceptibly insinuate themselves in your heart.[23] You would never be finished if you wanted to analyze continually the depths of your heart; by wanting to leave yourself behind in order to find God, you would just spend more time on yourself with such frequent examinations. Let us walk in simplicity of heart with peace and joy, which are the fruits of the Holy Spirit.[24] Whoever walks in the presence of God in the most trivial things has not ceased to do God's work, even though he might appear to be doing nothing solid or serious. My presupposition, of course, is that you are in God's plan and that you are in conformance with the laws of Providence in doing these trivial, indifferent things.

Most people, when they intend to convert or reform think about filling up their lives with certain difficult and extraordinary actions rather than by purifying their intentions and by dying to their natural inclinations in the most common actions associated with their position in life. They are much mistaken in this. It is much better to change fewer actions and to change more the disposition of your heart that causes you to do these actions. When you are already leading an honest and upright life it is far more urgent to change your inside rather than your outside in order to become truly Christian. God is not pleased either with mere words out of your mouth or with the posture of your body or of any exterior ceremonies. What he asks is a will that is not shared between himself and any other thing. It is a will malleable in his hands, that desires and rejects nothing, that wants unreservedly whatever he wants and that never wants under any pretext anything that God does not want.

Madame, take this simple will, this will all filled with God's will, wherever his Providence leads you. Seek God in the hours that seem so empty and they will become full for you since God will support you. Even the most useless amusements can turn into good works if you enter into them only with the object of respecting decency and conforming yourself to God's plan. How large our heart becomes when God opens this path of simplicity! We then walk as do little children, whom their mother leads by the hand and who let themselves be led without worrying about where they are going. We are then happy to be subjected; we are happy to be free; we are ready to speak; we are ready to be silent. When we cannot say edifying things, we say anything else with as much good nature. We enjoy what Saint Francis de Sales calls cheerfulness; in this way we can relax and also put others at ease.[25]

You will tell me, maybe, that you would prefer to be occupied with something more serious and more solid. But God does not prefer this for you because he chooses what you would not choose. You know that his taste is better than yours is. Yes, you would find more consolation in solid things for which he has given you a penchant; but it is this consolation that he wants to take away from you. It is this penchant that he wants to mortify in you, although it is both good and salutary. Even virtues need to be purified in their exercise by the setbacks that Providence has them undergo in order to better detach them from your own will. Oh, how simple, sweet, convenient, lovable, discreet, and sure in all its ways piety is when it is understood from the fundamental principle of God's will, without consulting your penchants, or temperament, or the outpourings of excessive zeal! You live more or less like others do, without affectation, without appearance of austerity, with a sociable and easygoing manner. But you live in a perpetual subjection to all your duties; in a relentless renunciation of all that does not enter in some way or other in God's ordering for us; finally, with a pure view of God to whom you sacrifice all irregular movements of nature. Here is the worship in spirit and in truth that Jesus Christ and his Father seek.[26] All the rest is only religion and ceremony and the shadow rather than the truth of Christianity.

Doubtless you will ask me by which means you can manage to preserve for yourself that purity of intention in a life so common and that seems so frivolous. "I have great difficulty," you will say, "in protecting my heart and soul against the flood of passions and wicked examples of the world when I am constantly on guard against myself. How can I, therefore, hope to hold up if I expose myself so readily to amusements that poison me or that at the very least corrupt a Christian so dangerously?"

I recognize the danger, and I believe it to be greater than one could even say. I agree to the necessity of guarding yourself against so many pitfalls. Here is how I would like to sum up the precautions to take.

First, I believe that you must make reading and prayer your foundation of everything. I am not at all talking about idle reading for curiosity in order to make you more learned concerning questions of religion. Nothing is more vain, more indecent, or more dangerous.[27] I would only like you to have simple reading material, far removed from the least nuance, limited to practical, sensible things, all of which are conducive to nourish your spirituality.[28] Avoid all that excites your mind and that would cause you to lose that blessed simplicity that makes your soul docile and submissive to all that the church teaches. When you engage in your readings, not to know more but to learn how better to be on guard against yourself, they will be beneficial for you. Add prayer to your reading and meditate in profound silence on some great truth of religion. You can do this by visualizing some action or some word of Jesus Christ.[29] After having convinced yourself of the truth of the act or word on which you are meditating, then apply it seriously and precisely to your own life for the minute correction of your faults. Form new resolutions before God and ask that he give you strength to accomplish what he has given you the courage to promise him. When you see that your mind is wandering during this exercise, bring it gently back to the subject without getting worried and without becoming discouraged by the inconvenience of these distractions, which are so stubborn. While they are involuntary they cannot harm you. On the contrary, they will serve to furnish you more than one prayer accompanied by very tangible consolation and fervor because they will humble you, mortify you, and accustom you to seek God purely for himself without mixture of any selfish pleasure. Provided that you are faithful in allotting these fixed times morning and evening in order to practice these things, you will see that they will work like an antitoxin for you against the dangers that surround you. I say morning and evening because you must renew your soul's nourishment from time to time as well as you do for the body to prevent it from fainting away through the fatigue of everyday human activity. But you must be firm with yourself and with others to reserve this time always. You must never allow yourself to be dragged into exterior occupations—however good they might be—if it means losing this time to nourish yourself.

The second precautions that I believe necessary is to take certain days—according to whether you are free and you feel the need—to go on a complete retreat in order to engage in private prayer. It is there that you can heal all your soul's wounds and erase all the malevolent impression of the world in private at the feet of Jesus Christ. This will even be useful for your health, for, provided that you know how to use these short spiritual retreats humbly, they will relax your body no less than your spirit.

Third, I am assuming[30] that you are limiting yourself to amusements that are appropriate to the profession of piety that you make and to the good example that the world expects of you. For the world, as worldly as it is, wants those whom it despises not to waver in the scorn that they have for it. It cannot prevent itself from having esteem for those who despise it in good faith. You well understand, Madame, that true Christians must rejoice that the world is such a harsh critic of itself; they must rejoice to be thereby in a more urgent necessity not to do anything that is not edifying.

Finally, I believe that you must only engage in the amusements at court to be obliging and only then as much as it is desired.[31] This way, all the times that you are neither called on nor desired, you must not ever appear to look to ask, even indirectly, for invitations. In this way you will give to your domestic affairs and to your exercise of piety all that you are free to give. The public, or at least reasonable people—those not embittered toward virtue—will be equally edified both to see you so discreet in making spiritual retreats when you are free and so sociable in engaging obligingly in innocuous diversions when you are called to do so.

I am convinced that by adhering to these rules, which are simple, you will call upon yourself an abundance of blessings. God, who will lead you by the hand in these amusements, will support you. He will make himself felt. The joy of his presence will be sweeter to you than all the pleasures that are offered to you. You will be moderate, discreet, and pensive without constraint, without affectation, without that harshness that is off-putting to others. You will be, according to the quotation from Saint Paul, in the middle of these things as if you were not there, and, by demonstrating nevertheless a cheerful and obliging personality, you will be all things to all people.[32]

If you see that boredom or depression are getting you down or that your joy is evaporating, come back gently and without being anxious to the bosom of your heavenly Father, who always holds out his arms to you. Expect joy and freedom of spirit from him even in the midst of sadness; expect moderation and reflection even in the midst of joy, and you will see that he will not let you lack for anything. A look of confidence to him, a simple beating of your heart for him, will refresh you. And, although you often feel your soul to be numb and discouraged, in every moment in which God will call you to do something he will give you the capability and the courage according to your needs. Here is the daily bread that we ask in each and every hour and for which we shall never want, for our Father—far from abandoning us—actually only seeks to find our hearts open so that he might pour floodwaters of grace therein.

Letter III—
Chains of Gold[33]

Madame,

Chains of gold are not any less chains than chains of iron. You are exposed to envy and you are worthy of compassion. Your captivity is not preferable to that of a person unjustly held in prison.[34] The only thing that ought to give you real consolation, Madame, is that God is taking away your freedom, and it is this consolation that might even support an innocent person in prison—such a one as I spoke of above. Therefore you have nothing more than that person except a mirage of glory, which, while giving you no substantial advantage, actually puts you in danger of being blinded and deceived.

But this consolation of finding yourself, by an order of Providence, in the situation in which you are is an inexhaustible consolation. With it you can never lack for anything. By it the chains of iron are changed—I won't say into golden ones, for we have seen how contemptible chains of gold are—but into happiness and freedom. What good to us is that natural freedom of which we are so jealous? To follow our unbounded inclinations, even in innocent things, and flatter our own will, is the worst use that we can make of ourselves.

Blessed are those whom God tears from their own will to attach them to his own! As much as they who chain themselves by their passions are miserable, so those whom God delights in chaining by his own hands are free and happy. In this ostensible captivity they no longer do what they would like. So much the better, from morning to evening—against their inclination—they do whatever God wants them to do. He holds them as if bound hand and foot to his will. He never allows them a single minute to themselves. He is jealous of this tyrannical ego that wants everything for itself. He leads, without letup, from constraint to constraint, from one unwelcome disturbance to another. He makes you accomplish his greatest plans even by means of boredom, puerile conversations, and useless activities of which one might be ashamed. He oppresses the faithful Christian and will not let him breath. Hardly has one irksome visitor left you when God sends another to move his work along. You would like to be free to talk to God, but you are more united with him in his crucifying will than in reassuring yourself by pleasant and affectionate thoughts of his blessings. You would like to be wrapped up in yourself in order to be more wrapped up in God. You don't even consider that nothing is less conducive for belonging to God than to still want to belong to yourself. This "me," this ego to which you want to return in order to serve God, is a thousand times farther from him than the most ridiculous frivolity, for there is in this ego a subtle poison that is not found in childish amusements.

It is true that you should take advantage of free time to relax. You must even, in preference to all the rest, set aside some hours for yourself to unwind—both mind and body—in a state of reflection and meditation. But for the rest of the day let the flood carry you along in spite of yourself; you must let yourself be dragged along without any regrets. You will find God in this torrent. You will find him, Madame, in a way all the more pure in that you will have not chosen this means to seek him.[35]

The pain that you suffer in that state of subjection is a natural lassitude that seeks consolation and not an attraction of God's Spirit. You believe that you miss God, but actually it is yourself that you miss because what you find most disagreeable in this tiresome and agitated state is that you cannot be free with yourself. It is the taste for the ego that you still have and that wants a calmer state to enjoy, in its own way, your mind, your feelings, and all your good qualities in the company of certain delicate persons who would be able to have you feel all that the ego has that is flattering. Or you would like to delight in God's presence in silence and in the pleasure of devotion instead of God's wanting to delight in you and break you in order to mold you to his will.

He leads others by the bitterness of privations. You, Madame, he leads by overwhelming you with the enjoyment of vain prosperity. He makes your situation hard and painful by putting in it what blind folk would believe makes life perfectly pleasant.[36] Thus he accomplishes two salutary works in you: he teaches you by experience and causes you to die[37] by things that uphold the corrupt and malignant life of the rest of humanity. You are like that king who could not touch anything without it turning to gold under his hand.[38] So much wealth made him miserable. You, Madame, will be happy by letting God have his way and by not desiring to find him except in what he wants for you.

While thinking about the misery of your privileged position, about the servitude from which you cry out in pain, the words of Jesus Christ to Saint Peter came to my mind: "In times past you used to walk where you would; but when you are in a more advanced age, another—a stronger one—will guide you and will lead you where you will not want to go."[39] Let yourself go and be guided, Madame, and do not hesitate along the path. You will walk like Saint Peter whither nature—jealous of its life and its freedom—does not want to go.[40] You will go to pure love, to perfect renunciation, to total death of your own will while accomplishing that of God who leads you according to his good pleasure.

Letter XXXVII—On Pure Love[41]

We know that we must suffer and that we deserve it. Still, we are always surprised at suffering, as if we don't think we either deserve it or need it. Only true and pure love loves suffering because it is only true and pure love that surrenders itself.[42] Resignation makes us suffer, but there is in it something that suffers from suffering and that resists. Resignation that gives nothing to God except moderately and while thinking about oneself may want to suffer, but it hesitates and vacillates often, fearing to suffer badly. Properly speaking, we are like two people in resignation: the one masters the other and watches over him to prevent him from rebelling. In pure love, which discards everything and is totally given over to God, the soul is nourished in silence by the cross and by union with Jesus Christ crucified without any second thoughts about its own suffering. At this point there is only one, unique, simple will that lets itself be seen by God exactly as it is, without thinking about looking at itself. The Christian says nothing, notices nothing. What does he do? He suffers. Is that all? Yes, that's all; that's all he has to do. Love can be felt well enough without speaking and without thinking. Love does the only thing that it knows how to do, which is to not desire anything when it is lacking all consolation. A will that is filled with God's will, even while everything else is taken from it, is the purest of all loves.

What a relief to think that we don't really have to be worried about pushing ourselves constantly to be patient and to be always on guard and stressed in order to keep up the appearance of virtue on the outside![43] It suffices just to be childlike and to surrender ourselves even in our pain.[44] This is not about courage; it is something both more and less: less in the eyes of the average virtuous person, more in the eyes of pure faith. It is a humbling of oneself, which elevates the soul to God's greatness. It is a weakness that removes all our strength and yet gives the omnipotence of God. "Whenever I am weak, then I am strong,"[45] says Saint Paul. "I can do all things in him who strengthens me."[46]

So, it is sufficient for you to nourish yourself by some short reading appropriate for your state and your taste. But leave it aside often in order to relieve your senses and to allow room for your inner spirit that leads to meditation. A few simple words, without reasoning and full of divine unction, are hidden manna. You might forget these words, but they work secretly and you are nourished by them; your soul is fattened up by them.[47] Sometimes we suffer without even knowing that we are suffering; other times we suffer and we find that we suffer badly and we put up with our impatience like a second cross heavier than the first. But nothing will stop us because true love always continues, since it does not go for itself, and since it accounts itself as nothing. Thus, we are truly happy. The cross is no longer a cross when there is no longer an ego to suffer from it and to appropriate to itself both fortune and misfortune.

Letter VIII—Fidelity in Small Things[48]

Saint Francis de Sales says that there are great virtues and small acts of faithfulness, just as there is salt and sugar. Sugar has a more exquisite taste, but it is not of such frequent usage; conversely, salt goes in every food necessary to life.[49] Great virtues are rare; the opportunity for them rarely comes. When these opportunities arise, we are prepared for them by all that has gone before. We are animated by the greatness of the sacrifice; we are upheld either by the brilliance of the deed that we are doing in the eyes of others or by the self-satisfaction we achieve by this effort we believe to be extraordinary. Small opportunities are unforeseen; they come by at any given moment; they constantly put us in conflict with our pride, our laziness, our arrogance, our recklessness and our pain. They go around breaking our will in everything and leaving us no reserve if we want to be faithful. Human nature never has time to catch its breath and must die to all its inclinations. We would a hundred times rather undergo great sacrifices for God, no matter how violent or painful, provided that we make up for them with the freedom of being able to follow our desires and habits in all other little matters. However, it is only by faithfulness in little things that the grace of true love is maintained and distinguishes itself from the ephemeral fervor of human nature.

Piety can be like a budget for temporal possessions. If we do not pay careful attention, we end up being bankrupt more through minor expenses rather than great luxury items. Whosoever can profit from small things, in the spiritual realm as in the temporal, can amass great wealth. All great things are only great in that they are the result of small things that we have carefully gathered together. Whosoever does not lose anything will quickly become rich.

Moreover, keep in mind that God does not seek so much our actions as the motive of love that causes the actions to be done and the flexibility that he demands of our will. Society almost always only judges our actions by what is on the outside; God, however, counts for nothing in our actions all that shines most in the eyes of men. What he desires is a pure intention, a will that is ready for anything and malleable in his hands, a sincere detachment from oneself. All this is accomplished more frequently, with less danger for pride, and in a manner that tests us more rigorously in everyday occasions rather than in extraordinary ones. Sometimes we are even more attached to a trivial thing than to an important thing. We have more repugnance in tearing ourselves from some amusement than in making a donation of some great sum of money.

We deceive ourselves all the more easily concerning small, insignificant things inasmuch as we believe them innocent and in that we imagine ourselves to be less attached to them. Nevertheless, when God takes them away from us, we can easily recognize by the pain of their privation how much our attachment to them and our use of them was excessive and inexcusable. Moreover, if we are negligent in these little things, we constantly scandalize our family, our servants, and even the greater public. People cannot imagine that our piety is in good faith when our conduct appears slack and irregular. Why should anyone believe that we would, without hesitating, make the greatest of sacrifices when we give in as soon as it is a question of the smallest sacrifices?

But what is the most dangerous is that our soul, by negligence in these little things, becomes accustomed to infidelity. We sadden the Holy Spirit. We rely on ourselves. We think nothing of neglecting God. However, true love sees nothing as little; everything that can please or displease God seems to the eyes of love always to be great. It is not that true love causes the soul troubles and scruples, but that it establishes no limits to faithfulness. Love simply acts in concert with God; since love does not trouble itself with things that God does not demand, it never hesitates a single instant concerning things that God does demand, whether they are great or small. Thus it is not by anxiety or trouble that we become faithful and exact in the smallest of things; it is by a feeling of love, which is exempt from those thoughts and fears of worried and overly scrupulous Christian souls. We are dragged along by love of God; we only wish to do what we do and we do not want anything at all of what we do not do.[50] At the same time that God jealously pressures us and pushes us relentlessly on the most minor details and seems to remove all freedom from us, we actually find ourselves set free and enjoying a profound peace in him. Oh, how happy the Christian soul is!

Moreover, those persons who are naturally less assiduous are those who should make an inviolable law for themselves about little things. They are tempted to scorn them; they have a habit of accounting them as negligible. They do not at all consider the repercussions of these small things. They do not sufficiently visualize the insidious progress that passions can achieve. They even forget the most disastrous experiences that they have undergone due to their passions. They prefer promising themselves an illusory fortitude and trusting in their own courage (so often misleading) than to subject themselves to a continual faithfulness. "It's a little nothing," they say. Yes, it is a "nothing," but it is a nothing that has become everything for you. A nothing that you love so much that you refuse it to God. A nothing that you despise in words in order to have a pretext for refusing it to God. But, in the end, it is a nothing that you keep for yourself against God and that will bring about your spiritual destruction.

It is not elevation of the spirit to scorn these little things; on the contrary, it is a too narrow viewpoint that considers things as insignificant that actually have such vast consequences. The more difficulty we have in guarding against these little things, the more we should fear neglecting them, the more we should mistrust our own motives, the more we should set up invincible barriers between ourselves and moral relapse: "Qui spernit modica, paulatim decidet."[51]

In the final analysis, you must yourself be your own judge. Would you put up with a friend who owes everything to you and yet who only serves you—through a sense of duty—during those rare occasions that we term great and would not want to subject himself to showing you in the everyday walk of life either kindness or consideration?

Do not fear being constantly attentive to those little things. You will need courage, but it is a penance that you deserve, that you need, and that will bring you peace and security: outside of these, there is only trouble and backsliding. Little by little God will make this situation easy and pleasant. True love is attentive, without awkwardness and without contentious spirit.

Letter LXVI—
To the Chevalier Colbert on Return to Faith

1688

Sir,[52]

You have forgotten me, but it is not in my power to do as much to you. In the bottom of my heart I carry something that always speaks to me of you and that makes me always anxious to ask about news of you. This is what I've felt particularly during the perils of your campaign.[53] Your forgetfulness, far from pushing me away, actually touches me all the more. In the past you have shown me a friendship whose impression is never erased and which moves me almost to tears when I remember our conversations. I hope that you remember how pleasant and cordial they were. Have you found, since that time, anything sweeter than God when one is worthy of feeling him? The truths that excited you then, are they no longer present to you? The pure light of God's kingdom, is it snuffed out? The nothingness of the world, can it have received some new luster?[54] That which was only a miserable dream, is it no longer that?[55] The God in whose bosom you used to open your heart and who caused you to enjoy a peace that passes all human understanding, is he no longer worthy of your love?[56] The eternal beauty, always renewed for pure eyes, has it no longer any attraction for you? The spring of heavenly pain, of guiltless pleasures, that are found in the Father of mercy and in the God of all consolation, has it dried up? No, for he is putting in my heart too urgent a desire to call you back to him. I can no longer resist it. For some time now I have vacillated, saying to myself, "I'll only bother him." Even beginning this letter, I promised myself to remain within the bounds of discretion; but at the fourth line my heart got the better of me. Even were you not to answer me, even were you to find me ridiculous, I would not cease speaking to God about you—with bitterness, not being able to speak to you yourself. So, once again, Sir, pardon me if I go beyond the rules.[57] I see this as well as you do, but I feel myself pushed forward and dragged along. God has not forgotten you yet, since he acts in me so ardently for your salvation.

What does he ask of you except that you yourself should want to be happy? Have you not felt that one is happy when one loves him? Have you not felt that one can never truly be happy—no matter what stupor one might seek in pleasures of the senses outside of him? Since you know, therefore, where the fountain of life is found, and that you have, in the past, plunged your heart in there to quench its thirst, why search now for half-opened and corrupt cisterns? Oh, happy days! Oh, wonderful times! Times that were brightened only by the soft rays of loving mercy, when will you return? When will it be granted to me to see once more this dear child of God called back under his powerful hand, filled with his favors and the delights of his sacred feast—causing all of heaven to rejoice, crushing the world underfoot, and drawing from experience of human weakness a source of inexhaustible humility and fervor?

I won't tell you, Sir, what it is you have to do. God will tell you well enough himself according to your needs, provided that you listen to him inside yourself and that you courageously scorn despicable people. But, ultimately, he wants *you.* Follow him. What can we refuse to him who wishes to give us everything by giving to us of himself? Therefore, Sir, do what you want, but love God.[58] And let his love, brought back to life in you, be your only guide. I have often thanked him for having kept you safe from the perils of this campaign, wherein your soul was more exposed to danger than your body. Often have I trembled for you. Put an end to my fears. Give back to me my heart's joy. I could not feel a greater joy than to find myself with you again—forming only one heart and one soul in the house of God, waiting for our blessed hope and the glorious coming of Almighty God who will intoxicate us both with the flood of his chaste delights.[59] Your ears are not yet unaccustomed to this sublime vocabulary of truth. Your heart is made to respond to the charms of these words. Here is the delicious bread that we eat every day at the table of our Father.[60] Why have you left it? With such support we should never fear needing anything else. But here is the last request I make of you. Even though you might not feel that you have the strength to come back to the happy place where you were before, at least answer me; at least, don't run away from me. I know what it is like to be weak. I am a thousand times weaker than you. It is very useful to have experienced that we are weak. But don't add to the weakness inherent to humanity separation from that which can lessen the weakness. You will be the master of our correspondence. I will never speak to you of anything except what you want to hear. I will keep the secret of God in my heart, and I will always be yours with tenderness and inviolable respect.

Letter LXVIII—
To Chevalier Colbert on Spiritual Reading

Paris, October 30, 1688

You mustn't believe, Sir,[61] that you move away from God when you lose the freedom of reading good books. We owe God the faithfulness of using so great an aid when he lets us have it; but when he removes it from us by some real necessity, he makes up for this by his mercy. So, he becomes himself our inner book. He presents himself in the middle of all the upheaval. He has us hear the sweetness of his voice even in the depths of the soul. He makes us feel the vanity, the corruption and the misery of all that is outside, and he writes himself in our hearts, by his Holy Spirit, a living and indelible law. Be happy, therefore, Sir, while you are not able to do otherwise, to be attentive in saying your Breviary, without upsetting your routine too much.[62] Whatever in the words of the Office[63] may have touched you the most will remain in your heart, and you will be able to remember it in dens of iniquity where it is permitted neither to pray nor to read.[64] So, the world[65] will not be able to prevent you from feeling how contemptible it is or from raising your heart toward God for whom alone you keep it, or from invoking him with confidence when in need, or from being mindful of your words according to his law.

Here is, Sir, an invisible worship that escapes this world and that the world cannot censure. When involuntary faults prevent you from having good thoughts, do not be discouraged. Alter them gently; put yourself back in your place under God's hand and you will be almost as if you had never left it. In the beginning, make a rule for yourself to raise your heart to God and to offer yourself to him at certain hours and on certain important occasions. In this way you will acquire, almost imperceptibly, the habit of acting in his presence. This routine will become pleasant and easy.

I am, Sir, very perfectly yours.

Letter to the Duc de Bourgogne on the Occasion of His First Communion[66]

It has finally arrived, Milord, this day that you have so desired and awaited: this day that must obviously decide all the others of your life until the day of your death. "Ecce Savator tuus venit, et merces ejus cum eo."[67] He comes to you under the appearance of the most familiar food in order to nourish your soul, just as bread nourishes your body each day. He will only appear to you as a morsel of ordinary bread, but God's power will be hidden therein and your faith will be able to find it there. Tell him, as Isaiah said: "Vere tu es Deus absconditus."[68] He is a God hidden by love; he veils his glory from us for fear that our eyes be dazzled by it and so that we might approach him more familiarly. "Accedite ad eum," says a psalm, "et illuminamini, et facies vestrae non confundentur."[69] It is there that you will find hidden manna, with the various flavors of all heavenly virtues. You will eat the bread that is above all substance. He will not change in you, vile and mortal man, but you will change in him so as to be a living member of the Savior. Let faith and love cause you to taste the gift of God. "Gustate, et videte quoniam suavis est Dominus."[70]

Letter to Louis XIV

The person, Sire, who takes the liberty of writing you this letter, has no interest in this world.[71] He writes it neither from hurt nor from ambition, nor from any desire to become involved in important affairs of state. He loves you without being known by you. He sees God in your person.[72] With all your might, you cannot give him any reward that he desires, and there is no pain that he would not suffer willingly in order to make you understand the truths necessary for your salvation. If he speaks to you forcefully, do not be amazed; it is that the truth is free and strong. You are hardly accustomed to hearing it. People accustomed to being flattered easily mistake for spite, for bitterness, and for exaggeration that which is only the pure truth. But it is to betray the truth to not show it to you in all its dimensions. God is witness that the person who speaks to you here does this with a heart full of zeal, of respect, of loyalty, and of tenderness for all that which touches your real interests.

You were born, Sire, with a fair and upright heart, but those who raised you only gave you for lessons of governing mistrust, jealousy, absence of virtue, the fear of any striking merit, the inclination for pliable and sycophantic men, pride and attention to your personal interest alone.[73] For around thirty years now your principal ministers have shaken and even overthrown the ancient maxims of the state in order to raise your authority (which had become theirs) to the heights because it was in their hands. Neither the state nor its rules have been spoken of any longer. We have heard tell only of the king and his good pleasure. They have increased your revenues and your expenses to an infinite degree. They have raised you up to the heavens in order to, so they said, erase the greatness of all your predecessors put together; that is to say, for having impoverished all of France in order to introduce at court a monstrous and irremediable luxury.[74] They have desired to raise you up on the ruins of all classes in the state, as if you could only be great by ruining all your subjects on whom your greatness is founded. It is true that you have been jealous of your authority, perhaps even too much so regarding outward things. But, down deep, each minister has been master in all areas of his administration. You believe that you have been governing because you have set the limits between those who were governing. They have well shown their power to the public, and we have felt it only too well. They have been hard, haughty, unjust, violent, and duplicitous. They have known no other rule, neither for the administration of the interior of the state nor in foreign negotiations, than to threaten, to crush, and to annihilate anything that stood in their way. They have counseled you only to distance you from any person of merit who could cause them inconvenience. They have accustomed you to receive constantly outrageous praise that borders on idolatry and that you should have, for your own honor, rejected with indignation. They have made your name odious and the whole French nation insufferable to all our neighbors. They have preserved no former ally because they have wanted only slaves. For more than twenty years they have been the cause of bloody wars.[75] For example, Sire, they had your majesty undertake a war against Holland in 1672 ostensibly for your glory and to punish the Dutch, who had occasioned some mockery from the depths of the bitterness in which we had put them by upsetting the rules of commerce established by Cardinal de Richelieu.[76] I cite in particular this war because it was the source of all the others. It had for cause only a motive of glory and vengeance, which can never make a war just. Whence it follows that all the borders that you have enlarged by that war are unjustly acquired in their origin. It is true, Sire, that the subsequent peace treaties seem to cover and repair that injustice, since they have given you these conquered lands. But an unjust war is nonetheless unjust for its being successful. The peace treaties signed with the vanquished are not freely signed. They sign with a knife at their neck. They sign in spite of themselves to avoid even greater losses. They sign, like you give your purse, when you have to give it or die. Sire, we have to go back to the origin of this war with Holland in order to examine before God all of your conquests.

It is useless to say that they were necessary to your kingdom. Other people's possessions are never necessary to us. What is truly necessary to us is to observe exact justice. You must not even claim that you are in your right always to keep certain places because they serve as a security for your borders. It is up to you to look for that security by good alliances, by your moderation, or by locations that you can defend within your borders.[77] In the final analysis the need to be vigilant regarding our security never gives us warrant to take our neighbor's land. Consult with learned and honest advisors on this matter. They will tell you that what I am saying is as clear as day.

All this is enough, Sire, for you to realize that you have spent your entire life outside the path of truth and justice and, consequently, outside of the gospel's path. So many horrible troubles that have devastated Europe for more than twenty years now, so much blood shed, so many scandals committed, so many provinces ravaged, so many cities and towns reduced to ashes: these are the fateful consequences of this war of 1672 undertaken for your glory and for the punishment of Dutch newspaper editors and medal makers.[78] Along with honest men and without flattering yourself, examine whether you can keep all you possess consequent upon the treaties to which you have reduced your enemies by such an unfounded war.

That war is still the real source of all the misfortunes that France is suffering. Ever since that war, you have always wanted to grant peace as a master and impose conditions instead of settling them with fairness and moderation. This is what has caused peace not to last. Your enemies, shamefully brought low, have dreamed only of raising themselves back up and uniting against you.[79] Should you be surprised at this? You have not even abided by the terms of that peace that you yourself had so haughtily granted. In time of total peace you waged war and made prodigious conquests. You established a commission to be both judge and jury.[80] This was adding insult to injury and mockery to usurpation and violence. You have sought ambiguous terms in the Treaty of Westphalia in order to attack Strasbourg.[81] In all these years never had any one of your ministers dared, in any negotiation, to interpret the terms of the treaty as giving a basis for laying the least claim to that city. This type of conduct has reunited and enraged all of Europe against you. Even those who have not dared declare themselves against you openly impatiently wish for your weakening and your humiliation as the only resource for freedom and for the tranquility of all Christian nations. You, Sire, who could acquire so much real and peaceful glory by being the father of your subjects[82] and the mediator between your neighbors, have been made the common enemy of your neighbors and have been made to seem a harsh master in your own kingdom.[83]

The strangest effect of this bad advice is the duration of the alliance formed against you. The Allies prefer making war unsuccessfully rather than concluding peace with you, because they are convinced—based on their own experience—that that peace would not be a true peace, that you would not keep it any more than the others, and that you would use it to crush separately, without difficulty, each of your neighbors as soon as they were disunited. So, the more victorious you are, the more they fear you and unite against you to avoid the slavery with which they fear themselves threatened. Not being able to defeat you, they intend to at least wear you down in the long run. In short, they no longer hope for any security from you except by putting you in a position of impotence with regard to harming them. Put yourself for a minute in their place, Sire, and see what it is to have preferred your own advantage to justice and good faith.

Moreover, your people, whom you should love as your children and who have been up to now so fervent for you, are dying of hunger.[84] Cultivation of the fields is almost abandoned. The cities and the countryside are losing population. All the trades are languishing and can no longer provide for the workers. All commerce is destroyed. Consequently, you have destroyed half of the real strength within your realm in order to make, and then defend, vain conquests without. Instead of taking money from these poor folks, you should have given alms and fed them. All of France is no longer anything but a huge hospital, decimated and without means. The magistrates are degraded and worn out. The aristocracy whose property is threatened with seizure lives only from royal pensions.[85] You are constantly harassed by those who seek favors and who murmur against you. Yet it is you, Sire, who have brought all these problems on yourself, because, the entire kingdom being ruined, you have everything in your own hands and no one can live any longer except from your gifts. Here is this great kingdom, flourishing so much[86] under a king who is daily portrayed to us as the savior of the people, and who could indeed be that if flattering advice had not poisoned him.

The common folk themselves (since everything must be said), who loved you so much and who had so much confidence in you, now begin to lose their friendship, confidence, and even respect. They no longer rejoice in your victories and conquests. They are full of bitterness and despair. The fires of sedition are being lit little by little in all corners. The people believe that you have no pity on their distress, that you love only your authority and your glory. They say: If the king had a father's heart for his people, wouldn't he find his glory in providing bread for them and in letting them catch their breath after so many disasters, rather than keeping a few places on the border that only cause war? What answer is there to that, Sire? Unrest among the people, which had been unknown for so long, now is becoming frequent. Paris itself, so close to you,[87] is not immune. The magistrates are constrained to tolerate the insolence of rioters and to channel money to them to appease them. And thus we pay those whom we ought to punish. You are thus reduced to the shameful, deplorable position of either letting sedition go unpunished and having it grow stronger because of this impunity, or inhumanly massacring these common folk whom you have driven to despair by depriving them—through your war taxes—of the bread that they try to earn by the sweat of their brow.

But while they lack bread, you yourself lack money and you refuse to see the urgency of the position to which you have been reduced. Because you have always been fortunate, you cannot imagine that you could ever cease to be. You are afraid to open your eyes. And you are afraid for anyone else to open them for you. You are afraid of being forced to give up some of your glory. This glory that hardens your heart is more dear to you than justice, than your own peace of mind, than the preservation of your people, who perish daily from the illnesses caused by famine; indeed, it is more dear to you than your eternal salvation—so incompatible with this idol of glory.

So, there it is, Sire, the shape that you're in. You live as if you had a baneful blindfold over your eyes. You congratulate yourself on the variable successes that decide nothing, yet you cannot see the big picture: that the nation's business in general is disintegrating, imperceptibly, without any aid to it. So, while on the harsh field of combat you take cannon from your enemies and storm their positions, you don't realize that you are fighting on terrain that is giving beneath your feet and that you are going to fall in spite of your victories.

Everyone sees this, and no one dares point it out to you. You will see it perhaps too late. True courage consists in not flattering oneself and in taking a firm stand in necessity. You only willingly lend your ear, Sire, to those who flatter you with vain hopes. The people whom you yourself judge to be the most reliable are nevertheless those whom you fear and avoid the most. You should go straight to the truth, since you are king, and press people to tell you the truth without sweetening it and encourage those who are too timid. On the contrary, however, you seek only to avoid digging deep into the truth. But God finally will be able to lift the veil that covers your eyes and show you that which you avoid seeing. He has had his arm raised against you for a long time now. But he is slow to strike you because he has pity on a prince who has been his entire life obsessed with flatterers and because, moreover, your enemies are his. But he will know how to separate his just cause from your own, which is not just, and humiliate you in order to convert you, for you will be Christian only in humiliation. You do not love God at all. You only fear him with the fear of a slave. It is hell and not God that you fear.[88] Your religion consists only in superstitions, in petty superficial devotions. You are like the Jews of whom God said: While they honor me with their lips, their heart is far from me.[89] You are scrupulous with respect to trifles yet hardened with respect to horrible evils.[90] You only love your own glory and your ease. You center everything around yourself as if you were God on earth and everything else were created only to be sacrificed to you. However, it is you whom God put on the earth for your people. But, alas, you do not understand these truths. How could you appreciate them? You do not know God at all. You do not love him at all. You do not pray to him at all with your heart, and you do nothing to try to know him.

You have a scandalous, corrupt archbishop—incorrigible, false, cunning, artful, an enemy of all virtue—a man who causes all good people to groan. You are satisfied with him because he only thinks of pleasing you by his flattery. By prostituting his honor for more than twenty years now, he has enjoyed your confidence. You hand over good people to him; you allow him to tyrannize the church; and no virtuous prelate is treated as well as he.[91]

As far as your confessor is concerned, he is not an evil man, but he fears solid virtue and he only likes secular and easygoing people.[92] He is jealous of his authority, which you have pushed beyond all limits. Never has a king's confessor alone been able to make bishops and decide all affairs of conscience. You alone in France, Sire, are ignorant of the fact that he knows nothing, that his mind is shallow and common, and that he nevertheless has a certain artifice even within his crudeness of spirit. The Jesuits themselves despise him and are indignant at seeing him so given over to the ridiculous ambition of his own family. You have thus made a minister of state out of a monk. He does not understand men any more than he understands anything else. He is the dupe of all those who flatter him and who give him gifts. He neither doubts nor hesitates over any difficult question. Any other enlightened and honest man would not dare to decide these questions all alone. Yet, as for himself, he fears only having to deliberate with people who know the rules.[93] He goes merrily along, never fearing to lead you astray. He always leans toward moral laxity and keeping you in ignorance. At least he only leans on the side of those living in conformity with the church's rules when he is afraid of scandalizing you otherwise. Thus, he is the blind leading the blind, and, as Jesus Christ says, they will all fall into the same ditch.[94]

Your archbishop and your confessor have got you mixed up in this bad business in Rome, the difficulties over the question of the vacant bishoprics.[95] They have let you become embroiled, through Monsieur de Louvois, in those of Saint-Lazare and would have let you die with this injustice if Monsieur de Louvois had outlived you.[96]

We had hoped, Sire, that your privy council would remove you from this path so misguided. But your council has neither force nor vigor for good. At least Mme. de Maintenon and the Duc de Beauvilliers ought to have used your confidence in them to enlighten you. But their weakness and their timidity dishonor them and scandalize everyone. France is up against the wall. What are they waiting for, to speak to you frankly? That everything be lost? Are they afraid of displeasing you? They do not love you, then, because we have to be prepared to anger those whom we love rather than flatter them and betray them with silence. What are they good for if they don't show you that you must give back those lands that do not belong to you, that you must prefer the lives of your subjects to a false glory, that you must remedy the wrongs that you have done to the church, and that you must become a true Christian before death comes upon you unawares? I well know that when anyone speaks with this Christian freedom, we run the risk of losing the favor of kings. But is your favor more precious to them than your salvation? I well know also that we should pity you, console you, comfort you, and speak to you with zeal, kindness, and respect. But, ultimately, the truth must be told. Woe, woe to them if they do not tell the truth, and woe to you if you are not worthy of hearing it![97] It is shameful that they should have your confidence without making good use of it for so long.[98] It is up to them to retire if you are too moody and if you want only flatterers around you. Perhaps, Sire, you will ask what they should be telling you. Well, here it is: They should tell you that you must humble yourself before God's powerful hand if you do not want him to humble you. You must ask for peace and, by this act of shame, expiate all the glory that you have made your idol. You must reject unjust advice of flattering politicians. Finally, you must give back to your enemies as quickly as possible all your conquests (which, moreover, you cannot retain without injustice) in order to save the state. Are you not still too blessed even in the midst of your misfortunes? Should God not put an end to this prosperity that has blinded you? Should he not constrain you to make this restitution essential to your salvation—reparations that you would never have been resolved to make in a peaceful and triumphant realm? The person who tells you these truths, Sire, far from being opposed to your interests never ceases praying for you and would actually give his life to see you such as God would want you to be.

The Maxims of the Saints

Preface

I have always believed that one should speak and write as soberly as possible concerning the interior paths.[1] Although they do not contain anything that is not manifestly in conformity with the immutable rule of faith and the evangelical virtues, it seems to me—nevertheless—that this subject demands extreme discretion. The average reader is not prepared to glean fruitful understanding from such weighty matter. This would be, indeed, to expose what is most pure and sublime in religion to the derision of the profane, in whose eyes the mystery of Jesus Christ crucified is already a scandal and folly. This would be putting into the hands of the least reflective and the least experienced of men the ineffable secret of God in our heart, and these men are simply not capable of either being instructed or being edified thereof. Furthermore, this would be like setting a trap for all gullible and indiscreet souls[2] in which they might fall prey to falsehood; for they might easily delude themselves into believing they are already in all the mystical states described in books and thus they become visionaries and rebels. Instead, if they are kept in ignorance of these mystical states that are beyond their own, they could only enter into the path of disinterested love and contemplation by means of grace alone, without mystical readings having any part in inflaming their imagination. These reasons, therefore, are what have persuaded me that one should keep silent inasmuch as possible about this matter lest one excite the curiosity of the general public, which has neither the experience nor the indwelling of grace necessary to examine the works of the saints. For our brutish nature can neither discern nor appreciate divine things such as the interior paths. But since the public's curiosity has become so widespread in recent days I believe it is now as necessary to address this issue as it once was to remain silent about it.

I propose as my goal in this work to explain the experiences and the expressions of the saints in order to prevent their being exposed to the derision of the impious. At the same time I want to enlighten the mystics as to the true sense of these holy authors so that they can know the true value of their expressions. When I speak of holy authors I mean to limit myself to those who are canonized or whose memory is cherished throughout the whole church, those whose writings have been officially approved after many critiques. I only mean here to speak of saints who have been canonized and admired by the entire church for having practiced and taught others to practice the sort of spirituality that is described in all their writings. It is surely not permissible to reject such authors as these, or to accuse them of having introduced novel innovations against the church's tradition.

I want to show how far these holy authors are from harming the dogma of our faith or from favoring any falsehood. I want to show the mystics that I am not diluting any approved doctrine or experience of these authors who are our models. By these means I want to lead them to believe me when I show them the precise limits that these same saints have delineated for us, beyond which limits it is never permissible for us to tread. The mystics I am addressing are neither fanatics nor hypocrites who hide the mystery of iniquity under a pretense of perfection. God forbid that I should speak the word of truth to those men who have no indwelling of the mystery of faith in a pure conscience; they only deserve our indignation and horror. Rather, I am speaking to the simple, innocent, and docile mystics. They need to know that falsehood and error have always closely followed behind the most perfect spiritual paths. From the very beginnings of Christianity the false Gnostics, execrable men, attempted to blend in with the true Gnostics, who were contemplatives and the most perfect of Christians. Again, the Beghards[3] falsely imitated true contemplatives such as Saint Bernard and Richard and Hugh of Saint Victor during recent centuries. Bellarmine remarks that mystical authors' terminology has often been criticized for its ambiguity. "It often happens," he says, "that they who deal with mystical theology are criticized in their choice of words by some and praised by others because these same expressions are not understood by everyone in the same sense."[4] Cardinal Bona says that "those who are in a state of passive contemplation are the least able to express themselves, yet are the most excellent in practice and experience." In fact, nothing is so difficult as making others understand the states that consist of operations so simple, so delicate, and so detached from the senses, or to always put in order all the necessary caveats to prevent misunderstanding of them, or to explain their theological underpinning in a rigorous manner. This is what has scandalized a good part of the reading public that has read the mystical works, and what has lead many others into error. In the last century, for example, while Spain was full of so many saints endued with wonderful grace, the Alumbrados[5] were discovered in Andalucia, which rendered suspect even the greatest saints. As a consequence, Saint Teresa, Balthazar Alvarez, and the blessed John of the Cross felt the need to defend themselves. Ruusbroec, whom Bellarmine calls a great contemplative, and Tauler, that apostolic man so celebrated throughout Germany, have both needed defending, the former by Denis the Carthusian and the latter by Blosius. Saint Francis de Sales himself has not been spared criticism because his critics have not been able to appreciate his joining of a precise and exacting theology with the eminent light of grace. We have seen this in the saintly Cardinal de Bérulle's feeling it necessary to pen an apologia for his doctrine. Thus has the chaff so often obscured the wheat that even the purest authors treating the interior life have needed defending lest their wording—taken in an evil sense—alter pure doctrine.[6]

These examples must make mystics sober and judicious. If they are humble and docile they must leave decisions in matters of doctrine as well as the choice of the most appropriate manner to use to define doctrine to the church's pastors. Saint Paul refuses to eat meat rather than scandalize the least of his brethren for whom Jesus Christ died.[7] How can we, therefore, stay attached to any expression as soon as it scandalizes a tender soul? Let the mystics clear away any doubt, since they now know that some have abused their terminology in order to corrupt that which is most holy. Further, may those who have spoken without forethought in ways both improper and exaggerated explain themselves and leave nothing to be desired toward the church's edification. Moreover, may those who have been mistaken in matters touching essential doctrine be content not only with condemning their error but rather let them admit to having believed it. May they give glory to God. May they feel no shame in having erred, for this is the common lot of mankind. May they humbly confess their errors since these will no longer be errors once they are humbly confessed. It is in order to separate the true from the false in so delicate and important a matter that two great prelates have given the public thirty-four propositions that contain in essence all the doctrine pertaining to the interior paths. I only claim in this volume to explain these principles in greater detail.[8]

All interior paths tend toward pure or disinterested love. This pure love is the highest degree of Christian perfection. It is the end of all the paths that the saints have experienced. Whosoever will go no further than this remains within the bounds of tradition. Whosoever goes past this boundary is already lost. If anyone doubts the truth and perfection of this love, I propose to show him the universal and obvious Catholic tradition from the apostles to Saint Francis de Sales without any interruption. Moreover, I will give to the reading public whenever it is desired a collection of all the passages from the fathers, the Scholastics, and the mystics, who all speak unanimously on this subject.[9]

In this volume it will be seen that the ancient fathers spoke as forcefully as Saint Francis de Sales and that they made the same suppositions that scornful critics have so mocked when they find them in the saints of recent centuries about the selflessness of love concerning salvation. Saint Augustine himself, whom several people have thought opposed this doctrine, teaches it no less than the others. It is true that it is imperative to explain pure love well and to indicate precisely the boundaries beyond which its disinterestedness can never go. Its disinterestedness can never exclude the desire to love God without limits, or love's degree, or its duration. It can never exclude conformity with God's will which desires our own salvation and which wants us to desire it as well—with him for his glory. This selfless love, always inviolably attached to the written law, performs all the same acts and accomplishes all the same distinct virtues as selfish love with the sole difference that it accomplishes them in a simple, peaceful manner, detached from all self-centered motives.[10]

The holy indifference so praised by Saint Francis de Sales is only the selflessness of this love, which is always disinterested and without selfish will for itself. Rather, it is focused, wanting positively all that which God would have us want by means of his scriptures and by the attraction of his grace.

In order to attain this state, one must purify love; all interior trials consist only in love's purification. Contemplation itself, even the most passive, is only the tranquil, uniform exercise of this pure love. One only passes imperceptibly from meditation, consisting in methodical, discursive acts, to contemplation, whose acts are simple and direct, in commensurate measure to one's passing from selfish love to selfless love. The passive state and transformation with the mystical wedding and the essential, immediate union are only the entire purity of this love whose state is habitual in a small number of souls without ever being either unchangeable or exempt from venial faults. When I speak of all the different degrees (of mystical union) whose names are so little known by the average Christian, I only do this because these terms are hallowed by usage by a large number of saints approved by the church who have described their experiences by these terms. Moreover, I only refer to them in order to explain them with the utmost caution. In the final analysis all interior paths lead to pure love as their destination, and, in life's pilgrimage, the highest of all degrees is the habitual state of this love. It is the foundation and roof of the whole structure. Nothing would be more rash than to combat the purity of this love so worthy of our God, to whom all is owed, so worthy of his perfection and of his jealousy, which is a consuming fire. But, equally, nothing would be more rash than to want to remove from this love, by misguided refinement, the reality of its acts in the practice of distinct virtues. Finally, it would be no less rash or dangerous to impute the perfection of interior paths in some mysterious state above and beyond the fixed term of pure love's habitual state.

It is to anticipate all these possible dangers that I propose to discuss in this work the subject in its entirety by means of what I call articles, listed according to the differing degrees and stages that the mystics have indicated for us in describing the spiritual life. Each article comprises two parts. The first will be the true one, which I approve and which includes all that which is authorized by the experiences of the saints—that which defines a healthy doctrine of pure love. The second part will be the false one, through which I will explain the exact spot wherein falsehood's danger begins. Therefore, by including in each article that which is excessive I will define it and condemn it with all theological rigor in my command.

Thus, my articles will be in their first part a collection of precise definitions concerning the saints' expressions, in order to reduce them all to an incontrovertible definition that will neither lend itself to ambiguity nor alarm even the most fearful souls. This will be a sort of dictionary with definitions so the reader will know the precise value of each term. These definitions gathered together will form a simple and complete system of all interior paths. This work will have a perfect unity because everything will be clearly seen to relate to the practice of pure love, as forcefully taught by all the early church fathers as by the most recent saints.

Conversely, the second part of my articles will show all that false principles entail, that they enable the most dangerous sort of deception contrary to faith and morals under the appearance of perfection. In each article I will attempt to indicate where misunderstanding begins and to condemn all that is bad therein without ever diluting anything the saints' experiences authorize. If they are willing to listen to me without prejudice, mystics will clearly see that I understand them and that I take the meaning of their terminology in the proper measure of its true sense. I let them judge if I do not explain their propositions with more precision than most of them have been able to do heretofore because I have applied myself to reducing their expressions and terminology to succinct, clear ideas—precise ideas approved by tradition without diluting the essence of their matter. All mystics who love only truth and the church's edification will surely be satisfied with this plan. I could have included a prodigious quantity of passages from the earliest church fathers, Scholastics, and mystical saints, but that endeavor would have thrown me into innumerable repetitions and made this work so prolix as to frighten the reader. This realization led me to suppress from this volume passages that have already been catalogued elsewhere. To spare the reader boredom, therefore, I intend to presuppose on his part a good working knowledge of this constant and evident mystical tradition in the church. I will limit myself to presenting a clear and coherent system regarding theological definitions. The dryness of this method seems to me a very unfortunate disadvantage as a writer but much less a disadvantage than that of interminable, oppressive citations.

It, therefore, only remains to me now to execute this plan that I have just described. I wait upon strength to do so, not from myself but from God, who is pleased to use the vilest and most unworthy instruments. My doctrine, thus, must never be my personal doctrine but that of Jesus Christ, who sends forth pastors. Woe to me if I should say anything coming only from myself. Woe to me if, in the task of instructing others, I were not myself the most docile and submissive son of the Roman, catholic, and apostolic church.

I shall begin the execution of this plan by a simple exposition of the various meanings that one can give to loving God in order clearly and precisely to lay out the current state of discussion in this matter, after which the reader will find my articles that approve what is true and condemn what is false in each question regarding interior paths.

Exposition of Various Types of Love by Which One Can Love God

1. We can love God, not for himself, but for blessings apart from him that nevertheless depend on his power and that we hope to obtain from him. Such was the love of the carnal Jews who observed the Law so that they would be rewarded by dew from heaven and by fertility of the earth. This love is neither chaste nor filial but purely servile. Properly speaking, it is not loving God; it is loving one's self and seeking only for one's self, not loving and seeking God but rather that which comes from him.

2. Even when we have faith, we may not have any degree of charity.[11] We know that God is our only source of happiness; that is, the only object whose sight can make us blessed. If, in this state, we loved God only as the sole instrument capable of making us happy and because of this inability of achieving happiness in any other object; if we looked upon God as only a means of felicity, used solely as a means to an end, then that love would be a love of ourselves rather than a love of God. At the very least it would be contrary to the divine order because, in looking at God only as an object or means of our happiness, it would bring him down to our level of use only for our happiness.

Although this love might have led us to seek no other reward than God alone, still it would be a purely venal love, having the nature of pure covetousness. "The soul," as Saint Francis de Sales says, "that would only love God for love of herself, putting her own pleasure as an end to the love that this soul bears God, alas! she would commit a heinous sacrilege. The soul that loves God only for love of herself, this soul loves herself when she should be loving God and she loves God in a way that she should love herself. It is as if someone would say: 'The love that I bear myself is the reason for which I love God.' So that the love of God becomes dependant, inferior, and subordinate to love of oneself which is an unparalleled impiety."[12]

3. We can love God with a love called hopeful love. It is not entirely selfish, for it is commingled with the beginnings of loving God for himself. But the motive of our own self-interest is its main and dominant motive. Saint Francis de Sales speaks of this type of love in these words: "I am not saying that it is in our nature that this love should make us love God only for our own self-love…Indeed, there is a great difference between saying 'I love God for the blessings that I expect from Him,' and saying 'I only love God for the blessings that I expect from Him.'"[13] This hopeful love is so called because the motive of self-interest is still dominant therein. It is, therefore, the beginning of conversion to God, but it is not yet true righteousness. It is of this hopeful love that Saint Francis has said: "The greatest love is only in charity: in hope love remains imperfect because it does not lead to a love of God's infinite goodness in and of itself but rather only inasmuch as it is good for us… Therefore no one can truly observe God's commandments or have eternal life by means of this love alone."[14]

4. There is a love called charitable love which is still mixed with some vestiges of self-interest but which is nevertheless true salvific love because selfless motives predominate therein. It is of this love that Saint Francis de Sales speaks in the passage cited above: "The greatest love is only in charity." This love seeks God for himself and prefers him to all other things without exception.

It is only through this preference that it is able to justify us. It does not prefer God or his glory any less than it does ourselves or our interests or any creatures that are around us. And here is the reason: it is that we are not any less vile creatures, unworthy to compare ourselves to God, than the rest of creation. God who did not create us for other creatures did not create us for ourselves either, but rather for himself alone.

He is no less jealous of us than of other external objects that we might love. Properly speaking, the only thing he is jealous of in us is ourselves, for he clearly sees that it is ourselves that we are tempted to love even in the enjoyment of all other external objects. He is incapable of being mistaken in his jealousy. All our affections are summed up in one: the love of self. Everything that does not spring from the principle of charity, as Saint Augustine so often says, comes from cupidity. Thus, it is this love, unique root of all evil, that God's jealousy attacks in us especially.[15] While we have only a love born of hope wherein self-interest takes precedence over the glory of God, a soul is not yet justified. But when selfless love, a love born of charity, begins to prevail against the motive of self-interest, then the soul that loves God is truly loved by him. This true charity is nonetheless not yet entirely pure; that is to say, without any mingling, still the love born of charity prevailing over the selfish motive of hope is called the state of charity. The soul then loves God for himself as well as for herself but so that she mainly loves God's glory; this soul seeks her own happiness therein only as a means that she uses and subordinates to the ultimate goal, which is the glory of her creator. It is not necessary that this preference for God and his glory rather than for ourselves and our interests, be always explicit in the justified soul. Faith assures us that God's glory and our happiness are inseparable. It is sufficient that this preference—so right and necessary—be real, albeit implicit, for all life's ordinary occasions. This preference only needs to become explicit in life's extraordinary occasions in which God wishes to put us to the test to purify us. Thereupon, he would grant us—commensurate to the test—courage and wisdom to bear the trial and to develop this preference in our hearts. Beyond that, it would be dangerous to seek this preference deep in our hearts.

5. One can love God with a love born of pure charity, without any mingling of motive of self-interest. At which stage one loves God in the midst of trials and tribulations in such a way that one could not love him more even if he showered the soul with consolation. Neither the fear of punishment nor the desire of reward has any part in this love. One no longer loves God, either for the merit, the perfection, or the happiness that one finds in loving him. One would still love him as much even if—supposing an impossible hypothesis—he did not know that we loved him or if he decided to damn eternally those who loved him.

We love him even so, as the sovereign and infallible good for those who are faithful to him. We love him as our personal property, as a promised reward, as our all.[16] But in this state we do not love him any longer from the precise motive of our own happiness and personal reward. It is what Saint Francis de Sales expressed with the most rigorous precision in these words: "It is two different things to say: 'I love God for myself,' as opposed to 'I love God for love of myself'...One is the holy affection of the Bride...The other is impiety."[17] Elsewhere he says again: "The purity of love consists in wanting nothing for oneself, envisaging only God's will for which one would be willing to prefer eternal torment to glory." The selfless soul in the state of pure charity awaits, desires, hopes for God as her own, as her reward. The soul wants him for herself but not for love of herself. She wants him for herself in order to be in conformity with God's will, which wants this for the soul. But the soul does not want God at all from love of herself, because it is now no longer self-interest that motivates her.

Such is the perfect and pure love that accomplishes the same acts of virtue as mixed love, with this sole difference: pure love banishes all fear as well as all worries; it is even exempt from the anxiousness of selfish love.

For the rest, I maintain that to avoid any misunderstanding in a subject matter where it is so dangerous to be ambiguous and difficult not to be, I will make it a rule to observe rigorously the definitions that I now give to these five sorts of love in order to better differentiate among them.

1. The love of the carnal Jews for the gifts of God, distinguished from him and not for him, can be named purely servile love. But since we will have no need at all to discuss it in this work, I shall say no more about it.
2. The love by which one only loves God as a means or sole instrument of acquiring happiness that one uses only and absolutely in relation to oneself, as a final goal, can be called concupiscent love, that is, a love deriving from pure concupiscence.
3. The love in which the motive of our own happiness is prevalent over that of God's glory is named hopeful love.
4. The love in which charity is still commingled with a motive of self-interest, yet this motive is subordinate to the main motive and the ultimate goal, which is the pure glory of God, should be named charitable or mixed love. But as we shall need presently to contrast this love to that love called pure or entirely selfless, I am obliged to give to this mixed love the

name of selfish love because, in fact, it is still mixed with the remains of self-interest, although it is a love that prefers God to oneself.

5. The love of God alone, considered in and of himself and without any mixture or commingling of selfish motives or of fear or of hope is pure love: perfect charity.

Article I

TRUE

Purely concupiscent or entirely mercenary love by which one would desire only God but God for the sole interest of one's own happiness, believing that only in him can we find the only instrument of our felicity, would be a love unworthy of God. One would love him as a miser loves his money or as a hedonist loves his pleasure, so that one would see God only in relation to oneself, as a means to an end. This reversal of order would be, according to Saint Francis de Sales, "a sacrilegious love and an unparalleled impiousness."[18] But this love born of pure concupiscence—that is, entirely mercenary—should never be confused with the love that theologians term preferential, which is a love of God commingled with our self-interest in which our own self-interest is always subordinate to the main goal, which is God's glory. Purely concupiscent or mercenary love is a love of oneself rather than a love of God. It may well prepare us for righteousness, inasmuch as it counterbalances our passions and makes us prudent and lets us know where our real treasure lies. But it is against the essential nature of the creature and can only really be a beginning of true interior righteousness.[19] Conversely, preferential love, albeit selfish, can justify the soul provided that self-interest be brought down and subordinated to the dominant love of God and that his glory be the main goal. Thus we prefer God no less sincerely than ourselves or than all other creatures. Nevertheless, this preference does not always have to be explicit, provided that it is real. Because God, who is familiar with the clay from which he molded us and who has pity on his children, only asks for an obvious and well-developed preference in cases where he gives them, by his grace, the courage to endure the trials wherein this preference needs to be explicit.

To speak in these terms is to speak without in any way distancing ourselves from the doctrine of the Council of Trent that preferential love in which the motive of God's glory is the main motive to which our self-interest is subordinate is not a sin. The council condemns those who maintain "that the righteous sin in all their works if, other than the principal desire that God be glorified, they envisage also eternal reward to move them from their lethargy and to encourage them to run the good race."[20] To speak in this manner is to speak like Saint Francis de Sales and like all the Scholastics seconded by the mystics.

FALSE

All selfish love, or love mixed with self-interest concerning our eternal happiness, even if brought in line with and subordinate to the main motive of God's glory, is a love unworthy of him. The souls imbued with this love need to cleanse themselves of it as of real filth or sin. One cannot even use concupiscent or mercenary love to prepare sinful souls for conversion, suspending therein their passions and their habits in order to put them into a state to listen tranquilly to the words of faith.

To speak in this way is to contradict the formal decision of the holy Council of Trent, which declares that mixed love wherein the motive of God's glory dominates is not a sin. Moreover, speaking thus is to go against the experience of all the holy pastors who often see solid conversions prepared in advance by concupiscent love and by purely servile fear.

Article II

TRUE

There are three different degrees, or three habitual sorts of the righteous on earth. Those of the first bear a preferential love for God, since they are justified, but this love, although principal and dominant, is still mixed with fear for their own self-interest. Those of the second sort are in even more of a state of preferential love, but this love, although principal and dominant, is still mixed with hope for their self-interest. This is why Saint Francis de Sales says that "holy resignation still harbors selfish desires, but they are controlled."[21] These two loves are comprised in the fourth, which I have termed selfish love in my definitions. Those in the third group of Christians, incomparably more perfect than the other two sorts of justified Christians, have an entirely selfless love that has been termed pure, to define it as being without any mixture of any other motive other than that of loving God's beauty in and for itself. This is what all the early fathers meant by speaking of three states. The first is that of the righteous who are still fearful due to the remnants of a spirit of slavery. The second is that of those who are still anxious for their own self-interest due to the remnant of a mercenary spirit. The third group comprises those who deserve to be called children of God *because they love the Father without any selfish motive, either of hope or of fear.*[22] This is what the authors of the last few centuries have expressed; it is exactly the same under other equivalent terms. They have listed three states. The first is the purgative life, in which one struggles against vices with a love commingled with a selfish motive of fear regarding eternal suffering. The second is the illuminative life, in which one acquires fervent virtue born of a love still commingled with the selfish motive of heavenly bliss. Finally, the third is the contemplative, or unitive, life, in which one is united with God by the peaceful exercise of pure love. In this last state one never loses either filial fear of the Lord or hope, characteristic of God's children, although one does lose all selfish motives of fear and hope.

Fear perfects itself by the process of purifying itself. It becomes a refinement of love and a serene, filial reverence. So, it is a chaste fear that remains from age to age. Similarly, hope—far from being lost—is perfected by love's purity. Thus, it is a real desire and a sincere expectation of promises fulfilled, not only in a general and absolute manner, but also promises being fulfilled in us and for us according to God's good pleasure and for the sole motive of his good pleasure, without mixing with it our self-interest. This pure love is not content with not wanting any reward apart from God himself. Any mercenary person, even a purely mercenary person, who might have a faith distinct from revealed truths could conceivably not want any reward other than God alone because he would understand clearly that God is infinite good, being himself alone a true reward and, indeed, the only instrument of happiness. This mercenary person would desire in future life only God alone, but he would want God as an objective beatitude or object of his happiness in order to use God as a means of formal blessing, that is to say, to bring him to himself to make himself blessed, his own beatitude being, therefore, his ultimate goal. On the other hand, he who loves with a pure love without any mixture of self-interest is no longer compelled by the motive of his own interest. He would desire beatitude for himself only because he knows that God also desires this, and that he wants each of us to desire it also for his glory. If, imagining an impossible case,[23] given God's purely gracious promises, in which God would wish to annihilate the souls of the righteous at the moment of their corporal death, or seek to deprive them of his vision and keep them eternally in the temptations and miseries of this life, as Saint Augustine postulates, or even would wish to have them suffer far from him the pains of hell for all eternity, as Saint John Chrysostom postulates, following Saint Clement, the souls who are in the third state of pure love would neither love God less nor serve him with any less faithfulness. Again, it is true that this supposition is impossible because of God's promises, because he gave himself to us as a Rewarder.[24] We can thus no longer separate our beatitude from our love of God, persevering to the end, but things that cannot be separated with respect to the object can very well be separated with respect to motives. God cannot fail to be the beatitude of the faithful soul, but the soul can love him with such selflessness that the beatific vision of God would not increase in any way the love she bears him without any thought for herself, and the soul would love him just as much even if God were never to be her beatitude. To say that this precise definition of motives is a vain subtlety would be to show ignorance of God's jealousy and that of the saints against themselves. It would be to define as vain subtlety the refinement and perfection of pure love that the tradition of all the ages has put in this very precision of motives.

To speak this way is to speak precisely like the general tradition of Christianity, from the earliest fathers up to Saint Bernard; like all the most famous Scholastic doctors, from Saint Thomas up to those of our century; finally, like all the canonized and approved mystics from throughout the church, in spite of the accusations they have endured. There is nothing more obvious in the church than this tradition and nothing would be more rash than to combat it or to attempt to evade it. This supposition of the impossible case that was just mentioned above, far from being an indiscreet or dangerous one coming from recent mystics, is on the contrary formally found in Saint Clement of Alexandria, in Cassian, in Saint John Chrysostom, in Saint Gregory Nazianzus, in Saint Anselm, and in Saint Augustine—a tradition that a great many saints have followed.

FALSE

There is a love so pure that it does not desire reward, which is God himself. It does not seek the reward in and for itself, although faith teaches us that God wants the reward in us and for us and that he commands us to want it as we want him for his glory. This love takes its selflessness and abnegation to the extreme of being willing to hate God eternally or to stop loving him. It goes to the point of abandoning all filial fear, which is nothing more than the refinement of jealous love. This love goes so far as to stifle in us all hope inasmuch as the purest hope is a peaceful desire to receive in us and for us, without any mixture of self-interest, the effect of God's promises made to us according to his good pleasure and for his pure glory. Again, this love goes as far as having us hate ourselves with a real hate so that we cease to love God's work in ourselves and his image as we love him by charity in our fellow man.

To speak this way is to give, by means of a horrible blasphemy, the name of pure love to a brutal and impious despair and to a hate of the Creator's handiwork. With monstrous extravagance it is to want the principle of conformity to God to set us against him. It is to desire, by means of an illusory, chimerical love, to destroy love itself. It is, indeed, to erase Christianity from our hearts.

Article III

TRUE

We must let souls exercise love still mixed with the motive of their own self-interest for as long as grace's influence leaves them therein. We must even revere these motives, which are scattered throughout all the books of holy scripture, in all the most precious monuments of tradition, and in all the church's prayers. We must use the motives to repress passions, to strengthen all virtues, and to detach souls from all that the present life entails.

This love, although less perfect than that which is totally selfless, has nevertheless formed a great number of saints throughout the ages. Most holy souls never manage to achieve love's perfect selflessness in this life. It would upset them and lead them into temptation to remove from them any possibility of self-interest as a motive. This motive being subordinate to love upholds them and strengthens them in dangerous occasions. It is useless and tactless to propose to them a higher love, which they cannot attain because they have neither the inner wisdom nor the attraction of grace. Even those who have either the wisdom or grace's attraction are still yet infinitely far from experiencing the reality of this love. And those who experience an imperfect reality of this love are very far from having the consistent exercise of it or enjoying the habitual state of it.

What is imperative in spiritual direction is only to have the penitent[25] follow grace step by step with infinite patience, caution, and delicacy. *It is necessary to limit oneself to letting God act and to never encourage pure love except when God by the workings of an inner anointing begins to open a heart to this word, which is so harsh to souls still attached to themselves and so liable to scandalize them or to cast them into anxiety.*[26] One should not remove from the penitent the support that selfish motives bring even when, following the evolving workings of grace, one begins to show him pure love. It is sufficient to show him on certain occasions how lovable God is in himself without turning the soul away from having recourse to the support conferred by mixed love.

To speak in this manner is to speak as the spirit of grace and the experience of interior paths will always have us speak. It is to put souls on guard against error.

FALSE

Selfish love is a base love, vulgar and unworthy of God—a love that noble souls should scorn. One must hasten to cause them to feel disgust for it and to have them aspire—from the outset of spiritual direction—to a totally selfless love.

One must take from them any motives of fear of death, of God's judgment, or of hell, which is only fitting for slaves. One must remove their desire for their heavenly home and repress all selfish motives of hope. After having had them taste of totally selfless love, one must assume that they now have both the attraction and the grace. One must distance them from all practices that are not in keeping with the perfection of this totally pure love.

To speak this way is to show ignorance of the ways of God and the operations of his grace. It is to want the Holy Spirit to blow where we desire rather than where he pleases. It is to confuse the different degrees of the interior life. It is to inspire in souls the spiritual ambition and avarice of which blessed John of the Cross speaks.[27] It is to distance them from the true simplicity of pure love, which is content to follow grace without attempting to anticipate it. It is to turn to scorn the foundations of Christian righteousness; I mean by that the fear of the Lord that is the beginning of wisdom and the hope by which we are saved.

Article IV

TRUE

In the habitual state of the most pure love, hope, far from disappearing, is actually perfected and conserves its distinction from charity. (1) The habit of hope remains infused in the soul and it is in conformity to the acts of that virtue which must be produced. (2) The exercise of this virtue always remains distinguished from that of charity. This is how: It is not the variety of the ends that makes the variety or the specificity of virtues. All virtues must have only one goal, although they might be distinguished one from another by true specification. Saint Augustine assures us that "charity alone exercises all virtues and it takes diverse names according to the various objects to which it applies itself."[28] Saint Thomas says that "charity is the form of all virtues," because it puts them all into practice and channels them all to one end: the glory of God.[29] Saint

Francis de Sales, who excluded so decisively and repeatedly all selfish motives from all virtues of perfect souls, followed precisely in the steps of Saint Augustine and Saint Thomas, whom he quoted. They all followed the universal tradition that posits a third degree of justified Christians, who banish all selfish motives from the purity of their love. It is, therefore, part of the constant tradition that we must not seek to find in this state a hope motivated by selfish motives; otherwise this would undo with one hand what has been done with the other. It would be to want to find the motive of self-interest in totally selfless love. We must remember that it is not the variety of ends or of motives that makes the distinction or specification of virtues. What makes the distinction is the diversity of formal objects. So hope may remain truly distinguished from charity. Now, the fact is that in the habitual state of the most selfless love the two formal objects of these two virtues remain very different. Therefore, these two virtues conserve in this state a real distinction and specificity in all Scholastic rigor. The formal object of charity is God's goodness or beauty considered simply and absolutely in itself without any idea that relates to us. The formal object of hope is God's goodness, defined as good for us and difficult to acquire. Now, it happens that these two objects, considered with the most rigorous precision and following their formal concept, are very different. The difference of the objects conserves the distinction or specificity of these two virtues. It is an immutable fact that God, inasmuch as he is perfect in himself and without relation to me, and God, defined as my possession that I want to try to acquire, are two very different formal objects. There is no confusion regarding the object that specifies the virtues; there is only confusion regarding the goal, and this confusion must remain. It alters nothing regarding the specification of virtues.

The only difficulty that remains is to explain how a totally selfless soul can want God, God being defined as her possession. Is this not, one might say, to fall short of selflessness's perfection? Is this not to backtrack in the way of God and to return to a motive of self-interest in spite of the tradition of the saints from all centuries who bar from the third state of the righteous any selfish motive? It is easy to answer that the purest love does not prevent us from wanting—indeed, it would have us to want positively—all that God wants us to desire. God wants me to want him inasmuch as he is my property, my treasure, my happiness, and my reward. I want him certainly, given this precise and nuanced understanding, but I do not want him only for the precise motive of his being my treasure. The object and the motive are different. The object is my self-interest, but the motive is not selfish because it is a question of God's good pleasure. I want this formal object and this "reduplication" (to quote the Scholastics),[30] but I want him in obedience and in conformity to his will that would have me want him. The formal object is the hope common to all the righteous. And it is the formal object that specifies virtues. The end is the same as that of charity, but we have seen that the unity of the goal never confuses virtues. I can doubtless want my sovereign good, inasmuch as it is my sovereign good, inasmuch as it is my reward and not another's, and want it in conformity to God, who wants me to want it. So, I want what is really—and what I know to be—in my greatest interest without any selfish motive determining my decision. In this state hope remains distinguished from charity without altering the purity of selflessness of its state. It is what Saint Francis de Sales explained in these words that are so theologically precise: "It is a very different thing to say 'I love God for myself' than to say 'I love God for love of myself.' The former is the holy affection of the bride; the latter is an unparalleled impiousness."[31]

To speak in this manner is to conserve the distinction of the theological virtues in the most perfect states of the interior life and consequently not to depart in any way from the Council of Trent's doctrine. At the same time, it is to explain the tradition of the fathers, the Scholastic doctors, and the holy mystics who posited a third degree of the righteous who are in a habitual state of pure love without any motive of self-interest.

FALSE

In this third degree of perfection a soul no longer desires her salvation as salvation, God as sovereign good, or reward as reward, although God wants us to have this desire. It follows that in this state one can no longer perform any act of true hope as distinguished from charity. That is, one can no longer desire or expect the effect of God's promises in and for oneself.

To speak thusly is to define perfection as the formal resistance to the will of God who desires our salvation and who wants us to want it as well as our own reward for his glory. At the same time it is to confuse the exercise of the theological virtues, opposing the decision of the Council of Trent.

Article V

TRUE

There are two different states among justified souls. The first is holy resignation. The resigned soul wants or would like several things for herself due to the motive of self-interest. Saint Francis de Sales says that "this soul still has selfish desires but they are tamed."[32] She represses and subordinates her own selfish desires to God's will, which she prefers to her own self-interest. In so doing this resignation is good and meritorious. The second state is that of holy indifference. *The indifferent soul no longer seeks anything for herself from motives of her own self-interest.*[33] She no longer has selfish desires to repress because she no longer harbors any selfish desire. It is true that she still has involuntary inclinations and aversions that she suppresses, but *she no longer has voluntary or deliberate desires for her self-interest except in occasions where she does not cooperate faithfully with all grace given to her.*[34] This indifferent soul, when she has recourse to grace, no longer wants anything except for God alone and in the way that God wants her to want him by this attraction.

She loves, it is true, several things apart from God, but she only loves them for the love of God alone and the love of God himself; for it is God that she loves in all that he has her to love. Holy indifference is nothing more than the selflessness of love, as holy resignation is only selfish love that submits self-interest to God's glory. Indifference always spreads as far and never farther than love's perfect selflessness. As indifference is love itself, it is a very real and positive principle. It is a formal and positive will that makes us really want or desire all that God wills that is known to us. This is not a benumbed indolence, an inner inaction, a lack of will, a general suspension, a perpetual equilibrium of the soul. On the contrary, it is a positive and constant determination to want and to want nothing, as Cardinal Bona says.[35] *One desires nothing for oneself but one wants everything for God. One wants nothing in order to be perfect or blessed, for one's own self-interest. But one wants total perfection and beatitude insofar as it pleases God to have us want these things, by the imprint of his grace,*[36] following his written law, which is always our inviolable rule. *In this state we no longer want salvation for the sake of salvation, as an eternal deliverance, as a reward for our merits, as the greatest of our interests, but we want it with our full will, like the glory and good pleasure of God—as a thing that he wants and that he wants us to want for his sake.*[37]

It would be a flagrant extravagance to refuse, from motive of pure love, to seek the blessings that God wants to give us and that he commands us to want. Even the most selfless love must want what God wants for us, as he wants this for our neighbor. The absolute determination on our part to desire nothing would no longer be selflessness but rather the extinction of love that is a true desire and will. It would not be holy indifference either, for indifference is the state of the soul equally willing to want or not want. That is, to want all God wants for his sake, and never to want for oneself that which God does not want. Instead, that senseless willfulness in wanting nothing is an impious resistance to all God's wishes made known to us and to all the workings of his grace. It is therefore an easy misunderstanding to clear up to say that we do not desire our own salvation. We want it fully, as it is God's will. It would be a horrible blasphemy to reject it in this sense, and we must always speak of this matter with a great deal of caution. It is only true that we do not desire it insofar as it is only our reward, our property, and our treasure. It is in this sense that Saint Francis de Sales said, "If more of God's good pleasure were found in hell, the saints would leave heaven to go there."[38] And elsewhere, "The desire for eternal life is good but we must only desire God's will."[39] And again, "If we could serve God without gaining merit we should want to do so."[40]

Elsewhere he says: "Indifference is higher than resignation, for indifference loves nothing except inasmuch as it is for God's will. For nothing leaves the heart indifferent in the presence of God's will. The indifferent heart is like a ball of wax in God's hands, malleable to all the impressions of his good and eternal will. It is a heart without choice, equally willing to accept anything without any other object of its will than the will of its God, and which does not put its love in things that God wants but rather in the will of God that wants them."[41] Elsewhere he says, speaking of Saint Paul and Saint Martin, "They see heaven open for them; they see a thousand tasks on earth. One and the other are the same to them and only God's will can weigh in the balance of their hearts."[42] He says later on, "If he knew that his damnation were more pleasing to God than his salvation, he would leave his salvation and would run to his damnation."[43] He speaks elsewhere thus, "It is not only required for us to rest in divine providence with respect to temporal things but much more for that which belongs to our spiritual life and our perfection."[44]

Elsewhere he says, "Whether it be for things concerning the interior or whether it be for things concerning the exterior, desire only what God would want for you."[45] Finally, he says in another passage: "I have practically no desires but if I were to be born again I would not have any at all. If God came to me, I would go to him also. If he did not want to come to me, I would remain where I was and not go to him." The other saints of recent centuries who are authorized throughout the church are full of similar expressions. These expressions all amount to saying that one no longer has any selfish or egocentric desires concerning either merit or perfection or eternal life.

To speak in this manner is to leave no misunderstanding in a matter so delicate that no ambiguity should ever be allowed. It is to anticipate any abuses that could be made out of the most precious and holiest thing that is on earth; by that I mean, pure love. It is to speak like all the fathers, like all the principal Scholastic doctors, and like all the holy mystics.

FALSE

Holy indifference is an absolute suspension of the will, a total non-will, an exclusion of all desire, even selfless. This indifference goes farther than the perfect selflessness of love. It does not want for us the eternal rewards that the written law teaches us God wants to give us and that he wants us to want to receive in us for the sake of his glory. All desire, even the most selfless, is imperfect. Perfection consists in not wanting anything any longer, in no longer wanting not only God's gifts but even God himself. It consists in letting God act in us however it pleases him, without our contributing for our part any real or positive will.

To speak in this way is to confound all ideas of human reason. It is to put an illusory perfection in an absolute extinction of Christianity and even of humanity. One cannot find terms odious enough to describe such a monstrous extravagance.

Article VI

TRUE

Holy indifference, which is only the selflessness of love, far from excluding selfless desires, is the real and positive principle of all selfless desires that scripture commands us to fulfill and all those that grace inspires in us. It is thus that Daniel was called the man of desires. It is thus that the Psalmist said to God, "All my desires are before your eyes."[46] Not only does the indifferent soul fully desire her salvation, inasmuch as it is God's good pleasure; but also perseverance, amendment of faults, the increase of love by the increase of grace and, generally without any exception, all spiritual and even temporal goods that are, in the order of Providence, a preparation of the means for our salvation and that of our neighbor. Holy indifference admits not only distinct desires and express requests for the fulfillment of all God's wishes known to us, but also general desires for all God's wishes that we do not know.

To speak thus is to speak according to the true principles of holy indifference and in conformity with the feelings of the saints whose terminology, when examined closely by what precedes and what follows, amounts to this pure and healthy explanation in faith.

FALSE

Holy indifference does not admit of any distinct desire or any formal request for any good thing either spiritual or temporal, regardless of whatever relation it may have to our salvation or that of our neighbor. We must never accept any of the pious and edifying desires to which, in ourselves, we find ourselves leaning.

To speak this way is to oppose God's will under the pretext of being more purely obedient to it. It is to violate the written law that commands us to have desires, although it does not order us to form them in a selfish manner, or an anxious or even always distinct manner. It is to stifle true love by a senseless refinement; it is to condemn with blasphemy the words of scripture and the prayers of the church, which are full of requests and desires. It is to excommunicate oneself and put oneself beyond the means of ever being able to pray either from the heart or with the mouth in a gathering of the faithful.

Article VII

TRUE

There is no state either of indifference or of perfection known in the church that gives to souls a miraculous or extraordinary inspiration. The perfection of interior paths only consists in a path of true love that loves God without any interest and of pure faith wherein one only walks in shadows, without any light save that of the same faith that is common to all Christians. This darkness of pure faith admits of no extraordinary light. It is not that God, who is master of his gifts, cannot give ecstasies, visions, revelations, or inner communications. But they do not belong to the path of pure faith. The saints teach us that we should not voluntarily tarry with these extraordinary phenomena but rather to go beyond them, as blessed John of the Cross says, and to remain in the barest and most obscure faith. All the more so should we be sure not to suppose any miraculous intervention in the paths of which we are speaking, or any extraordinary intervention by means of which indifferent souls direct themselves. They should have as their rule only the precepts and the counsels of the written Law and actual grace, which is always in conformity with the Law. With respect to the Law, they must always presuppose, without hesitating or reasoning, that God abandons no one if God has not been already abandoned by him. Consequently, prevenient grace always inspires them to fulfill the Law in cases where it should be fulfilled. Thus it is for the soul to cooperate in all the force of her will to not come short of grace by a transgression of the Law. In the cases where counsel does not turn into precept, they should without constraint perform acts either of love in general or of certain distinct virtues in particular, following the inclination of grace's inner workings—to this or that act according to the circumstance. What is certain is that grace prepares them for each deliberate action. Grace, which is the inner breath of God's Spirit, inspires them therefore in each occasion. This inspiration is only that which is common to all the righteous and does not ever exempt them in any way from the full measure of the written Law. This inspiration is only stronger and more special in the souls raised up to the level of pure love than it is in those souls who only have selfish love, because God communicates more with the perfect than with the imperfect. Therefore, when some holy mystics have allowed certain inspired desires and have rejected others, we must be sure not to believe that they intended to exclude the desires and other acts commanded by the written Law and to allow only those inspired in an extraordinary manner. This would be to blaspheme against the Law and at the same time to raise above the Law a fanatical inspiration. The desires and other inspired acts that the saints meant to speak about are those that the Law commands or those that the scriptural counsels approve and which are formed in an indifferent and selfless soul by the inspiration of grace, always prevenient, without any selfish zeal of the soul acting therein to anticipate grace. Thus, everything comes back to the letter of the Law and to the prevenient grace of pure love, with which the soul cooperates without anticipating.

To speak in this way is to explain the true sense of the good mystics. It is to clear away all ambiguity that might seduce some and scandalize others. It is to forewarn souls against all that is suspect of illusion. It is to "hold fast to the form of sound words," as Saint Paul recommends.[47]

FALSE

Souls already established in holy indifference no longer experience any desire, even selfless, that the written Law obliges them to have. They must no longer desire any but those things that miraculous or extraordinary inspiration leads them to desire—

without any dependence on the Law. They are motivated by God and taught by him about everything so that God alone desires in them and for them without their having to cooperate therein with free will. Their holy indifference, which eminently contains all desires, dispenses these souls from ever forming any. Their inspiration is their only rule.

To speak thus is to evade all precepts and all counsels under the pretext of fulfilling them in the most eminent way. It is to establish a sect of impious fanatics in the church. It is to forget that Jesus Christ came into the world, not to abolish the Law or to diminish its authority, but rather to fulfill its authority and to perfect it in such a manner that heaven and earth shall pass away before the Savior's words, pronounced to confirm the Law, pass away. Finally, it is to grossly contradict all the best mystics and to overthrow from one end to the other their entire system of pure faith, which is manifestly incompatible with miraculous or extraordinary inspiration that a soul would voluntarily follow as her rule and her support in order to avoid fulfilling the Law.

Article VIII

TRUE

Holy indifference, which is nothing but the selflessness of love, becomes in the most extreme trials what the holy mystics have named abandonment. That is, the selfless soul gives herself totally and without reservation to God for everything touching her own self-interest, but she never renounces either love or any of the things that interest the glory and the good pleasure of the Beloved. *This abandonment is only the abnegation or renouncing of self that Jesus Christ asks of us in the gospel after we have left everything else behind. This abnegation of ourselves is only for self-interest* and must never prevent selfless love that we owe to ourselves as to our neighbor for the love of God.[48] *Extreme trials in which this abandonment must be exerted are the temptations by which our jealous God wants to purify love, having love see no resource or hope for its own self-interest, even an eternal one.*[49] These trials are represented by a great number of saints as a terrible purgatory that can exempt souls suffering with total faithfulness from the purgatory of the afterlife. Cardinal Bona assures us that it is only "senseless and impious people who refuse to believe these secret and sublime things and to scorn them as false, although they are not clear, when they are witnessed to by men of very venerable virtue who speak about their own experience of what God does in our hearts."[50] These trials last only for a time. The more faithful souls are to grace, letting themselves be purified of all self-interest by a jealous love, the shorter these trials are. Usually it is a secret resistance of souls to grace under specious, fair-sounding pretexts, it is their harried and selfish effort to keep the sensual supports of which God wants to deprive them that makes their trails so long and painful, for God does not have his creature suffer for the sake of suffering, without any benefit. It is only to purify us and conquer our resistance. Temptations that cleanse love of all self-interest are not like other common temptations. Experienced spiritual directors can discern them by definite traits. But nothing is so dangerous as to consider temptations common to beginners as trials having as their goal the total purification of love in the most eminent souls. This is the source of all error. This is what makes misguided souls fall into frightful vices. We, therefore, should only assume these extreme trials in a very small number of very pure and mortified souls, in whom the flesh has for a long time been entirely in submission to the spirit and who have solidly practiced all the evangelical virtues. These must be humble and innocent souls who are prepared to make public confession of their misery. These must be souls that are docile to the point of never voluntarily hesitating about any of the harsh and humiliating things that one might demand of them. They must be souls unattached to any consolation or any liberty. They must be detached from everything, even the path that teaches them this detachment. They must be willing to engage in all the practices that one would wish to impose on them. They must make no account of any form of prayer, or experiences, or readings, or persons that they formerly consulted with confidence. Their temptations must be tested to make sure that they are of a different nature than common temptations, inasmuch as the real means of calming them is to not want to find any visible support for their self-interest therein.

To speak in this way is to repeat word for word the experiences that the saints have recounted themselves. It is, at the same time, to anticipate the dangerous disadvantages in which one might fall by credulity if one admitted too easily in practice these trials that are very rare because there are very few souls that have reached this stage of perfection, at which there is nothing more to purify, where the vestiges of self-interest are commingled with divine love.

FALSE

Interior trials remove forever physical, visible, and tangible graces. They suppress forever distinct acts of love and virtues. They put the Christian in a real and absolute incapacity to open up to his superiors or to obey them with respect to the essential practice of the gospel. They cannot be distinguished from common temptations. In this state one can hide from one's superiors, evade obedience, and seek in books and people without authority the relief and the wisdom that one needs, even if ecclesiastical superiors forbid it.

The director can assume that the penitent is undergoing these trials without having thoroughly tested the state of the penitent's soul concerning docility, mortification, or humility. He can right away have this Christian soul purge himself of all self-interest in temptation, without having him perform any act in his own self-interest to resist the temptation that presses upon him.

To speak in this manner is to poison souls. It is to remove from them weapons of faith necessary to resist the Enemy of our salvation. It is to mix up all of God's ways. It is to teach rebellion and hypocrisy to the children of the church.

Article IX

TRUE

A soul that during extreme trials abandons herself to God is never abandoned by him. If she asks, in the throes of her agony, to be delivered, God only refuses to answer this prayer because he wants to perfect her courage in weakness and to show that his grace is sufficient to her. She loses, in this state, neither the true and complete power to fulfill the laws, nor that of following the most perfect counsels according to her vocation and her present degree of perfection, nor the real, interior acts of her free will to fulfill these things. She loses neither prevenient grace nor explicit faith nor hope, insofar as hope is a selfless desire for God's promises. Nor does she lose her love of God or hatred of sin—even venial—or the intimate and momentary certainty, which is necessary for the rectitude of conscience. She only loses the physical taste for goods, only the fervid and selfish acts of virtue, only the consoling and affectionate fervor, only the certainty that comes after the fact and by selfish reflection gives one a comforting witness of its fidelity. These direct acts, which escape the soul's notice but are very real and which conserve in her all spotless virtues, are—as I have already said—the operation that Saint Francis de Sales has named the height of the spirit and the peak of the soul.[51] This troubled and dark state that is only for a time is not without peaceful intervals during which certain glimmerings of grace are like bolts of lightning against a dark, stormy night sky, leaving no trace behind them.

To speak thus is to follow Catholic dogma and the experiences of the holy mystics.[52]

FALSE

In these extreme trials a soul, without having previously been unfaithful to grace, loses the true and full power to persevere in her state. She falls into a real impotence, incapable of fulfilling the laws in the cases where the laws press upon her. She ceases to have explicit faith in cases where faith must act explicitly. She ceases to hope, that is, to expect and even to desire in a selfless manner the effect of God's promises in herself. She no longer has a love of God, either perceptible or imperceptible. Nor does she have any longer a hatred of sin; indeed, she loses not only the tangible and well-considered hatred of it but also the most direct and intimate hatred of sin. She no longer has any immediate and intimate certainty that can preserve the rectitude of her conscience when she acts. All the acts of the virtues essential to the interior life cease, even in their most direct and least reflective operations, which is—according to the language of the holy mystics—the height of the mind and the peak of the soul.

To speak thus is to destroy Christian piety under the pretext of perfecting it. It is to make out of trials destined to purify love a complete shipwreck of Christian faith and virtue. It is to utter that which the Christian faithful, nourished by the words of faith, should never hear without stopping up their ears.

Article X

TRUE

God's promises concerning eternal life are purely free.[53] Grace is never owed to us; otherwise it would not be grace. God never owes us either final perseverance or eternal happiness after our corporal death. Nor does he owe to our soul the right to exist after this life. He could let her fall back into her nothingness from her own weight.[54] If it were otherwise, God would not be free to determine the duration of his creature, and it would become a necessary being. But although God never owes us anything as an obligation, he has deigned to give us rights founded in his purely free promises. By these promises he has given himself as a supreme blessing to the soul that is faithful to him with perseverance. It is true, therefore, in this sense, that any hypothesis supposing one is excluded from eternal life from loving God is an impossible one because God is faithful in his promises. He never desires the death of the sinner,[55] but rather desires that he live and be converted. *By this, it is evident that all the sacrifices that the most selfless souls make ordinarily for their eternal beatitude are conditional.*[56] We say, "My God, if by an impossible supposition, you should want me to be condemned to eternal torment in hell without thereby losing your love, I would not love you any less." *But this sacrifice cannot be absolute in our ordinary state. There is only the case of the final trials in which this sacrifice becomes in some sense absolute.*[57] *So, a soul can be invincibly persuaded, with a well thought-out persuasion and not one of the intimate depths of the conscience, that she is rightly damned by God.*[58] Saint Francis de Sales was feeling this way when he found himself in the church of Saint Etienne-des-Grez.[59] A soul in this state of anxiety sees herself opposed to God on account of her past infidelities and her present hardness of heart, which seem to her to fill to the brim the cup of her damnation. She sees her inclinations to evil as deliberate desires, and she does not see at all the real acts of her love or her virtues, which, by their extreme simplicity, escape her reflection. She becomes in her own eyes covered with the leprosy of sin, albeit imaginary and not real. She cannot stand herself. She is scandalized by those who try to calm her down and take away this idea from her. There is no use trying to explain to her the precise dogma of faith concerning God's wish to save all humankind or about the belief that we should all hold, that God wishes to save each of us in particular. This soul does not question God's benevolent will, but she believes her own will evil because she sees in herself only the apparent evil that is exterior and tangible and not the good that is always real and intimate but is hidden from her eyes by God's jealousy. In the midst of the involuntary and invincible anxiety nothing can reassure her or show her in her inner self whatever it pleases God to keep hidden from her.[60] She sees God's anger enormous and hanging over her head like the waves of the sea, ever ready to submerge her. *It is at this point that the soul is conflicted. She dies on the cross with Jesus Christ, saying, "O my God, my God, why hast thou forsaken me?"*[61] *In this involuntary gesture of despair, she makes the absolute sacrifice of her own self-interest for the sake of eternity* because the impossible case seems to her to be possible and real at the present moment especially in the troubled and dark state in which she finds herself.[62] Once more, it is not here a question of reasoning with her, for she is incapable of being reasoned with. It is only a question of a conviction that is not intimate but that is apparent and insuperable. *In this state a soul loses all hope of her own self-interest, but she does not ever lose in the higher part, that is, in her direct and intimate acts, the perfect hope that is the selfless desire to have God's promises fulfilled.*[63] She loves God more purely than ever. Far from being willing to hate him, she does not even indirectly agree to cease loving him for one instant or to lessen in any degree her love or ever to put any voluntary limits to the growth of that love or to commit any sin, even venial. *A spiritual director can then allow this soul to acquiesce in a simple loss of her own self-interest and in the righteous condemnation that she believes to be from God.*[64] This usually serves to put her in a tranquil state and to calm temptations, and is destined only for that effect—I mean, for the purification of love. But a penitent should never be counseled or permitted by a spiritual director to believe positively by a voluntary and free persuasion that he is damned and that he should no longer desire the fulfillment of God's promises by a selfless desire. Even less should the spiritual director allow his penitent to be willing to hate God or to stop loving him or to break his Law, even by the most venial sins.

To speak thus is to speak according to the experiences of the saints, with all the precaution necessary to preserve the dogma of the faith and to not expose Christians to any error.

FALSE

The soul that is undergoing trials can believe with an intimate persuasion, free and voluntary, contrary to the dogma of faith, that God has abandoned her without being abandoned by her, or that there is no more mercy for her, however sincerely she might desire it, or that she may consent to hate God because God wishes for her to hate him, or that she might consent to no longer love God because he no longer wishes to be loved by her, or that she might put voluntary limits on her love because God wishes her to set such limits, or that she might break his laws because he wishes for her to break them. In this state a soul no longer has faith or hope or selfless desire for God's promises, or any real and intimate love of God, or any hate—even implicit—of the evil that is sin, or any cooperation with grace. She is passive, without action, without will, without any interest for God or for herself, without acts of virtue either meditative or direct.

To speak in this way is to blaspheme about subjects of which one is ignorant and to be corrupted in what one knows. It is to lead souls into temptation under the pretext of purifying them of it. It is to reduce all Christianity to an impious and stupid despair. It is even to contradict all the good mystics who assure us that Christians in this state show a very lively love of God by the regret of having lost him and an infinite horror of evil by the impatience with which they often put up with those who try to console and reassure them.[65]

Article XI

TRUE

God never abandons the righteous individual without having been abandoned by him. He is the infinite Good that only seeks to communicate itself to us. The more we receive him, the more he gives of himself. It is only due to our resistance alone that limits or slows his gifts. The essential difference between the new Law and the old[66] is that the former did not lead humanity to anything perfect. The old Law indicated good without giving the wherewithal to accomplish it and evil without giving the wherewithal to avoid it. Conversely, the new Law is the law of grace, which gives the desire to accomplish and the ability, and which only commands that which it gives the power to accomplish. Those who observe the ancient Law were usually assured of not seeing a diminution of their temporal goods: *Inquirentes autem Dominum non minuentur omni bono.*[67] Souls faithful to their grace will never suffer any diminution of their grace itself, which is always prevenient and which is the veritable treasure of Christian law. Thus each soul, in order to be fully faithful to God, can do nothing solid or meritorious except by following grace constantly, without needing to anticipate it. To want to anticipate grace is to want to give oneself that which grace has not yet given. It is to expect something of oneself and of one's efforts or one's work. It is a subtle and imperceptible vestige of a semi-Pelagian zeal at the time that one desires grace the most.[68] It is true that one must prepare oneself to receive grace and to attract it to oneself, but one must only do this by cooperation with grace itself. Faithful cooperation with the grace of the present moment is the most efficacious preparation to receive and to attract grace of the moment that must follow. If we examine the thing up close, it is evident that everything comes down to the question of faithful cooperation with our full will and with all the forces of our soul with grace in every minute. Everything that we might add to that cooperation, understood correctly in all its ramifications, would only be an indiscreet and hasty zeal, an anxious and nervous effort of a soul centered on herself. It would be an excitement ill timed that would upset, would weaken, would retard the workings of grace instead of facilitating them and making grace more perfect. It is as if a man led by another whose impulses he was bound to follow wanted constantly to anticipate these impulses and to turn around at any given moment to see how far he had traveled. This movement, anxious and ill conceived with the main engine, would only slow down and encumber the two men in their race. It is the same with the righteous man in the hand of God. God moves him constantly with divine grace. All hurried and anxious excitement that anticipates grace for fear of not acting enough, all hurried excitation outside of the case of the Law to give oneself by an excess of selfish precaution the dispositions that grace does not inspire in these moments, because grace inspires others that are less comforting and less perceptible, all hurried and anxious excitation to give oneself, as by obvious jolts, a more noticeable movement, a movement of which one can instantly give a selfish witness, these are defective excitations for souls called to the peaceful selflessness of perfect love.[69] This worried and harried action is what good mystics have termed activity, which has nothing in common with action or with real, peaceful acts that are essential to cooperate with grace. When they say that we must no longer excite ourselves or make efforts, they only want to curb that anxious and harried excitation with which we want to anticipate grace or recall the physical sensations after they have disappeared or to cooperate with grace in a more sensitive and more marked way than grace asks of us. In this sense excitation or activities must indeed be curbed. But if we understand by excitation a cooperation of our entire will and of all the forces of the soul to grace at any given moment, we must conclude as a matter of faith that we must be moved in each moment to receive all possible grace. This cooperation, even though it is selfless, is no less sincere; even though peaceful, it is no less effective and fully of our voluntary will; even though without anxiety, it is no less painful with respect to the concupiscence that it overcomes. This is not an activity; it is an action that consists in very real and very meritorious acts. It is thus that souls called to pure love resist the temptations of the last trials. They fight tooth and nail against sin, but this struggle is peaceful because the Spirit of God resides in peace. They resist in the presence of God, who is their strength. They resist in a state of faith and love, which is a state of prayer. Those who still need selfish motives of fear and hope should have recourse to them even with some natural eagerness rather than expose themselves to failure. Those who find in an experience, constant and recognized by a good spiritual director, that their force is in affectionate silence and that their peace is in the most bitter bitterness, can continue to conquer temptation in this way. One should not disturb them because they are suffering enough already. But if by a secret infidelity these souls suddenly fell from their state, they would have to seek recourse in the most selfish motives rather than run the risk of breaking God's laws through an excess of temptation.

To speak this way is to speak according to the rule of the gospel without diluting in any way either the experiences or the maxims of all the good mystics.

FALSE

The activity that the saints want us to curb is the action of the will itself. Our will should no longer perform any acts. It no longer needs to cooperate with grace with all its strength or positively and fully to resist concupiscence or to perform any interior or exterior action that might be painful to it. It is sufficient for it to let God act in the will, performing acts that flow as from a stream and for which the will has no repugnance, even a natural one.

The will has no further need to prepare itself by the proper use of grace to an even greater use that should follow and that is tied to the first. The will has only to let itself, without reflection, go down all the slopes that it finds within itself without giving them to itself.[70] No further work should be undertaken, no violence, no constraint of nature. The will has only to remain without will, passive and neutral between good and evil, even in the midst of the most extreme temptations.

To speak thus is to speak the language of the Tempter. It is to teach Christians to hold out traps to themselves. It is to inspire in them indolence in evil that is the height of hypocrisy. It is to lead them into an acceptance of all vices, an acceptance no less real for being indirect and tacit.

Article XII

TRUE

The Christians attracted to pure love can be as selfless for themselves as for the neighbor because they only see and desire in themselves, as in their most distant neighbor, the glory of God, his good pleasure and the fulfillment of his promises. In this sense these souls are as strangers to themselves. They love themselves only as they love the rest of creation in the order of pure charity. It is thus that Adam, while still innocent, doubtless loved himself uniquely for the love of God. The abnegation of oneself and the hate of one's soul recommended in the gospel are not an absolute hate of our soul as the image of God. For God's handiwork is good, and we must love it for love of him. But we corrupt this handiwork by sin, and we should hate ourselves in our corruption. The perfection of pure love consists, therefore, in loving ourselves only for him alone. Vigilance of the most selfless Christians must never be directed according to their selflessness. God, who calls them to be as detached from themselves as from their neighbor, wants them at the same time to be more vigilant toward themselves (for whom they are charged with responsibility) than toward their neighbor, for whom God does not hold them responsible.

Indeed, they must keep an eye on what they do each and every day in relation to their neighbor, whose conduct Providence has confided to them. A good pastor keeps watch over the souls of his neighbor without regard to self-interest. He loves only God in his neighbor. He never loses sight of him. He consoles him. He corrects him. He supports him. It is in this manner that we must support ourselves without flattering ourselves and we must correct ourselves without letting ourselves be discouraged. We must be charitable with ourselves as with others, only forgetting ourselves in order to curb the spite and delicacies or self-interest; forgetting ourselves only to want not to please ourselves; forgetting ourselves only to curb the anxious and self-centered meditations when we are entirely in a state of pure love's grace. But it is never permissible to forget oneself to the point of ceasing to keep watch over oneself as we would keep watch over our neighbor if we were his pastor. It is necessary to add to this that we are never so charged with responsibility of our neighbor as we are of ourselves, because we cannot control all the inner will of another as we can of our own. Whence it follows that we must always keep an incomparably greater watch over ourselves than the best pastor can keep watch over his flock. We must never forget ourselves in order to curb even the most selfish meditations if we are still in the path of selfish love. Finally, we must never forget ourselves to the point of rejecting all sorts of reflections as imperfect things. For reflections have nothing imperfect in them per se and they do not become harmful to souls except inasmuch as souls sick with self-interest do not look at themselves except to lose patience or to wallow in self-indulgence. Moreover, God often inspires with his grace, even in the most advanced souls, very useful reflections, either about his plans for them or about his past mercies that he would have them praise, or about the dispositions of which they should give an account to their spiritual director. But, finally, selfless love keeps watch, acts, and resists temptation more than selfish love watches or acts or resists. The sole difference is that the vigilance of pure love is simple and peaceful, in contrast to selfish love, which is less perfect and which always has some remnant of anxiety or worry because it is only perfect love that can banish fear and all its attributes.

To speak in this way is to speak in a correct manner that should not be held suspect by anyone; this follows the language of the saints.

FALSE

A soul totally without self-interest in herself, no longer loves herself even for the love of God. She hates herself with an absolute hate, supposing that the handiwork of the Creator is not good, and she pushes renouncement and abandonment to that point. She carries hate of herself to the point of wanting with a deliberate wish her own damnation and eternal reprobation. She rejects grace and mercy. She only wants justice and vengeance. She becomes such a stranger to herself that she no longer takes any part in either in doing good or avoiding evil. She only wants to forget herself in all things and to lose sight of herself. She is not content with neglecting her own interest;

she wants to neglect herself with respect to correction of her faults as well and the fulfillment of God's Law in the interest of his pure glory. She no longer considers herself charged with responsibility for herself or with the duty of keeping watch over herself even with a simple, peaceful, and selfless vigilance over her own will. She rejects any reflection as imperfect because only direct visions (and not meditative) are worthy of God.

To speak thusly is to contradict the experiences of the saints, whose whole inner lives have been filled with very useful meditations and reflections formed by the impression of grace because they knew after the fact of past graces and the miseries of which God had delivered them and they finally realized the nature of a great many things that had happened in themselves. This is to make an impious hate of our soul from abnegation of self, supposing the soul bad by her nature, following the principles of the Manicheans,[71] reversing the divine order by hating what is good, that which God loves inasmuch as it is fashioned in his image. It is to destroy all vigilance, all faithfulness to grace, all attention to have God reign in us, all good use of our Christian liberty. In a word, it is the height of impiety and of sacrilege.

Article XIII

TRUE

There is a great difference between simple, direct acts and premeditated, well-considered acts. Every time we act with a clean conscience there is in us an intimate certainty of following the right path. Otherwise we would act in doubt of doing right or wrong, and we would not be acting in good faith. But this intimate certainty often consists in acts so simple, so direct, so rapid, so instantaneous, so devoid of all meditation that the Christian who well knows what he is doing at the moment when he does it can no longer find, subsequently, any durable or distinct trace of it. From this it follows that if he wants to reconsider, upon reflection, what he has done, he falls into doubt. He no longer believes that he has done what he was supposed to do; he is troubled by scruples; and he is even scandalized by the indulgence of his superiors when they try to reassure him about what has happened. Thus God gives him, in the instant in which he commits direct acts, all the certainty necessary for the uprightness of his conscience, and God takes from him, by his jealousy, the facility of finding through reflection and after the fact the certainty of this uprightness so that the Christian can neither take solace in it for his consolation nor justify himself in his own eyes. With respect to premeditated acts, they leave behind a durable, fixed trace that one can find whenever one so desires. It is this that causes Christians still having self-interest in themselves to want to perform constantly acts that are clearly distinguished and premeditated in order to assure themselves of their operation and in order to bear witness to them. By contrast, selfless Christians are indifferent as to performing distinct or indistinct acts, direct or premeditated. They perform premeditated acts each time God's laws demands them or whenever grace leads them to perform these acts. But they do not seek out premeditated acts, thereby preferring them to other acts through a selfish anxiety for their own safety. Ordinarily, in the extremity of trials God only grants them direct acts, the traces of which they later cannot perceive. This is what causes the torment and martyrdom of Christian souls, while they have any motive of self-interest remaining in them. These direct and intimate acts, without reflection that leaves any noticeable trace, are what Saint Francis de Sales has called the summit of the soul and the height of the spirit.[72] It is in these acts that Saint Anthony considered the most perfect form of prayer to be found. As he said, "Prayer is not yet perfect when the hermit knows he is praying."[73] To speak thus is to speak according to the experience of the saints, without damaging the rigor of Catholic dogma. It is even to speak of the soul's workings consistent with the ideas of all the best philosophers.

FALSE

There are no real acts except those that are premeditated and that we can feel and that we can perceive. As soon as we no longer perform these types of acts it may truly be said that we no longer perform any real acts. Whosoever does not have, concerning these acts, a well-considered and lasting certainty has never had any certainty in his acts. Whence it follows that Christian souls who are undergoing trials and in apparent despair are indeed in a true despair; the doubt that they are in after having acted shows that they have lost in their actions the intimate witness of conscience.

To speak thus is to overthrow all the precepts of good philosophy. It is to destroy the witness of the Holy Spirit of God in us in order to make us sons of God. It is to annihilate all interior life and all uprightness in Christian souls.

Article XIV

TRUE

It happens that during the final trials leading to the purification of love there is a separation of the superior part of the soul from the inferior inasmuch as the senses and the imagination have no part in the peace and communications of grace that God grants rather often to our understanding and our will in a simple and direct manner that surpasses all meditation or reflection. *It is thus that Jesus Christ, our perfect model, was happy on the cross*[74] inasmuch as he enjoyed heavenly glory through the superior part of his soul while he was still suffering in the inferior part[75] with a physical feeling of rejection by his Father. *The inferior part was not communicating with the superior part either its involuntary anxiety*[76] or its physical weakness. The superior part was not communicating to the inferior part either its peace or its beatitude. *This separation is effected by the difference between the real, albeit simple and direct, acts of the mind's understanding and the will that leave no visible, physical trace behind, and reflective, meditative acts that, leaving a physical trace, communicate themselves to the imagination and the senses, that which we call the inferior part, in order to distinguish them from that direct and intimate operation of the understanding and of the will that we term the superior part. The acts of the inferior part in this separation are of the nature of an entirely blind and involuntary unease because all that is intellectual and voluntary belongs to the superior part.*[77] But, although this separation understood in this sense cannot be absolutely denied, it is necessary nevertheless that spiritual directors take great care not ever to allow in the inferior part any of the disorders that must, in the natural course of things, be supposed voluntary and whose superior part must, consequently, be responsible. This precaution must always be found in the path of pure faith, which is the only one that we are presently discussing, and in which we allow nothing contrary to nature's order. For this reason it is not necessary to speak here of possessions, obsessions, or other extraordinary phenomena. We cannot absolutely reject them since scripture and the church have recognized them, but we must always approach them with an infinite precaution according to each particular case so as not to be deceived by them.[78] Moreover, this subject, common to all the inner paths, presents no particular difficulty that requires explaining regarding the paths of pure faith and pure love. On the contrary, one may maintain that this path of pure love and of pure faith is the one in which we see the fewest examples of these extraordinary phenomena. Nothing lessens them as much as not expecting them and always encouraging Christians to a simple conduct in love's selflessness and in the darkness of faith.[79]

To speak thus is to speak according to Catholic dogma and to furnish the greatest safeguards against heresy and error.

FALSE

During spiritual trials a total separation occurs between the superior part of the soul and the inferior. The superior part is united with God in a union that has in no time any physical or distinct trace for faith or for hope or for love or for the other virtues. The inferior part becomes entirely bestial in this separation, and everything that takes place in this part against the rule of morality must be seen to be neither voluntary nor unworthy of merit nor contrary to the purity of the superior part.

To speak thusly is to destroy the Law and the Prophets; it is to speak the language of the demons.

Article XV

TRUE

Those who are in the midst of rigorous trials should never neglect that universal sobriety of which the apostles so often spoke and which consists in a sober use of all things that surround us.[80] This sobriety extends throughout all the operations of our senses, through all those of imagination, and of the mind itself. This sobriety extends to the point of making our wisdom sober and temperate. It reduces everything to simple use, to necessary use. This sobriety entails a constant privation of all that we would indulge in only for our pleasure. This mortification, or rather this death, seeks to curb not only all voluntary movements of nature corrupted and rebellious by the voluptuousness of the flesh and by the pride of the spirit, but also to curb all those most innocent consolations that selfish love seeks with such ardor. This mortification is practiced in peace and simplicity, without anxiety and without bitterness toward oneself, without method, according to the occasion and the need, but yet followed really and without letting go.[81] It is true that those Christians overwhelmed by an excess of trials usually require, through obedience to an experienced spiritual director, to cease or lessen certain corporal austerities to which they are very attached. This leniency is often necessary in order to sooth their bodies, weakened by the rigor of inner pains that are the most terrible of all penance. It happens even occasionally that these Christians have been too attached to these austerities, and the difficulty that they have in the beginning to obey their director and deprive themselves of the austerities in their weakened state shows that they indeed placed too much importance on them. But it is actually their personal imperfection and not that of the austerities that we must accuse. Austerities according to their institution are useful and sometimes necessary; Jesus Christ gave us the example of them, which example has been followed by all the saints. They beat down rebellious flesh, serving to make up for faults already committed and to preserve us from future temptations. It is true, however, that they only serve to destroy the essence of self-interest or cupidity, which is the root of all vices, or to unite a soul to God inasmuch as they are inspired by the spirit of tranquil retreat, of love, and of prayer, failing which they would only soften the rudest passions and would, against their own purpose, make man full of himself. This would only result in a justice of the flesh.[82] It is still necessary to observe that people in this state, being deprived of all tangible graces and of the fervent exercise of all noticeable virtues, no longer have any taste, or tangible fervor, or noticeable attraction for all these austerities that they had practiced with so much zeal. So, their penance consists in bearing with a very bitter peace the wrath of God that they expect constantly and their obvious despair. There is no austerity or torment that they would suffer with joy and relief in the place of this inner pain. All their intimate longing is to bear their agony where they can say with Jesus on the cross: "My God, my God, why hast thou forsaken me?"[83]

To speak thusly is to recognize the perpetual need for mortification. It is to approve corporal austerities that are, of their institution, very salutary. It is to want the most perfect Christian souls to do penance proportionate to their strength, to their grace, and to the trials of their state.

FALSE

Corporal austerities only incite concupiscence and inspire in the one who practices them the complacency of the Pharisee. They are not necessary either to anticipate or to calm temptations. Tranquil prayer always is sufficient to bend the flesh to the spirit. One may voluntarily end these practices, considering them crude, imperfect and only appropriate for beginners.

To speak thusly is to speak as an enemy of the cross of Jesus Christ. It is to blaspheme against his examples and against all tradition. It is to contradict the Son of God, who says, "And from the days of John the Baptist until now the kingdom of heaven has suffered violence, and men of violence take it by force."[84]

Article XVI

TRUE

There are two sorts of attachment. The first is a sin for all Christians. The second is not a sin, even venial, but only an imperfection by comparison to something else that is more perfect, and this is not even a true imperfection except for those souls currently attracted by grace to the state of love's perfect selflessness. The first attachment is pride. It is a love of one's own excellence inasmuch as it is one's own and without any subordination to our essential end, which is the glory of God. This attachment is that which caused the sin of the first angel, he who was content with himself, as Saint Augustine says, instead of relating to God, and by this simple attachment to himself he did not remain in truth.[85] This attachment is in us more or less a great sin, according to whether it is more or less voluntary. The second attachment, which should never be confused with the first, is a love of our own excellence inasmuch as it is our own, but with subordination to our essential end, which is the glory of God. We only want the most perfect virtues. We want them principally for God's glory, but we want them also in order to derive from them merit and reward. We want them yet for the consolation of becoming perfect. It is the resignation that, as Saint Francis de Sales says, "still has its own desires but tamed."[86] These virtues, which are selfish for the goal of our perfection and our beatitude, are good because they relate to God as their principal goal. But they are less perfect than virtues practiced by holy indifference for the sole glory of God in us, without any other motive of self-interest or for our merit or for our perfection, or for our reward—even eternal.

This motive of spiritual self-interest, which always remains in virtue, while the soul is still in a state of selfish love, is that which the mystics have called property or attachment.[87] This is what blessed John of the Cross calls avarice and spiritual ambition.[88] The soul, which the mystics describe as "proprietary" or "attached to self," gives her virtues to God through holy resignation, and in that is less perfect than the purely selfless soul, which gives virtues to God through holy indifference. This attachment or "property," which is not a sin, is nevertheless called an impurity by the mystics.

That is not to say that it is a stain on the soul, but only to indicate that it is a mixture of various motives that prevent love from being pure and without mixture. They often say that they find this impurity or mixture of selfish motives in their prayer and in their holiest exercises. But we must be very wary of believing that they mean by this any sinful impurity.

When we understand clearly what the mystics mean by *attachment* we can no longer have any difficulty understanding what they mean by the term *detachment*. It is the operation of grace that purifies love and that makes it selfless in the exercise of all virtues. It is by trials that this detachment is known. It causes the loss of all virtues, according to the mystics, but this loss is only apparent and for a limited time. The essence of virtues, far from actually being lost, is in reality only perfected by pure love. The soul is stripped therein of all tangible graces, of all tastes, of all facilities, of all the sources of fervor that could console her and reassure her. She loses methodical and enthusiastic acts in order to bear witness to herself as a self-interested witness concerning her perfection. But she loses neither direct acts of love nor the exercise of distinct virtues in the case of the Law, nor the intimate hatred of evil, nor the instantaneous certainty necessary for the uprightness of conscience, nor the selfless desire of God's promises to have their effect in her. The appearance of her unworthiness alone suffices to create the most rigorous spiritual trial, to remove all noticeable support from her, and to leave no remaining resource to self-interest. Why, therefore, would we want to add any real evil therein, as if God could only perfect his creature by the use of real sin? On the contrary, the soul, provided that she remain faithful in the trials called loss and detachment, suffers no real lessening of her perfection and only grows without ceasing in the inner life. Finally, the soul that is purified through the experience of daily faults, hating her imperfection because it is contrary to God, nevertheless loves the abnegation that comes naturally from it because this abnegation—far from being sin—is on the contrary the humiliation that is the penance and the remedy itself for sin. She sincerely hates all her faults as much as she loves God, the Sovereign Perfection, but she uses her faults to humiliate herself tranquilly and, thereby, "her faults become the windows of the soul through which the light of God enters," according to the terminology of Balthazar Alvarez.[89]

To speak thusly is to develop the true sense of the best mystics. It is to follow a simple system, which is summed up uniquely in the selflessness of love and which is authorized by tradition of all the ages.

FALSE

The attachment of the mystics—that is, selfish love—is a real impurity. It is a stain on the soul. The virtues of this state are not worthy of merit. It is necessary indeed to lose entirely the essence of these virtues. It is necessary for us to cease producing from them the most direct and intimate acts. We must really lose the hatred of sin, the love of God, of virtues distinct from its state in the case of God's laws. We must truly lose the instantaneous certainty necessary for uprightness of conscience and even the selfless desire of God's promises having effect in us. We must love our abjection, so that we really love our sin itself, because it makes us abject and contrary to God. Finally, we must, in order to be entirely pure, strip ourselves of our virtues and make of them a selfless sacrifice to God by voluntary actions that violate his written Law and that are incompatible with these virtues.

To speak thusly is to make of selfish love a sin, contrary to the official decision of the holy Council of Trent. At the same time, it is to strip from Christian souls the garment of innocence and to crush all grace in them under the pretext of "detaching" grace from them. It is to authorize and approve the mystery of iniquity and to renew the impiety of the Gnostics, who also sought to purify themselves by the practice of impurity itself, as Saint Clement of Alexandria teaches us.

Article XVII

TRUE

There is a small number of Christians who are in the midst of these last trials wherein they are finalizing the process of purifying themselves of all self-interest. The remainder of Christian souls, without passing through these trials, still achieve some degree of very real sanctity, sanctity very pleasing to God. Otherwise we would have to define selfish love as nothing more than a Judaic cult—insufficient for eternal life—going against the decision of the holy Council of Trent.[90] The spiritual director must not allow himself easily to suppose that the temptations he sees facing a penitent are extraordinary temptations. We cannot be too wary of an overheated, fervid imagination that exaggerates everything that someone feels, or believes himself to feel. We must be wary of insidious pride, subtle and practically imperceptible, that always tends to flatter the Christian into believing himself a soul divinely guided in an extraordinary manner. Finally, we must be wary of the illusion that insinuates itself in us and would have us finish in the flesh after having begun sincerely with spiritual fervor.[91] It is, therefore, essential to suppose right off that the temptations of a Christian soul are only common temptations whose cure is interior and exterior mortification with all the acts of fear, and all the practices of selfish love.[92] One must be firm in order to allow nothing beyond these traditional practices without a complete conviction that these practices are absolutely useless and that the tranquil and simple exercise of pure love alone can calm temptation. It is in this occasion that delusion and the danger of erratic behavior are acute. If a spiritual director without experience or one too credulous mistakes a common temptation for an extraordinary temptation given for love's purification, he puts a soul at risk; he makes the penitent full of himself; and he casts him into an incurable indolence whence he cannot but fall into vice. To reject selfish motives when we still have need of them is to remove from a child the milk of his nursemaid and kill him cruelly by weaning him at the wrong time. Often Christian souls who are still imperfect and all full of themselves imagine, based on indiscreet readings that are inappropriate for their needs, that they are already in the most rigorous trials of pure love when, in fact, they are only undergoing natural temptations that they have brought on themselves by their debauched, pusillanimous, and sensual lives. The trials we are speaking of here have to do only with souls already consumed in other interior and exterior disciplines and who are not guided by inappropriate readings but by the sole experience of God's guidance on them, guidance that is redolent only of honesty and docility. We are speaking of penitents who are always ready to admit the possibility that they are mistaken and that they must adhere to the common path.[93] These Christian souls are not pacified in the midst of their temptations by any of the ordinary remedies that are the motives of a selfish love, at least while they are in the state of pure love's grace. There is only the faithful cooperation with the grace of this pure love that calms their temptations, and it is thereby that we can distinguish their trials from common trials. Christians who are not in this state inevitably fall into horrible excesses if one attempts to constrain them to perform only the simple acts of pure love against their needs. Those who have a true vocation to pure love will never be pacified by the ordinary practices of selfish love. Who has ever resisted God and found peace? But in order to make such delicate and important identification of souls, we must put them to the test so that we might know if they come from God, and there is only the Spirit of God who can plumb the depths of God.

To speak thusly is to speak with all the prudence and precaution necessary about such a matter wherein one cannot be too cautious, and it is to allow, at the same time, all the teachings of the saints.

FALSE

The simple, peaceful, and uniform exercise of pure love is the only remedy that we should use against all the temptations of the various spiritual states. We should assume that all spiritual trials tend toward the same end and necessitate the same remedy. All the practices of selfish love and all acts motivated by this motive only fill us with love of self, irritate the jealousy of God, and strengthen temptations.

To speak thusly is to mix together everything that the saints have so carefully separated. It is to love seduction[94] and to run after it. It is to push Christian souls off the cliff into the abyss by taking from them all the resources of their present state of grace.

Article XVIII

TRUE

The will of God is always our sole rule, and love is entirely reduced to a will that no longer wants anything except what God wants and would have it want. But there are several sorts of God's will. There is the positive and written will that commands good and forbids evil. That will is the sole invariable rule for our will and for all our voluntary actions. There is a will of God that reveals itself to us by inspiration or attraction of grace, which is found in all the righteous. That will of God must always be supposed to be entirely in conformity with the written will. It is not permissible to believe that this will might require anything of us other that the fulfillment of the precepts and the counsels contained in the divine law. The third will of God is a will of simple permission. It is that which permits sin without approving of it. The same will that permits sin condemns it. This will does not permit sin by actively or positively desiring it but only by allowing it to occur and by not preventing it. This will of permission is never our rule. It would be impious to desire our sin under the pretext that God desires it by permitting it.

1. It is false that God desires sin. It is only true that he does not have a positive desire to prevent it.

2. In the same time that he does not have the positive will to prevent sin, he has the present and positive will to condemn it and to punish it as essentially contrary to his immutable holiness, to which he owes everything.

3. One must never suppose God's acceptance of sin until we have actually committed the sin and when we can no longer prevent what is done to be done.

So we must guide ourselves by God's two wills. According to the first, we must condemn and punish whatever he condemns and desires to punish. According to the other, we must desire confusion and abjection, which is not sin, but, on the contrary, is penance and the remedy itself of sin because this salutary confusion and this abjection, which has all the bitterness of a medicine, is an actual good that God has positively willed to make from sin, although he has never positively desired sin itself. It is like loving the antidote that we make out of poison without loving poison itself.

To speak thusly is to speak like all the saints and in all the rigor and precision of Catholic dogma.

FALSE

We must align ourselves with all the wills of God and with his permission[95] as with all his other wills. We must, therefore, allow sin in ourselves when we believe that God will allow it. We must love our sin, although it may be contrary to God, because of its abjection, which purifies our love and which removes from us all arrogance and all sense of worthiness of reward. Finally, the attraction or inspiration of grace requires Christians to break God's written Law in order to become more selfless regarding the subject of eternal reward.

To speak thusly is to teach apostasy and to set up the abomination of desolation in the holiest of sites.[96] It is not the voice of the Lamb but that of the dragon.

Article XIX

TRUE

Vocal prayer without the mental component—that is to say, without the attention of the mind and the affection of the heart—is a superstitious cult that only honors God with lips while the heart is far from him. Vocal prayer is only good and meritorious inasmuch as it is guided and animated by the heart. It would be better to recite a few words with much contemplation and love of God than long prayers with little or no contemplation when they are not required by Law. To pray without concentration and without love is to pray as the pagans do who imagine their prayers to be favorably received due to the multitude of their words. We pray only in relation to what we desire, and we only desire in relation to what we love, at least what we love with a selfish love. We must nevertheless respect and advise others to practice vocal prayer, because it is appropriate to awaken within us the thoughts and affections that it expresses. Vocal prayer was taught by the Son of God to the apostles themselves, and it has been practiced by the whole church throughout the ages.[97] It would be impious to scorn this sacrifice of praise, this fruit of the lips that confess the name of the Lord. Vocal prayer can, indeed, be constraining to contemplative souls for a certain time—Christians who are still in the imperfect beginnings of their contemplation because their contemplation is more sensitive and affectionate than it is pure and tranquil. It can be burdensome to souls who are in the last spiritual trials because everything troubles those in this last state. But we must never offer them as a rule the abandonment, without permission of the church and without a real impotence recognized by ecclesiastical superiors, any vocal prayer that is obligatory.[98] Vocal prayer considered in its simplicity and without scruple, when it is required by Law, can indeed constrain or burden a soul with respect to the things that we have just indicated, but it is never contrary to the highest contemplation. Experience itself would have us see that the most eminent Christian souls, in the midst of their most sublime spiritual communications, have friendly chats with God and that they read or recite aloud and in a type of mystical transport certain inspired words of the apostles and the prophets.[99]

To speak thusly is to explain healthy doctrine in the most correct terms.

FALSE

Vocal prayer is nothing more than a crude and imperfect practice of beginners. It is entirely useless to contemplative Christians. These souls are exempt, by the eminence of their state, from the recitation of vocal prayers that are demanded of them by the church because their contemplation contains eminently all that the different parts of the Divine Office contain that is the most edifying.[100]

To speak thusly is to scorn the reading of the sacred books. It is to forget that Jesus Christ taught us a vocal prayer that contains the perfection of the highest contemplation. It is to ignore the fact that pure contemplation is never perpetual in this life and that in its intervals we can and must faithfully recite the Office that is required by Law and which by itself is so effective in nourishing the spirit of contemplation in Christian souls.

Article XX

TRUE

Reading should not be undertaken either by curiosity or by the desire to judge one's own state or to make a decision alone concerning one's reading material. Nor should it be undertaken by a certain taste for what is called wit and enlightened subjects. We must only read the holiest books and even scripture with the guidance of pastors or spiritual directors who take the place of pastors. It is up to them to judge if each Christian is sufficiently prepared, if his heart is sufficiently purified and docile for each different reading. They must discern what nourishment is proportionate to each one of us. Nothing causes so much deception in the interior life than the indiscreet choice of books. It is better to read little and take long breaks from reading for contemplation in order to let love impress on us Christian truths more profoundly. When contemplation makes us drop the book from our hands, there is nothing more for us to do than to let it fall without worry. We can always pick it up later and it will aid us itself in the course of things to renew our contemplation.

Love, when it teaches by its sweet persuasion, surpasses all the reasoning that we could make about books. The most powerful of all persuasions is that of love. We must nevertheless pick up the book that is on the outside of us when the interior book ceases to be open. Otherwise the empty mind would fall into a vague and imaginary state of prayer that would be a real and pernicious indolence. We would neglect then the proper instruction concerning the necessary truths. We would abandon the Word of God.[101] We would never lay solid foundations of the exact knowledge of God's Law and the revealed mysteries.

To speak thusly is to speak following tradition and the experience of holy Christians.

FALSE

Reading, even of the holiest books, is useless to those whom God teaches entirely and immediately himself. It is not necessary that these persons have laid the foundation of common Catholic instruction. They have only to wait for all the light and truth of their prayers. As far as readings are concerned, when one feels like reading one may choose, without consulting one's superiors, whatever books deal with the most advanced spiritual states. One may read books that are censured or suspect to our pastors.

To speak thusly is to destroy Christian education, which is the nourishment of faith. It is to substitute a fanatical inner inspiration for the pure Word of God. Moreover, it is to allow Christians to poison themselves by readings that are contagious or at least disproportionate to their real needs. It is to teach them dissimulation and disobedience.

Article XXI

TRUE

It is essential to distinguish meditation from contemplation. *Meditation consists of discursive acts that are easy to distinguish one from the other* because they are generated by a type of noticeable impulse;[102] because they are varied by the diversity of the objects to which they apply, because they derive a conviction about a truth from the conviction of another truth already known; because they derive an affection from several motives that are methodically grouped together—and finally, because they are made and remade by a reflection that leaves behind itself distinct traces in the brain. *This composition of discursive and reflective acts is inherent to the exercise of selfish love* because this imperfect love that does not banish fear needs two things.[103] The first is to often remember all the selfish motives of fear and hope. The other is to assure itself of its working by acts that are well marked and well thought out. In this way discursive meditation is the exercise appropriate to this love that is still commingled with self-interest. Fearful and selfish love can never be content to perform simple acts in prayer, acts without any variety of selfish motives. It could never be content to perform acts of which it would be unaware. On the other hand, contemplation is, according to the most famous theologians and according to the most experienced contemplative saints, the exercise of perfect love. It consists of acts so simple, so direct, so tranquil, so uniform that they have nothing noticeable about them by which one can distinguish them. It is the perfect prayer of which Saint Anthony spoke, and which is not noticed by the hermit who engages in it himself. Contemplation is equally approved by the early church fathers, by the Scholastic doctors, and by the holy mystics. It is called a simple or loving look, to distinguish it from meditation, which is full of methodical and discursive acts. When the habit of faith is great, when it is perfected by pure love, the soul who no longer loves God except for himself alone no longer needs to seek or to assemble selfish motives concerning each virtue for her own self-interest. Reasoning at this point, instead of helping her, actually burdens and tires her. She only wants to love. She finds the motive of all virtues in love.[104] There is no longer for her any necessity but one. It is in this pure contemplation that we may say, along with Saint Francis de Sales, "It is necessary that love be very powerful since it supports all alone without being supported by any pleasure or any pretentiousness."[105]

Affective and discursive meditation, although less perfect than pure and direct contemplation, is nevertheless an exercise very pleasing to God and very necessary to most good Christian souls. It is the ordinary foundation of the interior life and the exercise of love for all the righteous who are not yet in the state of perfect selflessness.

This meditation has given rise to a great number of saints in all the ages. There would be a scandalous temerity in turning Christians away from it under the pretext of introducing them to contemplation. There are often in the most discursive meditation even, and even more so in affectionate prayer, certain peaceful and direct acts that are commingled with imperfect contemplation.

To speak thusly is to speak according to the spirit of tradition and according to the maxims of the saints the most removed from any suspicion of heretical innovation or deception.

FALSE

Meditation is only a dry and sterile study. Its discursive and reflective acts are only a vain work that tires the soul without nourishing her. Its selfish motives only produce an exercise of self-love. Never can one advance by this path. We must, indeed, hasten to cause good Christian souls to feel disgust for it, to have them pass immediately into contemplation, wherein acts are no longer appropriate.

To speak thusly is to have Christians feel distaste for the gifts of God. It is to turn to scorn the foundations of the interior life. It is to want to remove that which God grants and to want to count, rashly, on that which it does not please him to grant. It is to snatch the breast from the suckling child before it is able to digest solid food.[106]

Article XXII

TRUE

A Christian may leave discursive meditation and enter into contemplation when he attains the three following characteristics: (1) He no longer derives the inner nourishment from meditation that he derived before, and on the contrary, he feels it is distracting him; he feels it is drying him up; he feels as if he is struggling against its attraction. (2) He only finds ease, occupation, and inner nourishment in the simple presence of the purely loving God, who renews and refreshes him for all the virtues of his state. (3) He has only taste or attraction for retreat,[107] so that his spiritual director who tests him, finds him humble, sincere, docile, detached from the world and from himself. A Christian soul may, by obedience, with these three marks of vocation, enter into contemplative prayer without tempting God.

To speak thusly is to follow the ancient church fathers, such as Saint Clement of Alexandria, Saint Gregory of Nazianzus; Pope Saint Gregory; Cassian and all the ascetics; Saint Bernard; Saint Thomas and all the Scholastics. It is to speak like the holiest mystics, who were the most opposed to falsehood.

FALSE

We might introduce a Christian soul to contemplation without waiting for these three characteristics. It is sufficient that contemplation be more perfect than meditation in order to prefer the one to the other. It would be only holding souls back and having them languish in an unproductive method of prayer not to introduce them right off to the freedom of pure love.

To speak thusly is to overthrow the discipline of the church. It is to scorn the spirituality of the holy fathers. It is to belie all the maxims of the holiest mystics. It is to cast souls into falsehood.

Article XXIII

TRUE

Discursive meditation is not appropriate for souls that God is presently calling to contemplation by the three characteristics mentioned above. These souls would only enter into these discursive acts on account of scruples and to seek their own self-interest, as opposed to the current attraction of their grace.

To speak thusly is to speak like the blessed John of the Cross, who in these exact same circumstances calls meditation a "lowly means, a dirty means."[108] It is to speak like all the canonized mystics or those authorized by the entire church after the most rigorous examination. It is even to be in evident conformity with the principles of an exacting theology.

FALSE

As soon as one has begun to contemplate, there is no further need ever to return to meditation. That would be to backtrack and to fall down. It would be better to expose oneself to all sorts of temptations and to inner laziness rather than to take up discursive acts again.

To speak thusly is to be ignorant of the fact that the passage from meditation to contemplation is like the passage from selfish love to pure love. It is to ignore that this passage is usually long, imperceptible, and a mixture of these two states, as the nuances of colors are a unnoticeable passage from one color to another wherein they are both commingled. It is to contradict all the approved mystics,[109] who say, along with Balthazar Alvarez, that we must take up the oars of meditation when the wind of contemplation no longer fills the sails.[110] It is, indeed, often to deprive souls of the only nourishment that God leaves them.

Article XXIV

TRUE

There is a state of contemplation so elevated and so perfect that it becomes a habitual state, so that each time that a Christian engages in prayer, his prayer is contemplative and not discursive. So, he no longer has any need of going back to meditation or to his methodical acts.[111] If, nevertheless, it were to happen—contrary to the ordinary working of grace and contrary to the common experience of the saints—that this habitual contemplation ended absolutely, it would be necessary, failing contemplation, to substitute acts of discursive meditation in its place, because a Christian soul must never stay in a vacuum or in indolence. We must even suppose that a soul, falling from such a state of high contemplation, would fall only through some secret lack of faith. For the gifts of God are from his part without fail. He only abandons those by whom he is abandoned and he diminishes his graces only for those who diminish their cooperation. It would be necessary to persuade this Christian that it is not God who is failing him but rather, it must have been he who failed God. A Christian in this degree[112] could also be put back into meditation by the order of a spiritual director who would wish to test him, but then, following the rule of holy indifference and that of obedience, he should be as content to meditate like beginners as to contemplate like the cherubim.[113]

To speak thusly is to follow the spirit of the church and to anticipate all possible dangers of error. It is to speak like the greatest saints whose books the church has, so to speak, canonized along with their authors.

FALSE

It is better to remain in a state of absolute inaction than to take up again the less perfect instead of the more perfect.[114] The habitual state of contemplation is so constant that we must never suppose that one could fall from it by a secret lack of faith.

To speak thusly is to inspire in humanity a reckless assurance. It is to cast souls into the obvious danger of perdition.

Article XXV

TRUE

In this life there is a habitual state, but not entirely immutable, wherein the most perfect souls perform all their deliberate actions in the presence of God and for the love of God, following the words of the apostle: "Let all that you do be done in love,"[115] and again, "So, whether you eat or drink, or whatever you do, do all to the glory of God."[116] This relation of all our deliberate actions with our unique goal is the constant prayer recommended by Jesus Christ when he counsels that "men ought always to pray, and not to faint,"[117] and by Saint Paul when he says, "Pray without ceasing."[118] But we should never confuse this prayer with pure, direct contemplation, considered, as Saint Thomas Aquinas says, as the most perfect act. Prayer that consists in the relationship with God of all our deliberate actions can be perpetual in a sense, that is to say, it can last as long as our deliberate acts. In this case it is only interrupted by sleep and the other failings of nature that make us stop doing any free or meritorious act. But pure and direct contemplation does not have even this type of constancy because it is often interrupted by the acts of distinct virtues that are necessary to all Christians and that are not the acts of pure and direct contemplation at all.

To speak thusly is to remove any misunderstanding or ambiguity in a matter wherein it is dangerous to have any. It is to prevent mystics ignorant of the dogmas of faith from holding out their state as if they were no longer pilgrims in this life.[119] Finally, it is to speak like Cassian, who says in his first *Conference* that "pure contemplation is never absolutely constant in this life."[120]

FALSE

Pure and direct contemplation is absolutely constant in certain souls. Even sleep does not interrupt it. It consists of a simple and unique act that is permanent, that never has need of being repeated, and that always subsists by itself unless it is revoked by some contrary act.

To speak thusly is to deny the pilgrimage of this life, the natural failings of the soul, and the state of sleep wherein acts are no longer either willful or meritorious. It is, at the same time, to exempt a contemplative Christian from the distinct acts of virtue necessary in his state, virtues that are not acts of pure or direct contemplation. Finally, it is to be ignorant of the fact that all action of the understanding or of the will is essentially ephemeral, that to love God for ten seconds it is necessary to accomplish ten successive acts of love, each different from the other, each of which cannot follow the other, each of which is so finished that nothing remains of it while the other, which did not exist, begins to occur. Finally, it is to speak in a manner as extravagant with respect to the first principles of philosophy as it is monstrous with respect to the rules of religion.

Article XXVI

TRUE

During the intervals that interrupt pure and direct contemplation a very perfect soul can exercise distinct virtues in all its deliberate acts, with the same peace and the same purity or selflessness of love, which she contemplates while the attraction of contemplation is present. The same exercise of love that is named contemplation or quietude when it is considered in general and is not applied to any particular function becomes each distinct virtue inasmuch as it is applied to particular occasions. It is the object, as Saint Thomas says, that specifies all virtues.[121] But pure and peaceful love always remains the same as to its motive and its end in all the various specifications.

To speak thusly is to speak like the most exact and prudent school.[122]

FALSE

Pure and direct contemplation is without any interruption, so that it admits of no intervals in the exercise of the distinct virtues that are necessary to every state. All the deliberate acts of the life of the contemplative relate to divine things, which are the precise object of pure contemplation. This state does not allow, with respect to the objects to which love applies itself, of any distinction or specification of virtues.

To speak thusly is to utterly destroy all the innermost virtues. It is to oppose not only the whole tradition of the holy doctors but the most experienced mystics as well. It is to oppose Saint Bernard, Saint Teresa, and the blessed John of the Cross, who limit their particular experiences of pure contemplation to a half hour, in order to have us understand that we should always suppose that contemplation has limits.

Article XXVII

TRUE

Pure and direct contemplation is negative in that it does not have to do voluntarily with any noticeable image and distinct and qualifiable idea, as Saint Denis says (that is to say, any limited and particular idea about divinity), but it goes beyond all that which is distinct and perceptible (that is to say comprehensible and limited), so that it only limits itself to the purely intellectual and abstract idea of being, which is without limits and without restriction.[123] This idea, although very different from all that can be imagined or understood, is nevertheless very real and very positive. The simplicity of this purely immaterial idea, which has not passed by the senses or by the imagination, does not prevent contemplation from having for distinct objects all the attributes of God, for essence without attributes would no longer be essence itself, and the idea of the infinitely perfect being essentially contains in its simplicity the infinite perfection of this being. This simplicity does not prevent the contemplative soul from contemplating yet distinctly the three divine Persons, because an idea, as simple as it might be, can nevertheless represent various objects truly distinguished one from the other. Finally, this simplicity does not exclude the distinct view of the humanity of Jesus Christ and of all his mysteries, because pure contemplation admits of other ideas along with that of divinity. It admits of all the objects that pure faith can present to us. With respect to divine things, it only excludes perceptible images and discursive operations. Although the acts that go directly and immediately to God alone are more perfect, if we consider them from the aspect of the object and with philosophical rigor, they are nevertheless as perfect from the aspect of principle, that is to say, as pure and as meritorious, when they have as objects the objects that God presents and which we care for only due to the impression of his grace. In this state a soul no longer considers the mysteries of Jesus Christ by a methodical and perceptible working of the imagination in order to etch the traces of them in the mind and to be moved by them with consolation. The soul no longer occupies herself with it by means of a discursive operation or by coherent reasoning in order to draw conclusions from each mystery. However, she sees in a simple and amorous look all the diverse objects as validated and made present by pure faith.[124] Thus, the soul can exercise in the highest degree of contemplation, the most explicit acts of faith. The contemplation of the blessed in heaven, being purely intellectual, has as its distinct objects all the mysteries of the humanity of our Savior, whose graces and whose victories they sing. All the more reason for the imperfect contemplation of the pilgrimage of this life not ever to be able to be altered by the distinct vision of all these objects.

To speak thusly is to speak in the same way as all Catholic tradition and as all the approved mystics have wanted to express themselves.

FALSE

Pure contemplation excludes any image. That is to say, it excludes any idea, even purely intellectual. The contemplative soul accepts no real and positive idea from God that distinguishes God from other beings. This soul must see neither the divine attributes that distinguish him from all creatures nor the three divine Persons, fearing lest this change the simplicity of her view. She must still less interest herself with the humanity of Jesus Christ, since this humanity is not of the divine nature, or of its mysteries, because they would augment contemplation too much. The souls of this state have no longer any need of thinking of Jesus Christ, who is only the path for reaching God, his Father, because these souls have already achieved their goal.

To speak thusly is to ignore what all the approved mystics themselves have attempted to say about the purest forms of contemplation. It is to destroy faith, without which contemplation itself is destroyed. It is to create a fanciful contemplation that has no real object and that can no longer distinguish God from nothingness. It is to destroy Christianity under the pretext of purifying it. It is to invent a type of deism that falls directly into atheism, wherein any real idea of God, as distinguished from his creatures, is rejected. Finally, it is to promulgate two sorts of heresies. The first is that of supposing that there is on earth a contemplative who is no longer a pilgrim and who no longer needs a pilgrim's path because he has already reached the end. The second is to ignore that Jesus Christ, who is the way, is not any less the truth and the life, that he is the fulfiller as well as the author of our salvation.[125] Finally, the angels themselves, in their most sublime contemplation, have desired to see his mysteries, and the blessed[126] sing without ceasing the canticle of the Lamb in his presence.

Article XXVIII

TRUE

Contemplative souls are deprived of the distinct, sensible, and thoughtful view of Jesus Christ in two different times,[127] but they are never deprived for always of the simple and distinct vision of Jesus Christ in this life. *First of all, in the incipient fervor of their contemplation, this exercise is still very imperfect; it only represents God in a confused manner.*[128] The soul, absorbed by her sensible taste for meditation, cannot yet be occupied by distinct views. These distinct views would be a type of distraction for her in her weakness and would cast her once again into the reasoning of meditation from which she has only just left. This inability to see Jesus Christ distinctly is not perfection, but, on the contrary, the imperfection of this exercise because it is now more physical than pure. *Second, a soul loses Jesus Christ from sight in the final trials because God then removes from the soul the possession and the thoughtful knowledge of all that which is good in her, in order to purify her of all self-interest.*[129] In this distraught state of confusion and involuntary darkness the soul no longer loses sight of Jesus Christ any more than of God. But all these losses are only apparent and ephemeral; after them Jesus Christ is returned no less to the soul than is God himself. Apart from these two cases, the most elevated soul can in the actual contemplation be occupied with Jesus Christ, made present by faith. And, in the intervals in which pure contemplation ceases, she is still occupied with Jesus Christ. One finds in practice that the most eminent souls with respect to contemplation are those that are the most occupied with Jesus. They speak to him at all times as wife to husband. Often they no longer see anything but him in themselves. They carry successively the profound imprints of all his mysteries and of all the states of his mortal life. It is true that he becomes something so intimate in their heart that they become accustomed to looking at him less as a foreign and exterior object than as the interior principle of their life.

To speak thusly is to repress the most damnable of all errors. It is to explain clearly the experiences and the expressions of the saints, which souls given over to heresy could abuse.

FALSE

Contemplative souls no longer have any need to view distinctly the humanity of Jesus Christ, who is only the way, since they have already arrived at the destination. The flesh of Jesus Christ is no longer an object worthy of these souls, and they no longer know him according to the flesh, even when rendered present by pure faith. They are no longer occupied with him outside of ongoing contemplation, except in pure contemplation itself. God, whom they possess in his supreme simplicity, is sufficient to them. They must no longer be occupied with either divine Persons or the attributes of divinity.

To speak thusly is to remove the cornerstone. It is to tear eternal life from the faithful—eternal life that only consists in knowing the true God alone and Jesus Christ, his son, whom he sent. It is to be the Anti-Christ, who rejects the Word made flesh. It is to deserve the anathema that the apostle pronounces upon all those who will not love the Lord Jesus.[130]

Article XXIX

TRUE

We could say that passive contemplation is infused, inasmuch as it infuses souls with a sweetness and peace greater than that of the other graces that enter into the common run of justified Christians. It is a grace all the freer in that all the others are given in order to merit, because it infuses into souls the purest and most perfect love. But passive contemplation is neither purely infused, since it is independent and meritorious, nor purely free, since the soul connects it to grace. It is not miraculous, since it consists in—according to the witness of all the saints—only a loving knowledge, and that grace without miracle is sufficient for the most lively faith and for the most purified love. Finally, this contemplation cannot be miraculous, since we suppose it to be in a state of pure and obscure faith in which the Christian is led by any other light than that of simple revelation and the authority of the church, which is common to all the righteous. It is true that several mystics have supposed that this contemplation was miraculous because within it we contemplate a truth that has not passed by the senses or by the imagination. It is true, also, that these mystics recognized a depth of the soul that was active in this contemplation without any distinct operation of the physical senses. But these two concepts came only from the philosophy of the Scholastics, with which these mystics were imbued. This great mystery evaporates as soon as we suppose, along with Saint Augustine, that we have intellectual ideas that have not come through the senses, and this without any miraculous intervention, or when we suppose, moreover, that the core of the soul is not really distinguishable from its properties.[131] Therefore all passive contemplation may be reduced to something very simple, which has nothing of the miraculous about it. It is a fabric of acts of faith and love so simple, so direct, so peaceful, and so uniform that they seem to form only one sole act, or even seem to be no act at all but rather the tranquil repose of pure union. This is what makes Saint Francis de Sales desire that we not call it union, fearing lest we express a movement or action toward union rather than a simple or pure unity. Whence it comes that some, such as Saint Francis of Assisi in his great canticle, have said that they could no longer accomplish acts; others, such as Gregory Lopez, have said that they performed one continuous act during their entire life. One and the other group, even though using expressions seemingly contradictory, actually mean the same thing. They no longer perform harried acts characterized by nervous fits and starts. They perform acts so peaceful and so uniform that these acts, although very real, very successive, and even sometimes interrupted, seem to them to be a single act without interruption or a continual state of repose. Whence it has come to be that this contemplation has been called prayer of silence or of quietude. Whence it has happened that this prayer has also been called passive. God forbid that we should ever call it thusly in order to exclude real action: actions positive, deliberate, and meritorious of the free will, or the real and successive acts that we must repeat at each moment. This prayer is called passive only to exclude activity or the selfish eagerness of Christians when they want to excite themselves in order to feel and see their operation that would be less noticeable if it were more simple and uniform.[132] Passive contemplation is only pure contemplation; active contemplation is that which is still mixed with those eager, harried, and discursive acts. Thus, when contemplation still has within it a mixture of selfish eagerness[133] that we call activity, it is still active. When contemplation no longer has any vestige of this activity, it is entirely passive, that is to say, peaceful and selfless in its acts. In summation, the more a soul is passive with respect to God, the more she is acting in respect to what she must do; that is to say, the more the soul is malleable to the divine touch, the more its movement is efficacious, albeit without fits and starts and nervous agitation. For it is always equally true that the more the soul receives from God, the more she must give back to him from what she has received. This is the flux and reflux that sustains the order of grace and all the faithfulness of the created being.

To speak thusly is to go beyond all illusions; it is to explain in depth passive contemplation that one could not deny without flagrant temerity, and on which one could not expatiate without extreme danger. It is to straighten out all that the saints have said in their terms that the subtlety of certain theologians has obscured.

FALSE

Passive contemplation is purely passive, in that the free will no longer cooperates with grace by any real and ephemeral act. It is purely infused, purely free, and without any merit on the part of the soul. It is miraculous and—as long as it lasts—it pulls the soul from the state of pure and dark faith. This contemplation is like a supernatural ravishing or seizure that anticipates the soul's action. It is an extraordinary inspiration that puts the soul outside and beyond all common rules. It is an absolute binding or expulsion of the powers inasmuch as the understanding and the will are then in an absolute impotence of doing anything, which is doubtless a miraculous and ecstatic suspension.

To speak thusly is to overthrow the system of pure faith, which is that of all the correct mystics and especially of blessed John of the Cross. It is to confuse passive contemplation, which acts freely of its own and is meritorious, with graces freely given that are not at all common.[134] The saints warn us that the latter graces must never be our voluntary occupation. This is to contradict all authors who describe this contemplation as an act of love—free and worthy—and consequently as real acts, yet simple acts, of these two agencies. It is to contradict Saint Teresa herself, who assures us that in the seventh heaven the soul no longer experiences any of these ravishings that oppose the order of nature and the operations of understanding and the will.[135] It is to contradict all the great mystics who have said that these suspensions of natural operations, far from being a perfect state, are on the contrary a sign that nature is not yet sufficiently purified and that such effects cease in commensurate measure with the soul's achieving greater purification and familiarity with God in the state of pure faith. It is mixing up the pain that a pure soul would have in accomplishing anxious and reflective acts for her own self-interest against the actual attraction of grace, with an absolute inability of performing these acts by a natural effort. A misunderstanding in this area can be in some an inexhaustible source of error or in others a subject of scandal wholly misdirected and unfounded.

Article XXX

TRUE

The passive state of which all mystical saints have talked so much is only passive in that contemplation is passive; that is, it excludes not the peaceful, selfless acts, but only the activity or the acts that are anxious and eager for our own self-interest. The passive state is that in which a soul no longer loving God with a mixed love performs all her acts deliberately with a full and efficacious will, yet tranquil and selfless. Sometimes she performs the simple and indistinct acts that we call quietude or contemplation; other times she performs the distinct acts of the virtues appropriate to her state. But she accomplishes one and the other with a manner equally passive, that is to say, peacefully and selflessly. This state is habitual, but it is not entirely immutable. For, apart from the fact that the soul can fall from this state, she can commit venial sins in this state. This passive state presupposes no extraordinary inspiration. It only contains an infinite peace and malleability of the soul letting herself be moved by all the workings of grace. A very light and dry feather, as Cassian says, is moved without resistance by the slightest puff of wind, and this puff quickly blows it in every direction, whereas if the feather were wet and weighed down, its own weight would make it less movable and less easy to pick up.[136] The soul, in the grip of selfish love, which is the least perfect, still has a vestige of selfish fear that makes her less light, less malleable, and less movable when the breath of the inner spirit moves her. Water that is disturbed cannot be clear, nor can it reflect the image of neighboring objects, but still water becomes like the pure glass of a mirror. It receives without alteration all the images of various objects, and it keeps none of them. The pure and tranquil soul is the same. God imprints on her his image and that of all other objects that he wishes to imprint. Everything is imprinted; everything is erased. This soul has no proper form, and she has equally all those that grace gives her. Nothing remains to her, and everything disappears as in water as soon as God wishes to make new impressions. Only pure love gives this peace and this perfect docility. This passive state is not a contemplation that is always at work. Contemplation that only lasts during limited periods is a part of this habitual state. Selfless love must not be less selfless, nor less peaceful in the distinct acts of virtues than in the indistinct acts of pure contemplation.

To speak thusly is to remove all misunderstanding and admit of a state that is only the exercise of pure love so consistently authorized by all tradition.

FALSE

The passive state consists of a passive contemplation that is perpetual, and this passive contemplation is a sort of continual ecstasy or miraculous binding of the faculties that puts them into a real inability of operating freely.

To speak thusly is to confuse the passive state with passive contemplation, and it is, moreover, to have a very false idea of passive contemplation. It is to assume a state of miraculous and perpetual ecstasy that excludes all path of faith, all freedom, all merit, and all demerit, in short, a state that is incompatible with the pilgrimage of this life. It is to show ignorance of the experiences of the saints and to jumble up all their ideas.

Article XXXI

TRUE

In the passive state there is a simplicity and a childlike quality evinced by the saints, but the children of God who are simple with respect to good are always cautious concerning evil. They are sincere, candid, peaceful, and without ulterior motives. They do not reject wisdom but only the attachment to wisdom.[137] They divest themselves of their wisdom as they do of all other virtues. They faithfully use in each moment all the natural lights of reason and all the supernatural lights of actual grace in order to act according to the written Law and according to the true proprieties.[138] A soul in this state is not wise, either from an anxious search of wisdom or from a selfish turning in on herself in order to assure herself that she is wise and to revel in wisdom in and of itself. But without thinking of being wise for its own end, she becomes wise in God, by allowing willingly none of the overeager and irregular movements of the passions or of moods or of self-interest, and by using—without owning it—all light both natural and supernatural of the present moment. This present moment has a certain moral breadth wherein we should contain all things that have a natural and proximate relationship to the business at hand. Thus, sufficient to the day is the evil thereof.[139] And the soul lets the light of the following day take care of itself because the light of the following day, which does not yet belong to her, will bring with it, if it comes, its own grace and light, which is our daily bread. Such souls deserve and attract to themselves Providence's particular care, in which care they live without worrying about predicting a distant future, just like little children on their mother's breast. They are not in possession of themselves as the sages who are wise in themselves in spite of the prohibition of the apostle.[140] But they allow themselves to be possessed, instructed, and moved on all occasion by actual grace that communicates to them the spirit of God. These souls do not believe themselves to be extraordinarily inspired. They believe, on the contrary, that they can err and they only avoid this by almost never judging anything. They allow themselves to be corrected and have neither senses nor will of their own. Such are the children that Jesus Christ wants to approach him. They have within their dove-like simplicity all the prudence of the serpent,[141] but a borrowed prudence that they do not own anymore than I own the rays of the sun when I walk out in its light. Such are the poor in spirit that Jesus Christ has declared "blessed"[142] and who detach themselves from their own talents even as all Christians detach themselves from their temporal goods. Such are the little ones to whom God reveals his mysteries with such kindness while he hides them from the wise and the prudent.[143]

To speak thusly is to speak according to the gospel and all tradition.

FALSE

Reason is a false light. We must act without consulting it, trample underfoot the proprieties, follow without hesitation all our first inclinations and assume them to be of divine inspiration. We must repress not only anxious thoughts but indeed all thoughts, not only the anxious forecasting of the future but also all thoughts of the future. It is not enough to not be wise in oneself; we must abandon ourselves to the point of no longer watching over ourselves with a simple and peaceful vigilance, indeed to the point of not letting ourselves fall into the natural movements of inspiration in order to receive only those of grace.

To speak thusly is to believe that reason, which is the first gift of God in the natural order, is an evil and, consequently, to renew the insane and impious error of the Manicheans. It is to want to change perfection into a continual fantasy. It is to want to tempt God in all of life's moments.

Article XXXII

TRUE

In the passive state there is a freedom for God's children that has no relation to the frenzied liberation of the children of the secular world. These simple souls are no longer inhibited by the scruples of those souls who fear and hope for their own self-interest. Pure love gives them a respectful familiarity with God, much like that of a bride with her bridegroom. They have a peace and a joy full of innocence. They take with simplicity and without hesitation the relaxation to the body and soul that is really necessary, as they also advise their neighbor to do. They speak of themselves without passing positive judgment but rather from pure obedience and in case of real need, according to the situation in which they find themselves at the time. So, they speak simply of their state either well or ill as they would speak of another, without any attachment either to appearances or to the good opinion that their simplest and most modest words might raise for themselves, and recognizing always with humble joy that, if there is some good in themselves, it only comes from God.

To speak thusly is to convey the experience of the saints without doing harm to the rule of evangelical morals.

FALSE

The freedom of passive souls is founded on an innocence of "detachment" that makes pure for them anything they feel like doing, however irregular or inexcusable in others. They no longer have any laws, because the Law is not made for the righteous, provided that he appropriate nothing for himself and that he do nothing for himself.

To speak thusly is to forget that it is written that if the written Law is not for the righteous it is because an inner law of love always takes precedence over the outward precept and that the great commandment of love contains all the others. It is to turn Christianity into an abomination and to have God's name blasphemed among the Gentiles. It is to give Christian souls over to a spirit of lies and of dizziness.[144]

Article XXXIII

TRUE

In the passive state there is a union of all love's virtues that never excludes the distinct exercise of each virtue. Charity, Saint Thomas says, echoing Saint Augustine, is the form or the principle of all virtues.[145] That which distinguishes or specifies them is the particular object to which love applies itself. The love that abstains from impure pleasures is chastity, and this same love, when it suffers tribulations, takes the name of patience. This love, without changing its simplicity, becomes successively all the different virtues. But it seeks none of them for its own sake, that is to say, with respect to its force, grandeur, beauty, regularity, or perfection. "The disinterested soul," as Saint Francis de Sales remarks, "no longer loves virtues because they are beautiful and pure, or because they are worthy of being loved, or because they beautify and perfect those who practice them, or because they are deserving of praise, or because they prepare the way for eternal reward, but only because they are the will of God."[146] And again, speaking of Mother Chantal,[147] he says, "The disinterested soul does not cleanse herself of her sins in order to be pure and does not adorn herself with virtues in order to be beautiful but rather to please her husband for whom she would have loved ugliness as well as beauty if ugliness had pleased him as much." *Therefore, we practice all the distinct virtues without thinking that they are virtues. We only think in every moment of doing what God wishes, and jealous love would have us not be virtuous for ourselves and that we never are so virtuous as when we are least set on being virtuous.*[148] *One might say that in this sense the passive and disinterested soul no longer even wants love as defined as perfection and as happiness but only in that it is what God wants of us.*[149] Whence comes Saint Francis de Sales's saying that "we come back into ourselves loving love instead of loving the Beloved."[150] Moreover, this saint says that "the desire for salvation is good, but it is more perfect yet to desire nothing."[151] He means by this that we should not even desire God's love for our own sake. Finally, in order to give to this truth all the necessary precision, this saint says that "we must try to find in God only the love of His beauty and not the pleasure that there is in the beauty of His love."[152] This distinction will seem subtle to those not yet taught by grace,[153] but this distinction is supported by the tradition of all the saints since the origin of Christianity, which we cannot scorn without despising these same saints who have considered perfection to be this delicate jealousy of love.

To speak thusly is to repeat what the holy mystics have said, echoing Saint Clement and the desert fathers, on the cessation of virtues, which must be explained with infinite precaution.

FALSE

In the passive state the exercise of distinct virtues is no longer appropriate because pure love, which contains all of them perfectly in its quietude, dispenses Christian souls absolutely from their exercise.

To speak thusly is to contradict the gospel. It is to put the stumbling block of scandal[154] on the path of the church's children. It is to give them the name of the living when they are dead.

Article XXXIV

TRUE

The spiritual death of which so many of the holy mystics have spoken, following the apostle (who says to the faithful, "You are dead"[155]), is none other than the complete purification or selflessness of love, so that the worries and anxieties that come from selfish motives do not weaken the working of grace and that grace acts in an entirely free manner. Spiritual resurrection is only the habitual state of pure love that we reach, ordinarily, after trials designed to purify it.

To speak thusly is to speak like all the most holy and most prudent mystics.

FALSE

Spiritual death is a total extinction of the old man and of the last sparks of concupiscence.[156] So, we no longer have any need to resist, even with a peaceful and disinterested resistance, our natural urges, or to cooperate with any of Christ's medicinal grace.[157] Spiritual resurrection is the total consummation of the new man in this age and in the fullness of the perfect man as in heaven.

To speak thusly is to fall into heresy and into an impiety that overthrows all Christian morals.

Article XXXV

TRUE

The state of transformation of which so many of both the ancient and the modern saints have so often spoken is none other than the most passive state, that is to say, the state that is the most exempt from all selfish activity or worry. The soul that is tranquil and flexible to all the most delicate impulses of grace is like a ball on a level plain; it has no longer any natural or proper placement. It rolls equally in all different directions and even the slightest push is sufficient to move it. In this state a soul has only one love and she only knows how to love. Love is her life. Love is her being and her substance, because it is the sole principle of all her affections. Since this soul makes no anxious movements, she makes no resistance to God's hand, which pushes her. Thus, she only feels a single movement, which is to know him that is imprinted on her, just like a person pushed by another no longer feels anything other than that propulsion when—that is—the person does nothing to resist by a counter movement. So, the soul says with all simplicity, like Saint Paul: "It is no longer I who live, but Christ who lives in me; Jesus Christ manifests himself in mortal flesh,"[158] just as the apostle wishes that God manifest himself in us. Therefore, the image of God, obscured and nearly erased in us by sin, is redrawn more perfectly and a resemblance is therein renewed—a resemblance that is called transformation. So, if this soul speaks of herself by simple conscience, she says, like Saint Catherine of Genoa, "I no longer find myself; there is no longer any other 'me' except for God."[159] If, however, she looks within herself by reflection, she hates herself inasmuch as she is something outside of God; that is to say, she condemns the ego inasmuch as it is separated from the pure impression of the spirit of grace, just as the same saint looked upon herself with horror. This state is neither fixed nor unchangeable. It is only true that we must not believe that the soul may fall from this state without some unfaithfulness on her part because the gifts of God are without second thoughts and souls that are faithful to their grace will not suffer any lessening or diminution. However, the slightest hesitation or the most subtle self-indulgence can make a soul unworthy of such an eminent grace.

To speak thusly is to accept terms hallowed by scripture and by tradition. It is to follow various early church fathers who said that the pure soul was transformed and deified.[160] It is to explain the terminology of the most approved saints. It is to preserve in its integrity both faith and dogma.

FALSE

This transformation is a real deification of the soul in her nature, that is, a hypostatic[161] union or a conformity to God that is unalterable and that dispenses the soul from being vigilant toward the ego, under the pretext that there is no longer in her any other ego than that of God.

To speak thusly is to speak horrible blasphemy; it is to want to transform Satan into an angel of light.

Article XXXVI

TRUE

Christian souls that have been transformed no longer ordinarily have need of certain arrangements either with respect to places or times, or even of specific formulas or of meticulously researched practices for their interior spiritual exercises. The great habit of their familiar union with God gives them an ease and a simplicity of loving union that is incomprehensible to those souls in an inferior state, and this example would be very pernicious for all those other Christians who are less advanced and who still need established, formulated practices for support. Transformed Christians must always, albeit without any cumbersome rules, produce with simplicity equally indistinct acts of quietude or pure contemplation as well as distinct acts, both tranquil and selfless, of all the virtues appropriate to their state in life.

To speak thusly is to correctly explain the expressions of good mystics.[162]

FALSE

Transformed Christians no longer have any need to exercise virtues in the case of law or of counsel. Outside of this time they can be in an absolute vacuum and inner inaction. They only have to follow their inclinations, their attractions, their first instinctual movement without paying any attention to them. Concupiscence is quenched within them, or rather, it is in a state of suspension so dormant that we should not believe that it may ever awake at all.

To speak thusly is to lead souls into temptation. It is to puff them up with a deadly pride. It is to teach demonic doctrine. It is to forget that concupiscence is always—whether active or dormant or latent—capable of awakening suddenly in our bodies, which are heirs to sin.

Article XXXVII

TRUE

The most transformed Christians still retain their free will to be able to sin, just like the first angel and the first man. They have, moreover, the matter of concupiscence, although the obvious effects of it may be suspended or slowed by medicinal grace. These Christians can commit mortal sin and err in a horrible way. They even commit venial sins for which they say every day along with the whole church, "Forgive us our trespasses, etc." The slightest hesitation in faith or the slightest selfish turning back to themselves could, unnoticed, cause their grace to dry up. They owe it to the jealousy of pure love to avoid even the slightest faults, as the common run of the righteous avoid great sins. Their vigilance, although simple and tranquil, must be all the more searching in that pure love, in its jealousy, sees more clearly than selfish love with all its worries and troubles. These Christian souls must never either judge themselves or excuse themselves unless it is through obedience and in order to lift some scandal. Nor should they justify themselves by a deliberate and thoughtful testimony, although the inner depth of their conscience may not reproach them for anything. They must let themselves be judged by their superiors and obey them blindly in everything.

To speak thusly is to speak according to the true principles of all the holy mystics and without doing harm to tradition.

FALSE

Transformed Christians are no longer free to sin. They no longer have any concupiscence. Everything in them is movement of grace and extraordinary inspiration. They no longer can pray with the church each day, saying, "Forgive us our trespasses, etc."

To speak thusly is to fall into the error of the Gnostics, later renewed by the Beghards, and condemned in the Council of Vienne, and most recently taken up by the Alumbrados of Andalucia during the past century.[163]

Article XXXVIII

TRUE

Transformed Christians can profitably—indeed, they should, even given the current discipline—confess their venial sins that they notice. *By confessing they must hate their faults, condemn themselves, and desire the remission of their sins, not as their own purification and deliverance but rather as a thing that God wants and that he wants us to want for his glory.*[164] Although a selfless soul no longer washes herself of her faults to be pure, as we have seen in Saint Francis de Sales, and indeed she would love ugliness as much as beauty if it were as pleasing to the Bridegroom, she knows nevertheless that purity and beauty are what the Bridegroom wants. Thus, she loves only for his good pleasure both purity and beauty, and she rejects with horror the ugliness that he rejects. When a Christian is truly and presently in a state of pure love, we must not fear that in the actual confession of his sin he is actually condemning what he has committed against the Beloved and consequently in the most formal, the purest, and the most efficacious contrition, although he no longer always produces noticeable acts with obvious and well-thought-out words or prayers. If venial faults are erased in an instant by the simple recitation of the Lord's Prayer, as Saint Augustine assures us, for the common run of the justified, yet imperfect Christians, how much more so are they erased in souls transformed by the exercise of the purest love. It is true that we are not obliged to confess as frequently when an enlightened spiritual director has reason to fear that such frequent confessions would makes us overscrupulous, or that they turn into a mere habit, or that they become an emotional outlet[165] and relief for a self-love more saddened to see itself not entirely perfect than faithful in wanting to do violence to itself in order to correct itself; or yet because these frequent confessions too much trouble certain souls and remind them too much of their state in some few passing pains; or because they see in themselves no voluntary fault committed since their last confession that would appear to the confessor a sufficient matter of sacramental absolution after their having put themselves at his feet, submitting without guile to the power and the judgment of the church.

To speak thusly is to speak a language in conformity with the experience of the saints and with the needs of many Christian souls without doing damage to the principles of tradition.

FALSE

Confession is a remedy that is appropriate only to imperfect Christians, for which advanced souls have no need except as a pro forma act lest they scandalize the public by not having recourse to it. Either they never commit any sins that merit absolution, or they should not be vigilant with the tranquil and selfless vigilance of pure and jealous love to notice everything that might sadden the Holy Spirit within them. Or they need have no recourse to the confessional because they are no longer obliged to feel contrition, which is nothing more than jealous love that hates with a perfect hatred all that which is contrary to the good pleasure of the

Beloved. Or they believe that they would commit an act of infidelity against love's selflessness and against perfect abandonment[166] if they sincerely asked with their heart as well as with their mouth for the remission of their sins that God, nevertheless, wants that they should desire.

To speak thusly is to annihilate for these Christians the true exercise of pure love of the supreme good that must be in this occasion the actual condemnation of supreme evil. It is to remove Christians from the sacraments and the discipline of the church by a reckless and scandalous presumption. It is to inspire in them the pride of the Pharisees. It is to teach them, at the very least, to make confession without the proper vigilance, without attention, without sincerity of the heart when they ask with their mouth for the remission of their sins. It is to introduce into the church a hypocrisy that would make heresy incurable.[167]

Article XXXIX

TRUE

Christians experiencing the first tangible attraction making them pass to contemplation sometimes pray in ways that seem disproportionate with major flaws that they still have, and this disconnect makes some spiritual directors who do not have enough experience judge their prayer to be false and full of error, as Saint Teresa tells us happened to her.[168] Christians who are put to the test by extraordinary trials sometimes show an inconstant state of mind, weakened by an excess of pain, and a patience almost exhausted, as Job appeared imperfect and impatient in the eyes of his friends. God often allows Christians, even those called transformed and in spite of the purity of their love, to retain certain imperfections that are due more to the infirmity of their natural state than to their will and that are, according to Pope Saint Gregory,[169] the counterbalance of their contemplation—as the thorn in the flesh was to the apostle,[170] being like Satan's angel to prevent him from taking too much pride in the greatness of his revelations. Finally, these imperfections, that are none of them a violation of the Law, are left in a soul so that we might see the marks of the great work that grace has needed to accomplish therein. These infirmities serve to bring a Christian down in his own eyes and to hold the gifts of God under a veil of infirmity that quickens the faith of this Christian and of the righteous that know him. Sometimes they even serve to bring scorn and crosses upon him or serve to make him more docile to his superiors or to remove from him the consolation of being accepted and approved in his spiritual journey, as happened to Saint Teresa with her incredible trials. Finally, they serve to hide the secret of the bride and the Bridegroom to the wise and to the cautious of this world.

To speak thusly is to speak in conformity with the experience of the saints without doing harm to the evangelical rule, because spiritual directors who have experience and the spirit of grace will always be capable of judging of the tree by its fruits,[171] which are sincerity, docility, and the detachment of the soul in all major occasions. Moreover, there will always be other signs that the unction of God's Spirit will give sufficiently to make itself felt if we only patiently examine closely the state of each soul.

FALSE

We may look upon a Christian as contemplative or even transformed while still finding him for some considerable time negligent as to his instruction of the principles of religion, inattentive to his duties, dissipated, worldly and not mortified, always ready to excuse himself regarding his faults, lazy, proud, or hypocritical.

To speak thusly is to allow the most dangerous imperfections in the most perfect state. It is to give the name of extraordinary states to faults that are the most incompatible with true piety. It is to give approval to the most blatant errors. It is to overthrow the laws by which we can put spirits to the test in order to know whether they come from God. It is to call evil good and to warrant the curse of scripture.

Article XL

TRUE

The transformed soul is entirely and directly united to God in three ways: (1) in that she loves God for himself alone without any ground of selfish motives, (2) that she contemplates him without a physical image or discursive operation, and (3) that she accomplishes his laws and his counsels without any arrangement of formulas in order to render a selfish witness.

To speak thusly is to say what the holy mystics have tried to say when they excluded from this state the practices of virtue, and it is an explanation that does no violence in any way to universal tradition.[172]

FALSE

The transformed soul is united to God without any means either of the veil of faith or of the weakness of flesh tainted since the fall of Adam, or of medicinal grace of Jesus Christ, which is always necessary, or of Jesus Christ's mediation, by which alone we may in any state go to the Father.

To speak thusly is to renew the heresy of the Beghards condemned at the Council of Vienne.

Article XLI

TRUE

The spiritual wedding immediately unites the bride to the Bridegroom with essence to essence, substance to substance. That is, with will to will by that totally pure love that we have discussed so often. Therefore, God and the soul are no longer but one spirit, just as the husband and wife in marriage are no longer but one flesh. He who adheres to God is formed in the same spirit with him by a total conformity of will that grace effects.[173] The soul enjoys a fulfillment and joy of the Holy Spirit that is only a foreshadowing of heavenly bliss. The soul is in a complete purity, that is to say, without any stain of sin (except the daily sins that the exercise of love can erase immediately) and, consequently, she can enter into heaven wherein nothing tainted can enter without passing through purgatory. Concupiscence, which remains always with us in this life, is not at all incompatible with this complete purity because it is not a sin or stain of the soul. But this soul does not have original innocence[174] because she is neither exempt from the daily sins nor from concupiscence, which are incompatible with that innocence.

To speak thusly is to speak with the salt of wisdom that must season all our discourse.

FALSE

The soul in this state is in a state of original innocence. She sees God face to face. She enjoys his presence completely, just as the blessed do.[175]

To speak thusly is to fall in the heresy of the Beghards.

Article XLII

TRUE

The union called essential or substantial by the mystics consists in a simple, selfless love that fills all the affections of the whole soul and that operates through actions so tranquil and so uniform that they seem all like one action alone, although they are several acts very distinguishable one from the other. Various mystics have named these acts essential or substantial to distinguish them from anxious acts; that is, acts that are inconstant and done as if by fits and starts of a love still mixed with selfish motives.

To speak thusly is to explain the true sense of the mystics.

FALSE

This union becomes really essential between God and the soul, so that nothing can either break it or alter it. This substantial act is permanent and indivisible like the substance of the soul itself.

To speak thusly is to teach an extravagance as contrary to all philosophy as to faith and to the true practice of piety.

Article XLIII

TRUE

God, who hides himself from the great and the wise, reveals himself and communicates to the meek and the simple. The transformed soul is the spiritual man of whom Saint Paul speaks,[176] that is to say, the man who is moved and directed by the spirit of grace into the path of pure faith. This Christian often has an understanding that the wise do not have with all their science and human knowledge rather than experience and pure grace, due to his grace and by experience for all things through simple practice in trials and in the exercise of pure love. He must nevertheless submit with his heart as well as with his mouth not only to all the decisions of the church but also to the direction of his pastors, because they have a special grace to direct all the sheep of the flock without any exception.

To speak thusly is to speak the truth with certainty.

FALSE

The transformed soul is Saint Paul's spiritual man in such a way that he can judge of all the truths of religion and not himself be judged by anyone. He is God's seed and he cannot sin. God's anointing teaches him everything, so that he has no need of being taught by anyone, or of submitting to his superiors.

To speak thusly is to abuse passages of scripture and to turn them to our own destruction. It is to show ignorance of the fact that the divine anointing that teaches everything teaches nothing as much as obedience, and that his anointing only proposes the truths of faith and of practice by inspiring a humble docility to the ministers of the church. In a word, it is to establish in the midst of the church a damnable sect of independents and fanatics.

Article XLIV

TRUE

Pastors and saints of all the ages have harbored a sort of economy or secret in order to speak of the rigorous trials and the most sublime exercise of pure love only to those Christian souls to whom God had already given the attraction and the understanding. *Although this doctrine was the pure and simple perfection of the gospel shown throughout all tradition, the ancient pastors normally only proposed to the common lot of the righteous practices of selfish love that were commensurate with the grace they possessed,*[177] therefore giving milk to children and bread to strong Christians.[178]

To speak thusly is to say that which is constantly found in Saint Clement, in Cassian, and in several other holy authors, both ancient and modern.

FALSE

There has always been among the contemplatives of all the ages a secret tradition unknown to the body of the whole church even. This tradition harbored hidden dogmas beyond the truths of universal tradition, or—rather—these dogmas were contrary to those of the common faith and they exempted Christians from practicing all the acts of explicit faith and of distinct virtue that are not less essential in the path of pure love than in that of selfish love.

To speak thusly is to annihilate tradition by multiplying it. It is to create a sect of hypocrites hidden in the bosom of Mother Church without her ever being able to discover their whereabouts or to deliver herself of them. It is to renew the impious secrets of the Gnostics and the Manicheans. It is to weaken all the foundations of faith and morals.

Article XLV

TRUE

All the most eminent interior paths, far from being above a habitual state of pure love, are only the road to get to this end of total perfection. All the inferior degrees are not yet this true state. The last degree, called by mystics the transformation or essential union without location, is only the simple reality of this love without self-interest. This state is the most assured when it is true because it is the most voluntary and the most worthy of all the states of Christian righteousness and because it is the state that gives everything to God, leaving nothing to his creature. On the contrary, when it is false and imaginary, it is the height of delusion. The pilgrim, after many dangers, sufferings, and exhaustion, arrives on the summit of a mountain and sees in the distance the city that is his home; it is the end of his journey and of all his pains. At first, he is seized by joy; he believes that he is already at the gates of that city and that only a bit of road is left for him—a straight shot. But, as he advances, the road seems longer and he finds difficulties that he had not foreseen at first sight. He now finds it necessary to descend the mountain by the precipices into the deep valleys where he loses sight of that city that he believed was almost within his grasp. It is now necessary for him to climb rugged rocks again. It is only by means of such pains and dangers that he arrives finally in that city that he had first believed to be so near to him and straight ahead.

It is the same with totally selfless love. At first sight it looks so easily attained. We think we have it already. We imagine that we are there already. At least, we see only a short distance between us and it—a straight shot. But the farther along we go toward this love, the more we feel that the road is long and painful. Nothing is more dangerous than to delude ourselves with this beautiful idea and to believe ourselves already practicing what we are not. He who would speculate about having achieved this love would tremble right to the marrow of his bones if God were to put him to the tests by which this love becomes purified and is achieved in Christian souls. Finally, we must be extremely careful not to believe that we have the reality of this love when in fact we only have the understanding of it and the attraction to it. Any Christian who would dare to presume, by a thoughtful decision, to have already arrived at this love shows by his presumption how far from it he really is. The very small number of those who are there already do not know always if they are really there each time they reflect within themselves. They are ready to believe that they are not there when their superiors say that they are. They speak about themselves with selflessness and without reflection, as they do of others, and they act with simplicity by pure obedience according to real need, without judging or trying to reason about their state. Finally, although it is true to say that no one can indicate the precise boundaries of God's operations within souls and that only the Holy Spirit can plumb the depths of that same spirit, it is nevertheless true to say that no interior perfection dispenses Christians from real acts that are essential for accomplishing the whole Law and that all perfection can be summarized by this habitual state of pure and unique love that creates in these souls, with a selfless peace, all that mixed love creates in the others with some leftover selfish anxieties. In a word, there is only self-interest that cannot and must not be found in the exercise of selfless love; everything else is found therein more abundantly than in the common ranks of the righteous.

To speak with this precaution is to remain within the boundaries set down by our fathers. It is to piously follow tradition. It is to call up, without any mixture of novelty, the experiences of the saints and the language that they used in talking about themselves with simplicity and pure obedience.

FALSE

Christians who have been transformed are capable of judging themselves and judging others and are capable of assuring themselves of their inner gifts without dependence on the ministers of the church. They are capable of directing, without the mark of extraordinary vocation or even with the mark of an extraordinary vocation against the express authority of the pastors.

To speak thusly is to teach a profane and novel doctrine and to attack the most essential of all the articles of the Catholic faith, which is that of complete subordination of the faithful to the body of pastors, to whom Jesus Christ said, "He who hears you, hears me."[179]

Conclusion

Holy indifference is nothing more than the selflessness of love. Its trials are nothing other than purification. Abandonment is only the exercise of love during tribulation. What is termed the detachment of virtues is only the shedding of spiritual complacency, of all consolation, and of all self-interest in the exercise of virtues by pure love. The retrenchment of all activity is only the pulling back from self-centered worry and anxiety through pure love. Contemplation is only the simple exercise of that love reduced to one sole motive. Passive contemplation is nothing more than pure contemplation without activity or anxiety. The passive state, whether it is in periods limited by pure and direct contemplation or in intervals in which one does not contemplate, excludes neither real activity nor specific acts of the will nor the specific distinction of virtues with respect to their proper objects, but only simple activity or selfish worry. It is a peaceful exercise of prayer and virtues by means of pure love. *The most essential and immediate transformation and union are no more than the habit of this pure love that alone makes up the inner life and that becomes, therefore, the only principle and the only motive of all deliberate and meritorious acts.*[180] But this habitual state is never fixed or unchanging or permanent:[181] "Verus amor recti," as Saint Leo says, "habet in se apostolicas auctoritates et canonicas sanctiones."[182]

Bibliography

Adam, Antoine. *Du mysticisme à la révolte: les jansenistes du XVIIe siècle.* Paris: Fayard, 1968.

———. *Histoire de la littérature française au XVIIe siècle.* Paris: del Duca, 1968.

This historical survey of seventeenth-century French literature is considered the classic introduction to the subject. The chapter devoted to Fénelon, although succinct, is insightful and thought-provoking.

Adler, Alfred. "Fénelon's Télémaque: Intention and Effect." *Studies in Philology* 55 (1958): 592–95.

Arnauld, Antoine. *De la fréquente communion.* Vol. 27 in *Oeuvres.* Paris: n.p., 1779.

Bayley, Peter. *French Pulpit Oratory.* Cambridge: Univ. Press, 1980.

An essential study of the sermon as art form in seventeenth-century France.

Bénichou, Paul. *Les Morales du grand siècle.* Paris: Gallimard, 1948.

Bérulle, Pierre. *Oeuvres.* Paris: Estienne, 1644.

———. *Bérulle and the French School.* New York: Paulist Press, 1989.

This volume of the Classics of Western Spirituality series includes selected works by Bérulle, Olier, de Paul, and Jean Eudes, translated in most cases for the first time in English, along with very useful footnotes and Introduction. This is the best introduction to the writers of the French School for the general public.

Bettenson, Henry. *Documents of the Christian Church.* Oxford: Univ. Press, 1963.

Probably the best one-volume collection of historical documents relating to several issues discussed in this volume, from Augustine's position on grace to the Jansenist controversy.

Bremond, Henri. *Histoire littéraire du sentiment religieux en France.* Paris: Colin, 1967.

Considered revolutionary when first published in its goal of rehabilitating Fénelon and other mystics of the sixteenth and seventeenth centuries, it remains the classic study of the French School of Spirituality.

Calvet, Jean. *La littérature religieuse en France de François de Sales à Fénelon.* Paris: del Duca, 1956.

Carcassonne, Ely. *Fénelon: l'homme et l'œuvre.* Paris: Boivin, 1946.

Although succinct at only 167 pages, this masterful work is penetrating in its insights to Fénelon's spirituality. The chapters dealing with his doctrine of pure love have never been surpassed. It is, by far, the finest one-volume study of Fénelon's life and work.

Carcassonne, Ely. *Etat présent des travaux sur Fénelon.* Paris: Belles Lettres, 1939.

For over sixty years this critical bibliography held sway as the finest available for Fénelonian studies. Although Carcassonne's commentary can still be read with interest, it has recently been supplanted by H. Hillenaar, *Nouvel état présent des travaux sur Fénelon* (Amsterdam: Rodopi, 1999).

Chadwick, Owen. *The Reformation.* London: Penguin, 1954.

Chamfort, Nicolas. *Maximes, pensées, caractères et anecdotes.* Paris: Flammarion, 1968.

Chérel, Albert. *De Télémaque à Candide.* Paris: del Duca, 1958.

———. *Fénelon au XVIIIe siècle en France.* Paris: Hachette, 1917.

———. *Fénelon et la religion du pur amour.* Paris: Denoel et Steele, 1934.

Cochois, Paul. *Bérulle et l'école française.* Paris: du Seuil, 1963.

Cognet, Louis. *La Mère Angélique et saint François de Sales.* Vol. 2 of *La Réforme de Port-Royal.* Paris: Flammarion, 1950.

Compayré, Gabriel. *Fénelon et l'éducation attrayante.* Paris: Deleplane, 1910.

One of the best studies of Fénelon's method of indirect instruction.

Dainville, François. *L'éducation des Jésuites.* Paris: Editions du Minuit, 1978.

Dagens, Jean. *Bérulle et les origines de la restauration catholique.* Paris; Desclée et Brouwer, 1952.

Daniélou, Madeleine. *Fénelon et le duc de Bourgogne.* Paris: Bloud et Gay, 1955.

This work concentrates on the ten years of Fénelon's preceptorate, emphasizing his relationship with Louis, Duc de Bourgogne. It provides a wealth of anecdotes from contemporary sources.

Davis, James. *Fénelon.* Boston: Twane, 1979.

Although concise, this is the best biographical study of Fénelon currently available in English for the general reader.

De Sales, François. *Oeuvres.* Paris: Gallimard, 1969.

Dupré, Louis, and Don Saliers, eds. *Christian Spirituality.* New York: Crossroad, 1989.

Includes useful bibliography for further reading.

Fénelon, François de. *Oeuvres complètes.* 10 volumes. Geneva: Slatkine Reprints, 1971.

This is the most complete version of Fénelon's work in print. It is a reprint of the Gosselin edition of Fénelon's work, originally published in Paris in 1851.

———. *Oeuvres.* 2 vols. Introduction and notes by Jacques Le Brun. Paris: Gallimard, 1983 and 1997.

Although this edition does not include Fénelon's complete works, it is the finest edition in print for the works included. A masterpiece of critical insight and meticulous scholarship, it is highly recommended for any serious student of Fénelon.

———. *Explication des maximes des saints.* Introduction and notes by Albert Chérel. Paris: Bloud, 1911.

This critical edition supplements the original Versailles edition and the Gosselin edition. Chérel's Introduction is still valuable for its discussion of the various key themes of the work.

———. *Correspondance.* Introduction and notes by Jean Orcibal. 15 vols. Geneva: Klincksieck, 1971–[89].

This is by far the finest critical edition of Fénelon's correspondence available. Every second volume is a detailed commentary on the previous volume of correspondence. A treasure trove of information on Fénelon's family and spiritual influences. The first volume of the series is in itself one of the best biographies of Fénelon in print.

Gautier, Jean. *La Spiritualité de l'école française du XVIIe siècle.* Paris: Le Rameau, 1953.

Gondal, Marie-Louise. *Madame Guyon.* Paris: Beauchesne, 1989.

Goré, Jeanne-Lydie. *Itinéraire de Fénelon.* Paris: P.U.F., 1956.

Originally written as a doctoral dissertation, this remains an insightful study of the early influences on Fénelon's intellectual development. Goré gives particular attention to the role of the Alexandrian mystics in Fénelon's spirituality.

Gouhier, Henri. *Fénelon, philosophe.* Paris: Vrin, 1977.

One of the best studies of Fénelon as a metaphysician and theologian.

Haillant, Marguerite. *Fénelon et la prédication* Paris: Klincksieck, 1969.

Hillenaar, Hink. *Fénelon et les jésuites.* Paris: La Haye, 1967.

Huvelin, Henri. *Quelques directeurs d'âmes au XVIIe siècle.* Paris: Gabalda, 1911.

King, Ursula. *Christian Mystics.* New York: Simon and Schuster, 1998.

Designed for the general public, this is a very readable introduction to the life and work of major Christian mystics from the second century to the present day.

Knox, Ronald. *Enthusiasm.* New York: Oxford Univ. Press, 1950.
An excellent study of heterodox religious movements in the Catholic church throughout history. Chapters 11 through 14 are devoted to Quietism, Mme. Guyon, and Fénelon.

Kolakowski, Leszek. *Chrétiens sans église.* Paris: Gallimard, 1969.

Lajeunie, E. M. *St. François de Sales et le salésienisme.* Paris: du Seuil, 1962.

Lemaître, Jules. *Fénelon.* Paris: Fayard, 1910.

Lombard, Alfred. *Fénelon et le retour à l'antique.* Neuchatel: Secrétariat de l'université, 1954.

Mallet-Joris, Françoise. *Jeanne Guyon.* Paris: Flammarion, 1978.
The result of over ten years of research by one of France's leading historical novelists, this is undoubtedly the best modern study of Mme. Guyon's life and work.

Minois, Georges. *Bossuet.* Paris: Perrin, 2003.

Olier, Jean-Jacques. *Oeuvres.* Paris: Migne, 1856.

Orcibal, Jean. *Saint-Cyran et le jansénisme.* Paris: Seuil, 1961.
An excellent study of this religious movement by one of the twentieth century's leading scholars of seventeenth-century Catholicism.

Pelikan, Jaroslav. *The Christian Tradition.* 5 vols. Chicago: Univ. of Chicago Press, 1974– .
A study of the history of the development of Christian doctrine, with emphasis on the Western church. Volumes 4 and 5 deal with the Reformation and Counter-Reformation.

Rancé, Armand-Jean Le Bouthillier de. *De la sainteté et des devoirs de la vie monastique.* Paris: Muguet, 1683.

Richardt, Aimé. *Fénelon.* Paris: In fine, 1993.

St. Cyres, Viscount. *François de Fénelon.* London: Methuen, 1901.

Although out of print and dated in its scholarship, this is the only full-length biography of Fénelon in English.

Sainte-Beuve. *Port-Royal.* Paris: Gallimard, 1953.

The classic study of Jansenism by one of France's preeminent literary historians.

Solminihac, Alain de. *Lettres.* Cahors: Delsaud, 1930.

Taveneaux, René. *Le catholicisme dans la France classique.* Paris: SEDES, 1980.

Varillon, François. *Fénelon et le pur amour.* Paris: du Seuil, 1957.

Offers selections, with commentary, from Fénelon's work concentrating on his doctrine of pure love.

Viller, Marcel, et al. *Dictionnaire de spiritualité.* Paris: Beauchesne, 1937– .

This multi-volume series is perhaps the best single reference work for the history of Christian spirituality and mysticism. The article "Fénelon" by Louis Cognet is particularly well written.

Notes

INTRODUCTION

1. Although Jean Orcibal in his Introduction to Fénelon's *Correspondance* (Geneva: Klincksieck, 1972), 1:31, describes the financial situation of the Salignac-Fénelon as "ruine," Fénelon never seems to have lacked of any of the necessities of life while growing up. Nevertheless, Orcibal's insights on Fénelon's childhood are invaluable. The introductory volume to his edition of Fénelon's correspondence is in itself a biography of Fénelon and a treasure trove of both critical insight and meticulous scholarship.

2. Letter to Chevalier Fénelon dated 1694, in Fénelon's *Oeuvres complètes*, 10 vols. (Geneva: Slatkine, 1971), 7:405. All references to Fénelon's work, unless otherwise indicated, are from this edition.

3. As Orcibal states, "the direct documents are rare." Orcibal, 10.

4. See François de Dainville, *L'éducation des jésuites* (Paris: Editions de minuit, 1978). This Jesuit college would have been the nearest to the Fénelon château, and Fénelon's knowledge of Latin and Greek, evident in his later writing, argues for his having received a solid grounding in classical studies. The *ratio studiorum*, the Jesuit program of study, was undoubtedly the most sound one in the Périgord at this time, as Dainville's studies have shown.

5. Jeanne-Lydie Goré, *Itinéraire de Fénelon* (Paris: P.U.F., 1956), 49.

6. Ely Carcassonne, *Fénelon: l'homme et l'œuvre* (Paris: Boivin, 1946), 7.

7. See Orcibal, 1:33–35, for a discussion of the biographical confusion concerning Fénelon.

8. Fénelon may well have been tutored either by a local priest or a local squire by the name of Menashié. This "excellent humanist" so praised by some historians, however, turns out on closer inspection to have been merely a kindly neighbor with a rudimentary knowledge of classical letters.

9. Jean Jacques Olier (1608–57), rector of the parish of Saint Sulpice in Paris, founded the seminary of Saint Sulpice in 1642 and would gain a reputation as a spiritual director, preacher, and theologian. As a friend and disciple of Bérulle, as well as a deeply profound and mystical thinker himself, he would come to be considered a leader of the French School of Spirituality and would influence many disciples, such as Condren and

Tronson, to continue to propagate the Christocentric spirituality for which he and Bérulle were known.

10. Letter, dated 1706, included in the Gosselin edition of Fénelon's *Oeuvres complètes*, 7:612. Translation: "I am too young, Holy Father, to have been able to know Vincent personally...But as a child deprived of my father and educated by relatives, it used to please me to hear them tell of the admirable words and deeds of Vincent. [Fénelon goes on to speak of the relationship between his uncle, the marquis, and Vincent de Paul and Olier.] He made use of Olier, the founder of the seminary of Saint Sulpice—that man full of God's grace and clearly apostolic—as director of conscience. And as Olier had been captivated by Vincent and was on terms of intimate friendship and veneration with him, my uncle, being dear to Olier, came also to know Vincent very intimately."

11. In the same letter to Clement XI mentioned above wherein Fénelon describes his uncle the marquis, he also describes his uncle the bishop: "The other relative [Fénelon had just described the marquis] was bishop of Sarlat. He was known for taking care of the poor and in restoring the church buildings in a munificent manner. He was a loving pastor to his flock and beloved of them—indeed a kindly man although sober in his praise of men" (pastor gregis amans, et gregi charus, benignus quidem, sed in laude hominum sobrius). Fénelon, 7:612.

12. "Fénelon, qui venait d'arriver, n'en perdit pas un mot." Jean Calvet, "Fénelon dans ses origines," in *Fénelon, Personlichkeit und Werke* (Baden-Baden, 1953). This is a collection of articles by various scholars published in celebration of the tercentenary of Fénelon's birth.

13. "Suivre les conférences des moyens de se tenir bien unis pour procurer la gloire de Dieu," in Alain de Solminihac, *Lettres* (Cahors: Delsaud, 1937), 587.

14. Orcibal, 1:10.

15. Quoted in the *Fonds Solminihac* TMs, Archives of the diocese of Cahors, unpublished and translated from the original French. These unpublished manuscripts from Solminihac shed much light on the workings of the Counter-Reformation in southwest France in the generation immediately prior to Fénelon.

16. "Dieu m'a fait la grâce et m'a donné cette consolation d'être le premier évêque du royaume qui ait impugné publiquement dans l'assemblée des Prélats et en particulier en toute rencontre la doctrine de Jansenius et l'avoir décrié d'abord qu'elle a paru dans le royaume" (*Fonds Solminihac*, bundle 7:25).

17. Quoted in Solminihac, *Lettres*, 166.

18. Solminihac, *Lettres*, 585.

19. French School of Spirituality: The French historian Henri Bremond popularized this term in his multi-volume *Histoire littéraire du sentiment religieux en France* (Paris: Colin, 1968). He included in this grouping all the great mystics and theologians of the later sixteenth and early seventeenth centuries in France and francophone countries. Saint Francis de Sales and the Cardinal de Bérulle were considered by Bremond the most illustrious figures of the school, but he included many eminent saints and theologians: Olier, Condren, Mme. Acarie, Jeanne de Chantal, Vincent de Paul, and others. Louis Tronson, Fénelon's teacher and mentor at Saint Sulpice in Paris, had been a student of Olier, who had himself been a disciple of de Paul and Condren, who had studied under Bérulle. Thus the spirituality that was passed on to Fénelon in the seminary can be said almost to have come down by way of apostolic succession. For Fénelon it would always be a living tradition to which he was sincerely attached and of which he saw himself as a part.

20. Although the discussion of the work of Bérulle, Olier, and other members of the French School of Spirituality will necessarily be limited in this Introduction, the reader is encouraged to consult *Bérulle and the French School* (New York: Paulist Press, 1989) in the Classics of Western Spirituality series as well as volumes in the same series devoted to precursors who influenced the French School, particularly Francis de Sales.

21. Orcibal, 2:9.

22. Orcibal, 2:302.

23. Carcassonne, 7.

24. Cf. John 10:34, "you are gods," and John 17:22, "The glory that you have given me I have given to them, so that they may be one, as we are one, I in them and you in me, that they may become completely one."

25. For a succinct description of Orthodoxy's views of *theosis* the reader may consult Timothy Ware, *The Orthodox Church* (Middlesex: Penguin, 1963), 28–30. See also the relevant articles on "divinisation" and "grace" in the multi-volume French reference work, the *Dictionnaire de spiritualité*, ed. Marcel Viller (Paris: Beauchesne, 1937–). This is a standard and much respected reference work on spirituality (hereafter the dictionary will be abbreviated *Dict. Sp.*) See also "Supernatural Adoption" in the multi-volume *Catholic Encyclopedia* (New York: Appleton, 1907).

26. Henry Suso (1295–1366): German Dominican. Author of several works including an autobiographical *Life;* the *Little Book of Truth*, a meditation on Christ's passion; and the *Little Book of Eternal Wisdom.* He was widely known as a preacher and author and also as a defender of the mystical doctrine of his fellow Dominican, Meister Eckhart (1260–1327). Johannes Tauler (1300–1361): Dominican, disciple of Eckhart, although

never writing in Latin or formulating an extensive mystical thelogy as Eckhart, nevertheless became famous as a spiritual director and preacher. His teachings, emphasizing the indwelling of God in the human soul, possibly influenced Fénelon in his concept of mystical union and the role of God's love and grace. Catherine of Genoa (1447–1510): Italian laywoman. After enduring an unhappy marriage she underwent a mystical experience in 1473 marked by union with God. She gathered a group of Christian mystics around her with whom she shared her experiences, which were written down in 1551 as *Vita e dottrina.* For a succinct description of the life and works of these and other mystics see Ursula King, *Christian Mystics* (New York: Simon and Schuster, 1998).

27. The question of chronology with respect to Fénelon's discovery of the mystical authors is a murky one, as is the question of his reading of the Quietists, especially Molinos. In a letter to the Abbé de Chanterac—dated October 30, 1698—at the height of the Quietist controversy, he maintains that he had not read Molinos before 1684—and only then at Bossuet's urging for polemical purposes: "Avant ce temps-la je n'avais rien lu ni de Molinos ni même des bons mystiques." Fénelon, 9:570. As for Bossuet, Fénelon claims in another letter to Chanterac that he was totally ignorant of the mystical tradition: "Alors tout le scandalisait; il n'avait lu aucun des auteurs spirituels." Fénelon, 9:202.

28. From Latin *in partibus infidelium*—"in the lands of the infidel": Although nominated to the see of Geneva by the Duke of Savoy, Geneva had been in the hands of Calvinist reformers ever since the mid-sixteenth century. De Sales could not, therefore, occupy his episcopal see and was forced to settle in Annecy, which was still under the control of the Catholic Savoy dynasty.

29. Also called *resignatio ad infernum* in Latin, this concept would be championed by Fénelon in the *Maxims of the Saints* and would be seen as the most vulnerable point of attack in his doctrine of pure love. Bossuet, among others, saw this concept as negating Christian hope in salvation. The apostolic brief *Cum alias,* which condemned various propositions taken from the *Maxims,* would also condemn this concept in the form in which Fénelon expounded it in his book. This was seen as an exaggeration of de Sales's spiritual doctrine.

30. For a full discussion of Bérulle's indebtedness to Jesuit theology, see Jean Dagens, *Bérulle et les origines de la restauration catholique* (Paris: Bloud et Gay, 1952) (hereafter referred to as Dagens).

31. Pierre Bérulle, *Oeuvres* (Paris: Estienne, 1644), 177. All citations from Bérulle will be from this edition. For English-speaking readers,

selections from Bérulle's work are included in *Bérulle and the French School* (New York: Paulist Press, 1989).

32. Bérulle, 188.

33. Bérulle, 311.

34. Quoted in the *Vie de M. Jean-Jacques Olier*, included in the *Oeuvres Complètes de M. Olier* (Paris: Migne, 1856), 9. All references to Olier's work will be to this edition.

35. "Tout sacrifier à Dieu," in Olier, 53.

36. Olier, 114.

37. Bremond, 3:10.

38. "Not change your appearance," Orcibal, 2:48. Even though Orcibal dates this letter as circa 1686, long after Fénelon's student days with Tronson, the advice herein is typical of all Tronson's correspondence to Fénelon.

39. Saint-Simon says of them that they were in the king's highest confidence: "tous deux étaient au plus haut point de la confiance du Roi et de Mme de Maintenon." Saint-Simon, *Mémoires* (Paris: Gallimard, 1983), 253. All references to Saint-Simon will be from this edition.

40. Aimée Richardt believes Fénelon was preaching as early as 1683 and perhaps earlier. See Aimée Richardt, *Fénelon* (Paris: In Fine, 1993), 43.

41. See Marguerite Haillant's *Fénelon et la prédication* (Paris: Klincksieck, 1969), chap. 5, for a fuller discussion of Fénelon's technique of sermon composition.

42. Carcassonne, 23.

43. "Que le plaisir fasse tout," from *De l'Education des filles*, in Fénelon, 5:577. Chapter 6 is devoted to the use of fictional stories both to instruct and to morally educate children. "Les enfans aiment avec passion les contes ridicules...Ne manquez pas de profiter de ce penchant," Fénelon 5:575.

44. Morris Bishop, *A Survey of French Literature* (New York: Harcourt and Brace, 1965), 254.

45. "Extant": I use this term advisedly since scholars believe some fables to have been lost.

46. These roman numerals refer to the numbering of the Gosselin edition of Fénelon's work cited above.

47. Fénelon, 6:208.

48. Number XXIV,

49. Fénelon, 6:215.

50. "l'attente de l'age d'or est un thème important de l'atmosphère messianique qui entourait le duc de Bourgogne." Jacques Le Brun, ed., *Fénelon: Oeuvres* (Paris: Gallimard, 1983), 1313 n. 2.

51. Fénelon, 6:218.

52. Fénelon, 6:218.

53. "Au moins, me voilà délivré de la nécessité d'écrire le petit billet." Quoted by Chamfort in his *Anecdotes* (Paris: Gallimard, 1977), 239. This story was not unique to Chamfort; it seems to have been well known to other contemporary memorialists and historians.

54. Fénelon, 6:221.

55. Louis Cognet, in *Littérature française* (Paris: Flammarion, 1955), 249, describes Louis as "de naturel orgueilleux,violent et sensuel, d'une inquiétante instabilité nerveuse."

56. Quoted by Gabriel Compayré in *Fénelon et l'education attrayante* (Paris: Deleplane, 1910), 59.

57. Fénelon, 6:221.

58. Fénelon, 6:218.

59. Fénelon, 6:195.

60. Fénelon, 6:195.

61. Fénelon, 6:196.

62. Fénelon, 6:209.

63. Fénelon, 6:209.

64. Fénelon, 5:575.

65. Cognet, 250. "L'artifice du procédé est aujourd'hui trop apparent pour notre goût."

66. James Davis, *Fénelon* (Boston: Twane, 1979), 250. This good, short introduction in English to Fénelon's life and work incorporates recent critical evaluation and historical research.

67. For a full discussion of Fontenelle's influence on Fénelon, see Robert Holly, "*Les Dialogues des Morts:* From Boileau to the Prince de Ligne: A Study in Form" (PhD diss., Yale Univ. 1971).

68. For a good account of the atmosphere in Fontenelle's dialogues, see Holly, 20–25.

69. Dialogues numbers XXIX, XXXVIIII, LXIV, and LXXIV appeared in print as early as 1700, but the present corpus of dialogues was not established until the so-called Versailles edition of Fénelon's works in 1823. This was the first serious attempt at a critical edition of Fénelon's complete works to be published.

70. For Fénelon's mature view of the role of the theater in society, see "Lettre à l'Académie française," Fénelon, 6:615–48.

71. "Christian curriculum": This was the case with many Jansenists, for example, Nicole, who saw attending the theater and reading plays as an occasion of sin, and Rancé, founder of La Trappe, who saw study as at best

a necessary evil, certainly not as an aid to piety. See, for example, Rancé's *De la sainteté et des devoirs de la vie monastique* (Paris: Muguet, 1683).

72. "Aucune douceur chrétienne ne modifie ses jugements": Madeleine Daniélou, *Fénelon et le duc de Bourgogne* (Paris: Bloud et Gay, 1955), 109. This is one of the best studies of the relationship between Fénelon and Louis, filled with revealing anecdotes of the day-to-day workings of Fénelon and his staff and how they implemented his educational program.

73. The term *mentor* as a common noun gained general currency in French, then in English, in fact, as a result of the tremendous popularity of Fénelon's third great pedagogical work for Louis, the *Adventures of Telemachus*, in which he will continue his moral instruction in the guise of Mentor, tutor to Telemachus.

74. John Toland, to name only one eminent historian to use similar techniques, has said that his fictional works dealing with World War II, for example, are far more "historically accurate" than his nonfictional histories because they better capture the spirit of the times.

75. Fénelon, 6:296.

76. Fénelon, 6:296.

77. Daniélou in her study of Fénelon's relationship to the Duc de Bourgogne and Lemaitre in his *Fénelon* (Paris: Fayard, 1910) agree that the dialogues were written on an ad hoc basis, probably in response to moral questions that arose in the princes' daily lives.

78. Fénelon, 6:308.

79. Fénelon, 6:308.

80. Fénelon, 6:308.

81. Jules Lemaître, *Fénelon* (Paris: Fayard, 1910), 123.

82. Goré, in her *Itinéraire de Fénelon*, devotes a chapter to the theologians of the Alexandrian school, and their influence on Fénelon. Clement of Alexandria was prominent among the theologians of this school and Fénelon was doubtless attracted to both his personality (his charity, love of learning, and moderation) and his theology (Platonic, mystical, and affective).

83. Phil 3:20: "But our commonwealth is in heaven." The allegory of the Christian as pilgrim was one of the most common ones for French seventeenth-century preachers to use in their sermons. Fénelon's mentor, Bossuet, had a predilection for it and used it often.

84. Saint-Simon, quoted in Richardt, 70.

85. Fénelon, 6:450.

86. Carcassonne, 81.

87. See Antoine Adam's multi-volume *Histoire de la littérature française au XVIIe siècle* (Paris: Del Duca, 1968), 5:169–75. This work is considered by many to be the definitive general study of seventeenth-century French literature and in its scope, as a survey of the entire century, it has not been surpassed. It is highly recommended.

88. Fénelon, 6:405.

89. Fénelon, 6:408.

90. Fénelon, 6:437.

91. See Alfred Adler, "Fénelon's Télémaque: Intention and Effect," in *Studies in Philology* 55 (1958): 592–95.

92. Idomeneus: The name had been previously encountered during Telemachus's sojourn on Crete. He had there heard the story of Idomeneus who, having vowed to the gods to sacrifice the first thing he saw upon returning safely home, was forced to kill his son. For this crime he was exiled by his people. There are several different versions of this story in classical literature, from Euripides to Pausanius, but all agree on Idomeneus's exile.

93. This passage from Teresa of Avila's *Life* is quoted in King, 140. See especially chapter 29 for the description of her mystical ecstasy, being pierced with the arrow of divine love.

94. Fénelon, 6:565.

95. Fénelon, 6:565.

96. Fénelon, 6:428.

97. Fénelon, 6:428.

98. Fénelon, 6:476.

99. Fénelon, 6:477.

100. Daniélou, 169.

101. Antoine Arnauld (1612–94) and Pierre Nicole (1625–95) were both celebrated leaders of and apologists for Jansenism. Armand-Jean Bouthillier de Rancé (1626–1700) although not a Jansenist himself, had affinities with the Jansenists and often allied himself with them during his controversy over monastic learning, for example, and over Quietism.

102. Paul Bénichou, *Les Morales du Grand Siècle* (Paris: Gallimard, 1948); for a discussion of the influence of the Jesuits and Christian humanism on French literature in the seventeenth century, see chap. 1.

103. Jean-Pierre Camus (1583–1642), bishop of Belley, was a close friend of Francis de Sales and the most celebrated author of religious literature of his time, including many novels. Bremond calls him "une âme droite, bonne, pieuse et magnanime" (Bremond 1:151).

104. "Indigne non seulement d'un évèque mais d'un prêtre et d'un chrétien." Cited in Alfred Lombard, *Fénelon et le retour à l'antique au XVIIIe siècle* (Neuchatel: Secrétariat de l'université, 1967), 92.

105. Gustave Lanson, *Histoire de la Littérature française* (Paris: Hachette, 1894), 614.

106. René Pomeau, *La Littérature française* (Paris: Arthaud, 1971), 175. Pommeau, like many other critics, considers the novel to be more of a prose poem than a novel, thus the word "poem."

107. The paper that Calvet gave unfortunately remained unpublished. We have notes taken by one of the conference's participants. They perhaps do not express the force of Calvet's complete argument. They state, however, that "le conférencier estime a reçu ces doctrines [i.e., the mystical doctrines] et s'en est nourri. La philosophie scolatisque et la théologie qu'il a étudiées ensuite, lui ont fourni un vocabulaire technique sans toucher le fond. Lorsque plus tard il a entendu Mme Guyon, il lui est apparu qu'elle donnait un nom à ce qu'il savait et vivait depuis longtemps."

108. The Gosselin edition of Fénelon's complete works is the basis from which the translations in this volume were made. Published in 1851, under the direction of Gosselin and the Sulpician fathers, it is also known as the Paris edition or the edition of Saint Sulpice. In spite of its age, it remains the standard text of Fénelon's works. The reader is encouraged to consult Jacques Le Brun's Pleiade edition of selected works by Fénelon, however, for those works included in it. It is a masterpiece of scholarship and research. Other critical editions to be consulted include Albert Cherel's critical edition of Fénelon's *Explication des maximes des saints* and Jean Orcibal's critical edition of Fénelon's correspondence. See the Bibliography herein for details.

109. Fénelon, 6:72.

110. Fénelon, 6:73.

111. Fénelon's admiration for the work of Clement of Alexandria has been previously noted. Fénelon also was an admirer of Saint Bernard of Clairvaux and would cite him often during the Quietist controversy as an authority for his interpretation of the mystical tradition.

112. Fénelon, 6:76.

113. This is, of course, the classic Augustinian position on grace and free will.

114. Fénelon, 6:77.

115. Fénelon, 6:77.

116. Fénelon, 6:77.

117. Fénelon, 6:73.

118. Fénelon, 6:73.

119. Fénelon, 6:76.

120. Jean Baptiste Colbert (1619–83): Famous minister of Louis XIV, serving in several capacities from finance minister to secretary of the navy and secretary of state, Colbert was among the Sun King's most trusted advisers. The king's confidence in him extended to his sons and daughters and by extension sons-in-law, the Duc de Beauvillier and the Duc de Chevreuse.

121. "Débonnaireté" in the writings of de Sales refers to the "gentleness" of God's love. It was a term consistent with recurring metaphors in Salesian writings of God as loving Prince, since it was a term associated with chivalry. Knights were expected to be "débonnaire" in that they were expected to be "gentle," "courteous," and "mild mannered" when dealing with those who sought their protection.

122. Fénelon, 8:507.

123. Fénelon, 8:522.

124. Orcibal interprets this word in a definite feudal sense and sees Fénelon playing on the chevalier's honor as a chivalrous soldier and vassal to his king. Orcibal, 3:149 n. 2.

125. Fénelon, 8:509.

126. Fénelon, 6:83.

127. Fénelon, 6:83.

128. Messieurs de Port-Royal were a group of illustrious men, many from the highest social and intellectual strata of seventeenth-century France, who converted under the rigorist influence of Saint-Cyran, Arnauld, Nicole, and other Jansenist directors and left their secular occupations to live as semi-hermits near the convent of Port-Royal des Champs. Here they spent their lives in prayer and meditation, for the most part, although some did eventually take up tutoring children. Racine is probably their most celebrated student. Many excellent books are available on the subject of Port-Royal. *Port-Royal* by Sainte-Beuve (Paris: Gallimard, 1953) is the classic study of the convent and those associated with it.

129. For a full treatment of the various questions involved the dating of the "Letter to Louis XIV," see Orcibal, 3:398–400. After sifting all the evidence available, this eminent Fénelonian scholar arrived at an approximate date of December 1693.

130. This is Orcibal's theory. See 2:418 note 84. "Elle (Mme de Maintenon) était en réalité la véritable destinataire de cette lettre, sorte d'aide-mémoire…"

131. "à qui elle fut remise au temps de M. de B.," cited by Orcibal, 3:398.

132. Bishop, 280.

133. Fénelon, 7:511.

134. P. Castex and P. Surer, *Manuel des études littéraires françaises: XVIIe siècle* (Paris: Hachette, 1966), 243.

135. Gustave Lanson, *Histoire de la Litterature Française* (Paris: Hachette, 1912), 619.

136. There have been several excellent studies of Quietism published. See the relevant articles on Quietism and the major figures—Fénelon, Guyon, and others—in the *Dict. Sp.* Jean Armogathe's *Le Quiétisme* is considered a standard reference (Paris: P.U.F., 1973). Françoise Mallet-Joris's biography of Guyon, *Jeanne Guyon* (Paris: Flammarion, 1978), is essential reading.

137. Ronald A. Knox, *Enthusiasm* (New York: Oxford Univ. Press, 1950), 260.

138. Bausset, in Fénelon, 10:57. Cardinal Bausset devotes a chapter in his *Vie de Fénelon* to a discussion of Molinos and his beliefs. Considered one of the leading Fénelon scholars of nineteenth century France, his life of Fénelon is still viewed as one of the best written. Although not available by itself in print, it is included in its entirety in volume 10 of the Gosselin edition of Fénelon's complete works.

139. Molinos, quoted in Georges Minois, *Bossuet* (Paris: Perrin, 2003), 583.

140. Molinos, quoted in Mallet-Joris, 669.

141. Although several biographies of Jeanne Guyon exist (the best and most recent being that of Mallet-Joris), no biography exists of François La Combe. The reader will consult with profit Jean Orcibal's article "La Combe" in *Dict. Sp.*, 9:36–40.

142. This question of Guyon's knowledge of the doctrine of authors condemned as Quietist by the church is probably insoluble. She herself always maintained that she had little or no knowledge of the mystics in question. This assertion is in some sense disingenuous, since we know that she met with and engaged in discussions of doctrine with François Malaval (1627–1719), the blind mystic of Marseilles, whose writings would be condemned by Rome. Moreover, her spiritual director, François La Combe, had lived in Rome at the height of Molinos's popularity and was doubtless influenced by his teaching.

143. In the *Moyen Court*, Guyon, speaking of the single act, says: "But, dearly beloved, whoever you are who sincerely wish to give yourselves up to God, I conjure you, that after having once made the donation, you take not yourselves back again; remember, a gift once presented, is no longer at the disposal of the giver." Jeanne Guyon, A Short and Very Easy Method to Prayer.

144. Knox, 273.

145. Guyon, quoted in Minois, 587.

146. Guyon, quoted in Knox, 273.

147. Mallet-Joris, 185.

148. Louis Dupré, "Jansenism and Quietism," in *Christian Spirituality: Post Reformation and Modern*, ed. Louis Dupré and Don Saliers (New York: Crossroad, 1989), 136.

149. Guyon, quoted in Mallet-Joris, 199.

150. Guyon, quoted in Mallet-Joris, 202.

151. As Knox points out, Bossuet made great satirical hay of this and other incidents in his *Relation sur le Quiétisme.* Bossuet mentions that Mme. Guyon was so "full " of grace that "it was often necessary to unlace her." Quoted in Knox, 330.

152. Guyon, quoted in Mallet-Joris, 199.

153. The bishop of Geneva "in partibus" was especially tolerant. He would write her a letter attesting to her faith and morals. This letter will later be cited by Guyon and Fénelon in defense of her doctrine. The bishop of Grenoble, while courteous, was less charmed by Mme. Guyon than his colleague and after allowing her to teach for a while in his diocese ultimately asked her to move on.

154. All these terms (and others even more extravagant, such as comparing herself to the Woman in Revelations) were later to shock and horrify Bossuet, who quotes them liberally in his polemical works against Fénelon and Guyon. For his part, Fénelon chided Maintenon for allowing herself to be misled by Bossuet into believing such terms were heretical when they were only "metaphorical expressions."

155. Tronson, of course, was Fénelon's friend and former seminary teacher. Bossuet was Fénelon's friend and mentor, and Noailles, a former classmate of Fénelon, had known him since childhood and was also considered favorably disposed to him. In spite of the bitterness that would later ensue and the recriminations exchanged between some of these participants (particularly between Fénelon and Bossuet), this commission was in no way stacked against Fénelon or biased against Guyon at the outset.

156. Bossuet, quoted in Richardt, 125. Richardt's chapter on the friendship between Fénelon and Mme. Guyon is well written and recommended to the reader wishing a general overview of their relationship.

157. Bossuet, letter to Mme. d'Albert, dated 1694, quoted in Mallet-Joris, 212.

158. There are several excellent histories available of Bossuet's correspondence and interviews with Mme. Guyon. Two of the most recent and readable accounts are found in the biography of Fénelon by Aimé

Richardt and Georges Minois's *Bossuet*. From Bossuet's perspective, however, the standard account of his dealings with Guyon remains his *Relation sur le Quiétisme*, included in the Pléiade edition of his *Oeuvres* (Paris: Gallimard, 1961). See page 1108 where he summarizes Guyon's mystical experiences as "absurdes communications," and "illusions." All future references to Bossuet's works will be from this edition.

159. Fénelon, 2:223.

160. For a description of the various documents and books consulted by the commissioners, see Bossuet, 1115–20. Bossuet betrays a growing frustration with Fénelon at this point, saying that the writings he sent the commissioners in defense of mysticism "multiplied day by day."

161. In his *Réponse à la Relation sur le Quiétisme* Fénelon would claim that Bossuet was nearly completely ignorant of the mystical tradition and its greatest exponents, such as Tauler, Saint Catherine of Genoa, Saint Teresa of Avila, and Francis de Sales. "Je voyais de plus qu'en cette affaire la doctrine des saints mystiques n'était pas moins en péril que moi. M. de Meaux ne les connaissait point" (Fénelon, 3:98).

162. Bossuet, 1115.

163. Fénelon, 2:226.

164. Bossuet, 1119.

165. A view Bossuet expressed in the *Relation sur le Quiétisme*, 1109–15.

166. Knox, 342.

167. Bossuet, 1126.

168. The last years of Guyon's life were spent in Blois under a sort of house arrest, what Mallet-Joris refers to as "la résidence surveillée" (Mallet-Joris, 594).

169. "Ce n'est pas l'homme ou le très grand docteur que je regarde en vous; c'est Dieu." Fénelon, quoted in Bossuet, 1117.

170. Fénelon, 9:81.

171. J. Calvet is not the only scholar to have pointed out the tortured distinctions Fénelon seems to make between the truth and falsity of many of the maxims. "Le procédé a quelquechose de sec et de lassant et d'aveuglant: on a l'impression que l'auteur affirme et nie successivement la même chose." *La Littérature religieuse de François de Sales à Fénelon* (Paris: del Duca, 1956), 402.

172. The hypostatic union (*hypostasis* in Greek) is the technical term from the Council of Chalcedon's definition of the union between Jesus as God and Jesus as man: "Christ, Son, Lord, Only-begotten, recognized in two natures, without confusion, without change, without division...the distinction of natures being in no way annulled by the union, but rather the characteristics of each nature being preserved and coming together to form

one person and subsistence." Quoted in Henry Bettenson, *Documents of the Christian Church* (London: Oxford Univ. Press, 1963), 51.

173. This is de Sales's doctrine of the "fine pointe de l'âme" from Bk. I, chap. 12 of the *Traité de l'Amour de Dieu.* Fénelon discusses this concept by name in Article IX of the *Maxims.*

174. In delineating this distinction between "empirical" and "mystical" personalities, I am indebted to Carcassonne's analysis, found in chapter 3 of his *Fénelon,* a penetrating study of Fénelon's mystical theology. See especially pp. 52–53.

175. "Je ne puis qu'estimer ce que j'entends, admirer ce que je n'entends pas." Letter dated March 22, 1696, included in the Gosselin edition of Fénelon's *Oeuvres complètes,* 9:86. Saint-Simon expressed similar consternation, writing that "this book shocked everyone: the ignorant because they didn't understand anything in it and the others because of its difficulty and its barbarous, novel language" (Saint-Simon, 369).

176. Saint-Simon, 369.

177. In Calvet's happy turn of phrase: "M. de Cambrai y soutenait des choses inouies; on ne les comprenait pas, mais on les disait dangereuses" (*La Littérature religieuse de François de Sales à Fénelon,* 403).

178. Fénelon, 9:201.

179. Fénelon, 9:337.

180. Fénelon, 9:516.

181. Knox, 346.

182. Fénelon, 9:517.

183. Innocent XII, *Cum alias,* quoted in Richardt, 201.

184. Saint-Simon says that Louis XIV "publicly showed his joy" ("en témoigna publiquement sa joie"), 603.

185. Duc de Beauvillier, quoted in Saint-Simon, 604.

186. Fénelon, 9:720.

187. Leszek Kolakowski makes this case in *Chrétiens sans Eglise* (Paris: Gallimard, 1969), 492–566.

188. Abbé Bossuet, quoted in Richardt, 204.

189. Knox, 347.

190. Knox, 348.

191. Anthony Levi, *Louis XIV* (New York: Carroll and Graf, 2004), 243.

192. Legend has it that, speaking about the faithfulness of his friends even after his banishment from Versailles, Fénelon quipped that there was no greater proof of the doctrine of pure love than that of courtiers still remaining faithful to a friend who had suffered such signal political disgrace.

Sermon for the Feast of Epiphany on the Vocation of the Gentiles

1. Preached before the Society for Foreign Missions in its church in Paris in 1687. See "Early Preaching" in the Introduction.

2. "Surge...": "Arise, shine; for your light has come, / and the glory of the Lord has risen upon you" (Isa 60:1). This was the text appointed by the lectionary for reading on the day (January 6) that Fénelon gave this sermon.

3. By "house" Fénelon means the Society for Foreign Missions.

4. "Today": Fénelon is, of course, referring to the fact that Epiphany commemorates the visit of the Magi to Bethlehem. Traditionally, many doctors of the church considered the Magi to be allegorical representations of the Gentile nations, acknowledging the divinity of Jesus.

5. "Light...darkness": Highly metaphorical language to designate Christ (the light to the Gentiles) and darkness (ignorance of the gospel). The "star," of course, is the star of Bethlehem, which lit the way for the Magi to find Jesus.

6. "Come, come": This anaphoric repetition calls to mind several hymns of the Christmas season, such as "Adeste Fideles," with its refrain of "venite, venite." Interestingly, this hymn is believed to date from approximately the same time period that Fénelon composed this sermon.

7. "New Magi...Indies": Fénelon is doubtless alluding to the Siamese ambassadors present at the sermon. They can be seen as princes from the East come to worship the true God at a Christian church.

8. Fénelon here invokes the aid of the Holy Spirit to preach his sermon effectively. This invocation would be familiar to an Anglican audience in that it echoes the collect derived from Psalm 19, often inserted by preachers at the beginning of their sermons: "Let the word of my mouth and the meditation of my heart be always acceptable in your sight, O Lord, my strength and my Redeemer."

9. This last paragraph forms what was commonly called in French the *chute* or transition to the rest of the sermon, prefaced invariably in Catholic preaching by the Hail Mary. This was one element typical to the Catholic sermon of seventeenth-century France that separated it from a Protestant sermon. The Ave Maria was felt so strongly by Protestants to be idolatrous that Fénelon often omitted it from his sermons during his mission to convert the Huguenots of southwest France after the revocation of the Edict of Nantes in 1685. He was criticized for this omission and was obliged to reinsert it. Cf. correspondence from Seignelay to Fénelon in volume two of the Orcibal edition. The letter dated February 7, 1686,

is of particular interest. In it Fénelon states: "nous avons cru devoir différer de quelques jours l'Ave Maria dans nos sermons." Orcibal, 2:27.

10. Cf. Isa 60:3: "Nations shall come to your light, / and kings to the brightness of your dawn."

11. Allusion to the conquest of Jerusalem in AD 70 by Emperor Titus, who reduced the city to ruble and sent into exile the majority of the Jewish population.

12. "Fallen short": *déchu* in French. The word choice by Fénelon is interesting and suggestive of his view of the Jews in relation to God. *Déchu* can mean in legal jargon "dispossessed," as a ruler who has been removed from the throne or a person who has been judged unfit to, for example, administer his or her property or act as executor for others. In a theological sense it refers to a fall from grace. Satan, for example, is referred to in French as the *Ange déchu*, the fallen angel. Here Fénelon seems to say that the Jews were removed from their status as the chosen people after their rejection of Christ and have subsequently fallen from God's grace. This opinion was widely shared among Christians of the seventeenth century. One of the most common representations of the synagogue and/or the Jewish people in visual arts from the Middle Ages up to the Renaissance was that of a woman with a blindfold over her eyes to symbolize the Jewish people's obstinate refusal to see the truth of the gospel.

13. Gal 4:26: "But the other woman corresponds to the Jerusalem above; she is free, and she is our mother."

14. "By the hand": one of Fénelon's favorite metaphors. This image of God leading humanity by the hand is found throughout the pedagogical works as well as in Fénelon's spiritual correspondence.

15. See Rom 10:20: "I have been found by those who did not seek me."

16. These are traditional metaphors from the patristic period to describe the relationship between Jesus, the Bridegroom, and his church, the Spouse. As early as the second century AD church fathers such as Origen were already interpreting books of the Bible (especially the Song of Solomon) in this allegorical sense. This metaphorical identification between Jesus as bridegroom to the soul later would be used by several famous mystics, such as Saint Teresa of Avila, to describe their experience of mystical union with God, the *noces spirituelles* or "spiritual wedding."

17. Fénelon is referring to the discovery of America in the fifteenth century.

18. Fénelon may have had in mind Thomas à Kempis's passage from the *Imitation of Christ:* "Homo proponit sed Deus disponit."

19. Dan 8:5: "As I was watching, a male goat appeared from the west, coming across the face of the whole earth without touching the ground."

20. I have kept the traditional, albeit somewhat confusing translation of "charity" instead of "love," because Fénelon himself insists in this sermon on translating the term by "charité" instead of the more common French word "amour." The reader is reminded that charity here refers to divine love, being derived in its etymological sense from *caritas*.

21. Isa 52:7.

22. "Their own blood": Fénelon could well have had in mind the martyrdom of the Jesuit missionaries (Jean de Brébeuf and his colleagues) in Canada between 1642 and 1649, which was widely reported in France.

23. See Isa 9:2: "The people who walked in darkness / have seen a great light; / those who dwelt in a land of deep darkness— / on them light has shined."

24. Ignatius: The Society of Jesus, the Jesuits, was founded in the sixteenth century by Saint Ignatius of Loyola.

25. According to Le Brun, this would be an allusion to P. Bagot, a Jesuit who turned down the offer to become the king's confessor in order to devote himself to founding a congregation of missionary priests. Le Brun, 1495.

26. Using a rhetorical device known as apostrophe, Fénelon addresses the Siamese king, Phra-Narai, as if he were present in the assembly.

27. As mentioned in note 7 above, Fénelon preached this sermon before several ambassadors from Siam to the court of Louis XIV.

28. "Indian": Siam was considered part of the vast oriental territories termed the East Indies by Europeans. Thus, the Siamese ambassadors were referred to as Indians.

29. Peter: Simon Peter, one of Jesus' twelve disciples. According to the Catholic Church, Peter went to Rome after the resurrection to preach the gospel there. He is therefore considered the first bishop of Rome and, consequently, the first pope. His successor at this time would have been Pope Innocent XI.

30. "Land of the Gentiles": In French, *gentilité* (from the Latin *gentilitas*); it is the corollary to *Chrétienté*, translated "Christendom."

31. This passage echoes Isaiah 40:4–5: "Every valley shall be lifted up, / and every mountain and hill be made low; / the uneven ground shall become level, / and the rough places a plain. / Then the glory of the Lord shall be revealed, / and all people shall see it together, / for the mouth of the LORD has spoken."

32. "Holy Pontiff": Allusion to François Pallu, missionary to China who had died in that country in 1684. Francis Xavier was a founding

member of the Society of Jesus, friend and disciple of Ignatius Loyola. He became famous for his missionary work in India, Japan, and China, where he died in 1552. He was canonized in 1622.

33. "Erring brothers": allusion to the Protestants among whom Fénelon had preached, and who represented, at this time, approximately one-quarter to one-third of the French population.

34. Cf. Matt 5:14: "You are the light of the world. A city built on a hill cannot be hid. No one after lighting a lamp puts it under the bushel basket, but on the lampstand, and it gives light to all in the house."

35. In this sermon we find some of Fénelon's typical arguments against the concept of the church championed by many Protestants. Fénelon's argument in this passage is that Christ intended for his church to be united and visible in its organization. The only united and visible church that was preaching the gospel to all the corners of the earth, according to him, was the Roman Catholic Church; ergo, she was obviously the only true church of God. In the pages that follow we see developments of this argument for Catholicity, such as the argument that since Christ left his Holy Spirit to guide the church, this visible church could not have fallen into error; moreover, since Christ left the church to preach the gospel to the poor and ignorant, he could not have allowed this church to fall into heresy because this would have endangered the salvation of the "simple folk" throughout the ages who innocently followed the church's teachings.

36. Donatist: A member of a schismatic sect that arose in northern Africa in the fourth century. "Manichean": A believer in Manichaeism, which was a dualistic religious philosophy taught by Mani, a Persian religious leader of the third century. Augustine of Hippo had been a devotee of Manichaeism before converting to Christianity and later, as bishop, was a fierce opponent of Donatism.

37. Luke 10:16.

38. Sir 45:27: "Ipse est enim pars eius, et hereditas."

39. Here I follow Fénelon's own translation of Exodus 32:26, in the Vulgate "si quis est Domini iungatur mihi." The New Revised Standard Version has the slightly different "Who is on the LORD's side? Come to me!"

40. Literally, "Dieu qui lit dans les cœurs et qui sonde les reins," which is a paraphrase of the Vulgate Jeremiah 17:10 "Ego Dominus scrutans cor, et probans renes." This would render into English as the awkward sounding "probe the kidneys." I have therefore preferred to follow the New Revised Standard Version of the same text: "I the LORD test the mind / and search the heart."

41. This passage echoes the themes and vocabulary found in Titus. 2:11–13: "For the grace of God has appeared in the present age bringing

salvation to all, training us to renounce impiety and worldly passions, and to live lives that are self-controlled, upright, and godly, while we wait for the blessed hope and the manifestation of the glory of our great God and Savior, Jesus Christ. He it is who gave himself for us that he might redeem us from all iniquity and purify for himself a people of his own who are zealous for good deeds."

42. An allusion to the Beatitudes (Matt 5:3–11) "Blessed are the poor…blessed are those who mourn."

43. The theme of glory being removed from the chosen people due to their sin is a common one in scripture. In 1 Samuel 4 we read of the Israelites allowing the Philistines to capture the ark of the covenant. Upon hearing this news Phinehas's wife gave birth to a child and called him Ichabod, "meaning 'the glory has departed from Israel,' because the ark of God has been captured."

44. Fénelon doubtless takes this metaphor from Saint Paul, who compares recently converted Christians to wild branches grafted onto a cultivated tree, the original olive tree being the Jewish people, the original chosen people (cf. Rom 11:17).

45. Allusion to the Gospel of John (1:5). Fénelon here seems, however, to be misinterpreting the original for his didactic purpose. In the Vulgate the text reads "Et lux in tenebris lucet, et tenebrae eam non comprehenderunt," which he translates "comprendre" in French, although the verb in French does not have the sense of "overcoming" that the Latin and original Greek verbs have.

46. The first major ecumenical councils of the church were held in the eastern part of the Roman empire: Nicea, Constantinople, Chalcedon.

47. Fénelon is alluding to the Muslim conquest of the Eastern Roman Empire beginning in the seventh century and culminating with the fall of Constantinople in 1453. Muslim rule saw a decline in numbers of Christians and the closing of many monasteries.

48. Augustine (354–430): Bishop of Hippo and author of many treatises defending his position on the role of grace in the work of salvation. His influence was tremendous throughout the history of Western Catholicism, particularly in the theological disputes of seventeenth-century France that pitted Jansenists against Jesuits.

49. Here Fénelon lists the major losses of national churches to Catholicism at the time of the Reformation. He is using one of the most common arguments employed by Catholic apologists of the Counter-Reformation against Protestants: The church is a living entity, nourished by the Holy Spirit. Once a group of Christians separates itself from this "stalk" it inevitably withers and dies. A proof of Protestants' lack of

spiritual nourishment, according to Fénelon, is their lack of missionary work. He was factually correct, in that the Protestant churches in the sixteenth and seventeenth centuries were concerned with consolidating their positions rather than with missionary endeavors. The great age of Protestant missions came in the eighteenth and nineteenth centuries.

50. Prov 20:26 (in the Vulgate): "Dissipat impios rex sapiens" (the wise king disperses the impious).

51. An allusion to the growing movement of the *libertins* or freethinkers in seventeenth-century France. Writers such as Montaigne had given impetus to skepticism in the sixteenth century and by Fénelon's time there was an influential group of skeptics, such as Fontenelle, who were widely discussing their views and publishing them.

52. "If they were capable of it": In this passage Fénelon appears to champion a radical Augustinian interpretation of the perseverance of the elect. Fénelon's concept of grace is one that seems to have evolved from his youth to his adulthood. Although sometimes seemingly contradictory and always full of nuance, Fénelon's earliest writings on the subject (this sermon—it will be remembered—is one of his earliest published works) seem to approximate Jansenist interpretations of irresistible grace. There were even rumors of Fénelon being a Jansenist himself during this period. In his mature writings, however, he will always champion the Jesuit position of prevenient grace requiring human cooperation and capable of being rejected by free will.

53. This is a free rendering of Isaiah 49:15: "Can a woman forget her nursing child, / or show no compassion for the child of her womb? / Even these may forget, / yet I will not forget you."

Fables

NUMBER I—AN OLD QUEEN AND YOUNG PEASANT

1. "Nearly coughed up a lung": a very liberal translation of an earthy, comic expression in French. Literally, "she coughed until she died."

2. "Uglier than an ape": literally, *guenuche*, a female monkey, which was a common term of derision in seventeenth-century France.

3. "Peronelle in the village": Rarely is the moral of a Fénelonian fable clearer than this one is. It is better for the Duc de Bourgogne to learn

how to be satisfied with his own life and fate than constantly to want to change his life. Fénelon, who was well versed in Latin and Greek, doubtless had in mind the quintessential Greek maxim *gnothi seauton* (know thyself).

NUMBER IX—PATIENCE AND EDUCATION

4. "lick": A very earthy term, which is true to life. Fénelon set out in his pedagogical works for the Duc de Bourgogne to teach various subjects, from history to anthropology to zoology. Bears, of course, actually do lick their young in nurturing them.

5. As occurs in nearly all of Fénelon's fables, there is a moral to the story. In this case he extols the virtues of patience and education.

NUMBER XXIV— NIGHTINGALE AND WARBLER

6. Alpheus River (also Alpheios): In Greek and Roman mythology a river associated especially with Hercules, who diverted it in order to clean out the Augean stables as one of his labors.

7. Graces: In Greek and Roman mythology, the Graces are three goddesses considered the embodiment of grace and loveliness.

8. Pan: In Greek and Roman mythology the god of woodlands, half man and half goat, often associated with mirth and merriment, sometimes of a licentious nature.

9. Philomela: In Greek and Roman mythology the sister of Prokne, who was married to Tereus, king of Thrace. Tereus seduced and raped Philomela. She was subsequently turned into a nightingale by the gods.

10. "young shepherd": This is obviously an allegorical representation of Fénelon's pupil, the Duc de Bourgogne.

11. Muses: In Greek and Roman mythology the nine daughters of the union of Zeus and Mnemosyne. They each preside over a branch of the arts: Kalliope is the Muse of epic poetry; Kleio of history; Euterpe of tragedy; Melpomene of lyric poetry; Terpsichore of dancing; Erato of hymns; Polyhymnia of dancing or flute playing; Urania of astronomy; and Thaleia of comedy.

12. Apollo: In Greek and Roman mythology the god of the sun and the patron of music, poetry, and art. Traditionally portrayed in classical art as an extremely handsome and graceful young man.

13. Admetos: In Greek and Roman mythology the king of Pherai to whom Apollo was indentured as a punishment after having killed one of the cyclops.

14. Minerva (Athena in Greek): In Greek and Roman mythology the goddess of wisdom. She is associated with the city of Athens, whose patroness she was.

15. Orpheus: In Greek and Roman mythology the son of Apollo and Kalliope, the Muse. He was such a wonderful musician that it was said that even wild beasts followed him and the trees bent to listen to his playing the lyre.

16. Hercules: In Greek and Roman mythology the son of Zeus and Alcmene. The greatest of the demi-gods, he was celebrated for his strength and courage in destroying various monsters.

17. Achilles: In Greek and Roman mythology the son of the mortal Peleus and the goddess Thetis, who supposedly dipped him in the river Styx to make him invulnerable to any human weapon. Unfortunately, she was obliged to hold him by his heel, and it was in this heel that he was shot and killed during the Trojan war. Although the great hero of the Greeks in Homer's *Iliad*, he is nevertheless portrayed as quick-tempered, reckless, and petulant—all faults that Fénelon saw as incipient in his pupil, the Duc de Bourgogne, and which he wished to restrain.

18. "cornucopia" (also called the horn of plenty): A goat's horn filled to overflowing with fruit and flowers. It was considered a symbol of prosperity and abundance.

19. "golden age": This is not mere poetic fancy on Fénelon's part or flattery of his royal pupil. Fénelon seriously hoped and believed that the Duc de Bourgogne would one day rule France and that he had the qualities and the intelligence to bring about a golden age in France. Fénelon imagined his pupil as incarnating the virtues of Saint Louis with the compassion of Henri IV.

20. This image is not as outlandish or bizarre as it may appear to a modern reader. It was common in mythology and legend to picture Orpheus, Apollo, and other inspired gods and demi-gods as bending nature to their song and causing flowers to grow along their path.

21. "satyrs and fauns": In Greek and Roman mythology woodland divinities usually pictured with the body of a man and the horns and feet of a goat.

22. Echo: In Greek and Roman mythology a nymph who was punished by Hera—wife of Zeus and queen of the gods—by having her repeat the last words she heard anyone saying.

23. "dryads": In Greek and Roman mythology divinities who presided over forests.

NUMBER XXI—
YOUNG BACCHUS AND THE FAUN

24. Bacchus: In Greek and Roman mythology the son of Zeus and Semele, the god of wine. As in so many Fénelonian fables, the allegory here is clear. The young god Bacchus represents the young Duc de Bourgogne, who must learn to correct his own faults before criticizing others.

25. Silenus: In Greek and Roman mythology a satyr who became Bacchus's tutor.

26. "This critic": the young faun.

27. "sacred to his cult": in Greek mythology Bacchus is often portrayed with a crown of grapevine and either wearing or holding bunches of grapes. These were symbols of his cult as the god of wine.

28. "bristling": in French *hérissée*, which means that the hairs were standing on end. An odd adjective to describe a fur but the impression that Fénelon wants to convey here, I believe, is that of a savage, unkempt appearance. The ancient Greeks associated Bacchus's cult with wild and drunken orgiastic rituals (whence the English word *bacchanal*), and he was seen in many ways as being the opposite of Apollo with his moderate and reasoned love of art and beauty. The analogy should not be stressed too much in this fable, however, since Fénelon's main purpose seems to be simply to show that the faun, being associated with Bacchus and his unbridled mirth, was not restrained by polite rules of etiquette and could therefore openly and honestly speak his mind.

NUMBER XXXII—
INDISCREET PRAYER OF NELEUS

29. Nestor: One of the protagonists of Homer's *Iliad*, famous for his wisdom and discretion.

30. Pisistratus: The son of Nestor in the Homeric epics. Telemachus meets him, along with Nestor, in Book Three of the *Odyssey* while searching for his father.

31. Pallas: One of the many cult names of Athena/Minerva, goddess of wisdom in Greek and Roman mythology.

32. "fill with your spirit": The reader will note the similarity of this prayer with the liturgies of baptism, confirmation, ordination, consecration, and coronation in the Catholic Church. This is no coincidence. Fénelon uses the goddess Minerva (and her alter ego, Mentor) as a metaphor for divine Wisdom and divine Grace in his third pedagogical work, the *Adventures of Telemachus.* This fables prefigures this comparison and underlines the didactic nature of the pedagogical works. Fénelon means for Louis, Duc de Bourgogne, to understand the importance of his role as a divinely sanctioned and blessed one. At his coronation he would receive graces of the Holy Spirit to enable him to accomplish his role as king of France by divine right.

33. "cut the thread": In Greek mythology it was actually the Fates (Atropos, spinning the past; Klotho, spinning the present; and Lachesis, spinning the future) who determined the span of human life. Atropos was usually held to be the Fate who cut the thread of days. Here Fénelon gives Athena even greater importance by investing her with this power.

34. Neleus: In Greek mythology the father of Nestor had been killed by Hercules after having been refused his blessing.

35. It is likely, as Jacques LeBrun suggests in his notes to the *Fables* (Le Brun, 1318), that this fable may have been written at about the same time that Fénelon was working on the first draft of the *Adventures of Telemachus.* The last chapter of the novel features a scene that is almost identical to this, with the difference being the substitution of Telemachus for Neleus at the altar, seeing the vision of Athena.

36. "nothing of the effeminate": Ironic, in that Minerva was a female goddess. This seeming inconsistency may be explained one of two ways: (1) Minerva was the most virile and warlike of the Olympian goddesses, often pictured in ancient art wearing armor and bearing arms; (2) Minerva was intended always to be, in the pedagogical works, a model for the Duc de Bourgogne to emulate. Fénelon was concerned by what he saw as incipient signs of effeminacy in his pupil—rumors circulated at court about the homosexual proclivities of his grandfather, Louis XIV—so he encourages a virile, manly conduct in the Duc de Bourgogne throughout the pedagogical works.

37. "any word": We may compare this theophany with many such manifestations in the Bible. As in this fable, the biblical theophanies to Moses, Isaiah, and other prophets were almost always accompanied by fear and trembling on the part of the prophets. (Cf. Isa 6:1, 4–5: "In the year that King Uzziah died I saw the Lord sitting upon a throne, high and lofty...The pivots on the thresholds shook at the voice of those who called, and the house filled with smoke. And I said: "Woe is me! I am lost, for I

am a man of unclean lips, and I live among a people of unclean lips; yet my eyes have seen the King, the Lord of hosts!")

38. "nectar...ambrosia": In Greek mythology nectar and ambrosia are the food and drink of the gods.

39. "ocean": The image of water, especially oceans and floods, symbolizing sin and temptation, is a recurring one in Fénelon's work. There is the very dramatic scene at the end of chapter 6 of the *Adventures of Telemachus* in which Minerva, under the guise of Telemachus's tutor Mentor, saves Telemachus from the ocean by holding him by the hand, thus leading him to safety. This is an obvious allegory of Christians' battles against temptations from which they can be saved by divine grace upholding them and leading them to salvation.

40. "palace": This seems to be a reference to Versailles, the magnificent palace built by Louis XIV, grandfather of Louis Duc de Bourgogne. We know from Fénelon's "Letter to Louis XIV," written around the same time that he was composing the *Fables*, that Fénelon thought the enormous expenditure of public monies on Versailles was unconscionable. (See "Letter to Louis XIV" in this volume.) One of the lessons that Fénelon repeatedly tried to instill in the Duc de Bourgogne was that of simplicity, as opposed to the corruption and luxury of the court of Versailles.

41. "daily occupations": Fénelon's aspiration was to become counselor (perhaps prime minister) to the future king that he hoped the Duc de Bourgogne would become. One of his main goals would then have been to bring France back, inasmuch as possible, to a medieval polity and social structure. Fénelon's own family being of old nobility and having ruled over manor and serfs, he had an idyllic image of the relationship between benign liege-lord in the castle and the contented, hard-working peasant in the field. He saw mostly deleterious consequences for France in the social upheaval of the sixteenth and seventeenth centuries, the rise of the bourgeoisie, and the concomitant abasement of much of the ancient nobility by Richelieu and Mazarin, serving Louis XIII and Louis XIV. The model king that he constantly held up to Louis, Duc de Bourgogne, was Louis IX, Saint Louis, medieval crusader and the only canonized king in French history.

42. "wisdom and justice": Here Fénelon calls to mind the gifts that the wisest of all Old Testament kings, Solomon, asked of God. Fénelon suggests that Neleus, and by extension Louis, Duc de Bourgogne, can rule as wisely as Solomon if he only seeks to rule in accordance with Christian principles and eschews vain luxury and sensual pleasures.

43. "How blind..." It is certainly no coincidence to see similarities between Neleus's *mea culpa* and the sacrament of confession. The three

essential elements of any sincere confession—(1) the recognition of the fault, (2) the request for forgiveness, and (3) the intention of amending one's future conduct—are all present here in Neleus's contrite conversation with Minerva.

The Dialogues of the Dead

DIALOGUE XXVIII—DIONYSIUS AND DIOGENES

1. Dionysius the Elder (431–367 BC): Tyrant of Syracuse who eventually carved out a kingdom stretching from Sicily to lower Italy. He was a poet and a patron of poets and artists; still, he acquired a reputation as a suppressor of liberty. It is this aspect of Dionysius's story that Fénelon emphasizes in this dialogue, using him as his satiric foil in order to condemn overweening ambition, unjust tyranny, corruption, and dissipation in personal life.

2. Diogenes (412–323 BC): Greek philosopher, founder of the Cynic school that stressed the vanity of worldly possessions as a means of acquiring happiness. He was famous for living in a sort of barrel or tub like a dog (*kyon* in Greek), hence the name of his philosophy.

3. "Macedonian": He is referring to Alexander the Great. According to ancient historians, when Alexander visited him and asked what he could do for him, Diogenes replied, "Just get out of my sun."

4. Rhegium: Dionysius captured the Italian city in 387, enabling him to exert control over most of lower Italy.

5. Fates: In Greek and Roman mythology the Fates were said to have the power to determine a person's lifespan. They were pictured as three sisters, spinning (Atropos, spinning the past; Klotho, spinning the present; and Lachesis, spinning the future); Atropos cut the thread of life.

6. "revels": This anecdote is related by several classic authors.

7. "disarmed": As has been mentioned before, the salient feature of the Fénelonian Hades is that it renders powerless all those tyrants and dictators who wielded absolute power on earth. The leitmotif in most of the dialogues recalls the Latin proverb "sic transit gloria mundi."

DIALOGUE L—
MARCUS AURELIUS AND ANTONINUS PIUS

8. Marcus Aurelius: Roman emperor (in the first century) celebrated for his beneficent rule and famous as the author of the *Sayings*, a collection of maxims based on Stoic philosophy.

9. "hardened virtue of the Stoics": literally *vertue insensible*, meaning "virtue that cannot feel anything," that is, that is inured to pain. Stoic philosophers taught that life can only be borne if we abstain from vice (revels, orgies, drunkenness, and so forth) and harden ourselves to disappointment and pain.

10. Antoninus: Antoninus Pius, emperor of Rome (86–161 AD) who adopted Marcus Aurelius and made him his heir. He was known for his benevolent, moderate rule.

11. Commodus: Son of Marcus Aurelius and Roman emperor from 161 to 192 AD. Unworthy successor of his father, he became increasingly mentally unbalanced and his reign degenerated into despotism. He was assassinated, and his death marked the end of the Antonine dynasty.

12. "honest man": The French term is *honnête homme*, which translates variously as "honest," "virtuous," or "ideal." The *honnête homme* was the ideal of seventeenth-century Frenchmen, similar to the *chevalier sans peur et sans reproche* of the Middle Ages or the *Corteggione* of the Renaissance.

13. "abstained": This word choice is probably not coincidental. The rule of the Stoics was *abstine et sustine*, literally translated as "abstain [from vice and worldly pleasures] and put up [with unavoidable wrongs and misfortunes]."

14. Faustina: The daughter of Antoninus Pius.

15. Avidius Cassius: Governor of the eastern provinces of the Roman Empire. He led a rebellion against Marcus Aurelius in 175, causing the emperor to head an expedition against him. He was assassinated before Aurelius arrived.

16. "He only dreamed": This is a historically accurate representation of Commodus as given to us by Roman historians such as Suetonius, with whose writings Fénelon was well versed. Commodus was, according to these contemporary historians, violent, vain, paranoid, and hedonistic.

DIALOGUE LVIII—
LOUIS XI AND CARDINAL BALUE

17. Louis XI (1423–83): King of France who increased the size of France and strengthened the monarchy. He was notorious, however, for his paranoia, his superstition, his vindictiveness, and his cruelty.

18. Balue: Jean Balue (1421–91): A French churchman, successively bishop of Evreux, Angers, and Cardinal. He enjoyed the favor of Louis XI until he plotted against him with Charles the Bold, Duke of Burgundy, whereupon the king had him arrested and imprisoned.

19. "We are all equal": Equality of the shades is the key literary device that Fénelon uses in the dialogues to foster debate among the characters. Since they are all dead and all equal now, all are free to speak their mind even to their former masters and torturers.

20. "lowly birth": Fénelon, like Saint-Simon in this matter, was vehemently opposed to peasants and bourgeois being given high posts in the government. He saw this as a sign of social upheaval and corruption of traditional values.

21. "purple": Received a bishopric.

22. "Pragmatic Sanction": Concordat between Louis XI and the Holy See that regulated affairs between the two.

23. "the cage": Louis XI was notorious for the various tortures and methods of punishment he had inflicted on his enemies, one of which was the cage, so called because it was a narrow box made of metal bars and resembling a cage. With hardly enough room for a man to stand up in it, it was a confining and harsh sort of imprisonment that left those incarcerated therein with deformed limbs.

24. Plessis-les-Tours: One of Louis XI's favorite palaces.

The Adventures of Telemachus

CHAPTER ONE

1. Calypso: Nymph who in Homer's *Odyssey* shelters Ulysses and falls in love with him. She attempts to keep him on her island, but after several years he decides to leave and continue his voyage to Ithaca, his home.

2. Ulysses: Greek hero of the Trojan War and protagonist of Homer's *Odyssey*, which relates his adventures on returning home from the war.

3. Telemachus: Son of Ulysses. He appears in the *Odyssey*, the continuation of which the *Adventures of Telemachus* undertake to relate.

4. Minerva: In Roman mythology the goddess of wisdom, counterpart to and assimilated with the Greek Athena. She will represent both secular and divine wisdom in the novel.

5. "white...purple...gold": The colors of Telemachus's garments are symbolic of his role as hero of the novel, the role that Calypso has planned for him as future consort and king of her island, and also allude to Telemachus's alter ego, Louis Duc de Bourgogne, for whom Fénelon wrote the novel, intending him to see the allegorical comparison between himself and the son of Ulysses. White was the traditional color of the French monarchy. Gold and purple are colors traditionally associated with royalty.

6. "Are these the thoughts…": Mentor, being in reality the goddess Minerva/Athena, can read Telemachus's mind and knows that the young man is already beginning to be dangerously tempted by the luxury he sees on Calypso's island. Not incidentally, these temptations of sensuality (in the form of the beautiful Calypso) and luxury (in the form of the opulent surroundings) were the very temptations that Fénelon feared Louis would begin to fall prey to at the time he was writing the *Adventures of Telemachus* for him. Louis would have been fifteen or sixteen years old at this time.

7. "weakness": In French *mollesse*, a term found throughout Fénelon's pedagogical works, where is always represents some defect or sin. It can be variously translated as "weakness," "softness," "indolence," and "effeminacy." I have used these various choices throughout, depending on the context of the passage.

8. "heart and soul": *Coeur* is usually translated as simply "heart." It is important for the reader to keep in mind when seeing this term in seventeenth-century French literature that *heart* had a much fuller meaning than it does in modern English. When a seventeenth-century French writer speaks of heart—especially in didactic, philosophical, or theological literature—the meaning is usually the essence of a person—physical, spiritual, and mental. So, *coeur* can variously be translated as "heart" or "soul" or both, depending on the context of the word. It often is best understood as meaning the whole person. "My heart," then, could mean "me."

9. "gods against the giants: In Greek and Roman mythology the Olympian gods were said to have battled against giants who were finally defeated when Minerva/Athena taught Vulcan how to forge thunderbolts with which Jupiter/Zeus struck them.

10. "Jupiter and Semele": In Greek and Roman mythology Semele was a mortal woman, the mother of Bacchus/Dionysus, and the god of wine.

11. Silenus: The satyr who in Greek and Roman mythology raised Dionysus after the death of his mother.

12. Atalanta and Hippomenes: Characters from Greek mythology. Atalanta refused to wed anyone who could not defeat her in a foot race. The penalty for defeat was death. But Hippomenes, favored by Aphrodite, was given three golden apples, which he threw to the ground during the race. Atalanta bent down to pick them up, and thus Hippomenes was able to outrace her.

13. Hesperides: In Greek mythology the land at the farthest reaches of the known world, understood to be either northwest Africa or perhaps the strait of Gibraltar.

14. "centaurs and Lapiths": In Greek and Roman mythology centaurs were represented as half man and half horse. They battled with the Lapiths, a Thessalian tribe, at a wedding feast after becoming intoxicated and attempting to carry away some of the Lapith women.

15. "Orpheus and Eurydice": Well-known myth from Greek and Roman mythology. Orpheus, a gifted musician and beloved of the gods, went to the underworld in an effort to persuade Pluto to give back his dead wife, Eurydice. Pluto granted his wish with the proviso that Orpheus lead her by the hand back to earth and not look back at her until they reached the upper world. Just before reaching the earth above, Orpheus turned to look back at Eurydice, and she was immediately sent back to Hades.

16. "good fortune": Literally, *bonheur*, "happiness." The happiness or good fortune to which Calypso is referring is, of course, the good fortune of being loved by her and not, as the casual antecedent would suggest, Telemachus's shipwreck.

17. "he has yet to see": The *Adventures of Telemachus* was conceived as a sequel to the *Odyssey*. It is, more precisely, not so much a sequel, as a prequel, in that to understand the plot of the *Telemachus* we must remember that Telemachus has set out to find his father because Ulysses has not reached home yet. So, actually, the novel is set in the middle of the plot line of the *Odyssey*.

18. "buried under the waves": Fénelon is summarizing here Book Five of the *Odyssey*, in which Ulysses' ship is sunk by a storm summoned up by Neptune. Ulysses is saved by washing up on shore where Nausicaa, daughter of the king of the Phaeacians, finds him and cares for him.

Letters of Spiritual Direction

LETTER XL—ON CHARACTER

1. Written as early as 1689, this is one of the first letters extant between Fénelon and Mme. de Maintenon. In it he proposes to describe and analyze her character and lay down means by which to establish a working relationship between them as spiritual director and penitent. For this reason it serves well as an introduction to other letters in the Fénelon-Maintenon correspondence.

2. The term here translated as "pride in your reputation" is another one of those subtle French words—*gloire,* in this case—that translate with difficulty into English. In the seventeenth century *gloire* could mean "glory" or "fame," but it also had the meaning of the pride that one has in one's own self-worth, the satisfaction that one has in knowing that one has done one's duty or, again, simply concern for one's reputation.

3. "honest folk": literally, *honnêtes gens.* This term is more capacious than the adjective "honest" would imply. Indeed, the term *honnête homme* (honest man) was considered the ideal of seventeenth-century France. In the same way that the Courtier and his *sprezzatura* was held up as an ideal for the Renaissance man, *honnêteté* or "honesty" was the ideal to which seventeenth-century gentlemen and women aspired. Cotgrave's *Dictionarie of the French and English Tongues*, a contemporary French-English dictionary, translates the word as, among other things, "virtue," "goodness," "courtesy," "civility," and "a noble disposition" (Columbia: Univ. of South Carolina Press, 1950).

4. Cf. 1 Cor 3:2: "I fed you with milk, not solid food, for you were not ready for solid food. Even now you are still not ready."

5. Literally, Fénelon writes "through sacrifice of your reason." He does not, however, mean to imply that Mme. de Maintenon, even as a sincere Christian, should no longer think rationally or use her powers of reason; he means to attack once again what he sees as her pride in her own intelligence and ability to reason instead of abandoning herself in absolute humility to God's will.

6. Fénelon's opinion as to the advisability and efficacy of Mme. de Maintenon's involving herself in government was to change drastically within the next four to five years. While in this letter, believed to have been written 1689 or 1690, he counsels her not to mix herself up in politics, by the time he writes his famous "Letter to Louis XIV" (actually considered by most historians to have been intended for Mme. de Maintenon and written in 1693–94), he will strongly advise her to use all her influence

on the king to change his bellicose policies. Indeed, Fénelon will chastise her for not having involved herself more in political decisions that could have avoided so many years of warfare and misery (see "Letter to Louis XIV" in this volume).

7. Louis XIV, whose companion Mme. de Maintenon had been and to whom she was now married.

8. If this advice seems harsh, even unnatural, we must keep in mind that Fénelon's spirituality—in common with so many other members of the French school of spirituality—centers on the concept of total renunciation of self, total abandonment to God's will. Human ties and affection—whether friendship or romantic love—can only stand in the way of complete subjection to God's will. This is a recurring theme throughout his work, and there are many letters of spiritual direction in which this advice is reiterated, including one to a cloistered nun whom he warned of developing friendships with her fellow religious because these friendships would be a distraction from her complete devotion to and worship of God. As is true with most complex personalities, however, Fénelon seems not always to have followed his own advice. As he says in this very letter, once he cared for someone, he was a warm and tender friend. It has been suggested by more than one historian that his friendship for Mme. de Guyon—as much as his agreement with her theology—led to his unceasing support for her and thus to his ultimate banishment from court and to political disgrace.

9. Cf. John 6:60: "This teaching is difficult." Fénelon's prose is permeated with references to scripture—so many, indeed, that it is difficult (and distracting to the reader) to note each one. Fénelon here reiterates the gospel message that the gate is narrow that leads to salvation. It requires sacrifice and the cross. Fénelon however, constantly modulated his spiritual direction according to his interlocutor. While he comes back again and again in his correspondence with Mme. de Maintenon to themes of sacrifice and renunciation of ego, with disciples he considered more mature and advanced in the spiritual path he highlights the gospel themes of freedom in Christ.

10. John 16:12.

11. A recurring theme in Fénelon's work, whether theological as in the *Maxims of the Saints* or personal such as his correspondence, is the necessity of reforming the inner man or woman and not the exterior. Faithful to Salesian spirituality, Fénelon repeatedly tells his readers that one may find holiness in any walk of life as long as one has the pure love of God in one's heart. Exterior marks of piety such as fasting and wearing hairshirts, crosses, scapulars, and the like Fénelon found to be affectation at best and sinful hypocrisy or pride at worst.

12. Freedom is another recurring theme in Fénelon's work that might surprise a Protestant reader, for example, who has associated images of ritualism and exterior fasting and devotions with the Roman Catholic Church—the sorts of things that Luther and other leaders of the Reformation decried—as opposed to real, sincere inner conversion and a personal relationship with Christ that we usually associate with the Protestant faith traditions: the "freedom of a Christian" so dear to Luther. Fénelon, as we see in this letter, however, was indifferent if not hostile to exterior acts of devotion; what mattered for him was not outward acts but inner conversion to God's will. Once this conversion takes place the converted Christian will be obedient to God's will irrespective of outward shows of piety. Fénelon will repeatedly say in his correspondence to his readers: "Where there is love, there is freedom."

LETTER I—ON THE USE OF TIME

13. The letter was addressed to Mme. de Maintenon.

14. Here Fénelon uses a common mystical metaphor in speaking of Mme. de Maintenon's progress in the spiritual life: a journey or a path. It occurs throughout his work, frequently in his correspondence.

15. A paraphrase of Matt 7:16: "You will know them by their fruits."

16. An allusion to Mme. de Maintenon's—and by extension each Christian's—spiritual director. For a Catholic, the priest in a very real way takes the place of God on earth. In his sacred ministry, in granting absolution, in offering the sacrifice of the Mass, and so on, the priest is an *alter Christus* (another Christ).

17. Simplicity is a recurring theme in Fénelonian spirituality. It is found throughout his correspondence. "Ego" here translates the French *amour-propre*, which was a concept that obsessed many writers of the seventeenth century, clergy and secular alike. The famous moralist LaRochefoucaud, for example, was haunted by the thought of our being deceived by our duplicitous ego, which manipulates us to act in ways foreign to and contrary to our conscious will.

18. Acts 9:6.

19. Ps 143:10.

LETTER II—ON DIVERSIONS

20. Fully consistent with the moral teaching of Saint Francis de Sales and the French School of Spirituality. Nearly all the spiritual direction of the

Salesian and the Berullian traditions tend not to the avoidance of secular life but rather to the sanctification of it.

21. "moaning and groaning": Fénelon seems clearly to be alluding to the Jansenists and others of what I have termed the Rigorist party at court, who proscribed court amusements such as ballet, theater, and opera. This group wielded enormous power and influence in France in the seventeenth century. For an excellent overview, see Alexander Sedgewick, *Jansenism in Seventeenth Century France* (Charlottesville: Univ. of Virginia Press, 1977).

22. Simplicity is one of the key recurring themes in Fénelon's work.

23. Mme. de Maintenon was of a notoriously scrupulous nature (one is reminded of Luther before his conversion in the thunderstorm), going to confession often and worrying about the sinfulness of every action she was engaged in. Fénelon throughout his early letters of direction to her tries to calm her fears, telling her that the only important thing is to love God and abandon herself meekly to God's will. All the rest will flow from that one simple act. Only later, when their relationship turned sour during the vehemence of the Quietist controversy, during which Maintenon took Bossuet's side against Fénelon, does the tone of the letters grow harsher, more curt, and Fénelon seems to imply that Maintenon was acting falsely with him, not showing good faith.

24. Gal 5.22: "the fruit of the Spirit is love, joy, peace, patience, kindness, generosity, faithfulness, gentleness, and self-control. There is no law against such."

25. As Jacques Le Brun points out in the Pléiade edition of Fénelon, Saint Francis de Sales apparently never actually used this word in his work. Le Brun suggests that Fénelon was probably quoting from memory, as he often did when it came to the Bible, the church fathers, and other works he knew intimately. He was possibly thinking of the word *joliété*, which de Sales uses, for example, in the *Introduction to the Devout Life:* "It is nothing, Philothée, to tell little white lies, to be a little lax in speaking, in your actions or in respect to your clothes, your gayness *[jolietés]*, your games or dances provided that as soon as the spiritual spiders enter into your conscience you chase them out and banish them just like honey bees do with corporal spiders" ([Paris: Gallimard, 1969], 74).

26. John 4:23: "But the hour is coming, and is now here, when the true worshipers will worship the Father in spirit and truth, for the Father seeks such as these to worship him." As we see throughout Fénelon's correspondence, he is so familiar with scripture and the church fathers that he often cites them from memory or paraphrases them without using quotation marks or citing an exact text. When dealing with a correspondent

such as Mme. de Maintenon, well versed in scripture herself from her Calvinist upbringing, he could assume that she would understand his allusions and respond to them. We notice again, of course, Fénelon's predilection for the gospel themes of freedom, spirit, and truth as opposed to biblical condemnations of sin, which he rarely cited. Once again we see him as faithful to the spirituality and moral direction of both de Sales and the French School.

27. Although Fénelon was not misogynistic—indeed, as the author of the celebrated *On the Education of Girls* he is considered a precursor in women's rights—he shared the prejudices of his time concerning women intellectuals. Not only did seventeenth-century French society in general condemn women who desired intellectual attainments (we recall Molière's trenchant satire *Les femmes savantes*) but the church in particular was highly suspicious of any layperson—particularly laywomen—who meddled in theology, calling this *libido sciendi* (sinful lust for knowledge).

28. "spirituality": The word Fénelon uses is *coeur*, literally translated as "heart." In seventeenth-century French, especially under the pen of theologians and philosophers, *coeur* often has the meaning "soul" or "spirituality." I have, therefore, translated the word variously as "heart" or "soul" or "spirituality," depending on the context of the passage.

29. This process of visualization calls to mind Saint Ignatius's *Spiritual Exercises*. This should not be surprising, given that Fénelon admired Ignatian spirituality and was a friend of the Jesuits in France having been championed by most of them not only in his Quietist controversy with Bossuet but also in his polemical war with the Jansenists.

30. "assuming": In answering her original question about whether amusements and diversions at court were permitted to a Christian.

31. "as much as it is desired": The wording is ambiguous in the original—*autant qu'on le désire*—allowing two possible translations: (1) that Mme. de Maintenon can lawfully engage in as many court diversions as she herself desires (as long as she does so with the intention of obeying God's will); or (2) that she should only engage in the diversions as much as is desired of her (by the king, for example) so that she would not be considered too puritanical or harsh. This second interpretation seems more plausible.

32. 1 Cor 9:22: "To the weak I became weak, that I might win the weak. I have become all things to all people, that I might by all means save some."

LETTER III—CHAINS OF GOLD

33. This letter, although undated and found without the name of its addressee, is believed to have been written for Mme. de Maintenon, perhaps in 1692. See Orcibal 2:252.

34. This striking image of Mme. de Maintenon being like a prisoner, even if her chains are of gold, calls to mind an author with whom Fénelon disagreed profoundly on a theological level but whom he greatly admired as an intellect and a prose stylist: Pascal. We recall that Pascal in his *Pensées* often compares suffering humanity to a prisoner on death row—miserable and desperately searching for meaning for his suffering and relief for his pain and yet hopeless without God's grace. See, for example, Pensée 163, edition Louis Lafuma (Paris: du Seuil, 1962).

35. This advice about allowing herself to be dragged along by God and finding him in this very renunciation of her own will is typical of Fénelon's spiritual counsel. Repeatedly in his letters of direction he advises his readers to be more humble and childlike, allowing themselves to be led along by God's hand as a parent leads a child along by the hand, knowing what is best for the child even if the child is tempted to resist.

36. Fenelon reminds us of Jesus' description of those who would not understand his message as being blind and deaf. Those who consider Mme. de Maintenon's situation to be ideal simply because she lives in a palace and is surrounded by riches are blind to what is essential to her happiness: her salvation.

37. "to die": That is, to her old self, to die to sin. Fénelon often echoes the biblical injunction of the necessity to die to one's former life in order to be reborn in Christ: "We know that our old self was crucified with him so that the body of sin might be destroyed, and we might no longer be enslaved to sin. For whoever who has died is freed from sin" (Rom 6:6–7).

38. "that king": King Midas, according to Greek mythology, was punished by Dionysos for his cupidity by having everything he touched turn to gold.

39. Fénelon, perhaps citing from memory, paraphrases Jesus' words to Peter in the Gospel of John (John 21:18): "When you were younger, you used to fasten your own belt and to go wherever you wished. But when you grow old, you will stretch out your hands, and someone else will fasten a belt around you and take you where you do not wish to go." Fénelon may also have had in mind the note that the Evangelist follows these words with. He comments that Jesus said this to Peter to show him that by his death "he was to glorify God." In like manner, Fénelon is endeavoring to

show Mme. de Maintenon that by sacrificing her ego, her will, to God's will and by dying to her old self she will be glorifying God as well.

40. "nature": The term again means here the the Pauline "old man," Mme. de Maintenon's natural inclination to selfishness and sin.

LETTER XXXVII—ON PURE LOVE

41. The autograph copy of this letter bears no salutation or name of addressee. In its style and content it is similar to letters written in the late 1680s and early 1690s.

42. "surrenders itself": Meaning surrenders itself to God. See the Introduction for a fuller explanation of Fénelon's spirituality and his views on the necessity for Christians to surrender totally and to abandon themselves to God's will, discarding their own will.

43. For Fénelon, true virtue and true mortification consist in inner surrender to God and love of God, not outward acts of devotion.

44. *Être petit*, literally "to be small." Fénelon means small in the sense of becoming like a child—a biblical metaphor that he uses often in his correspondence.

45. 2 Cor 12:10.

46. Phil 4:13.

47. "fatten up": In French *engraisser*, a very earthy word choice for Fénelon. He underlines the richness of God's Word to nourish us spiritually, to put—as we might say in colloquial English—meat on our bones.

LETTER VIII—FIDELITY IN SMALL THINGS

48. This letter, now in the Bibliothèque Nationale in Paris, is anonymous. It apparently came from a collection of letters belonging to the Beauvilliers; thus, it was probably addressed to one of the family.

49. *Introduction à la vie dévote*, chap. 1, part 3: "Sugar is more excellent than salt but salt is more frequently and generally used" (my translation).

50. "of what we do not do": That is, once the Christian surrenders completely to God's will and is led along by God's love, then he or she no longer desires to do anything that is not in conformance with God's will. Such a person only wants to continue doing whatever God's grace would have him or her do.

51. "Qui spernit modica...": Sir 19:1: "One who despises small things will fail little by litte."

LETTER LXVI—TO THE CHEVALIER COLBERT ON RETURN TO FAITH

52. Although no addressee is named on the autograph copy of this letter, Jean Orcibal believes it to have been written to the Chevalier Colbert. Antoine-Martin Colbert, third son of Louis XIV's finance minister Colbert, was a close friend of Fénelon, as were most of the extended Colbert family. Orcibal's exhaustive critical edition of Fénelon's correspondence is currently in the process of being published. Any reader wishing to delve more deeply into Fénelon's correspondence will find a treasure trove of detail in Orcibal's notes and commentary to each volume therein. I have consulted this edition freely and recommend it warmly.

53. "campaign": The military campaign referred to here is the German campaign of 1688.

54. Fénelon uses "world" here in the traditional Christian metaphorical sense of evil and secular temptation.

55. Faithful here not only to the Christian deprecation of worldly pleasures but also to the Baroque disdain of life's inherent mutability and inconstancy, Fénelon alludes here to the world as a dream. We are reminded of myriad seventeenth-century examples expressing similar disdain, such as Calderon's *La Vida es sueño* (Life is a dream).

56. "peace that passes...": An allusion to Phil 4:7.

57. "the rules": Fénelon is referring to the rules of discretion and friendship that he had mentioned previously.

58. Almost an exact translation of Augustine's well-known maxim, "Dilige et quod vis fac" (Love and do what you will).

59. "intoxicate": The verb used here is *enivrer*, which usually is translated "to intoxicate" or "to make drunk." Fénelon means that in giving himself to God, the Chevalier Colbert will experience a greater "high" than that of any worldly pleasure or intoxicant.

60. "table of our Father": An allusion to the Eucharist.

LETTER LXVIII—TO CHEVALIER COLBERT ON SPIRITUAL READING

61. "Sir": Although no addressee is named, this letter, like others addressed to "a soldier," were probably written for Antoine-Martin Colbert, the Chevalier Colbert, third son of Louis XIV's minister Colbert.

62. Literally, Fénelon says *sans trop vous gêner*, which can be translated various ways, usually "without being too bothered," "without putting

yourself out." He seems to be telling his young friend that he is aware of military routine and that the Chevalier should pray the Breviary as his military obligations allow him to do so. The reader is reminded that the Breviary is the officially sanctioned prayer book of the Roman Catholic Church. It is incumbent upon priests and members of most religious orders to recite the Breviary during the canonical hours (Matins, Prime, Terce, Sexte, None, Vespers, and Compline) throughout the day. If it would seem odd that a young soldier, a layman, should even have a copy of the Breviary, historians have noted that Colbert's father, Louis XIV's finance minister, had a personal devotion to the Breviary and indeed had had a private printing done for his family so they could each have a copy.

63. "the office": *Divine Office* is another term for the Breviary.

64. "dens of iniquity": In French, *lieux de dissipation*, which is another term that is fluid and difficult to translate exactly into English. *Dissipation* can mean "debauchery" and "iniquity," but is far more subtle than this and can also mean simply "shirking of duty" or "cutting up" (in class, for example, with respect to a rowdy student). Since we are dealing here, however, with a young man on military duty exposed to drink, gambling, camp followers, and so on, the stronger sense of the term seems to apply.

65. "world": Again, the word is used in the biblical sense of secular temptations and activities devoid of God. Fénelon always evinces a deep concern in his writings for the world as such, being God's creation.

LETTER TO THE DUC DE BOURGOGNE ON THE OCCASION OF HIS FIRST COMMUNION

66. Of the voluminous correspondence addressed by Fénelon to the Duc de Bourgogne nearly nothing remains because, at Bourgogne's death in 1712, Louis XIV had all the letters destroyed. One of the few letters remaining is this one written to Louis on the occasion of his first communion on April 11, 1694. It is now preserved in the archives of the seminary of Saint-Sulpice in Paris.

67. Isa 62:11: "See, your salvation comes; / his reward is with him."

68. Isa 45:15: "Truly, you are a God who hides himself."

69. Ps 34:5: "Look to him, and be radiant; / so your faces shall never be ashamed."

70. Ps 34:8: "O taste and see that the LORD is good."

FÉNELON

LETTER TO LOUIS XIV

71. The use of the third person singular pronoun is significant in this letter, as well as the use of the word *person.* Having sent this letter anonymously, Fénelon wishes to conceal his identity as much as possible. In French the word *person* achieves this goal all the more so since its gender is feminine (*la personne* in French) and therefore gives the impression that the author of the letter might have been female.

72. This is a striking affirmation of the doctrine of the divine right of kings. Fénelon holds Louis XIV to be a divinely appointed monarch: "l'oint du Seigneur," king of France by the grace of God and the immutable character of his coronation. By virtue of his consecration by the church to rule France, Louis XIV shares in the divine attributes of sovereignty and majesty—and thus represents God's power and justice on earth.

73. Although the extent of Louis's mistreatment as a child is a matter of debate among historians, there is a consensus among them in saying that the young Louis, as Dauphin, was influenced by his father, who was widely known as a suspicious and mistrustful monarch, as well as by Mazarin, his counseler and possible stepfather, who reinforced Louis's mistrust of others as well as his obsession with his personal grandeur and importance. For an interesting treatment of Louis's relationship with and possible molestation by Mazarin, see Michel de Grèce, *Louis XIV: l'envers du soleil* (Paris: Flammarion, 1988).

74. Luxury is a recurring theme in Fénelon's work. We see it criticized in his letters of spiritual direction, and we see it attacked as well in the pedagogical works written for the Duc de Bourgogne, especially in the *Telemachus* (see Mentor's changes on Salente in chap. 10).

75. It may be recalled that Louis XIV's foreign policy was a bellicose one throughout his reign. From the War of the Dutch Devolution at the beginning of his reign in the 1660s to the War of the Spanish Succession at the end of his reign (1701–14) he engaged constantly in conflicts with his neighboring monarchs in order to enlarge the borders of France and to punish those (such as William of Orange) whom he saw as hostile to him. As archbishop of Cambrai, Fénelon saw firsthand the devastation wrought by the War of the Spanish Succession and spent generously of his diocesan treasury to succor the poor and homeless displaced by the war.

76. Here Fénelon refers to a customs duty put in place at the beginning of Louis XIV's reign and offensive to the Dutch.

77. Fénelon accurately points out one of Louis XIV's frequent justifications for waging war: to secure his borders from invasion. The

fortifications designed by Vauban, Louis's favorite military architect, still remain in border towns such as Besançon on the German border.

78. "punishment": literally "embarrassment," but the sense here seems clearly to refer to the punishment alluded to previously in the letter.

79. An allusion to the League of Augsburg, 1686.

80. *Chambre des réunions* was a commission established by Louis XIV to investigate historical claims by France to certain lands along the border of France and neighboring countries to the east. Fénelon asserts that this commission was biased in Louis's favor and served in reality merely to find pretexts to acquire territory by covering these conquests with a veil of historical legitimacy.

81. Occupied in 1681, Louis XIV indeed relied on his own interpretation of the treaty to justify this military action. Strasbourg and the Alsace region were integrated into France at that time and provided cause for conflict between France and Germany for the next three hundred years.

82. "father of your subjects": This is a favorite and recurring theme in Fénelon's work. In his political treatises, his correspondence with political figures, and in his pedagogical works (especially the *Telemachus*) Fénelon insists repeatedly on the concept of the king being a father to his subjects, whom he should love and care for as his children. Thus, Fénelon's model king was Louis IX, Saint Louis, whom Fénelon saw as the medieval embodiment of a just and loving monarch, interested not in war or conquest but in the welfare of his people.

83. In the original French the word Fénelon uses here is *on*, usually translated "they" (they have made you the common enemy), implying again that Louis XIV has allowed himself to be flattered and mislead by his ministers and courtiers. In many parts of the letter, for example, Fénelon puts the blame squarely on Louis XIV's shoulders by the repetition of *vous-même;* it is "you yourself" he tells the king, who has made these decisions.

84. This was no exaggeration on Fénelon's part. Historians estimate the up to one-tenth of France's population died of starvation during the 1690s due to poor harvests and the consequences of Louis's wars.

85. "pension": *lettre d'état* in French. These were royal writs suspending judicial procedures for a certain length of time for anyone working for the Crown. "Pension" seemed a more apt translation than "judicial waiver," since Fénelon seems to be speaking here generally of the royal favors accorded by the king to keep the nobility pliant and under his control. Legal waivers, tax exemptions, and pensions were all part of this same strategy to make the nobility subservient to Louis XIV.

86. "flourishing": An example of Fénelonian irony.

87. "Paris...": The palace of Versailles, Louis XIV's residence, is located only a few miles west of Paris.

88. With this damning indictment of Louis XIV's irreligion, Fénelon consigns the king's faith to the lowest level of the various ways of loving God delineated in the *Maxims of the Saints*—that of purely "servile," "carnal" love—in reality not a love of God at all but rather "a love of oneself."

89. Isa 29:13: "Because these people draw near with their mouths / and honor me with their lips, / while their hearts are far from me."

90. Historians agree with Fénelon that Louis XIV was scrupulous with respect to the outward practice of religion, attending Mass regularly, and yet—as Fénelon states—was able to inure himself to the suffering brought upon his people by his frequent wars of aggression.

91. "archbishop": Fénelon here refers to François de Harlay de Champvallon, archbishop of Paris, a man notorious for his scandalous life. He always was hostile to Fénelon, and this, along with his reputation, doubtless occasioned this scathing attack.

92. Louis XIV's confessor, Father de La Chaise, was well known in court circles both for his nepotism and his indulgence toward the king's vices. Fénelon sees him as an opponent not only of the religious party at Versailles (his friends the Beauvilliers and Chevreuses, among others) but also of common virtue and decency. He accuses him of being complicit in Louis XIV's egotism and arrogance and in the moral laxity prevailing at the court.

93. According to Orcibal (2:417 n. 78) these "rules" refer to the primitive canons of the church, which were being contravened by La Chaise's cupidity and self-aggrandizement.

94. Matt 15:14: "If one blind person guides another, both will fall into a pit."

95. Fénelon refers here to the Affaire de la Régale, which pitted Louis XIV against Pope Innocent XII. The *régale* was the revenue that the king could claim during the period in which a diocese was without a bishop, between the death of one bishop and the installation of his successor. In the seventeenth century it was within the king's purview to nominate bishops, which the pope would then either approve or reject. Louis XIV abused this royal prerogative by allowing dioceses to remain without bishops for lengthy periods of time, infuriating the pope who pressed for rapid appointments.

96. Saint-Lazare refers to a military order, dating from the Middle Ages, for which Louvois—Louis XIV's minister of war—had been named vicar general. His intention was to divert the funds from the order to the

royal treasury, but he died before this could be accomplished. For Fénelon, this seems to be yet another example of Louis XIV allowing himself to be involved in sordid, mercenary dealings against the best interests of the church and his own salvation.

97. Fénelon seems to echo many scriptural verses here and allude to familiar biblical themes of the duty of Christians to acknowledge Christ and preach the truth and the thematic corollary of warning to those who have ears to hear the gospel but will not (cf. Matt 11:15; 1 Cor 9:16; and others).

98. "without making use...": literally, *sans fruit* (without fruit).

The Maxims of the Saints

1. The word Fénelon uses here is *voie*, the French equivalent of the Latin *via*, translated as "road," or "way," or "path." In traditional Christian mystical theology three ways or paths have been formulated: the *via purgativa*, in which time the soul suffers through a knowledge of its own sinfulness and a desire to unite with God; the *via illuminativa*, in which the soul becomes enlightened to the means to attain union with God; and finally, the *via unitiva*, the highest state, in which the soul attains a form of union with God.

2. "souls": The word Fénelon uses here is *âme*, which literally means "soul." This is a word he uses throughout the *Maxims*. It flows easily from Fénelon's pen for three reasons: First, it was a common metaphor for person in French seventeenth-century literature. In this sense Fénelon uses it in the same way that we might say in English, "Ten thousand souls live in this town." Second, Fénelon often seeks to emphasize the spiritual nature of human will, in which case he uses "soul" where we might more easily use "mind," "will power," "intellect," or "self." And, then, there are times in which he literally means soul, in the same sense as we do when referring to the immortal part of our nature created by God. In translating Fénelon's works I have tried inasmuch as possible to follow his style and usage. So, I have translated *âme* most often by "soul," unless the context makes such a rendering confusing—in cases where he obviously means simply a person, a Christian, or a penitent, for example, in which cases I have chosen these terms instead of "soul." The question of gender is a thorny one as well. In French *âme* is feminine, and often Fénelon uses this particularity of French grammar to highlight the soul's connubial relationship to God, as in Article XXXVIII when speaking of Bride and Bridegroom. Therefore, instead of translating the possessive adjectives

and pronouns associated with *âme* by the more impersonal "it," "itself," and so on (antithetical to Fénelon's style), I have opted generally to use feminine ones when referring to *âme* as translated by "soul" and masculine ones when referring to *âme* as translated by "Christian" or "penitent."

3. The Beghards were a reformist group of Flemish Christians. They ressembled the Italian group, the Humiliati, and the Dutch Brethren of the Free Spirit, in tending to live together in houses without taking monastic vows and in their criticism of the church for owning property. They were condemned as heretical by the Council of Vienne in 1311.

4. Fénelon has translated from Bellarmine's *De Scriptoribus ecclesiasticis*. The following quotation from Cardinal Bona is also Fénelon's own translation from a Latin edition.

5. Alumbrados were a group of Spanish mystics who declared all prayers, rites, and ceremonies of the church useless in their search for complete abandonment to God. They were condemned by the Inquisition in 1524 and were later often cited as early heretics by opponents to Quietism.

6. Fénelon here lists several of the mystics whom he admired most and to whom he felt the most indebted for his own mystical theology. *Saint Teresa of Avila* (1515–82), Spanish Carmelite reformer of the Carmelite Order and author of her spiritual biography as well as several other works; *Saint John of the Cross* (1542–91), Spanish Carmelite, friend of Saint Teresa and fellow reformer of the Carmelite Order. Author of mystical prose and poetic works such as the *Ascent to Mount Carmel; John Tauler* (1300–1361), German mystic, Dominican theologian, and author of *Sermons; Jan van Ruusbroec* (1293–1381), Flemish mystic and author of *The Sparkling Stone* and *Book of Supreme Truth; Balthazar Alvarez* (1533–80), Spanish mystic and spiritual director of Saint Teresa of Avila; *Saint Francis de Sales* (1567–1622), Savoyard mystic and bishop *in partibus* of Geneva, probably Fénelon's favorite mystic and author of *Treatise of the Love of God*, wherein he champions such concepts as holy indifference, passive acceptance of God's will, pure love, and other ideas taken up and defended in the *Maxims of the Saints* by Fénelon; *Pierre de Bérulle* (1575–1629), French theologian and cardinal, leader of the Counter-Reformation in France and one of the founders of the French School of Spirituality, of which Fénelon may be considered a late member.

7. See Rom 14:21.

8. "two great prelates": Bossuet and Noailles, bishops of Meaux and Châlons, who along with Louis Tronson drafted the thirty-four articles of Issy condemning Quietist doctrine (see "The Quietist Controversy and the *Maxims of the Saints*" in the Introduction).

9. Fénelon had originally planned the *Maxims* to be a voluminous apologia of mysticism, containing multiple quotations from various approved mystics and running into the thousands of pages. Noailles, archbishop of Paris, and Tronson, director of Saint-Sulpice, dissuaded him from this project. What was finally published as the *Maxims* is only the commentary on the authors without the quotations.

10. Fénelon, always at pains to distinguish his doctrine from Quietist error, draws up in this and the following paragraphs a list of several tenets imputed to Quietists—their belief that they were exempt from moral law, that their perfect state, once achieved, was immutable, and so on—which, he says, form no part of his own beliefs.

11. "charity": Consistent with the Greek linguistic distinction between *eros* and *agape* and the Latin distinction between *amor* and *caritas*—the former in each pair generally connoting a romantic or sexual love and the latter a spiritual love—Fénelon often uses the French word *charité* in the specialized sense of the soul's love of God. When speaking of human desire, however, he always uses the more common French term for love: *amour.* To complicate matters further, however, he also uses *amour* to describe the purest form of loving God: *pur amour.* Nevertheless, since Fénelon himself is careful to maintain a distinction between the two terms *amour* and *charité* in the *Maxims*, I have followed his lead by translating *charité* as "charity" and *amour* as "love."

12. De Sales, *Traité de l'Amour de Dieu*, 2.17, in *Oeuvres* (Paris: Gallimard, 1969). All citations from Francis de Sales will be from this edition and will be indicated by book number and chapter number, following traditional practice. Page numbers will only be indicated for purposes of clarification.

13. De Sales, *Traité de l'Amour de Dieu*, 2.17.

14. De Sales, *Traité de l'Amour de Dieu*, 2.17.

15. "cupidity": In French, *cupidité* coming directly from the Latin *cupiditas*, meaning "a sinful desire contrary to God's will." This is the desire that 1 Tim 6:10 translates as the "love of money" being the root of all evil. In the Vulgate: "Radix enim omnium malorum est cupiditas." Even though in modern French *cupidité* has exclusively taken on the meaning of "love of money," in Fénelon's time it could still commonly be understood in a broader sense. Cotgrave, for example, in his seventeenth-century dictionary still translates it as "covetousness," "lust," "wanton affection," and "dishonest love."

16. In Article II of the *Maxims* Fénelon will describe God as *Rémunérateur*; that is, "he who rewards."

17. De Sales, *Traité de l'Amour de Dieu*, 2.17.

18. De Sales, *Traité de l'Amour de Dieu*, 2.17.

19. "righteousness": The French word used here by Fénelon is *justice*. He uses variants of this word throughout the *Maxims: juste*, *justifier*, *justification*. Following the common tradition of English biblical translators I have normally translated this word as "righteousness." Likewise, I have generally translated *les justes* as "the righteous," and occasionally by "the just" or "the justified." However, again following tradition, I have generally translated *justifié* as "justified" and *justification* as "justification." The reader, however, should be aware that the same word is at the origin of these various translations: the Greek *dikaios* and the Latin *justus*, as in Saint Paul's famous text from Rom 1:17, "The just shall live by faith." The question of justification, the "making right" a Christian's relationship to God, was of course of the utmost importance in seventeenth-century France, which saw the continuing debate between Huguenot and Catholic theologians over Calvin's interpretation of justification as well as the more recent Jansenist contribution to the debate by the publication of Jansen's *Augustinus* in 1640. Faithful to the Erasmian humanistic position, Fénelon championed the role of free will to cooperate with grace in the role of justification, against the Jansenists, who held a more deterministic, Calvinistic, position. The Council of Trent had earlier promulgated canons on justification that attempted to strike a nuanced tone, both condemning the proposition that "man can be justified before God by his own works" (canon 1) and that "the free will of man...does not cooperate at all...[in]...the grace of justification" (canon 4).

20. Council of Trent, Session 6, c. 11.

21. De Sales, *Traité del'Amour de Dieu*, 9.3. Fénelon's doctrine of pure love was constantly susceptible to refinement, and his defense of it open to development. In marginal notes to his first edition (attested to by Chérel and LeBrun in their critical editions of the *Maxims*) Fénelon quotes Bernard of Clairvaux's doctrine of "cupiditas ordinata," which he apparently saw as a corollary to de Sales's "soumission" of concupiscence. He apparently intended to make much use of this Bernardine doctrine in the planned revision of the second edition of the *Maxims*, an edition never published due to the papal condemnation of the first edition.

22. The italicized statement was condemned by article 2 of *Cum alias*. Throughout the text of the *Maxims* italicized portions will indicate propositions that were condemned by the papal brief.

23. This is the famous *cas impossible* that Fénelon inherited, so to speak, from the medieval mystics such as Tauler and most recently from Francis de Sales. It would be seized upon by Bossuet, among others, and used as a polemical weapon against Fénelon. Bossuet claimed that

Fénelon's apparent acceptance of the impossible case proved that he negated the role of Christian hope in salvation.

24. "Rewarder": In French, *rémunérateur*, from the Latin *remunerator*; literally, "he who rewards."

25. As mentioned above, the word here translated by "penitent" is *âme*, literally, "soul." Fénelon, however, uses *âme* throughout the *Maxims* to designate human beings as either people in general (in which case I've translated by "person"), people as members of the church (in which case I've translated by "Christian"), or people who, having put themselves under the guidance of a spiritual director, accept his authority and follow his counsel. This practice of spiritual direction was a common one in seventeenth-century France, as it remained in many Catholic and Orthodox communities right into the twentieth century.

26. This proposition was condemned by article 3 of *Cum alias.*

27. See John of the Cross, *Dark Night*, 1.3

28. Saint Augustine, *De moribus ecclesiae*, Book I, chap. 25, cited in the margin of Fénelon's original 1697 edition.

29. Thomas Aquinas, *Summa Theologica*, IIa, IIal, q. 23, a. 8, ad. 3.

30. "Reduplication": In Scholastic theology there is reduplication when to a term there is added "as" or some other similar expression in order to indicate the meaning in which the first term is to be taken. For example, "Christ as man suffered but not Christ as God." In this article Fénelon suggests that as long as the soul selflessly loves God *as* God, she may love him *as* "treasure" or "beatitude" as well without impiety.

31. De Sales, *Traité de l'Amour de Dieu*, 2.17.

32. De Sales, *Traité de l'Amour de Dieu*, 9.3.

33. By "indifferent" Fénelon does not mean indifferent in the commonly accepted sense of "not mattering" or "not caring." Rather, he is using this adjective in a specifically theological sense, referencing his doctrine of holy indifference ("sainte indifférence"), a product of pure love ("pur amour"). It is that passive state in which the soul follows God's grace without attempting to anticipate it. This is the state in which, according to Albert Chérel, "the soul no longer has any voluntary or deliberate desires for her self-interest." For a good, concise discussion of this term, see the Introduction to Chérel's edition of the *Explication des Maximes des Saints* (Paris: Bloud, 1911), 43–45. This proposition was condemned by article 4 of *Cum alias.*

34. This proposition was condemned by article 4 of *Cum alias.*

35. Bona, *Via Compendii*, XIX. Fénelon was apparently citing from memory; the source is unidentifiable.

36. This proposition was condemned by article 5 of *Cum alias.*

37. This proposition was condemned by article 6 of *Cum alias.*

38. De Sales, *Third Spiritual Conference.*

39. De Sales, *Questions following the Conferences*, 1296.

40. De Sales, *Sixth Spiritual Conference.*

41. De Sales, *Traité de l'Amour de Dieu*, 9.4.

42. De Sales, *Traité de l'Amour de Dieu*, 9.4.

43. De Sales, *Traité de l'Amour de Dieu*, 9.4.

44. De Sales, *Third Spiritual Conference.*

45. Although Fénelon does not reference this quotation or the next, they are similar to ones found in De Sales's *Third Spiritual Conference.*

46. Ps 37:10, from the Vulgate: "Domine, ante te omne desiderium meum."

47. See 2 Tim 1:13.

48. This proposition was condemned by article 7 of *Cum alias.*

49. This proposition was condemned by article 7 of *Cum alias.*

50. Bona, *Via Compendii*, IV.

51. De Sales, *Traité de l'Amour de Dieu*, 1.12.

52. Although Fénelon's prose is somewhat turgid, what he's getting at here is that, even in the midst of mystical trials, revelations, and so forth, the soul does not separate herself from the Christian community or the precepts of the church. She may lose her selfish and "comforting" fervor—really just a form of spiritual pride in her own righteousness—but she never loses her hatred of sin, as the church defines it, or her ability and desire to follow the commandments of God as defined by the church. For God communicates with the faithful soul even in the midst of her trials and spiritual aridity and inspires her to persevere.

53. Fénelon's work is informed by a thorough knowledge of scripture. Even when not being quoted verbatim, we hear in Fénelon's work biblical echoes at every turn. Here, see Rom 8:2.

54. Faithful to a long tradition in Christian mystical writings, Fénelon maintains that we are created and sustained by God and that it is only God's grace that keeps us from returning to the nothingness, the dust from which we were formed. This is a common theme among authors of the French School of Spirituality.

55. See again scriptural echoes: Ezek 18:32.

56. This proposition was condemned by article 8 of *Cum alias.*

57. This proposition was condemned by article 8 of *Cum alias.*

58. This proposition was condemned by article 9 of *Cum alias.*

59. A reference to an episode in the life of Francis de Sales in which he felt abandoned by God.

60. Much polemical hay was made by Bossuet in his *Relation sur le quiétisme* over this concept of "trouble involontaire," which, in comparing the mystic's involuntary sufferings to Christ's, Fénelon seems to assert that Christ was at times powerless to control his will and actions.

61. Matt 27:46. In emphasizing the identification that we must make with the human, suffering, incarnate Jesus Fénelon shows the influence of de Sales and Bérulle, in particular, as well as most theologians and mystics of the French School of Spirituality (see especially Bérulle's *Grandeurs de Jesus*). Fénelon also admired Saint Bernard, thus the Christocentric spirituality of the Cistercians is in evidence in Fénelon. This proposition was condemned by article 10 of *Cum alias.*

62. The "impossible case" referred to here is the famous *cas impossible* so hotly debated in the seventeenth century. The "impossible" nature of the "impossible case" is that the soul loves God so much that she would be willing to sacrifice her own salvation if it were God's will. The church waffled a good deal (seeming to approve expression of the "impossible case" in the work of Francis de Sales and Teresa of Avila, for example) before condemning its extreme expression in the work of the Quietists, including the writings of Jeanne Guyon.

63. This proposition was condemned by article 11 of *Cum alias.*

64. This proposition was condemned by article 12 of *Cum alias.*

65. Once again we see a continuation of the recurring theme of the "impossible case." Fénelon throughout the *Maxims* attempts to defend the mysticism of "pure love" as being orthodox. To do so, he repeatedly draws distinctions between the mystic who, following de Sales, Bérulle, and others, would be willing to sacrifice eternal happiness if God so wished, and the mystic who believes that doing so is the only way to be in a state of pure love—even if this state contradicts the teachings of the church regarding salvation and the Christian's need to desire his own salvation.

66. Here Fénelon means the Old and New Testaments.

67. Ps 34:9: "Those who fear him have no want."

68. Semi-Pelagian was a mitigated form of the doctrine of grace taught by Pelagius (360–420). It held that fallen humans retained the ability to turn to God without the assistance of grace. Fénelon considered himself a true disciple of the bishop of Hippo in questions of grace and free will; therefore, he opposed the Calvinist-Jansenist position affirming the irresistibility of grace. Thus, in this article, we see his support of the Erasmian (and Jesuit) position of Christians' ability, through free will, to cooperate with God's prevenient grace in their salvation.

69. Fénelon was constantly on guard against the criticism leveled against him on account of his association with Mme. Guyon, seeming

thereby to defend her eccentric, extraordinary behavior—visions, ecstasies, fits, seizures, etc. Here he makes it clear to the reader that pure love does not require "jolts" and "excitation"; on the contrary, pure love is peaceful and sober and obedient to the church.

70. Here again Fénelon addresses the Quietist error that maintains that the soul should remain totally passive in the hands of God; accordingly, Quietists no longer need actively to obey the commandments or precepts of the church. They believe we no longer need to make active decisions of our will because God will guide us to do what he desires. Fénelon, as he does throughout the *Maxims*, condemns this position as heretical.

71. "Manicheans": A religious movement founded by the Persian prophet Mani in the third century; it preached a dualistic struggle between good and evil.

72. The allusion is to Francis de Sales's doctrine expounded in his *Traité de l'Amour de Dieu*, 1.2, of the two layers of consciousness in the soul: the superior level called by him the "cime" or "fine pointe de l'âme," which communicates with God; and the lower level of sensory perception, which is capable of suffering even while the superior level is in union with God.

73. John Cassian (360–435): One of the Latin church fathers who traveled extensively in Egypt and studied under the desert monks and hermits there. His two most influential works are the *Institutes*, which describes the monastic life of the Egyptian monks, and the *Conferences*, which relate conversations he claimed to have had with some of the most famous desert fathers, including Saint Anthony. This citation is from *Conferences*, 9.31 (quotations from Cassian are from John Cassian, *Conferences*, trans. Colm Luibheid [New York: Paulist Press, 1985]).

74. This proposition was condemned by article 13 of *Cum alias*.

75. "was still suffering": The term Fénelon uses here, *l'homme des douleurs*, translates literally "a man of suffering," which is a scriptural reference to Isa 53:3: "He was despised and rejected by others; / a man of suffering."

76. "anxiety": The word used here is *trouble*, which is a difficult word to translate, ranging in meaning from simple embarrassment or discomfort to unease, confusion, or anxiety. It was tempting in this case to translate *trouble* by "pain"; however, there are so many stronger words in French to describe pain and suffering that Fénelon could certainly have chosen one of those had he wished. I, therefore, followed his stylistic choice and translated *trouble* by "anxiety." This proposition was condemned by article 13 of *Cum alias*.

77. This proposition was condemned by article 14 of *Cum alias.*

78. Fénelon here, as elsewhere throughout the *Maxims* and indeed all his writings, urges the utmost precaution on the reader's part regarding extraordinary manifestations of grace such as visions, ecstatic trances, and so forth. These can, he clearly states, often be diabolical in nature. He was especially sensitive to this issue because many of his fellow disciples of pure love—Father LaCombe and Jeanne Guyon in particular—had experienced phenomena of this nature and had been condemned by the church for either distorting or misunderstanding them. As a consequence, throughout the eighteenth century in France mystical experiences of this nature were strongly discouraged by ecclesiastical authorities, which led to a near extinction of the mystical tradition in France until the Romantic revival of the nineteenth century. Jesuit Father Pierre de Caussade is a notable exception to this rule, but he was often in trouble with his superiors for his defense of mysticism. It may be remembered that other great mystics such as Saint Teresa of Avila and Saint John of the Cross were also regarded with great suspicion by church authorities at first—indeed imprisoned by the Inquisition—until they were able to convince their superiors of the authenticity of their mystical experiences.

79. "darkness of faith": An allusion to the experiences of many mystics who experienced periods of spiritual sterility and barrenness as often or more so than visions and ecstasies. We are reminded, naturally, of Saint John of the Cross, for example, and his experiences of *noche oscura*, or "dark night of the soul."

80. The purpose of article XV seems manifestly to defend adherents of pure love and mystics in general from the charge leveled by Bossuet and others that they neglected corporal austerities, supposing themselves to be in a state beyond the need of such physical disciplines (cf. Bossuet's comments in his *Relation sur le Quiétisme*, for example). However, it is interesting and important to note that even while defending the traditional use of corporal austerities, Fénelon strikes a very personal tone—one very reminiscent of Saint Francis de Sales—in maintaining that the leading of a sober Christian life, imbued by God's pure love, is more important than the inflicting of physical discipline. This position is in sharp contrast not only with Bossuet but also with the rigorist Jansenist morality (cf. Pierre Nicole's attacks on literary and intellectual pursuits, court amusements, and so on in his *Essais de morale*).

81. Simplicity and peace are recurring themes in all Fénelon's work. In Fénelon's view, living in a state of pure love of God means a state of innocent, childlike dependence on God and faith in him.

82. "justice": Here, as throughout the *Maxims*, meaning justification in God's eyes: righteousness.

83. Matt 27:46.

84. Matt 11:12.

85. "The devil, too, wished to live according to himself when he did not abide in the truth" (Book 14, chap. 3) (Augustine, *The City of God*, trans. Marcus Dods [New York: Random House, 1950], 445).

86. De Sales, *Traité de l'Amour de Dieu*, 9.3.

87. In *propriété*, the concept of attachment, is a central theme of Fénelonian spirituality. Christians seeking the highest states of pure love and union with God must seek to "detach" themselves from any vestiges of self-interest represented by *propriété*.

88. See John of the Cross, *Dark Night*, 1.3. The theme of detachment of oneself is an important and recurring one in John of the Cross's work. In the *Ascent of Mount Carmel*, 1.4, for example, Saint John discusses the absolute necessity of the soul to detach itself from any creature (which he defines as any physical, intellectual, or even spiritual thing apart from God himself): "The necessity of passing through this dark night (the mortification of the appetites and the denial of pleasure in all things) for the attainment of the divine union with God arises from the fact that all of man's attachments to creatures are pure darkness in God's sight" (*The Collected Works of St. John of the Cross*, trans. Kieran Kavanaugh [Washington: Institute of Carmelite Studies, 1973], 77; quotations from John of the Cross are from this edition).

89. This quotation is taken from a seventeenth-century translation of a Spanish *Life of Fr. Balthazar Alvarez.*

90. The Council of Trent defended the theology of self-interest enshrined in the use of external devotions, disciplines, and the like as means of grace, of building merits in heaven and avoiding years in purgatory. The council also defended the theology of indulgences, which is, by its very nature, based on self-interest as opposed to the Protestant doctrines of *sola gratia* and *sola fide.*

91. During his trial by the Roman Inquisition, Molinos admitted to having succumbed to sexual temptation with several of his disciples. This cloud of sexual immorality hung heavily over all those subsequently accused of Quietism. Hence the provocative, almost inflammatory, nature of Bossuet's identification of Fénelon and Jeanne Guyon as Montanus and Priscilla, thus seeming to suggest an inappropriate connection between them beyond that of Quietist doctrine.

92. If Fénelon seems to be insisting on the necessity of traditional and exterior acts of faith—formal prayer, disciplines, fasting, and so

forth—it is useful to recall the context in which he is writing the *Maxims*. Not only does he have in mind the prejudice of his fellow prelates—particularly Bossuet—against mysticism, but he also is defending the doctrines of pure love and the passive state against the backdrop of the unfortunate excesses in the interpretation of this doctrine committed, according to public gossip, by Mme. Guyon and Father LaCombe as well as the young female protégées of Mme. de Maintenon at Saint-Cyr, which had been the catalyst for the Conferences of Issy.

93. "common path": Here Fénelon means the common, traditional practices that the church enjoins upon practicing Catholics: formal prayers and liturgy, assistance at Mass, fasting, and so forth.

94. "seduction": The term should be understood here as diabolical seductions, the wiles of the devil.

95. "permission": Here meaning permission or allowance for sin to occur.

96. See Matt 24:15.

97. This is an allusion to the Lord's prayer, used by the Catholic Church and other liturgical churches to justify the continued practice of set or formal liturgical prayer in church as opposed to the more radical Protestant reformers, who insisted that all prayer should be either extemporaneous or, as in the case of the Quakers, silent.

98. "obligatory": For Catholics, attendance at Mass, for example, is obligatory. Among the beliefs and practices of the Quietists condemned by the church in the sixteenth and seventeenth centuries was the teaching that public acts of faith such as vocal prayer and attendance at Mass were unnecessary to the mystic perfected by pure love.

99. "inspired words": Literally, "words on fire" (*paroles enflammées*")

100. "Divine Office": The set of formal, liturgical prayers required of all contemplative religious orders (and to a lesser degree, by all priests, monks, and nuns) throughout the day: Matins, Prime, Terce, Sext, None, Vespers, and Compline.

101. "Word of God": The Bible. One accusation made against Quietists was that, considering themselves in a state of perfection, they felt they had no further need to read the Bible, the Breviary, or other devotional literature.

102. This proposition was condemned by article 15 of *Cum alias.*

103. This proposition was condemned by article 15 of *Cum alias.*

104. In this article Fénelon distinguishes two stages of approaching and communicating with God: meditation, marked by external acts of prayer and devotion; and contemplation, the higher, purer level, marked by constant, simple love of God. We constantly hear echoes of one of

Fénelon's favorite biblical passages: "Whoever does not love does not know God, for God is love" (1 John 4:8).

105. De Sales, *Traité de l'Amour de Dieu*, 9.11.

106. An echo of Saint Paul's admonition to the Corinthians, who were yet young in the faith and who wanted too quickly to advance to the mystical life and its inherent gifts of visions, glossolalia, spiritual union with God and so forth: "And so, brothers and sisters, I could not speak to you as spiritual people, but rather as people of the flesh, as infants in Christ. I fed you with milk, not solid food, for you were not ready for solid food" (1 Cor 3:1–2).

107. "retreat": I am translating the French *recueillement*, a difficult word to express in English because it lends itself to many different translations, from "contemplation" and "meditation" to "spiritual recollection" and even "reverence" due to a superior. I have found that Fénelon often uses this term, as I believe the case is here, to mean "retreat" or "withdrawal" from the world (especially "world" considered in its ecclesiastical sense of the secular, sinful world). On other occasions I translate *recueillement* as "contemplation" or "prayer," according to the context.

108. A problematic citation. Although Fénelon cites from Saint John of the Cross's *Fire of Love*, cant. 3, the exact reference to "mud/dirt" *(boue)* is not found in this text. Fénelon, a great admirer of John of the Cross, is perhaps confusing this text with another passage of the Spanish Carmelite.

109. "approved mystics": Literally, "good mystics," but the adjective "good" *(bon)* is more nuanced than its English equivalent and often can mean "correct" or "right" or "justifiable" or "approved" as well as simply "good." In this sentence, for example, I have chosen to translate *bons mystics* by "approved mystics," concluding that this is the most logical sense of Fénelon's words.

110. This is a particularly effective metaphor in evoking Fénelon's concept of the two types of communing with God: meditation, which is seen as a noticeable, external, manual act; and contemplation, which is seen as an invisible, imperceptible act infused with celestial intervention.

111. This proposition was condemned by article 16 of *Cum alias.*

112. "in this degree": That is, having advanced this far along the path of contemplation.

113. "cherubim": An order of angels distinguished as guardians or throne-bearers. They are high ranking, second only to the seraphim.

114. "the less perfect...": The less perfect means the act of meditation, as defined by Fénelon; the more perfect is the state of contemplation.

115. 1 Cor 16:14.

116. 1 Cor 10:31.

117. Luke 18:1.

118. 1 Thess 5:17.

119. Fénelon here hearkens to a long metaphorical tradition in the church of comparing Christians to pilgrims who are only passing through this vale of tears in order to reach their true home, in heaven. Compare Saint Paul's Letter to the Philippians (especially 3:20), wherein he says that "our citizenship is in heaven." This was a very frequent and popular theme in French preaching of the seventeenth century. Bossuet, for example, uses it to great effect in his *Sermon on Death* and other works. See, for example, his *Panégyrique de Saint Thomas de Cantorbery*, in *Oeuvres* (Paris: Gallimard, 1961), 581: "L'Eglise est dans le monde comme une étrangère...elle ne s'y arrête donc pas, mais elle y passe; elle ne s'y habitue pas, mais elle y voyage...etc."

120. Cassian, *Conferences*, 1.13.

121. Saint Thomas Aquinas, *Summa Theologica*, II, 2; q. 23, a. 8, ad. 3.

122. "school": School of thought or group of theologians, as the Scholastics.

123. In using the term *negative* Fénelon is referencing the apophatic theology of the Eastern church fathers, such as Dionysius the Areopagite, which emphasized the impossibility of describing God's essence—hence "apophatic" or "negative," from the the Greek *apophasis* for "denial." The reference is to the Pseudo-Dionysius, *Mystical Theology*, chaps. 2–5.

124. "amorous look": This *regard amoureux* is what was referred to by the Eastern Fathers as the "apprehension of the heart" or the "prayer of the heart." According to Timothy Ware, this prayer is "not merely said by the lips, not merely thought by the intellect, but offered spontaneously by the whole being of man—lips, intellect, emotions, will, and body. The prayer fills the entire consciousness, and no longer has to be forced out, but says itself. This prayer of the heart cannot be attained simply through our own efforts, but is a gift conferred by the grace of God" (Ware, *The Orthodox Church*, 74).

125. Fénelon alludes to Jesus' proclamation in Matt 5:17: "Do not think that I have come to abolish the law or the prophets; I have come not to abolish but to fulfill."

126. "the blessed": That is, the blessed in paradise. Cf. Rev 15:2–3: "And I saw what appeared to be a sea of glass mixed with fire, and those who had conquered the beast...standing beside the sea of glass with harps of God in their hands. And they sing the song of Moses, the servant of God, and the song of the Lamb."

127. This proposition was condemned by article 17 of *Cum alias*.

128. This proposition was condemned by article 17 of *Cum alias*.

129. This proposition was condemned by article 17 of *Cum alias*.

130. 1 Cor 16:22: "Let anyone be accursed [in Greek, *anathema*] who has no love for the Lord."

131. This article elaborates upon Fénelon's doctrine of the two levels of the soul, borrowed from Francis de Sales, according to which the superior part of the soul communicates directly and lovingly with God without means of the sensory perception of the inferior part of the soul. The word translated by "properties" is *puissances*, which lends itself to several nuances from "powers" and "capabilities" to "properties." For a fuller discussion of this aspect of Fénelonian thought, see Henri Gouhier, *Fénelon philosophe* (Paris: Vrin, 1977), 108–9.

132. Fénelon uses the term *opération*, which lends itself to several meanings in French, from actual actions—military operations, for example—to intellectual processes and the inner workings of the Spirit. Here Fénelon refers to those Christians, still weak in their faith, who need to see visible manifestations or effects of their piety instead of relying on a peaceful, albeit interior, union with God.

133. The word I translate by "eagerness" is *empressement*, which also gives the sense in French of "fussiness" or "business," or in adjectival form "hectic" or "harried," similar to other descriptive nouns and adjectives used by Fénelon in the *Maxims*—such as *agité* and *inquiet*—used to describe the anxious, troubled piety of these still imperfect souls. I believe Fénelon here is once again underlying the traditional contrast between the active virtues and the passive.

134. Here Fénelon is making the distinction between the merit of passive contemplation, which he says is "free" inasmuch as it is freely chosen by the Christian in order to unite with God, and the sometimes spectacular spiritual gifts—also "free" in that God grants them without regard to the Christian's worthiness—given to certain Christians, such as the stigmata, glossolalia, and so forth. In the first case he uses the word *libre* and in the second *gratuit*. Although both French words are normally translated as "free," the former is commonly used to describe human action while the latter is the normal word to describe divine action. Grace, for example, in French is called a *don gratuit*, a "free gift" of God.

135. See Saint Teresa of Avila, *Interior Castle*, 7.1–4.

136. Cassian, *Conferences*, 9.4.

137. Fénelon saw this *propriété de la sagesse* as one of his greatest temptations to overcome in the spiritual path to pure love. He often speaks in his correspondence with Mme. Guyon of his struggle to overcome his

reliance on his intellect and his pride in his worldly knowledge, *sagesse*, in order to humble himself.

138. "proprieties": The word Fénelon uses here is *bienséances*, which was in current usage in seventeenth-century France and understood to mean "appropriate conduct," "etiquette," "politeness." Here Fénelon seems to appropriate the word to mean conduct appropriate for a Christian.

139. An allusion to Matt 6:34.

140. Although the allusion is vague, Fénelon could be referring to any of Christ's injunctions (as related by the apostles) to childlike simplicity. More plausible is a reference to Saint Paul (often referred to by Fénelon as "the apostle") in his urging of avoiding worldly wisdom in favor of a childlike dependence on God (see Phil 2:14; Rom 8:15).

141. "prudence of the serpent": An allusion to Matt 10:16.

142. An allusion to the Beatitudes (Matt 5:3–11).

143. An allusion to Matt 11:25.

144. Throughout the Bible the sacred writers contrast God, as Author and Father of truth, with Satan, the author and father of lies (see Ps 101:7; Hab 2:18; see also 2 Thess 2:11, where Saint Paul speaks of false prophets who "send them a powerful delusion, leading them to believe what is false").

145. Thomas Aquinas, *Summa Theologica*, II, II, qu. 23, a. 8, ad. 3.

146. Both this quotation and the following are taken from the de Sales, *Twelfth Spiritual Conference*.

147. Mother Chantal: Saint Jeanne de Chantal (1572–1641), friend, disciple, and collaborator of Saint Francis de Sales.

148. This proposition was condemned by article 18 of *Cum alias*.

149. This proposition was condemned by article 19 of *Cum alias*.

150. De Sales, *Traité de l'Amour de Dieu*, 9.9.

151. De Sales, *Eighteenth Spiritual Conference*.

152. De Sales, *Traité de l'Amour de Dieu*, 9.10.

153. The word Fénelon uses here is *onction*, which may be translated as "oil," "unction," or "anointing." Here I believe he means to refer to our anointing with grace.

154. The metaphor of the stumbling block is a recurring theme in scripture. For example, see Saint Paul: "Let us…resolve never to put a stumbling block or hindrance in the way of another" (Rom 14:13).

155. Col 3:3. Fénelon follows the Vulgate in translating *Mortui enim estis*. In the NRSV this passage is rendered "you have died." The necessity of dying to oneself is one of the most constant Fénelonian themes in his spiritual correspondence as well as in the *Maxims*.

156. The terminology Fénelon uses here, "old man" and "new man," come from Saint Paul. See, for example, Col 3:9: "the old self." The old self (old man) symbolizes our state before grace; the new self (new man), our state after being reborn in Christ.

157. "medicinal grace": This alludes no doubt to Christ's statement to the disciples that he had not come into the world to save the healthy, but rather to cure the sick: "Those who are well have no need of a physician, but those who are sick" (Matt 9:12).

158. Although the majority of this quotation is taken from Gal 2:19–20, Fénelon—perhaps quoting from memory—alters the original text, which reads: "I have been crucified with Christ; and it is no longer I who live, but it is Christ who lives in me. And the life I now live in the flesh I live by faith in the Son of God, who loved me and gave himself for me."

159. Fénelon is quoting Saint Catherine's autobiographical *Life*, chapter XIV.

160. Drawing upon a rich and varied mystical tradition, particularly in the early Eastern church, Fénelon's doctrine of transformation echoes concepts of deification and sanctification elaborated by Saint Clement of Alexandria, Saint Gregory of Nyssa, and Dionysius the Areopagite.

161. "hypostatic": The terminology of *hypostasis* is derived from the christological debates of the fourth century dealing with the union of the divine and human natures in the Person *(hypostasis)* of the Word. Fénelon is condemning the most extreme concept of deification, which would have our human nature become blurred with or identical to God's nature.

162. "good mystics": "Good" here could be read as "orthodox" or "right-thinking" or "approved."

163. The Beghards were a group of medieval Christians (primarily thirteenth-fourteenth centuries) who strove to live an ideal of Christian life without the constraints of a formal monastic rule. They were condemned by the Council of Vienne in 1311. The Alumbrados were a group of Spanish mystics, condemned in 1525 and after. They were later associated in the minds of those opposed to this strain of spirituality with the Quietist doctrines promulgated by Miguel de Molinos. Molinos's chief mystical work, the *Guia espiritual* (1675), was viciously attacked by the anti-mystical faction of the church and was condemned in the brief *Coelestis Pastor* in 1687. Fénelon is at pains in the *Maxims* to distance himself from any association with the Beghards or the Alumbrados, since such association brought with it the taint of Quietist heresy.

164. This proposition was condemned by article 20 of *Cum alias.*

165. "emotional outlet": *Décharge du coeur* literally translates as a "discharge of the heart." Fénelon apparently means to address the problem of

those overscrupulous penitents who use the confessional for inappropriate ends: either to assuage a morbid sense of guilt or as a means of emotional release or affective sublimation.

166. "abandonment": Abandonment is a recurring theme in the writings not only of Fénelon but of the approved, orthodox mystical writers such as Francis de Sales, Bérulle, and others of the French School of Spirituality, and also of writers condemned by the church as heretical, such as Molinos, Mme. Guyon, and others deemed Quietist. Bossuet had recently implied in his *Instruction sur les états d'oraison* that Mme. Guyon had fallen into Quietist heresy and that those who supported her were guilty by association. Faithful to his friend as well as to his conviction that Guyon had not consciously taught heretical doctrine, Fénelon refused to approve Bossuet's work. Within the year Bossuet in his *Relation sur le Quiétisme* would be comparing Fénelon and Mme. Guyon to Montanus and Priscilla, founders of the Montanist heresy.

167. "heresy": The word Fénelon uses here is *illusion*, but it seems clear that he has in mind the illusion or error of heresy or false doctrine.

168. Saint Teresa of Avila in her spiritual autobiography (*Life*, chap. 13) describes being misunderstood and even criticized by certain spiritual directors and confessors who did not have enough knowledge or experience with mystical prayer.

169. Pope Saint Gregory: Pope and doctor of the church (540–604) known for his piety . His *Moralia* is a commentary on the book of Job.

170. Saint Paul speaks of his "thorn in the flesh" (2 Cor 12:7). Biblical scholars still debate the exact nature of this infirmity. Fénelon's argued that even the greatest of saints sometimes display weakness of character and, in the cases of Saint Peter and Saint Paul, occasionally scandalous breaches of Christian discipline and charity, but they were no less marked by divine grace for all their weakness and quick temper.

171. Christ says, "Each tree is known by its own fruit" (Luke 6:44).

172. This proposition was condemned by article 21 of *Cum alias.*

173. This is an implied reference to 1 Cor 6:17, a key text on mystical union.

174. "innocence": Fénelon uses the word *intégrité*, which in modern French means "honesty" but in the seventeenth century still could have the meaning "innocence."

175. "blessed": *Bienheureux*" is a term used in Catholic devotion to speak of souls who, although awaiting the Day of Judgment, already see God.

176. 1 Cor 2:15.

177. This proposition was condemned by article 22 of *Cum alias.*

178. Fénelon is referring to various Pauline strictures concerning tailoring doctrinal teaching according to the abilities of the student. For example, Saint Paul differentiates between the spiritual instruction that can be given to those Christians who are still children in the faith and the more advanced doctrine that can be given to mature Christians: "I fed you with milk, not solid food, for you were not ready for solid food. Even now you are still not ready" (1 Cor 3:2).

179. Luke 10:16.

180. This proposition was condemned by article 23 of *Cum alias.*

181. "permanent": *Inamissible* is a theological term referring most often to grace and meaning that it is incapable of being lost, once it is given. Yet again, Fénelon takes pains to differentiate his doctrine of pure love from that of the Quietists, who held that the state of quietude or perfectibility, once acquired, was permanent.

182. "Verus...": Among the many quotations Fénelon uses in the *Maxims*, this is only the second one that he cites in the original Latin. Perhaps he wanted to impress upon his reader the importance of this statement by relying upon the sonority and gravitas that Latin would have conveyed to his audience. It translates: "True upright love resides in the apostolical authority and the canonical sanctions." Here, once again, as he has done repeatedly in the *Maxims*, Fénelon is assuring us of his sound orthodoxy and submission to the authorities of the church as being superior to personal inspiration and inner gift, however pure or holy their origin.

Index

Other Volumes in This Series

Abraham Isaac Kook • THE LIGHTS OF PENITENCE, LIGHTS OF HOLINESS, THE MORAL PRINCIPLES, ESSAYS, LETTERS, AND POEMS
Abraham Miguel Cardozo • SELECTED WRITINGS
Albert and Thomas • SELECTED WRITINGS
Alphonsus de Liguori • SELECTED WRITINGS
Anchoritic Spirituality •ANCRENE WISSE AND ASSOCIATED WORKS
Angela of Foligno • COMPLETE WORKS
Angelic Spirituality • MEDIEVAL PERSPECTIVES ON THE WAYS OF ANGELS
Angelus Silesius • THE CHERUBINIC WANDERER
Anglo-Saxon Spirituality • SELECTED WRITINGS
Apocalyptic Spirituality • TREATISES AND LETTERS OF LACTANTIUS, ADSO OF MONTIER-EN-DER, JOACHIM OF FIORE, THE FRANCISCAN SPIRITUALS, SAVONAROLA
Athanasius • THE LIFE OF ANTONY, AND THE LETTER TO MARCELLINUS
Augustine of Hippo • SELECTED WRITINGS
Bernard of Clairvaux • SELECTED WORKS
Bérulle and the French School • SELECTED WRITINGS
Birgitta of Sweden • LIFE AND SELECTED REVELATIONS
Bonaventure • THE SOUL'S JOURNEY INTO GOD, THE TREE OF LIFE, THE LIFE OF ST. FRANCIS
Cambridge Platonist Spirituality •
Carthusian Spirituality • THE WRITINGS OF HUGH OF BALMA AND GUIGO DE PONTE
Catherine of Genoa • PURGATION AND PURGATORY, THE SPIRITUAL DIALOGUE
Catherine of Siena • THE DIALOGUE
Celtic Spirituality •
Classic Midrash, The • TANNAITIC COMMENTARIES ON THE BIBLE
Cloud of Unknowing, The •
Devotio Moderna • BASIC WRITINGS
Dominican Penitent Women •
Early Anabaptist Spirituality • SELECTED WRITINGS
Early Dominicans • SELECTED WRITINGS
Early Islamic Mysticism • SUFI, QUR'AN, MI'RAJ, POETIC AND THEOLOGICAL WRITINGS
Early Kabbalah, The •
Elijah Benamozegh • ISRAEL AND HUMANITY
Elisabeth of Schönau • THE COMPLETE WORKS
Emanuel Swedenborg • THE UNIVERSAL HUMAN AND SOUL-BODY INTERACTION
Ephrem the Syrian • HYMNS

Other Volumes in This Series

Fakhruddin 'Iraqi • DIVINE FLASHES
Francis and Clare • THE COMPLETE WORKS
Francis de Sales, Jane de Chantal • LETTERS OF SPIRITUAL DIRECTION
Francisco de Osuna • THE THIRD SPIRITUAL ALPHABET
George Herbert • THE COUNTRY PARSON, THE TEMPLE
Gertrude of Helfta • THE HERALD OF DIVINE LOVE
Gregory of Nyssa • THE LIFE OF MOSES
Gregory Palamas • THE TRIADS
Hadewijch • THE COMPLETE WORKS
Henry Suso • THE EXEMPLAR, WITH TWO GERMAN SERMONS
Hildegard of Bingen • SCIVIAS
Ibn 'Abbād of Ronda • LETTERS ON THE ṢŪFĪ PATH
Ibn Al'-Arabī • THE BEZELS OF WISDOM
Ibn 'Ata' Illah • THE BOOK OF WISDOM AND KWAJA ABDULLAH ANSARI: INTIMATE CONVERSATIONS
Ignatius of Loyola • SPIRITUAL EXERCISES AND SELECTED WORKS
Isaiah Horowitz • THE GENERATIONS OF ADAM
Jacob Boehme • THE WAY TO CHRIST
Jacopone da Todi • THE LAUDS
Jean Gerson • EARLY WORKS
Jeremy Taylor • SELECTED WORKS
Jewish Mystical Autobiographies • BOOK OF VISIONS AND BOOK OF SECRETS
Johann Arndt • TRUE CHRISTIANITY
Johannes Tauler • SERMONS
John Baptist de La Salle • THE SPIRITUALITY OF CHRISTIAN EDUCATION
John Calvin • WRITINGS ON PASTORAL PIETY
John Cassian • CONFERENCES
John and Charles Wesley • SELECTED WRITINGS AND HYMNS
John Climacus • THE LADDER OF DIVINE ASCENT
John Comenius • THE LABYRINTH OF THE WORLD AND THE PARADISE OF THE HEART
John of Avila • AUDI, FILIA
John of the Cross • SELECTED WRITINGS
John Donne • SELECTIONS FROM DIVINE POEMS, SERMONS, DEVOTIONS AND PRAYERS
John Henry Newman • SELECTED SERMONS
John Ruusbroec • THE SPIRITUAL ESPOUSALS AND OTHER WORKS
Julian of Norwich • SHOWINGS
Knowledge of God in Classical Sufism • FOUNDATIONS OF ISLAMIC MYSTICAL THEOLOGY

Other Volumes in This Series

Luis de León • THE NAMES OF CHRIST
Margaret Ebner • MAJOR WORKS
Marguerite Porete • THE MIRROR OF SIMPLE SOULS
Maria Maddalena de' Pazzi • SELECTED REVELATIONS
Martin Luther • THEOLOGIA GERMANICA
Maximus Confessor • SELECTED WRITINGS
Mechthild of Magdeburg • THE FLOWING LIGHT OF THE GODHEAD
Meister Eckhart • THE ESSENTIAL SERMONS, COMMENTARIES, TREATISES AND DEFENSE
Meister Eckhart • TEACHER AND PREACHER
Menahem Nahum of Chernobyl • UPRIGHT PRACTICES, THE LIGHT OF THE EYES
Nahman of Bratslav • THE TALES
Native Mesoamerican Spirituality • ANCIENT MYTHS, DISCOURSES, STORIES, DOCTRINES, HYMNS, POEMS FROM THE AZTEC, YUCATEC, QUICHE-MAYA AND OTHER SACRED TRADITIONS
Native North American Spirituality of the Eastern Woodlands • SACRED MYTHS, DREAMS, VISIONS, SPEECHES, HEALING FORMULAS, RITUALS AND CEREMONIALS
Nicholas of Cusa • SELECTED SPIRITUAL WRITINGS
Nicodemos of the Holy Mountain • A HANDBOOK OF SPIRITUAL COUNSEL
Nil Sorsky • THE COMPLETE WRITINGS
Nizam ad-din Awliya • MORALS FOR THE HEART
Origen • AN EXHORTATION TO MARTYRDOM, PRAYER AND SELECTED WORKS
Philo of Alexandria • THE CONTEMPLATIVE LIFE, THE GIANTS, AND SELECTIONS
Pietists • SELECTED WRITINGS
Pilgrim's Tale, The •
Pseudo-Dionysius • THE COMPLETE WORKS
Pseudo-Macarius • THE FIFTY SPIRITUAL HOMILIES AND THE GREAT LETTER
Pursuit of Wisdom, The • AND OTHER WORKS BY THE AUTHOR OF THE CLOUD OF UNKNOWING
Quaker Spirituality • SELECTED WRITINGS
Rabbinic Stories •
Richard Rolle • THE ENGLISH WRITINGS
Richard of St. Victor • THE TWELVE PATRIARCHS, THE MYSTICAL ARK, BOOK THREE OF THE TRINITY

Other Volumes in This Series

Robert Bellarmine • SPIRITUAL WRITINGS
Safed Spirituality • RULES OF MYSTICAL PIETY, THE BEGINNING OF WISDOM
Shakers, The • TWO CENTURIES OF SPIRITUAL REFLECTION
Sharafuddin Maneri • THE HUNDRED LETTERS
Spirituality of the German Awakening, The •
Symeon the New Theologian • THE DISCOURSES
Talmud, The • SELECTED WRITINGS
Teresa of Avila • THE INTERIOR CASTLE
Theatine Spirituality • SELECTED WRITINGS
'Umar Ibn al-Fāriḍ • SUFI VERSE, SAINTLY LIFE
Valentin Weigel • SELECTED SPIRITUAL WRITINGS
Vincent de Paul and Louise de Marillac • RULES, CONFERENCES, AND WRITINGS
Walter Hilton • THE SCALE OF PERFECTION
William Law • A SERIOUS CALL TO A DEVOUT AND HOLY LIFE, THE SPIRIT OF LOVE
Zohar • THE BOOK OF ENLIGHTENMENT